BARRON'S
How
To
Prepare
For
The
POSTAL
CLERK-CARRIER
Examination

by
Philip Barkus
Director, Training for Results

BARRON'S EDUCATIONAL SERIES, INC.
Woodbury, New York • London • Toronto • Sydney

All inquiries should be addressed to:
Barron's Educational Series, Inc.
113 Crossways Park Drive
Woodbury, New York 11797

Library of Congress Catalog Card No. 82-24296
International Standard Book No. 0-8120-2524-5

Library of Congress Cataloging in Publication Data
Barkus, Philip.
  Barron's how to prepare for the Postal Service
clerk-carrier examination.

  1. Postal service—United States—Examinations,
questions, etc. 2. Civil service—United States—
Examinations. 3. Postal service—United States—
Employees. I. Barron's Educational Series, inc.
II. Title. III. Title: How to prepare for the Postal
Service clerk-carrier examination.
HE6499.B29   1982   383'.145'076   82-24296
ISBN 0-8120-2524-5

PRINTED IN THE UNITED STATES OF AMERICA
3 4 5 6 004 9 8 7 6 5 4 3 2 1

CONTENTS

CHAPTER 5
Memory for *Numbered* Addresses—How to Improve Your Score _____ 97

A FINAL REVIEW

CHAPTER 6
Practice Test 1 _____ 133

Introduction

WHAT THIS BOOK IS ALL ABOUT

This book has its origin in a series of exam preparation courses attended by several hundred candidates for the most recent Postal Service Clerk-Carrier tests. The courses taught these men and women techniques for taking the test that were based on years of successful test preparation experience. Special research was done to develop the best methods for taking this examination. The end result—success on the actual test—has been the final and best way we know to show the value of these methods and the course. Now you, too, can benefit from our research. You can use this book at home to help you pass—and *pass high*—when you take your examination.

This book will provide practical information on the following.

- How and when to apply
- Eligibility requirements
- Why you should study
- What the U.S. Postal Service Clerk-Carrier Examination is like
- Complete test-taking strategies and techniques
- How to study and apply what you've learned

Our format is simple. First, you will be given a clear description of the application and testing procedures. Sample questions will show you exactly what the real test is comprised of. Then you will take a diagnostic practice test modeled after the actual examination to help you evaluate your present strengths and weaknesses. The strategies and techniques used to score high on these questions will be clearly explained, step-by-step. Throughout the book, you will be working on timed practice drills and examinations that show how to apply these techniques under realistic test conditions. Throughout your work, you will follow a diagnostic system whereby you can keep track of your progress. If you study and practice the way this book directs, you will master these kinds of questions when they appear on the real test.

One more benefit. You will find that the abilities you develop as you use this book are transferable to your job in the Post Office and to your everyday life. Improving your reading and memorization skills will help you become a better worker. How? The abilities, which the examination tests for, are directly related to learning and performing the Postal Service Clerk and Carrier jobs well. In addition, being a faster, more accurate reader and being able to remember more items, for a longer time, are assets that can enlarge the personal, social and educational aspects of your life.

DO I REALLY NEED TO STUDY?

Picture these figures: 225,000 men and women signing up to take the U.S. Postal Service Clerk-Carrier Examination in New York City versus 2,500 to 3,000 job openings; 8,000 people applying for the test in St. Louis, Missouri, versus 50 jobs; 2,500 test applicants versus 94 jobs in Amarillo, Texas. There were similar statistics throughout the country. Why? These Postal Service jobs are extremely attractive in terms of salary, working conditions, and other job benefits. (The *starting* salary of a full-time, regular letter carrier, for instance, is now over $19,000.) Undoubtedly, the size of these turnouts is also a reflection of the recession and increased unemployment. But, regardless of the times, a job with the Postal Service, particularly since its reorganization in 1971, is quite a good one. It offers a career opportunity with fringe benefits that match or exceed those in many other private agencies and the public sector. In the next chapter you will receive specific information on salaries, benefits, and on the job itself.

Right now, the most important point to consider about the above statistics, is the probable size of your competition on the next test, and what you can do to meet it. Obviously, not everyone who applies and passes will be appointed because the number of vacancies are too limited. Those who pass will be considered for a job appointment in accordance with their score placement and the rest of the competition. The higher your test score, the higher your standing on the placement list and the better your chance for early appointment. Even *one* extra point can boost you hundreds of places on the job appointment list. This, of course, means hard, cold (and welcome) money to you.

Numerous studies and our first-hand experience show that those who prepare for this test have a tremendous advantage over those who take the test cold. This book will help you gain that advantage.

How to Use This Book

Chapter 1 includes important background information on eligibility and application for the test. Be sure to review the test description and do the sample questions.

You will then be ready to take the Diagnostic Practice Test in **Chapter 2.** Your results on this test will help you to see where your present strengths and weaknesses lie. Record these results on the Personal Progress Record Card and on the special Diagnostic Chart that accompanies each chapter. With these in hand, you can effectively plan your study program and evaluate your progress as you go along.

Chapters 3, 4, and 5 are designed to help you to fully develop the two basic skills that prior examinations have tested for—Address Checking and Memory for Addresses. The test strategies and memory techniques presented in these chapters are related specifically to the kind of questions you will face. Each method is fully explained and illustrated.

If you wish, you may proceed to the appropriate part of each practice test (Part A on address checking or Part B on Memory for Addresses) in chapters 6 through 10 immediately after reading the corresponding chapters above.

The final section of this book, **Chapters 6 through 10,** is composed of five complete practice tests, each containing 95 questions on Address Checking and 88 questions on Memory for Addresses. As you complete each chapter, enter the results in the Diagnostic Chart within the chapter and the Personal Progress Record on page 231. Note any special areas of weakness and re-read the appropriate sections in Chapters 3 through 5. Do additional drilling as necessary before proceeding with the next practice test.

Note that the drills, as well as the practice tests, may be taken several times. The Personal Progress Record has space to record scores for three trials. Answer sheets for three trials are available in the Appendix for the practice tests; there is room in the drills themselves for three scores to be recorded. You should see progress as you continue practicing.

Be sure to read the important guidelines and summaries that appear at the beginning of Chapters 6 and 8 before you take Practice Tests 1 and 3.

A Recent Test Format

Part	Description	Number of Questions	Time Allowed
A	Address Checking	95	6 minutes
B	Memory for Addresses	88	5 minutes

This time allowance is for the time spent on the *rated* part of the test. You can, however, expect to spend approximately 2 hours in the examination room. See Chapter 1, page 4, for complete details.

The Application and Testing Procedures

HOW AND WHEN TO APPLY

Your first step is to keep informed of Postal Service job opportunities so that you don't miss taking the next examination that comes up. Often, local newspapers, unemployment offices, job referral centers and governmental personnel offices publicize forthcoming exams. However, to be certain about postal job opportunities, the best thing to do is to visit your local Post Office or local Federal Job Information Center to find out if they are accepting applications. If so, they will give you the proper application form to fill out. At the same time, you should read the official test announcement which contains specific, current information on such things as the test filing period, eligibility requirements, salary, job location, job duties, and the tests you must pass in order to be appointed.

ANSWERS TO FREQUENTLY ASKED QUESTIONS ABOUT ELIGIBILITY FOR THE CLERK-CARRIER TEST

Here are some highlights summarized from the most recent official test announcement and other official sources that answer the most frequently asked questions about applying for the Clerk-Carrier test:

What are the educational and experiential qualifications?
No experience is required; no minimum education is required.

Must I be a U.S. citizen?
You must be a U.S. citizen, or owe allegiance to the United States, or have been granted permanent resident alien status in the United States.

Are there any residence requirements?
There are no residence requirements.

How old must I be to be appointed?
You may be appointed at age 16 if you have a high school diploma or equivalent; you must be 18 if you are *not* a high school graduate. In general, there is no maximum age limit.

Are there any physical requirements?
You must be physically able to perform the duties of the position. Physical, medical, and vision examinations are required before appointment.

How is salary determined?
This is determined from collective bargaining agreements. (At the time of publication, those appointed as part-time, flexible schedule employees started at a salary of $9.05 per hour with a maximum of $10.38 per hour, including cost of living adjustments after eight years. Such employees are converted to Regular Status according to seniority and openings, at an annual salary range of between $15,000 and $18,000 plus COLA.)

Are there any special requirements for carrier positions?
Driving is required. You must demonstrate a safe driving record and pass a special road test prior to appointment. You must have a valid driver's license in the state in which you are appointed.

How are job vacancies filled?
The examination will be used to establish a register of eligibles or to expand the current register of eligibles from which future Clerk and Carrier vacancies will be filled.

What does the U.S. Postal Service Clerk-Carrier Examination consist of?
All applicants must pass a written examination designed to test aptitude for learning and for performing the duties of this position. The test consists of two parts: (1) Address Checking and (2) Memory for Addresses. A minimum score of 70 must be achieved. The official announcement for the test you take will contain current information on these and other subjects of interest. Make sure to read it when it becomes available.

Once you have read the official test announcement and have received the application form, be careful to fill it out accurately and return it *within the time period specified in the announcement*. You must file your application on time in order to receive your admission card. Without the admission card, you will not be allowed to take the test. A facsimile of the application form, which consists of two parts—the application card and the admission card— separated by a perforated line, appears on the next page.

The *application card* portion of the application form looks like this:

LAST NAME	FIRST NAME	MIDDLE INITIAL

ADDRESS (House/Apt. No. and Street)

CITY	STATE	ZIP CODE

BIRTH DATE (Mo., Day, Year)

DO NOT WRITE IN THIS SPACE

DATE OF THIS APPLICATION	TELEPHONE NUMBER

TITLE OF EXAMINATION

WHERE DO YOU WISH TO TAKE WRITTEN TEST
(City & State)

PS FORM 2479-A, Sept. 1980   **APPLICATION CARD**

The back of the application card has instructions to applicants on how to complete the form. It also indicates that you should mail or deliver in person the *entire* form (without separating the parts) to the Postmaster of the Post Office where you wish to be employed.

The *admission card*, the second part of the application form, appears below:

TITLE OF EXAMINATION	DATE OF THIS APPLICATION	WHERE DO YOU WISH TO TAKE WRITTEN TEST (City & State)
DATE OF BIRTH	SOCIAL SECURITY NUMBER	POST OFFICE APPLIED FOR

IF YOU HAVE PERFORMED ACTIVE DUTY IN THE ARMED FORCES OF THE UNITED STATES AND WERE SEPARATED UNDER HONORABLE CONDITIONS INDICATE PERIODS OF SERVICE
FROM (Mo. Day, Yr.)   TO (Mo. Day. Yr.)

DO NOT WRITE IN THIS SPACE

DO YOU CLAIM VETERAN PREFERENCE? ☐ NO ☐ YES IF YES, BASED ON

☐ (1) ACTIVE DUTY IN THE ARMED FORCES OF THE U.S. DURING WORLD WAR I OR THE PERIOD DECEMBER 7, 1941, THROUGH JULY 1, 1955, (2) MORE THAN 180 CONSECUTIVE DAYS OF ACTIVE DUTY (OTHER THAN FOR TRAINING) IN THE ARMED FORCES OF THE U.S. ANY PART OF WHICH OCCURRED BETWEEN JAN. 31, 1955 AND OCT. 14, 1976, OR (3) AWARD OF A CAMPAIGN BADGE OR SERVICE MEDAL

☐ YOUR STATUS AS (1) A DISABLED VETERAN OR A VETERAN WHO WAS AWARDED THE PURPLE HEART FOR WOUNDS OR INJURIES RECEIVED IN ACTION, (2) A VETERAN'S WIDOW WHO HAS NOT REMARRIED, (3) THE WIFE OF AN EX SERVICEMAN WHO HAS A SERVICE CONNECTED DISABILITY WHICH DISQUALIFIES HIM FOR CIVIL SERVICE APPOINTMENT, OR (4) THE WIDOWED, DIVORCED OR SEPARATED MOTHER OF AN EX-SERVICE SON OR DAUGHTER WHO DIED IN ACTION OR WHO IS TOTALLY AND PERMANENTLY DISABLED

PRINT OR TYPE YOUR NAME AND ADDRESS

FIRST, MIDDLE, MAIDEN, IF ANY, AND LAST NAME

HOUSE/APT. NO. AND STREET, OR R.D., OR POST OFFICE BOX NO.

CITY, STATE, AND ZIP CODE (ZIP Code *must* be included)

This card will be returned to you. Bring it, along with personal identification bearing your picture or description, with you when you report for the test. ID's will be checked, and a fingerprint or signature specimen may be required.

PS Form 2479-B, Sept. 1980   **ADMISSION CARD**

This card will be returned to you later, advising you when and where to report for the test.

WHAT IT'S LIKE AT THE TEST—
SOME THINGS TO REMEMBER

When you receive your admission card, it will be accompanied by a few sample questions like the ones you will take on the test. These are useful. Later, we will show you what these questions look like. First, let us complete the picture of what the testing procedure is like by describing what you may experience during the test itself as well as what happens afterwards.

On the day of the test, you will be one of a group of other test candidates assembled in a room. The exact number of test takers will depend on many things. The staffing needs of the post offices that are to be served by the exam and the employment situation in the area are two important deciding factors. Often, these tests are held in large public places, such as halls and schools, so that all those who want to take the examination can be accommodated. You may, therefore, find yourself to be one of 300 to 400 persons seated in small groups around tables placed throughout the room. Your identification and admission cards will be checked by Postal Service employees who act as test monitors. The monitor in charge of administering the test will direct you in filling out a form containing questions on your job preference,* veteran's status, date of birth, etc. You must indicate your answers by darkening the boxes on the form. (This is similar to the way you will indicate your answers on the test. In Chapters 3, 7, 8, 9, and 10, you will see and use this kind of answer sheet.) The monitor will also explain the test procedure fully and will emphasize that the various parts of the test are carefully timed. Follow these directions exactly. If you are not sure of something, ask for clarification.

Reminders

- If you are not certain about how to get to the test location or how long the trip will take, check these things out as soon as you get your admission card. If you have to rush in to the test, worried and out of breath, you will not be in the best condition to take the examination. If you come late, you will not be admitted. *Come early*.

- Do not forget to bring your admission card, two sharpened #2 lead pencils, and personal identification bearing your picture or description. The identification will be checked, and a fingerprint or signature specimen may be required. Make a note of your service dates if you are claiming veteran status, and jot down your Social Security number, too.

---

* This procedure allows you to select one of three job choices: Clerk (only), Carrier (only), or Clerk and Carrier. It is best for most applicants to select *Clerk and Carrier*. In this way, you would have increased your chances of being called in for *some* job. Remember that although a driver's license is needed to work as a Carrier, you would not need it *until the time of appointment*. That could be months from now. During the intervening period, you would be able to get the driver's license. Once your choice is made, it can*not* be changed later in any way during the life of the "register" or "list" (see page 7 for more information concerning this).

THE TEST ITSELF—
SAMPLE QUESTIONS

As the official announcement indicates, this test is definitely job-related. You will be able to see how true this is when you go over some of the sample questions recently sent to test applicants.

PART A—ADDRESS CHECKING

In this test you will have to decide whether two addresses are alike or different. This kind of question is included in the test because every member of the Postal Service staff is responsible for seeing that each piece of mail arrives at the right destination as quickly as possible. If addresses are misread, delays in delivery will result. In spite of various new developments in sorting and handling the mail that use electronic and computerized devices, the human element is crucial in providing fast and efficient service. Here are the instructions and the sample questions that go with them.

Questions

If the two addresses are alike in every way, darken space Ⓐ for the question. If the two addresses are different in any way, darken space Ⓓ for the question. Mark your answers to these questions in the grids provided.

1.	2134 S 20th St	2134 S 20th St	1 Ⓐ Ⓓ
2.	4608 N Warnock St	4806 N Warnock St	2 Ⓐ Ⓓ
3.	1202 W Girard Dr	1202 W Girard Rd	3 Ⓐ Ⓓ
4.	Chappaqua NY 10514	Chappaqua NY 10514	4 Ⓐ Ⓓ
5.	2207 Markland Ave	2207 Markham Ave	5 Ⓐ Ⓓ

Answers

1. A   3. D   5. D
2. D   4. A

The questions seem easy, but the test itself is not. At least, it's not easy if you want to score higher than your many competitors. In the latest test, candidates were given *95* pairs of addresses to compare in *6* minutes.

To pass with high scores, test takers had to work as fast and accurately as possible. They knew that every extra point they made meant they would be that much higher on the list for job appointment. When a list has thousands of names, *one* extra point will make a difference of *hundreds* of places on the list. Also, when there are a limited number of job openings, list position can mean the difference between getting a job or "dying" on the list. That is why merely passing is not good enough. In the next chapters, you will learn exactly what to do to earn those extra points.

PART B—MEMORY FOR ADDRESSES

The majority of postal clerks work behind the scenes sorting and distributing mail. They must be able to remember sorting schemes by which mail is organized for delivery. Carriers need to have a good memory too. One of their responsibilities is to arrange mail according to the delivery route they will follow that day. They must be able to learn and remember the streets and building addresses on their route. Now you know why memory questions appear on this exam. Here are some sample questions and instructions for answering them:

Questions

In this test, you will have to memorize the locations (A, B, C, D or E) of twenty-five addresses shown in five boxes below. For example, "Sardis" is in Box C, 5200–5799 West is in Box B, etc.

Study the locations of the addresses for *5 minutes*. As you study, sound them to yourself. Then cover the boxes and try to answer the questions below. Mark your answers for each question by darkening the space in the grids provided.

A	B	C	D	E
4700-5599 Table	6800-6999 Table	5600-6499 Table	6500-6799 Table	4400-4699 Table
Lismore	Kelford	Joel	Tatum	Ruskin
4800-5199 West	5200-5799 West	3200-3499 West	3500-4299 West	4300-4799 West
Hesper	Musella	Sardis	Porter	Somers
5500-6399 Blake	4800-5499 Blake	6400-7299 Blake	4300-4799 Blake	7300-7499 Blake

1. Musella   1 Ⓐ Ⓑ Ⓒ Ⓓ Ⓔ
2. 4300–4799 Blake   2 Ⓐ Ⓑ Ⓒ Ⓓ Ⓔ
3. 4700–5599 Table   3 Ⓐ Ⓑ Ⓒ Ⓓ Ⓔ
4. Tatum   4 Ⓐ Ⓑ Ⓒ Ⓓ Ⓔ
5. 5500–6399 Blake   5 Ⓐ Ⓑ Ⓒ Ⓓ Ⓔ
6. Hesper   6 Ⓐ Ⓑ Ⓒ Ⓓ Ⓔ
7. Kelford   7 Ⓐ Ⓑ Ⓒ Ⓓ Ⓔ
8. Somers   8 Ⓐ Ⓑ Ⓒ Ⓓ Ⓔ
9. 6400–7299 Blake   9 Ⓐ Ⓑ Ⓒ Ⓓ Ⓔ
10. Joel   10 Ⓐ Ⓑ Ⓒ Ⓓ Ⓔ
11. 5500–6399 Blake   11 Ⓐ Ⓑ Ⓒ Ⓓ Ⓔ
12. 5200–5799 West   12 Ⓐ Ⓑ Ⓒ Ⓓ Ⓔ
13. Porter   13 Ⓐ Ⓑ Ⓒ Ⓓ Ⓔ
14. 7300–7499 Blake   14 Ⓐ Ⓑ Ⓒ Ⓓ Ⓔ

Answers

1. B	5. A	9. C	13. D
2. D	6. A	10. C	14. E
3. A	7. B	11. A	
4. D	8. E	12. B	

Now imagine a test situation where you are given 5 minutes to answer *88* questions! This is what the memory test will be like. Very few people feel that this test is easy. But don't be like those who immediately give up on the memory part by saying, "either you've got it or you don't." The implication is that nothing can be done to improve their memory performance. This belief is not accurate. There are definite methods, universally recognized, that are used to train for memory improvement. We have selected, and refined, what we believe are the most helpful and practical of these methods for your use on the Memory for Addresses section of the Clerk-Carrier Test. You will be happily surprised at how good your memorization capabilities really are!

AFTER THE TEST

The answer sheets are sent to a special division of the Postal Service that prepares and rates examinations. After the papers have been scored and the registers (lists) established, you will receive a Notice of Rating by mail. (The register is established in the order of the scores on the test, subject to veteran's preference. If you request and are entitled to veteran's preference, you will receive extra points on your rating.) If you have passed, the Notice of Rating will also indicate on which Post Office registers your name has been placed and the date on which this was done. These locations are the ones you *should notify in writing* if you: (1) change your address, (2) have any change in your availability, (3) have any inquiries, (4) want to extend your eligibility. This last point is particularly important because it gives you an opportunity to remain on the list for an extra year. Normally, eligibility is good for two years only. However, you may receive an extension of your eligibility for an additional year if you send in a written request. Send your request in eighteen months from the date in which your name was placed on the register (unless, of course, you have been appointed in the interim). The maximum length of eligibility is three years.

Keep the Notice of Rating Card in a safe place—you will need it some day.

WHY APPLY TO THE POSTAL SERVICE?

When you work for the Postal Service, you will be working for an employer that does things in a big way—it is the world's largest mail system. In 1980, it handled over 106 billion pieces of mail, with 113 billion predicted for 1982. To do that, it employed over 666,000 people in over 30,000 post offices and 9,000 stations, branches, and other locations. It delivered more than 208 million parcel post packages and used a fleet of over 190,000 cars and trucks. It issued almost 27 billion stamps—enough to stretch around the globe 17 times. It operated on a 19.6 billion dollar annual budget, of which 16.5 billion went toward payroll expenses.

The Postal Service also performs many nonpostal services, ranging from the distribution of income tax forms and alien address reporting forms, to the preparation of wild fowl population surveys, and to the search for relatives of deceased persons for the Armed Services.

In 1971, the Postal Service was reorganized to remove the system from politics and political patronage and to permit various reforms affecting its management, financing, structure, and labor relations. Its track record since then shows advances in productivity, reduction in costs, and the introduction of new services (Computerized Forwarding System, Mailgram, Express Mail Service, Electronic Mail Service, etc.).

One very important aspect of its new look is in the area of personnel relations, which directly concerns you as a future employee. Since reorganization, the Postal Service has abolished political patronage in selecting postmasters and rural carriers, replacing it with a merit system. Now, candidates for the job are evaluated and selected by national and regional management selection boards. In 1971, the Service signed a historic agreement with employee unions, the first labor contract in the history of the federal government to be achieved through the collective bargaining process. Negotiations with the four major labor organizations representing the various postal employee groups determine wages and working conditions. A summary of some benefits and programs that can affect you as an employee is given below. (Unless otherwise specified; all figures apply to full-time regular employees.)

BENEFITS

Work Schedules and Classifications

Postal clerks and carriers are classified as *casual, part-time flexible, part-time regular*, or *full-time*. Casual workers are not career employees but are hired to help process mail during peak mailing or vacation periods. Part-time flexible workers are career employees who do not have a regular work schedule but who work as the need arises and usually work less than 40 hours per week. Part-time regulars have a set work schedule (for example, 4 hours a day). Full-time employees work a 40-hour week over five days.

Annual Leave

This includes leave for vacations, personal and emergency purposes, etc. The amount of paid leave you receive depends upon length of service (as an employee and in military service).

Length of Service	Leave Days Per Year
Less than 3 years	13 days
3 to 15 years	20 days
Over 15 years	26 days

Sick Leave

You are permitted 13 days of paid sick leave per year.

Wage Scale

(effective 5/15/82)

	Start	Maximum
Full-time Employees	$19,830	$22,492
Hourly Rate—Regulars	$9.53/hr	$10.81/hr
Hourly Rate—Flexible Employees	$9.80/hr	$11.13/hr

The maximum salary is reached in eight years.

COLA

COLA stands for Cost of Living Adjustment. These adjustments are pay increases that are based on the Consumer Price Indexes for March and September of each year. If they rise, your pay increases too, according to a special formula.

Special Pay Provisions

1. *Overtime.* This is paid at time-and-a-half your base hourly straight-time rate, after 8 hours in a day, or 40 hours in a week.
2. *Night pay.* A premium of 10% of your base hourly rate is paid for work done between 6 P.M. and 6 A.M.
3. *Holidays.* Employees receive 9 paid holidays a year.

Free Life Insurance

You will receive regular life insurance coverage of $10,000 plus an equivalent amount of accidental death and dismemberment insurance. As your base pay increases, your insurance coverage will rise to a maximum of $60,000 in the categories above.

Retirement

There are various liberal retirement options too complex to describe here. Basically, the benefits you receive will depend upon your age at retirement, length of service, salary, etc. Seven percent of your base pay will be deducted as your contribution to the retirement fund. The Postal Service has implemented the National Retirement Counseling System to help potential retirees explore the benefits and detriments of retirement. Through counseling, the dissemination of information, and improved processing of retirement requests, the program attempts to ensure that the transition from employment to retirement is a smooth one.

Low-Cost Health Insurance

The Postal Service pays 75% of the cost.

Program of Cash Awards for Suggestions

Training and Career Development Programs

1. *Advancement to supervisory positions.* A new system called PASS (Profile Assessment System For Supervisors), in which you participate, is used to select supervisors. There is no written test involved.
2. *In-Service training and guidance.* Various in-service courses are offered at the System's Technical Center and through a network of 180 training centers located throughout the country. Career guidance counseling is also offered.
3. *Correspondence courses.*

The Women's Program

The objective is to increase career opportunities for women in the Postal Service who now make up about one-fourth of the postal work force. This is done through attempts to identify talent, supply counseling, and conduct special seminars.

Equal Opportunity and Affirmative Action Programs

These focus on the need for equal opportunity and sensitivity toward minorities and the handicapped. All levels of managers are involved in planning and training to meet these objectives.

Rehabilitation Programs

These have been developed to assist employees with alcohol and drug-related problems.

THE NATURE OF THE WORK

Postal Clerks

Most people are familiar with the post office window clerk behind the counter who sells stamps and accepts parcel post. Window clerks also weigh packages to determine postage and suitability for mailing. They register, certify and insure mail, and answer questions about postage rates, mailing restrictions, and other postal matters. Occasionally they may help a customer file a claim for a damaged package.

Most postal clerks, however, are distribution clerks who sort incoming and outgoing mail in workrooms out of public view. Distribution clerks work at local post offices or at large mail-processing facilities. Those clerks at local post offices sort local mail for delivery to individual customers. Incoming mail gathered from collection boxes is forwarded to the nearest mail processing center, where clerks sort and prepare the mail for delivery.

About 300 mail processing centers throughout the country service post offices in surrounding areas. There, mailhandlers unload the sacks of incoming mail and separate it into groups of letters, parcel post, magazines, and newspapers. They feed letters through stamp-canceling machines and then take the mail to other workrooms to be sorted by postal clerks according to destination. Clerks operating electronic letter-sorting machines push keys corresponding to the zip code of the post office to which each letter will be delivered; the machine drops letters into proper slots. Other clerks sort odd-sized letters, magazines, and newspapers by hand. Finally, the mail is dispatched to local post offices for further sorting according to delivery routes.

Working Conditions

Working conditions for clerks differ according to the work assignment and the type of labor-saving machinery available. In small post offices, clerks may use a hand truck to move mail sacks from one part of the building to another and may sort mail by hand. In large post offices and mail processing centers, chutes and conveyors move the mail, and much of the sorting is done with machines. When they are not operating a letter-sorting machine, clerks are usually on their feet reaching for sacks and trays of mail and placing packages and bundles into sacks and trays.

Distribution clerks may have to work at night or on weekends because most large post offices process mail around the clock. Distribution clerks work closely with other clerks. Window clerks, on the other hand, have a greater variety of duties, have frequent contact with the public, generally have a less strenuous job, and rarely have to work at night. Window clerks must be courteous and tactful when dealing with the public, especially when answering questions or receiving complaints.

Most clerks begin as part-time flexible employees and become full-time clerks in order of seniority as vacancies occur. Full-time clerks may bid for preferred assignments such as day shift, or a window job. Advancement possibilities are unlimited. Clerks can look forward to obtaining a higher level, nonsupervisory position as expediter or window service technician, or promotions to supervisory positions.

Mail Carriers

Most mail carriers travel planned routes delivering and collecting mail. Carriers start work at the post office early in the morning, where they spend a few hours arranging their mail for delivery and taking care of other details.

A carrier may cover the route on foot, by vehicle, or by a combination of both. Foot carriers use a satchel or cart to deliver their mail. In some areas, a car or small truck is used to deliver mail. Carriers serving residential areas cover their routes only once a day, but some carriers assigned to a business district may make two trips a day. Deliveries are made door-to-door, to curbside or roadside mailboxes, to neighborhood delivery and collection boxes, to office buildings, and to apartment houses which have all the mailboxes located in the lobby.

Besides delivering and collecting mail, carriers collect money for postage-due and C.O.D. items and obtain signed receipts for registered, certified, and insured mail. If a customer is not home, the carrier leaves a notice that tells what the item is and where it is being held.

After completing their routes, carriers return to the post office with mail gathered from street collection boxes, homes, and business places. They turn in their delivery receipts and money collected during the day, and separate the letters and large flats they collected for further processing by clerks.

Many city carriers have more specialized duties. Some deliver only parcel post while others collect mail from street boxes and receiving boxes in office buildings. In contrast, rural carriers provide a wide variety of postal services. In addition to delivering and picking up mail, they sell stamps and money orders and accept parcels, letters, and items to be registered, certified, or insured.

All carriers answer customers' questions about postal regulations, services, and provide change-of-address cards and other postal forms upon request.

Working Conditions

Most carriers begin work early in the morning, in some cases as early as 4:00 A.M. if they have routes in the business district. Carriers spend most of their time outdoors in all kinds of weather delivering mail. Even those who drive often must walk when making deliveries and must lift sacks of parcel post when loading their vehicles.

The job, however, has its advantages. Carriers who begin work early in the morning are through by early afternoon.

New carriers are trained on the job. They may begin as part-time flexible city carriers and become regular or full-time carriers in order of seniority as vacancies occur. Advancement possibilities are unlimited. Carriers can look forward to obtaining preferred routes as their seniority increases, higher level jobs such as carrier technician, or promotion to supervisory positions.

JOB OUTLOOK

The employment of postal clerks and carriers is expected to increase through the 1980's due to increases in mail volume and housing starts. In addition, thousands of job openings will result annually from the need to replace experienced clerks and carriers who retire, die, or transfer to other occupations. Openings will be concentrated in areas with rapid population growth. Those employees who plan to continue or expand their education should be aware that there will also be a growing need for computer specialists and for electronic and electrical maintenance technicians as more and more sophisticated equipment is used to process the mail.

A FINAL WORD

You now have a good picture of most matters connected with the test— before, during, and after. You will be able to act in your best interests on things like applying, job choice, retaining eligibility, obtaining information, etc. You should also have gained a certain amount of confidence in knowing why and how certain things happen. Now we've come to the best confidence builder of all. That is, the confidence you get when you're thoroughly prepared to do well on the test itself. It is for that thorough preparation to which the rest of this book is dedicated.

Diagnosing
Your
Skills

ANSWER SHEET
DIAGNOSTIC PRACTICE TEST

Part A—Address Checking   Date _____

1 Ⓐ Ⓓ	25 Ⓐ Ⓓ	49 Ⓐ Ⓓ	73 Ⓐ Ⓓ
2 Ⓐ Ⓓ	26 Ⓐ Ⓓ	50 Ⓐ Ⓓ	74 Ⓐ Ⓓ
3 Ⓐ Ⓓ	27 Ⓐ Ⓓ	51 Ⓐ Ⓓ	75 Ⓐ Ⓓ
4 Ⓐ Ⓓ	28 Ⓐ Ⓓ	52 Ⓐ Ⓓ	76 Ⓐ Ⓓ
5 Ⓐ Ⓓ	29 Ⓐ Ⓓ	53 Ⓐ Ⓓ	77 Ⓐ Ⓓ
6 Ⓐ Ⓓ	30 Ⓐ Ⓓ	54 Ⓐ Ⓓ	78 Ⓐ Ⓓ
7 Ⓐ Ⓓ	31 Ⓐ Ⓓ	55 Ⓐ Ⓓ	79 Ⓐ Ⓓ
8 Ⓐ Ⓓ	32 Ⓐ Ⓓ	56 Ⓐ Ⓓ	80 Ⓐ Ⓓ
9 Ⓐ Ⓓ	33 Ⓐ Ⓓ	57 Ⓐ Ⓓ	81 Ⓐ Ⓓ
10 Ⓐ Ⓓ	34 Ⓐ Ⓓ	58 Ⓐ Ⓓ	82 Ⓐ Ⓓ
11 Ⓐ Ⓓ	35 Ⓐ Ⓓ	59 Ⓐ Ⓓ	83 Ⓐ Ⓓ
12 Ⓐ Ⓓ	36 Ⓐ Ⓓ	60 Ⓐ Ⓓ	84 Ⓐ Ⓓ
13 Ⓐ Ⓓ	37 Ⓐ Ⓓ	61 Ⓐ Ⓓ	85 Ⓐ Ⓓ
14 Ⓐ Ⓓ	38 Ⓐ Ⓓ	62 Ⓐ Ⓓ	86 Ⓐ Ⓓ
15 Ⓐ Ⓓ	39 Ⓐ Ⓓ	63 Ⓐ Ⓓ	87 Ⓐ Ⓓ
16 Ⓐ Ⓓ	40 Ⓐ Ⓓ	64 Ⓐ Ⓓ	88 Ⓐ Ⓓ
17 Ⓐ Ⓓ	41 Ⓐ Ⓓ	65 Ⓐ Ⓓ	89 Ⓐ Ⓓ
18 Ⓐ Ⓓ	42 Ⓐ Ⓓ	66 Ⓐ Ⓓ	90 Ⓐ Ⓓ
19 Ⓐ Ⓓ	43 Ⓐ Ⓓ	67 Ⓐ Ⓓ	91 Ⓐ Ⓓ
20 Ⓐ Ⓓ	44 Ⓐ Ⓓ	68 Ⓐ Ⓓ	92 Ⓐ Ⓓ
21 Ⓐ Ⓓ	45 Ⓐ Ⓓ	69 Ⓐ Ⓓ	93 Ⓐ Ⓓ
22 Ⓐ Ⓓ	46 Ⓐ Ⓓ	70 Ⓐ Ⓓ	94 Ⓐ Ⓓ
23 Ⓐ Ⓓ	47 Ⓐ Ⓓ	71 Ⓐ Ⓓ	95 Ⓐ Ⓓ
24 Ⓐ Ⓓ	48 Ⓐ Ⓓ	72 Ⓐ Ⓓ	

ANSWER SHEET
DIAGNOSTIC PRACTICE TEST

Part B—Memory for Addresses
List 1

Date _____

1 Ⓐ Ⓑ Ⓒ Ⓓ Ⓔ	31 Ⓐ Ⓑ Ⓒ Ⓓ Ⓔ	61 Ⓐ Ⓑ Ⓒ Ⓓ Ⓔ
2 Ⓐ Ⓑ Ⓒ Ⓓ Ⓔ	32 Ⓐ Ⓑ Ⓒ Ⓓ Ⓔ	62 Ⓐ Ⓑ Ⓒ Ⓓ Ⓔ
3 Ⓐ Ⓑ Ⓒ Ⓓ Ⓔ	33 Ⓐ Ⓑ Ⓒ Ⓓ Ⓔ	63 Ⓐ Ⓑ Ⓒ Ⓓ Ⓔ
4 Ⓐ Ⓑ Ⓒ Ⓓ Ⓔ	34 Ⓐ Ⓑ Ⓒ Ⓓ Ⓔ	64 Ⓐ Ⓑ Ⓒ Ⓓ Ⓔ
5 Ⓐ Ⓑ Ⓒ Ⓓ Ⓔ	35 Ⓐ Ⓑ Ⓒ Ⓓ Ⓔ	65 Ⓐ Ⓑ Ⓒ Ⓓ Ⓔ
6 Ⓐ Ⓑ Ⓒ Ⓓ Ⓔ	36 Ⓐ Ⓑ Ⓒ Ⓓ Ⓔ	66 Ⓐ Ⓑ Ⓒ Ⓓ Ⓔ
7 Ⓐ Ⓑ Ⓒ Ⓓ Ⓔ	37 Ⓐ Ⓑ Ⓒ Ⓓ Ⓔ	67 Ⓐ Ⓑ Ⓒ Ⓓ Ⓔ
8 Ⓐ Ⓑ Ⓒ Ⓓ Ⓔ	38 Ⓐ Ⓑ Ⓒ Ⓓ Ⓔ	68 Ⓐ Ⓑ Ⓒ Ⓓ Ⓔ
9 Ⓐ Ⓑ Ⓒ Ⓓ Ⓔ	39 Ⓐ Ⓑ Ⓒ Ⓓ Ⓔ	69 Ⓐ Ⓑ Ⓒ Ⓓ Ⓔ
10 Ⓐ Ⓑ Ⓒ Ⓓ Ⓔ	40 Ⓐ Ⓑ Ⓒ Ⓓ Ⓔ	70 Ⓐ Ⓑ Ⓒ Ⓓ Ⓔ
11 Ⓐ Ⓑ Ⓒ Ⓓ Ⓔ	41 Ⓐ Ⓑ Ⓒ Ⓓ Ⓔ	71 Ⓐ Ⓑ Ⓒ Ⓓ Ⓔ
12 Ⓐ Ⓑ Ⓒ Ⓓ Ⓔ	42 Ⓐ Ⓑ Ⓒ Ⓓ Ⓔ	72 Ⓐ Ⓑ Ⓒ Ⓓ Ⓔ
13 Ⓐ Ⓑ Ⓒ Ⓓ Ⓔ	43 Ⓐ Ⓑ Ⓒ Ⓓ Ⓔ	73 Ⓐ Ⓑ Ⓒ Ⓓ Ⓔ
14 Ⓐ Ⓑ Ⓒ Ⓓ Ⓔ	44 Ⓐ Ⓑ Ⓒ Ⓓ Ⓔ	74 Ⓐ Ⓑ Ⓒ Ⓓ Ⓔ
15 Ⓐ Ⓑ Ⓒ Ⓓ Ⓔ	45 Ⓐ Ⓑ Ⓒ Ⓓ Ⓔ	75 Ⓐ Ⓑ Ⓒ Ⓓ Ⓔ
16 Ⓐ Ⓑ Ⓒ Ⓓ Ⓔ	46 Ⓐ Ⓑ Ⓒ Ⓓ Ⓔ	76 Ⓐ Ⓑ Ⓒ Ⓓ Ⓔ
17 Ⓐ Ⓑ Ⓒ Ⓓ Ⓔ	47 Ⓐ Ⓑ Ⓒ Ⓓ Ⓔ	77 Ⓐ Ⓑ Ⓒ Ⓓ Ⓔ
18 Ⓐ Ⓑ Ⓒ Ⓓ Ⓔ	48 Ⓐ Ⓑ Ⓒ Ⓓ Ⓔ	78 Ⓐ Ⓑ Ⓒ Ⓓ Ⓔ
19 Ⓐ Ⓑ Ⓒ Ⓓ Ⓔ	49 Ⓐ Ⓑ Ⓒ Ⓓ Ⓔ	79 Ⓐ Ⓑ Ⓒ Ⓓ Ⓔ
20 Ⓐ Ⓑ Ⓒ Ⓓ Ⓔ	50 Ⓐ Ⓑ Ⓒ Ⓓ Ⓔ	80 Ⓐ Ⓑ Ⓒ Ⓓ Ⓔ
21 Ⓐ Ⓑ Ⓒ Ⓓ Ⓔ	51 Ⓐ Ⓑ Ⓒ Ⓓ Ⓔ	81 Ⓐ Ⓑ Ⓒ Ⓓ Ⓔ
22 Ⓐ Ⓑ Ⓒ Ⓓ Ⓔ	52 Ⓐ Ⓑ Ⓒ Ⓓ Ⓔ	82 Ⓐ Ⓑ Ⓒ Ⓓ Ⓔ
23 Ⓐ Ⓑ Ⓒ Ⓓ Ⓔ	53 Ⓐ Ⓑ Ⓒ Ⓓ Ⓔ	83 Ⓐ Ⓑ Ⓒ Ⓓ Ⓔ
24 Ⓐ Ⓑ Ⓒ Ⓓ Ⓔ	54 Ⓐ Ⓑ Ⓒ Ⓓ Ⓔ	84 Ⓐ Ⓑ Ⓒ Ⓓ Ⓔ
25 Ⓐ Ⓑ Ⓒ Ⓓ Ⓔ	55 Ⓐ Ⓑ Ⓒ Ⓓ Ⓔ	85 Ⓐ Ⓑ Ⓒ Ⓓ Ⓔ
26 Ⓐ Ⓑ Ⓒ Ⓓ Ⓔ	56 Ⓐ Ⓑ Ⓒ Ⓓ Ⓔ	86 Ⓐ Ⓑ Ⓒ Ⓓ Ⓔ
27 Ⓐ Ⓑ Ⓒ Ⓓ Ⓔ	57 Ⓐ Ⓑ Ⓒ Ⓓ Ⓔ	87 Ⓐ Ⓑ Ⓒ Ⓓ Ⓔ
28 Ⓐ Ⓑ Ⓒ Ⓓ Ⓔ	58 Ⓐ Ⓑ Ⓒ Ⓓ Ⓔ	88 Ⓐ Ⓑ Ⓒ Ⓓ Ⓔ
29 Ⓐ Ⓑ Ⓒ Ⓓ Ⓔ	59 Ⓐ Ⓑ Ⓒ Ⓓ Ⓔ	
30 Ⓐ Ⓑ Ⓒ Ⓓ Ⓔ	60 Ⓐ Ⓑ Ⓒ Ⓓ Ⓔ	

ANSWER SHEET
DIAGNOSTIC PRACTICE TEST

Part B—Memory for Addresses
    List 2   **Date** _____

1 Ⓐ Ⓑ Ⓒ Ⓓ Ⓔ	31 Ⓐ Ⓑ Ⓒ Ⓓ Ⓔ	61 Ⓐ Ⓑ Ⓒ Ⓓ Ⓔ
2 Ⓐ Ⓑ Ⓒ Ⓓ Ⓔ	32 Ⓐ Ⓑ Ⓒ Ⓓ Ⓔ	62 Ⓐ Ⓑ Ⓒ Ⓓ Ⓔ
3 Ⓐ Ⓑ Ⓒ Ⓓ Ⓔ	33 Ⓐ Ⓑ Ⓒ Ⓓ Ⓔ	63 Ⓐ Ⓑ Ⓒ Ⓓ Ⓔ
4 Ⓐ Ⓑ Ⓒ Ⓓ Ⓔ	34 Ⓐ Ⓑ Ⓒ Ⓓ Ⓔ	64 Ⓐ Ⓑ Ⓒ Ⓓ Ⓔ
5 Ⓐ Ⓑ Ⓒ Ⓓ Ⓔ	35 Ⓐ Ⓑ Ⓒ Ⓓ Ⓔ	65 Ⓐ Ⓑ Ⓒ Ⓓ Ⓔ
6 Ⓐ Ⓑ Ⓒ Ⓓ Ⓔ	36 Ⓐ Ⓑ Ⓒ Ⓓ Ⓔ	66 Ⓐ Ⓑ Ⓒ Ⓓ Ⓔ
7 Ⓐ Ⓑ Ⓒ Ⓓ Ⓔ	37 Ⓐ Ⓑ Ⓒ Ⓓ Ⓔ	67 Ⓐ Ⓑ Ⓒ Ⓓ Ⓔ
8 Ⓐ Ⓑ Ⓒ Ⓓ Ⓔ	38 Ⓐ Ⓑ Ⓒ Ⓓ Ⓔ	68 Ⓐ Ⓑ Ⓒ Ⓓ Ⓔ
9 Ⓐ Ⓑ Ⓒ Ⓓ Ⓔ	39 Ⓐ Ⓑ Ⓒ Ⓓ Ⓔ	69 Ⓐ Ⓑ Ⓒ Ⓓ Ⓔ
10 Ⓐ Ⓑ Ⓒ Ⓓ Ⓔ	40 Ⓐ Ⓑ Ⓒ Ⓓ Ⓔ	70 Ⓐ Ⓑ Ⓒ Ⓓ Ⓔ
11 Ⓐ Ⓑ Ⓒ Ⓓ Ⓔ	41 Ⓐ Ⓑ Ⓒ Ⓓ Ⓔ	71 Ⓐ Ⓑ Ⓒ Ⓓ Ⓔ
12 Ⓐ Ⓑ Ⓒ Ⓓ Ⓔ	42 Ⓐ Ⓑ Ⓒ Ⓓ Ⓔ	72 Ⓐ Ⓑ Ⓒ Ⓓ Ⓔ
13 Ⓐ Ⓑ Ⓒ Ⓓ Ⓔ	43 Ⓐ Ⓑ Ⓒ Ⓓ Ⓔ	73 Ⓐ Ⓑ Ⓒ Ⓓ Ⓔ
14 Ⓐ Ⓑ Ⓒ Ⓓ Ⓔ	44 Ⓐ Ⓑ Ⓒ Ⓓ Ⓔ	74 Ⓐ Ⓑ Ⓒ Ⓓ Ⓔ
15 Ⓐ Ⓑ Ⓒ Ⓓ Ⓔ	45 Ⓐ Ⓑ Ⓒ Ⓓ Ⓔ	75 Ⓐ Ⓑ Ⓒ Ⓓ Ⓔ
16 Ⓐ Ⓑ Ⓒ Ⓓ Ⓔ	46 Ⓐ Ⓑ Ⓒ Ⓓ Ⓔ	76 Ⓐ Ⓑ Ⓒ Ⓓ Ⓔ
17 Ⓐ Ⓑ Ⓒ Ⓓ Ⓔ	47 Ⓐ Ⓑ Ⓒ Ⓓ Ⓔ	77 Ⓐ Ⓑ Ⓒ Ⓓ Ⓔ
18 Ⓐ Ⓑ Ⓒ Ⓓ Ⓔ	48 Ⓐ Ⓑ Ⓒ Ⓓ Ⓔ	78 Ⓐ Ⓑ Ⓒ Ⓓ Ⓔ
19 Ⓐ Ⓑ Ⓒ Ⓓ Ⓔ	49 Ⓐ Ⓑ Ⓒ Ⓓ Ⓔ	79 Ⓐ Ⓑ Ⓒ Ⓓ Ⓔ
20 Ⓐ Ⓑ Ⓒ Ⓓ Ⓔ	50 Ⓐ Ⓑ Ⓒ Ⓓ Ⓔ	80 Ⓐ Ⓑ Ⓒ Ⓓ Ⓔ
21 Ⓐ Ⓑ Ⓒ Ⓓ Ⓔ	51 Ⓐ Ⓑ Ⓒ Ⓓ Ⓔ	81 Ⓐ Ⓑ Ⓒ Ⓓ Ⓔ
22 Ⓐ Ⓑ Ⓒ Ⓓ Ⓔ	52 Ⓐ Ⓑ Ⓒ Ⓓ Ⓔ	82 Ⓐ Ⓑ Ⓒ Ⓓ Ⓔ
23 Ⓐ Ⓑ Ⓒ Ⓓ Ⓔ	53 Ⓐ Ⓑ Ⓒ Ⓓ Ⓔ	83 Ⓐ Ⓑ Ⓒ Ⓓ Ⓔ
24 Ⓐ Ⓑ Ⓒ Ⓓ Ⓔ	54 Ⓐ Ⓑ Ⓒ Ⓓ Ⓔ	84 Ⓐ Ⓑ Ⓒ Ⓓ Ⓔ
25 Ⓐ Ⓑ Ⓒ Ⓓ Ⓔ	55 Ⓐ Ⓑ Ⓒ Ⓓ Ⓔ	85 Ⓐ Ⓑ Ⓒ Ⓓ Ⓔ
26 Ⓐ Ⓑ Ⓒ Ⓓ Ⓔ	56 Ⓐ Ⓑ Ⓒ Ⓓ Ⓔ	86 Ⓐ Ⓑ Ⓒ Ⓓ Ⓔ
27 Ⓐ Ⓑ Ⓒ Ⓓ Ⓔ	57 Ⓐ Ⓑ Ⓒ Ⓓ Ⓔ	87 Ⓐ Ⓑ Ⓒ Ⓓ Ⓔ
28 Ⓐ Ⓑ Ⓒ Ⓓ Ⓔ	58 Ⓐ Ⓑ Ⓒ Ⓓ Ⓔ	88 Ⓐ Ⓑ Ⓒ Ⓓ Ⓔ
29 Ⓐ Ⓑ Ⓒ Ⓓ Ⓔ	59 Ⓐ Ⓑ Ⓒ Ⓓ Ⓔ	
30 Ⓐ Ⓑ Ⓒ Ⓓ Ⓔ	60 Ⓐ Ⓑ Ⓒ Ⓓ Ⓔ	

Diagnostic Practice Test

One of the first questions that you may be asking yourself is—what kind of a test score can I make right now? Where would I stand in relation to others taking the same test?

To help answer these questions, we would like you to take the following Diagnostic Practice Test, which is modeled after actual Postal Service tests on address checking. After you have taken the test, we will show you how to score it and how that score will compare with the scores of typical test candidates. By knowing your present level of achievement and your strengths and weaknesses, you will be able to direct your improvement efforts. You will know exactly *what* and *how much* to study and practice. You will have a starting point against which to measure the progress you make as you go through this book. The satisfaction you get from seeing your score improve is the best motivating force we know.

DIAGNOSTIC PRACTICE TEST

PART A—ADDRESS CHECKING

WORK—*6 minutes*

In this test you are to decide whether two addresses are alike or different. If the two addresses are *exactly alike in every way*, darken space Ⓐ. If they are *different in any way*, darken space Ⓓ.

Mark your answers on the Answer Sheet for Address Checking at the beginning of this chapter. Tear it out, put today's date on it, and place it next to the questions.

Use any of the timing methods described in the Appendix, page 240, but remember to allow yourself *exactly 6 minutes* to do as many of the 95 questions as you can. If you finish before the time is up, re-check your answers.

1 ...	405 Winter Rd NW	405 Winter Rd NW
2 ...	607 S Calaveras Rd	607 S Calaveras Rd
3 ...	8406 La Casa St	8406 La Cosa St
4 ...	121 N Rippon St	121 N Rippon St
5 ...	Wideman Ark	Wiseman Ark
6 ...	Sodus NY 14551	Sodus NY 14551
7 ...	3429 Hermosa Dr	3429 Hermoso Dr
8 ...	3628 S Zeeland St	3268 S Zeeland St
9 ...	1330 Cheverly Ave NE	1330 Cheverly Ave NE
10 ...	1689 N Derwood Dr	1689 N Derwood Dr
11 ...	3886 Sunrise Ct	3886 Sunrise Ct
12 ...	635 La Calle Mayor	653 La Calle Mayor
13 ...	2560 Lansford Pl	2560 Lansford St
14 ...	4631 Central Ave	4631 Central Ave
15 ...	Mason City Iowa 50401	Mason City Iowa 50401
16 ...	758 Los Arboles Ave SE	758 Los Arboles Ave SW
17 ...	3282 E Downington St	3282 E Dunnington St
18 ...	7117 N Burlingham Ave	7117 N Burlingham Ave
19 ...	32 Oaklawn Blvd	32 Oakland Blvd
20 ...	1274 Manzana Rd	1274 Manzana Rd
21 ...	4598 E Kenilworth Dr	4598 E Kenilworth Dr
22 ...	Dayton Okla 73449	Dagton Okla 73449
23 ...	1172 W 83rd Ave	1127 W 83rd Ave
24 ...	6434 E Pulaski St	6434 E Pulaski Ct
25 ...	2764 N Rutherford Pl	2764 N Rutherford Pl
26 ...	565 Greenville Blvd SE	565 Greenview Blvd SE
27 ...	Washington DC 20013	Washington DC 20018
28 ...	3824 Massasoit St	3824 Massasoit St
29 ...	22 Sagnaw Pkwy	22 Saganaw Pkwy
30 ...	Byram Conn 10573	Byram Conn 10573
31 ...	1928 S Fairfield Ave	1928 S Fairfield St

32 ...	36218 Overhills Dr	36218 Overhills Dr
33 ...	516 Avenida de Las Americas NW	516 Avenida de Las Americas NW
34 ...	7526 Naraganset Pl SW	7526 Naraganset Pl SW
35 ...	52626 W Ogelsby Dr	52626 W Ogelsby Dr
36 ...	1003 Winchester Rd	1003 Westchester Rd
37 ...	3478 W Cavanaugh Ct	3478 W Cavenaugh Ct
38 ...	Kendall Calif 90551	Kendell Calif 90551
39 ...	225 El Camino Blvd	225 El Camino Ave
40 ...	7310 Via de los Pisos	7310 Via de los Pinos
41 ...	1987 Wellington Ave SW	1987 Wellington Ave SW
42 ...	3124 S 71st St	3142 S 71st St
43 ...	729 Lincolnwood Blvd	729 Lincolnwood Blvd
44 ...	1166 N Beaumont Dr	1166 S Beaumont Dr
45 ...	3224 W Winecona Pl	3224 W Winecona Pl
46 ...	608 La Calle Bienvenida	607 La Calle Bienvenida
47 ...	La Molte Iowa 52045	La Molte Iowa 52045
48 ...	8625 Armitage Ave NW	8625 Armitage Ave NW
49 ...	2343 Broadview Ave	2334 Broadview Ave
50 ...	4279 Sierra Grande Ave NE	4279 Sierra Grande Dr NE
51 ...	165 32d Ave	165 32d Ave
52 ...	12742 N Deerborn St	12724 N Deerborn St
53 ...	114 Estancia Ave	141 Estancia Ave
54 ...	351 S Berwyn Rd	351 S Berwyn Pl
55 ...	7732 Avenida Manana SW	7732 Avenida Manana SW
56 ...	6337 C St SW	6337 G St SW
57 ...	57895 E Drexyl Ave	58795 E Drexyl Ave
58 ...	Altro Tex 75923	Altra Tex 75923
59 ...	3465 S Nashville St	3465 N Nashville St
60 ...	1226 Odell Blvd NW	1226 Oddell Blvd NW
61 ...	94002 Chappel Ct	94002 Chappel Ct
62 ...	512 La Vega Dr	512 La Veta Dr
63 ...	8774 W Winona Pl	8774 E Winona Pl
64 ...	6431 Ingleside St SE	6431 Ingleside St SE
65 ...	2270 N Leanington St	2270 N Leanington St
66 ...	235 Calle de Los Vecinos	235 Calle de Los Vecinos
67 ...	3987 E Westwood Ave	3987 W Westwood Ave
68 ...	Skamokawa Wash	Skamohawa Wash
69 ...	2674 E Champlain Cir	2764 E Champlain Cir
70 ...	8751 Elmhurst Blvd	8751 Elmwood Blvd
71 ...	6649 Solano Dr	6649 Solana Dr
72 ...	4423 S Escenaba St	4423 S Escenaba St
73 ...	1198 N St NW	1198 M St NW
74 ...	Sparta Ga	Sparta Va
75 ...	96753 Wrightwood Ave	96753 Wrightwood Ave
76 ...	2445 Sangamow Ave SE	2445 Sangamow Ave SE
77 ...	5117 E 67 Pl	5171 E 67 Pl
78 ...	847 Mesa Grande Pl	847 Mesa Grande Ct
79 ...	1100 Cermaken St	1100 Cermaker St

80 ... 321 Tijeras Ave NW	321 Tijeras Ave NW
81 ... 3405 Prospect St	3405 Prospect St
82 ... 6643 Burlington Pl	6643 Burlingtown Pl
83 ... 851 Esperanza Blvd	851 Esperanza Blvd
84 ... Jenkinjones W Va	Jenkinjones W Va
85 ... 1008 Pennsylvania Ave SE	1008 Pennsylvania Ave SW
86 ... 2924 26th St N	2929 26th St N
87 ... 7115 Highland Dr	7115 Highland Dr
88 ... Chaptico Md	Chaptica Md
89 ... 3508 Camron Mills Rd	3508 Camron Mills Rd
90 ... 67158 Capston Dr	67158 Capston Dr
91 ... 3613 S Taylor Ave	3631 S Taylor Ave
92 ... 2421 Menokin Dr	2421 Menokin Dr
93 ... 3226 M St NW	3226 N St NW
94 ... 1201 S Court House Rd	1201 S Court House Rd
95 ... Findlay Ohio 45840	Findley Ohio 45840

STOP.

**If you finish before the time is up, go back
and check the questions in this section of the
test only.**

PART B—MEMORY FOR ADDRESSES

In this test you will have five boxes labeled A, B, C, D, and E. Each box contains five addresses. Three of the five are groups of street addresses, like 2100–2799 Mall, 4800–4999 Cliff, and 1900–2299 Laurel; and two are names of places. They are different in each box.

You will also be given two lists of addresses. You will have to decide in which box each address belongs. When you are working on the first list, you will have the boxes with the addresses *in front* of you. When you are working on the second list, you will *not* be able to look at the boxes. (The second list is the *real* test.)

Samples

A	B	C	D	E
2100-2799 Mall Ceres 4800-4999 Cliff Natoma 1900-2299 Laurel	3900-4399 Mall Cedar 4000-4299 Cliff Foster 2300-2999 Laurel	4400-4599 Mall Niles 3300-3999 Cliff Dexter 3200-3799 Laurel	3400-3899 Mall Cicero 4500-4799 Cliff Pearl 3000-3199 Laurel	2800-3399 Mall Delhi 4300-4499 Cliff Magnet 1500-1899 Laurel

Questions 1 through 7 show the way the questions look. You have to decide in which lettered box (A, B, C, D, or E) the address belongs and then mark that answer in the answer grid.

1.	3300–3999 Cliff	**1** Ⓐ Ⓑ Ⓒ Ⓓ Ⓔ
2.	Natoma	**2** Ⓐ Ⓑ Ⓒ Ⓓ Ⓔ
3.	Foster	**3** Ⓐ Ⓑ Ⓒ Ⓓ Ⓔ
4.	1500–1899 Laurel	**4** Ⓐ Ⓑ Ⓒ Ⓓ Ⓔ
5.	3900–4399 Mall	**5** Ⓐ Ⓑ Ⓒ Ⓓ Ⓔ
6.	Pearl	**6** Ⓐ Ⓑ Ⓒ Ⓓ Ⓔ
7.	3200–3799 Laurel	**7** Ⓐ Ⓑ Ⓒ Ⓓ Ⓔ

Answers

1. C	3. B	5. B	7. C
2. A	4. E	6. D	

STUDY—*3 minutes*

You will now have *3 minutes to spend memorizing the addresses in the boxes*. These are the addresses that will be in the test. Try to learn as many as you can. When the three minutes for studying are up, turn to page 22 to begin your practice test.

List 1

WORK—*3 minutes*

Tear out the Answer Sheet for this section of the test. For each question, mark the answer sheet to show the letter of the box in which the address belongs. Try to remember the location of as many addresses as you can. *You will now have 3 minutes to complete List 1*. If you are not sure of an answer, you should guess.

A	B	C	D	E
2100-2799 Mall Ceres 4800-4999 Cliff Natoma 1900-2299 Laurel	3900-4399 Mall Cedar 4000-4299 Cliff Foster 2300-2999 Laurel	4400-4599 Mall Niles 3300-3999 Cliff Dexter 3200-3799 Laurel	3400-3899 Mall Cicero 4500-4799 Cliff Pearl 3000-3199 Laurel	2800-3399 Mall Delhi 4300-4499 Cliff Magnet 1500-1899 Laurel

1. Magnet
2. Niles
3. 3400–3899 Mall
4. 1900–2299 Laurel
5. Cicero
6. Dexter
7. 2300–2999 Laurel
8. 3300–3999 Cliff
9. 3200–3799 Laurel
10. 2100–2799 Mall
11. Pearl
12. 3200–3799 Laurel
13. Ceres
14. 4500–4799 Cliff
15. 3900–4399 Mall
16. Delhi
17. 4300–4499 Cliff
18. 3000–3199 Laurel
19. Ceres
20. Foster
21. Natoma
22. 4400–4599 Mall
23. Cedar
24. 2300–2999 Laurel
25. 1500–1899 Laurel
26. 4000–4299 Cliff

27. Dexter
28. Magnet
29. 3300–3999 Cliff
30. 3400–3899 Mall
31. Niles
32. 2100–2799 Mall
33. 1900–2299 Laurel
34. Cedar
35. Pearl
36. 2800–3399 Mall
37. 4800–4999 Cliff
38. 3900–4399 Mall
39. Foster
40. 3000–3199 Laurel
41. Ceres
42. Niles
43. 3400–3899 Mall
44. Delhi
45. 2300–2999 Laurel
46. 4500–4799 Cliff
47. Dexter
48. Magnet
49. 3300–3999 Cliff
50. Cicero
51. 4300–4499 Cliff
52. 3900–4399 Mall

53. Natoma
54. 3200–3799 Laurel
55. Pearl
56. 4000–4299 Cliff
57. 4500–4799 Cliff
58. 2100–2799 Mall
59. Foster
60. 4400–4599 Mall
61. 4800–4999 Cliff
62. Ceres
63. 2800–3399 Mall
64. 1500–1899 Laurel
65. Natoma
66. 3000–3199 Laurel
67. 4000–4299 Cliff
68. Niles
69. 2300–2999 Laurel
70. Magnet
71. Delhi
72. 4400–4599 Mall
73. Cicero
74. Cedar
75. 2800–3399 Mall
76. 1900–2299 Laurel
77. Dexter
78. Pearl

79. 4300–4499 Cliff
80. 3900–4399 Mall
81. Foster
82. 4800–4999 Cliff

83. Delhi
84. Ceres
85. 1500–1899 Laurel
86. Natoma

87. 2800–3399 Mall
88. Niles

STOP.

**If you finish before the time is up, go back
and check the questions in this section of the
test only.**

List 2

STUDY—*5 minutes*

You are now about to take the test using List 2. (*This is the test that counts!*)

    Turn back to the first page of Part B of this test and study the boxes again. You have *5 minutes to restudy the addresses.* When the time is up, tear out the Answer Sheet for List 2. Use it for this test.

WORK—*5 minutes*

For each question, mark the answer sheet to show the letter of the box in which the address belongs. You will have *5 minutes to do the test.* During the 5 minutes for this test, do *not* turn to any other page.

1. Cedar	31. 3000–3199 Laurel	61. Natoma
2. 4300–4499 Cliff	32. Niles	62. 3000–3199 Laurel
3. 4400–4599 Mall	33. Delhi	63. 4300–4499 Cliff
4. Natoma	34. 3900–4399 Mall	64. Cedar
5. 2300–2999 Laurel	35. Cicero	65. 4400–4599 Mall
6. 4500–4799 Cliff	36. Dexter	66. 1500–1899 Laurel
7. Ceres	37. 4800–4999 Cliff	67. 4800–4999 Cliff
8. 3400–3899 Mall	38. 2300–2999 Laurel	68. Delhi
9. Delhi	39. 2100–2799 Mall	69. Pearl
10. Dexter	40. 3300–3999 Cliff	70. 2300–2999 Laurel
11. 1900–2299 Laurel	41. 3400–3899 Mall	71. 4500–4799 Cliff
12. 3300–3999 Cliff	42. 4300–4499 Cliff	72. Niles
13. Cicero	43. Ceres	73. 4000–4299 Cliff
14. 4000–4299 Cliff	44. Foster	74. 3400–3899 Mall
15. 2100–2799 Mall	45. Magnet	75. 1900–2299 Laurel
16. Foster	46. 3200–3799 Laurel	76. 2800–3399 Mall
17. Magnet	47. Pearl	77. Ceres
18. Ceres	48. 1500–1899 Laurel	78. Magnet
19. 2800–3399 Mall	49. 4500–4799 Cliff	79. Cicero
20. 3200–3799 Laurel	50. 1900–2299 Laurel	80. 3200–3799 Laurel
21. 4300–4499 Cliff	51. Niles	81. 3000–3199 Laurel
22. Pearl	52. 3300–3999 Cliff	82. 3900–4399 Mall
23. 3900–4399 Mall	53. 2800–3399 Mall	83. Natoma
24. Natoma	54. Cicero	84. 3300–3999 Cliff
25. 4800–4999 Cliff	55. Delhi	85. 3400–3899 Mall
26. 1500–1899 Laurel	56. 4000–4299 Cliff	86. Foster
27. Cedar	57. Dexter	87. 2100–2799 Mall
28. 4400–4599 Mall	58. Magnet	88. 4300–4499 Cliff
29. 4500–4799 Cliff	59. 3000–3199 Laurel	
30. Dexter	60. 3900–4399 Mall	

END OF EXAMINATION.

**If you finish before the time is up, go back
and check the questions in this section of the
test only.**

ANSWER KEY

PART A—ADDRESS CHECKING

1.	A	26.	D	51.	A	76.	A
2.	A	27.	D	52.	D	77.	D
3.	D	28.	A	53.	D	78.	D
4.	A	29.	D	54.	D	79.	D
5.	D	30.	A	55.	A	80.	A
6.	A	31.	D	56.	D	81.	A
7.	D	32.	A	57.	D	82.	D
8.	D	33.	A	58.	D	83.	A
9.	A	34.	A	59.	D	84.	A
10.	A	35.	A	60.	D	85.	D
11.	A	36.	D	61.	A	86.	D
12.	D	37.	D	62.	D	87.	A
13.	D	38.	D	63.	D	88.	D
14.	A	39.	D	64.	A	89.	A
15.	A	40.	D	65.	A	90.	A
16.	D	41.	A	66.	A	91.	D
17.	D	42.	D	67.	D	92.	A
18.	A	43.	A	68.	D	93.	D
19.	D	44.	D	69.	D	94.	A
20.	A	45.	A	70.	D	95.	D
21.	A	46.	D	71.	D		
22.	D	47.	A	72.	A		
23.	D	48.	A	73.	D		
24.	D	49.	D	74.	D		
25.	A	50.	D	75.	A		

PART B—MEMORY FOR ADDRESSES

List 1

1.	E	13.	A	25.	E	37.	A
2.	C	14.	D	26.	B	38.	B
3.	D	15.	B	27.	C	39.	B
4.	A	16.	E	28.	E	40.	D
5.	D	17.	E	29.	C	41.	A
6.	C	18.	D	30.	D	42.	C
7.	B	19.	A	31.	C	43.	D
8.	C	20.	B	32.	A	44.	E
9.	C	21.	A	33.	A	45.	B
10.	A	22.	C	34.	B	46.	D
11.	D	23.	B	35.	D	47.	C
12.	C	24.	B	36.	E	48.	E

49.	C	59.	B	69.	B	79.	E
50.	D	60.	C	70.	E	80.	B
51.	E	61.	A	71.	E	81.	B
52.	B	62.	A	72.	C	82.	A
53.	A	63.	E	73.	D	83.	E
54.	C	64.	E	74.	B	84.	A
55.	D	65.	A	75.	E	85.	E
56.	B	66.	D	76.	A	86.	A
57.	D	67.	B	77.	C	87.	E
58.	A	68.	C	78.	D	88.	C

List 2

1.	B	23.	B	45.	E	67.	A
2.	E	24.	A	46.	C	68.	E
3.	C	25.	A	47.	D	69.	D
4.	A	26.	E	48.	E	70.	B
5.	B	27.	B	49.	D	71.	D
6.	D	28.	C	50.	A	72.	C
7.	A	29.	D	51.	C	73.	B
8.	D	30.	C	52.	C	74.	D
9.	E	31.	D	53.	E	75.	A
10.	C	32.	C	54.	D	76.	E
11.	A	33.	E	55.	E	77.	A
12.	C	34.	B	56.	B	78.	E
13.	D	35.	D	57.	C	79.	D
14.	B	36.	C	58.	E	80.	C
15.	A	37.	A	59.	D	81.	D
16.	B	38.	B	60.	B	82.	B
17.	E	39.	A	61.	A	83.	A
18.	A	40.	C	62.	D	84.	C
19.	E	41.	D	63.	E	85.	D
20.	C	42.	E	64.	B	86.	B
21.	E	43.	A	65.	C	87.	A
22.	D	44.	B	66.	E	88.	E

EVALUATING YOUR PROGRESS

PART A

Computing Your Score

Check your answers against the Answer Key. Score yourself by using this formula:

$$\begin{array}{r} \text{Number right} \\ \underline{-\ \text{Number wrong}} \\ \text{YOUR SCORE} \end{array}$$

For example, if you completed 52 questions and got 8 wrong,

$$\begin{array}{rr} \text{Number right} = & 44 \\ \underline{-\ \text{Number wrong} = -} & \underline{8} \\ \text{Your score} = & 36 \end{array}$$

Notice that you do *not* figure in the questions that you did not answer.

Guidelines

How good is the score you just made?

        52 or higher...............Good
        Between 32 and 52 ......Fair
        Below 32 ....You need to improve

These are commonly accepted figures. We believe, however, that you should not be satisfied with anything *less* than 52. Our experience in training many people to prepare for this test shows that most serious test candidates who use the preparation program described in this book (Chapter 4 covers Address Checking) will be able to raise their score to the upper sixties and seventies.

Personal Progress Record

One of the most satisfying things that can happen while you are working toward a goal is to see signs of progress. The improvement you make on Address Checking can readily be seen by examining the scores you make on the practice tests and exercises in this book. We think that keeping track of your growing skill is so important that a Personal Progress Record has been furnished for your use on page 231.

The following is a sample of this Personal Progress Record to familiarize you with it. The entries on this sample are based on the example above.

Personal Progress Record—Sample

		ADDRESS CHECKING								
		Initial Tests					Repeated Tests			
Date	Test	Number Completed	Number Correct	− Number Wrong	= Score		Date	Score	Date	Score
5/15	Diagnostic Practice Test	52	44	− 8	= 36					
5/16	Practice Test 1	64	54	− 10	= 44					
5/18	Practice Test 2	66	57	− 9	= 48					
5/20	Practice Test 3	70	60	− 10	= 50					
	Practice Test 4			−	=					
	Practice Test 5			−	=					

Now turn to page 231. Look at the table entitled "Personal Progress Record—Address Checking." Make the proper entries on the line for the Diagnostic Practice Test you just took. This table will help you record your progress as you take additional practice tests.

PART B

Computing Your Score

Check the answers on your answer sheet against the Answer Key. Calculate your score by using these four steps:

1. Enter the number of answers you got right ....____
2. Enter the number of answers you got wrong..............____
3. Divide the number wrong by 4 (or multiply by ¼) .... −____
4. Subtract Line 3 from Line 1......................YOUR SCORE =____

Follow this example to make sure that you have figured your score correctly. We will assume that you completed 32 questions, of which you got 24 right and 8 wrong.

Line 1...............Number right... 24
Line 2...............Number wrong 8
Line 3...............¼ of line 2 = ¼ × 8...................... − 2
Line 4...............24 − 2..........................YOUR SCORE = 22

Notice that just as for Address Checking, questions that are not answered are *not* taken into account.

Guidelines

How good is the score you just made?

> 44 or more ....Good
> 26 to 43 ....Fair
> 25 or less ....You need to improve.

If your score on this test was low, don't be discouraged. *Just about everyone who takes this memory test "cold" has the same experience.* Yet, most of them go on to make a vast improvement in their score after they have studied what lies ahead in Chapters 5 and 6. If you are like the average person that we have worked with and are willing to invest a little time in study and practice, you can confidently set your sights on a mark well above 44. In fact, scores of 60 and above are attainable by those who prepare themselves thoroughly.

Personal Progress Record

Turn to page 231. Look at the table entitled "Personal Progress—Memory for Addresses." Use it to keep a permanent record of your scores on the practice tests. A sample is printed below to familiarize you with it. The entries are based on the preceding example.

Personal Progress Record—Sample

		MEMORY FOR ADDRESSES										
		Initial Tests							Repeated Tests			
Date	Test	Number Completed	Number Correct **A**	Number Wrong	× ¼ =	Points off **B**	Score **(A − B)**		Date	Score	Date	Score
5/15	Diagnostic Practice Test	32	24	8	× ¼ =	2	22					
5/16	Practice Test 1	46	38	8	× ¼ =	2	36					
5/18	Practice Test 2	58	52	6	× ¼ =	1½	50½					
5/20	Practice Test 3	64	60	4	× ¼ =	1	59					
	Practice Test 4				× ¼ =							
	Practice Test 5				× ¼ =							

Make the proper entries on the record for the Diagnostic Practice Test that you just took. Use it to keep a record of all the practice tests you take. You should be pleasantly surprised at how much higher your next entry on this card will be.

HOW ADDRESSES MAY DIFFER

Now that you have completed the Diagnostic Practice Test and checked your answers, you can see that the differences between address pairs fall into four main categories.

1. **Number Differences.** A street address or a zip code may be:
   a. *Transposed.*

   6<u>35</u> La Calle Mayor   *versus*   6<u>53</u> La Calle Mayor

   b. *Changed.*

   Washington DC 200<u>13</u>   *versus*   Washington DC 200<u>18</u>

   c. *Omitted.*

   1047<u>6</u> Eastern Avenue   *versus*   1047_ Eastern Avenue

2. **Directional Differences.** These can occur *before* or *after* the street name.

   1166 <u>N</u> Beaumont Dr   *versus*   1166 <u>S</u> Beaumont Dr

   758 Los Arboles Ave <u>SE</u>   *versus*   758 Los Arboles Ave <u>SW</u>

3. **Abbreviation Differences**
   a. *Streets, Drives, Avenues.*

   2560 Lansford <u>Pl</u>   *versus*   2560 Lansford <u>St</u>

   6434 E Pulaski <u>St</u>   *versus*   6434 E Pulaski <u>Ct</u>

   b. *States.*

   These abbreviations are particularly important now that the new, 2-letter abbreviations of state names are replacing many of the longer, easy-to-distinguish ones. For example, the *Postal Service Directory* abbreviates California by CA, *not* CAL or CALIF. Their abbreviation for Minnesota is MN, *not* MINN. Because many states now have 2-letter abbreviations beginning or ending with the same letter, there is a greater chance to overlook the differences if they appear on the test. For example:

   Sparta <u>G</u>A   *versus*   Sparta <u>V</u>A

   Shreveport <u>L</u>A   *versus*   Shreveport <u>I</u>A

   Portland O<u>R</u>   *versus*   Portland O<u>H</u>

   (A complete list of the 2-letter state abbreviations appears on page 225 with which you may practice.)

4. **Spelling Differences**
   a. *Single letters may be added, transposed, or changed.*

   22 Sa<u>gn</u>aw Pkwy   *versus*   22 Sa<u>ga</u>naw Pkwy

   3302 W A<u>v</u>alon Rd   *versus*   3302 W A<u>l</u>avon Rd

   8406 La C<u>a</u>sa St   *versus*   8406 La C<u>o</u>sa St

   b. *Small groups of letters may be substituted.*

   3282 E D<u>ow</u>nington St   *versus*   3282 E D<u>un</u>nington St

   565 Green<u>ville</u> Blvd SE   *versus*   565 Green<u>view</u> Blvd SE

   (Very often these are endings that commonly look or sound somewhat alike. A brief list of these groups is given in the table on page 49.)

DIAGNOSTIC CHART

PART A—ADDRESS CHECKING

Type of Difference	"D" Questions	Number of "D" Questions Wrong		
		TRIAL 1	TRIAL 2	TRIAL 3
Numbers: transposed	8, 12, 23, 42, 49, 52, 53, 57, 69, 77, 91			
changed	27, 46, 86			
omitted	29, 60			
Directions	16, 44, 59, 63, 67, 85			
Abbreviations: streets, roads, avenues, etc	13, 24, 31, 39, 50, 54, 78			
states	74			
Spelling: single letters	3, 5, 7, 22, 37, 38, 40, 56, 58, 62, 68, 71, 73, 79, 88, 93, 95			
groups of letters	17, 19, 26, 36, 70, 82			
Total Number of Each Type	53			
	Use the columns on the right to enter the question numbers of those "A's" you marked "D"			

This chart will help you to pinpoint the kinds of errors you have made on this Practice Test. Use it as directed below after you have taken and marked the test.

The first column on the left, "Type of Difference," contains the same categories whereby addresses may differ (see opposite). On the same line across, the second column gives the number of the questions that fall within each category. In the third column, you are to enter the number of the questions you had wrong. Do not include those you did not do. Use the space indicated in this column to list the number of any "A" questions you answered as "D." Checking these addresses may reveal a problem on which you will want to work.

After you have made all the entries, you will be able to see the areas in which you need to improve. Then turn to the appropriate part of Chapter 3, Address Checking: How to Improve Your Score, and read it. Then practice those drills that can help. For example, if you find you have been making too many errors picking out number differences, read page 52 and do Drills 18 through 21. If you have a problem with single letters because of reversals like *b* and *d*, or if you have been overlooking the difference between *a, e,* and *o*, read page 49. Examine the table and work on Drills 10 and 11 if the problem persists.

Remember that this chart is designed for diagnostic purposes and guidance on further practice. It has been drawn so that you can enter the results each time you retake a Practice Test. In this way you will be able to see how you are progressing. It is not necessary to try to score it. That is best done by using the Personal Progress Record Card.

PART B—MEMORY FOR ADDRESSES

Kind of Address		Number of Questions	Number Wrong		
			TRIAL 1	TRIAL 2	TRIAL 3
Direct:					
	list 1	40			
	list 2	36			
Numbered:					
	list 1	48			
	list 2	52			

The purpose of this chart is to help you evaluate your performance on the two kinds of memory questions that appear in the Practice Test—the questions on the direct (name) addresses and the questions on the numbered addresses. Use it as directed below after you have taken and marked the entire test.

The first column on the left, "Kind of Address," is divided by category into "Direct Address" versus "Numbered Address." The second column gives the number of questions in each category. Use the third column to enter the total number of questions in each category that you answered incorrectly. There is room for you to make additional entries if you take the Practice Test more than once.

At a glance, you will be able to see which area you need to concentrate on and how well you are progressing as you take repeat trials. Use Chapter 4 and the drills in it to improve your memory for the direct addresses. Use Chapter 5 for the numbered addresses.

Remember to use the Personal Progress Record Card (Memory for Addresses) to keep track of your actual scores as you keep studying and practicing.

Learning
the
Special
Techniques

Address Checking—How to Improve Your Score

TEST STRATEGY

Before we get into the specific ways to increase speed and accuracy, let's discuss test strategy. One definition of strategy is, "a plan, method or series of maneuvers for obtaining a specific goal or result." You can see the importance of effective strategy everywhere. Effective strategy makes the difference between champions and also-rans in every field of human endeavor—from fighting a war to managing a baseball team. That is why great, big-league managers earn so much. They have been known to take teams that ranked in fifth or sixth place under former managers and mold them into league champions. How? By using ways to make the most of their team's ability. Using *your* ability to the best advantage is what effective test strategy is all about. This is what we will now discuss.

DON'T GO FOR 100%

On the Address Checking test, your goal is, of course, to get the highest score you can. It is to your advantage to work as quickly and accurately as possible since the test score is based on the number of wrong answers as well as the number of right answers. The problem is that for most of us, the faster we work, the more errors we make. But everyone is different in his or her speed and skills. Therefore, each of us has to know what combination of speed and accuracy will yield the best results. Practice, and trial and error, will determine the correct combination for *you*. To illustrate these ideas, here are a couple of illustrations:

Joe Smith is preparing to take the Post Office Clerk-Carrier test. He decides to work very carefully, as he did in school, and to avoid any errors. After taking the test, his results on the Address Checking part show that he has completed 32 questions and has gotten only 2 wrong. If he were graded the way he used to be in school, he would have a score of 94 percent!

But that's not the way this test is actually scored. His true score will be calculated by the formula you saw before:

$$\begin{array}{r} 30 \text{ Right} \\ -\ 2 \text{ Wrong} \\ \hline 28 = \text{Joe Smith's Score} \end{array}$$

This score is definitely too low according to the criteria on page 27.

A few years later, Joe has another opportunity to take the Clerk-Carrier test in this city. This time he prepares for it, and he rethinks his test strategy. He decides to push on a bit faster, even though he is not sure whether he can be as accurate as before.

Here is what happened:

He answered 44 questions and got 5 wrong.
His percentage score = 88%, quite a drop; *but* . . .
his actual test score = 34 (39 − 5).

His new strategy paid off—he raised his score from 28 (below par) to 34 (fair) even though he got more than twice as many wrong!

GUESSING

This discussion of test strategy wouldn't be complete without discussing the matter of guessing. After all, why not raise the number of possible right answers by making sure you've answered all 95 questions even if you have to guess blindly at the last 20 or 30? Guessing is *not* advisable if you consider the odds involved. You have a 50–50 chance on each question. If you guess, you will probably get as many wrong as you get right. The net result is zero—nothing gained. You might even be unlucky and get more wrong than right. In that case, you would be penalized because each wrong answer would deduct a point from your score. You would also stand to lose time better spent working at your usual pace, which you *know* would net you a few extra points.

Because everyone is different, you, the reader, will need to work out your individual test strategy on this and other parts of the test. You will learn how fast you can proceed while still maintaining reasonable accuracy. If you study and practice the techniques described in the following pages, you will increase speed and accuracy and keep raising your score. Use the Personal Progress Record on page 231 to help you see what your optimum speed is to yield the best score.

As was mentioned before, it is within the realm of possibility to score in the high eighties on this section of the test. The wonderful thing about this program is that *you are in charge* of your progress—you can go as fast and as far as your talent and persistence allow.

TECHNIQUES FOR INCREASING
YOUR ADDRESS CHECKING SKILLS

In any activity requiring skill, whether in bowling, chess, or typing, the key to success is knowing the correct techniques and then practicing them. A good example of what proper technique and training can accomplish is seen in the advances that have been made in track and field sports.

Barely 38 years ago, a world record of 4 minutes and 6.2 seconds for the one-mile run was set by the "Flying Swede," Gunder Haegg. Running experts at that time were sure it would never be broken. The 4-minute mile wasn't even on the horizon. But things have sure changed. Recently, 7 out of 11 runners competing in a one-mile race broke the once invincible 4-minute barrier! What happened to explain this phenomenal performance? For one thing, the sport was scientifically studied to learn more about running techniques and training methods. Everything was scrutinized, including length of stride, recovery time, track shoe design, pacing, diet, and the psychology of running. Anything and everything, no matter how minute, was considered, as long as it led to faster time. Then, too, increased interest and participation in running led athletes to start their careers and training at an earlier age. Athletes trained longer and harder. Sports medicine used scientific methods to establish the best training regimens. We can see how the two factors—correct technique and diligent practice—have paid dividends.

Correct technique and diligent practice are also the basis for this book. Every technique that can help you raise your score has been carefully considered and explained. Learn and practice each of them. Remember, when you raise *your* speed record, you get that much closer to a job appointment.

(Incidentally, the present world record is 3 minutes and 47.33 seconds, and no one talks about limits too much any more.)

USE BOTH HANDS PROPERLY

When you take the Postal Service test, you will find that the questions are printed on a separate page from the answer sheet (the way it has been done in this book). Nevertheless, many candidates lose time by not using their hands correctly. The most common error is for the candidates to leave one or both hands idle and out of position while they read each address line. When they have decided on Ⓐ or Ⓓ, they then have to bring their pencil up to the correct line on the answer sheet. Valuable fractions of a second are lost performing this movement. Sometimes the test taker loses his place on the question sheet or on the answer sheet. This wastes more time and may even result in putting an answer on the wrong line. That could lead to disaster. Every succeeding answer will then appear on the wrong line.

The remedy is simply to *keep both hands in the correct position relative to the question and answer sheets*. Assuming you are right-handed, you should keep your left hand on the question sheet as a guide, slowly moving it down for each question. Your right hand, holding the pencil, should be poised on the corresponding question number on the answer sheet. Keep both hands working together in this way as you take the test.

Wrong Hand Position

Correct Hand Position

MAKING YOUR MARK

The instructions you receive at the time of the official test will include directions on how to fill out the answer sheet. Make sure you follow these directions, but be careful that you don't misinterpret them and do what is unnecessary and time-wasteful.

We are referring to the way you are supposed to mark the answer sheet. You are instructed to darken completely the answer space that you have selected. You must keep your mark neat and stay within the circle.

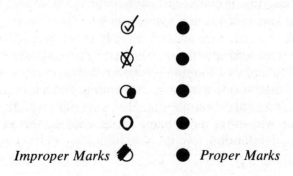

Improper Marks   *Proper Marks*

But we have seen many test candidates spend as much, or more, time carefully outlining and darkening the spaces as they did in examining the question and in deciding on the answer! This is *not* an artistic competition. Don't waste time! You could be completing perhaps 50% to 100% more questions using the time wasted making that beautiful mark.

Here is what to do. Prepare your pencil point so that it is broad enough to darken the interior of the circle or bar in one or two strokes. Bring two or three such pencils to the examination room. Train yourself to darken the circles properly and speedily. Special answer sheets to help you drill on this is provided on pages 45 through 48 of this chapter.

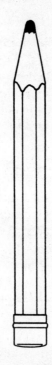

Shape of Preferred Pencil Point

A DIFFERENT KIND OF "READING"

Notice that this test is called "Address Checking." *Checking* is not the same as ordinary reading. For example, you can check a letter to see if it has a return address or not without reading that address. Similarly, you can quickly check a "Help Wanted" column to see if there are any job openings for "receptionists" and/or "engineers," without really reading the details in the ads. Did you ever have the experience of driving a car and suddenly realizing that, for a few minutes, you had not been aware of driving? Yet the car and you were still in one piece. Obviously, you had seen, heard and reacted to the traffic about you, but in a special way. In other words, there are differences in the amount and quality of what you see and how it registers, depending upon the kind of "looking" you are doing.

In the first illustration, what you have done is to look at the envelope just long enough and hard enough to *perceive* an address. You could not tell what the address was in terms of name, number, etc., because you had not focused your understanding on it. You did not really *read* it—you just *scanned* it. This difference is of major importance to you in a test situation such as this, where speed is important. Reading for comprehension would slow you down, and it is not necessary for this type of test. Your brain would need time to translate the written symbols into meaningful words. You would not be able to read faster than you think. The remedy? Do *not* read for comprehension. Just scan the addresses to perceive any differences between the two.

To see how a slowdown caused by reading for comprehension can occur, check these two pairs of addresses:

2461 Cherry St., Springfield	2461 Sherry St., Springfield	Ⓐ Ⓓ
195 Vloovook, La Canton	195 Vloovool, La Canton	Ⓐ Ⓓ

The first pair of addresses has familiar words, especially Cherry and Sherry. If you let yourself visualize Cherry as a bunch of fruit and Sherry as a bottle of wine, you have attached meaning to these words. That momentary mental pause for recognition slowed you down. Your job was only to see that Cherry was different from Sherry and to mark choice Ⓓ.

When you looked at the second pair, you may have fallen into *two* time-consuming traps. First, you may have allowed yourself to reflect momentarily on that weird, unusual name—"Vloovook." Maybe you tried to connect it to something or someplace you heard of . . . Eskimos, perhaps?

Second, you may have sounded it out. Whether you whispered it aloud or to yourself, you lost time. Sounding it out lowered your speed of perception to that of your oral reading speed, which is far slower than your silent speed. Many people who read this way are largely unaware that they do so. To make sure that you are not moving your lips or subvocalizing, conduct this simple test. As you read, put your fingers gently alongside your lips and your throat. You will feel a slight muscle movement or vibration if you are vocalizing. The cure lies first in becoming aware of the habit. Then, you must keep trying to let your brain register what your eyes see, in an instantaneous flash of recognition. Keep your lips still. Don't even *think* about how the words sound. Try keeping a pencil clenched between your teeth when you do the practice exercises in this book or whenever you read anything.

To summarize, your task is to compare Vloovook with Vloovool and to notice the difference between "k" and "l." You must be able to perceive the distinctions in shape,* spacing, and position whether in letters, numbers, or names, as quickly as you can. That's all! Many test takers prepare themselves mentally for address checking by imagining that their eyes are picking

---

* NOTE: There are letters and letter combinations that may cause perceptual problems. For example, the letters *b* and *d* are often mistaken for each other by people who *reverse* them. Reversal can occur vertically with the letters *m* and *w*. Errors may occur with words or parts of words, e.g., "was" versus "saw." Some people are more prone to these difficulties than others. If you find you have this kind of problem, spend extra time practicing the letters and words that cause you trouble. Use the table "Some Common Perception Errors Made in Reading" on page 49, which has a sampling of commonly confused letters and groups of letters or words.

up images the way a camera or an optical scanner does. It may seem silly, but for the purpose of this test, say to yourself, "*I am a camera.*"

Use the exercises on pages 50 through 53 to develop your perceptual speed and accuracy. Here's one to try right now: Quickly read the sentence below:

> Two trees on the left and one shrub standing in between are attractive.

Now count the *t*'s in the sentence *one time*—don't go back to double check. Write the number here _____. The answer is nine *t*'s. Did you get it right?

WIDEN YOUR EYE SPAN

To see how this important technique can help, imagine that you are timing two test candidates, Tom and Barbara, as they check these addresses on their test:

> 1462 Church Av Eaton Ill   1462 Church Av Eaton Ind

Results: Both candidates correctly selected choice Ⓓ.

> Tom took a total of 6 seconds to come up with the answer; Barbara took only 4 seconds.

Although both of them got the right answer, Barbara worked 50% faster than Tom. At that rate, she could answer 75 questions in the time it would take Tom to do 50! Her test score would then be in the upper ranks, while Tom's would be far, far behind.

One of the factors working in Barbara's favor may have been her wider eye span, i.e., her ability to perceive more at a glance than Tom could. To understand what eye span, or *span of perception*, really means, we need to examine how the eye works.

Our eyes are controlled by six tiny muscles as they move along a line of print. This eye movement is not smooth; it is more like a series of jumps and stops. It is during these stops, called *fixations*, that we actually perceive words. The amount of numbers and letters our eyes pick up at each stop is called our *eye span*. The wider our eye span, the faster we can go. To illustrate, let's see how Barbara and Tom each read the line below:

BARBARA

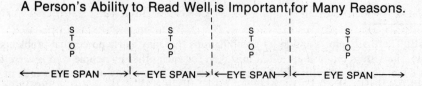

A Person's Ability to Read Well is Important for Many Reasons.

Notice that Barbara reads this sentence, stopping four times. At each stop or fixation, her eye has spanned an average of three words.

Tom has not developed his eye span sufficiently. He reads the same line this way:

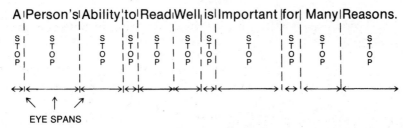

Tom has stopped for a fixation on every word. His average eye span is only *one* word. The result? He has read the line far slower than Barbara.

Word-by-word reading, with its greater number of fixations, slows a reader down dramatically. (On page 39 it was noted that "sounding out" words could be another one of the reasons for reading words in a sentence one at a time.) What makes matters worse is that many people who read this way are unaware of it. Now that we have established that Tom is one of these people, let's compare the way Tom and Barbara read the address on page 40. In the samples below, dots (•) have been used to indicate points above which the eye focuses at each fixation; a solid line underscores the width of the eye span. Eye span width is measured by counting the units of type included in each fixation. (It includes the spaces between words as well.)

TOM

Number of fixations = 5 per side.
Average eye span = 5 type units.

BARBARA

1462 Church Av Eaton Ill   1462 Church Av Eaton Ind

Number of fixations = 3 per side.
Average eye span = 8 type units.

These diagrams clearly show the reason that Barbara is going fifty percent faster than Tom. But even Barbara's performance can be improved! It is possible to see each side in two, or in even in *one* fixation if you train yourself to widen your eye span. You can learn to use your peripheral vision to widen your perception span to its maximum by using the exercises given on pages 59 through 64. As your eyes become able to grasp larger and larger "bunches" of each address at a time, your checking speed will increase.

There is still another benefit that comes with increased eye span. You save extra time because your eyes move back and forth fewer times as you compare the two addresses. If Barbara's eye movements could be seen as they sweep back and forth between the left and right hand columns, their path would look like this:

BARBARA

(The loops have been exaggerated to make the diagram clearer.)

Barbara made three "eye sweeps" going from the left side to the right side (plus the returns). She compared the "eyeful" gathered during each fixation on the left with the corresponding part of the address on the right. If Tom worked the same way, he would need more time because his eyes would have to make five sweeps (one for each fixation).

There is still room for improvement! Barbara could work even faster if she checked the entire address on the left side and *then* compared the mental images of the three fixations with the corresponding parts of the address line on the right.

DON'T GO BACK—DON'T REGRESS

One day, a student who had just begun one of our exam preparation classes took the Address Checking portion of the Diagnostic Practice Test and scored only 15. When we asked if he would describe any special difficulty he was having, he shamefacedly said, "I really feel awful about my score. If anything, I should have come out higher than most. After all, I work for a printer as a proofreader!" We asked a few more questions about his job, and the reason for his troubles became clear. He had formed a tendency, reinforced by years of proofreading, to scrutinize all printed matter with the utmost care so that absolutely no errors appeared in the magazines his firm published. He developed into a perfectionist as far as catching errors in his on-the-job reading matter. Sad to say, he carried these proofreading habits over to *everything* he read, including the addresses on the Postal Service test. As a result, his test score was drastically low. On pages 34 through 35 we discussed test strategy and why absolute perfectionism was *not* a good idea. His case makes the point perfectly. Others, whose occupation may lead them into the same problem, include stenographer-typists, file clerks, and accountants.

If you find yourself re-reading work or pausing over an item in an address for too long a period of time, you can end the habit by (1) re-reading the explanation on test strategy and (2) pushing yourself ahead to greater and greater speeds using the special exercises at the end of this chapter.

There are still other reasons for regression:

1. Some adults carry over habits formed in school when they read and studied for exams. When someone is reading difficult material which they must remember and understand thoroughly, they naturally read at a slower pace. There is often a need to re-read and reflect until the material sinks in. Obviously, address checking is a kind of reading that is a world apart. So why not change your reading style to fit the task at hand?
2. Many of us regress because we feel we have missed something, and we must look back to make sure we didn't.
3. We don't concentrate effectively. We daydream or let outside thoughts enter our consciousness. At that point, our work suffers. We may slow up. We may *really* miss seeing words. How can we learn to concentrate better? By focusing our attention and not allowing internal or external distractions intrude. Become a machine! Pretend nothing can stop you— that you're an electronic scanning device passing over a succession of word and number images.

Regardless of the reason, you can stop yourself from regressing. Each time you catch yourself ready to look back—force yourself to go on! Psyche yourself into believing that you are really not going to miss that much or make many errors if you keep on going. To help you build that kind of confidence, special exercises have been provided that are aimed at overcoming regression. Turn to page 65 of this chapter for directions.

WORK RHYTHMICALLY

As you do the practice tests and drills in this book, you should carefully time yourself. Soon you will get the feel of how fast you are going without looking at a clock. You will know when you are going at a pace that balances speed and accuracy for best results. Learn to feel that pace in your bones. Translate it into a rhythm, as your eyes sweep from one address to the other. If you keep the rhythm without letting regression or distractions get the better of you, you will *consistently* complete a certain number of lines in a given time.

To help you visualize how to go about finding, feeling, and using rhythm on the test, another illustration will be used. Let's assume that our friend Tom becomes able to check an address in two fixations. He now needs only two eye sweeps to complete a typical address like this:

TOM

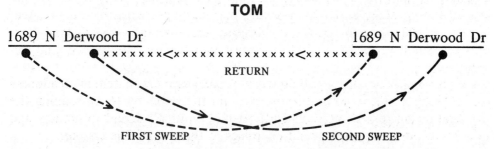

(The loops have been exaggerated to make the diagram clearer.)

Furthermore, we will assume that he has learned how to work at a rhythmic pace.

Tom then takes another practice test, completes 70 of the 95 questions, and gets 10% of his answers wrong. His score is: 63 right − 7 wrong = 56. Rhythm cannot be discussed without mentioning time, so let's calculate how long it took him to do *one* line. Divide 6 minutes (360 seconds) by 70. This works out to approximately 5 seconds per line (including the time needed for Tom to mark down his answer and move to the next line).

Because Tom has been practicing, he can really feel what a 5-second period is like. It is as though he has a mental metronome keeping time for him. His brain, eye movements, and hands all work together at the right rhythm to drive him along at the rate of 5 seconds per line.

How about you? Do you know what a 5-second period of time feels like? Or a 4-second period of time? Try this experiment:

Assume you are working to reach a 4-second-per-line speed. First, practice getting the feel of 4 seconds and the right rhythm by counting off 4 seconds as you look at a sweep second watch face. Do that several times. Then, chant out loud a few times—"1 - 2 - 3 - 4," etc. Now, chant it mentally. When you think you've got the feel of a 4-second time period, use it to check the address below. Fit your movements into that 4-second time slot. Establish the right rhythm. Try to move smoothly.

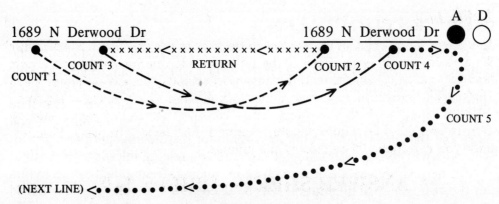

(The loops have been exaggerated to make the diagram clearer.)

RHYTHMIC CYCLE

Count 1 Initial *fixation* on the first half of the address in the left column.
Count 2 *Sweep* to the right column—*fixation* to compare.
Count 3 Return to *fixation* on the second half of the address in the left column.
Count 4 *Sweep* to the right column—*fixation* to compare.
Count 5 Mark answer and *sweep* to the next line.

Repeat this cycle a few times. This experiment was intended only to illustrate the technique of working in rhythm. The 4-second cycle is probably too fast for you . . . *now*. Only you will be able to feel what is right for you at this stage. Experiment with the various practice tests in this book.

SPECIAL EXERCISES FOR BUILDING ADDRESS CHECKING SKILLS

You now have the "tools." You have learned the strategies and techniques that make a high score possible. Now you must be certain that you can apply them at test time. That means practice.

This section contains various exercises and drills. They will help you to eliminate any bad habits that you may have and to build the address checking skills you need. Work on them as needed. As you practice, remember that your progress may not be steady. Dramatic improvements are often followed by plateaus, times when your scores level off for a while. Sometimes there are even dips. All this is perfectly natural and occurs in all skills training. Just keep on practicing in the sure knowledge that your scores must rise. (Remember that four-minute mile!)

Note that an Answer Key may be found on page 71. In order to check your progress, since you may wish to take a number of exercises more than once, refer to the Personal Progress Chart on pages 233 to 234 to record your scores.

DRILLS TO INCREASE SPEED IN MARKING ANSWERS

Drills 1–9

Use pages 45 through 48 to develop speed. There are nine answer drills with 95 answer lines in each. Four of the drills are laid out horizontally; five are laid out vertically. On the test, the answer sheets may be laid out either way. Darken *one* space on each line, either box Ⓐ or Ⓓ. Pick boxes at random; it doesn't matter which you select. The idea is to practice making the entries cleanly and quickly. Time yourself. Prepare your pencil properly. Practice until you can make 95 entries in one minute.

ANSWER SHEET—DRILLS 1–9

DRILL 1

1 ⒶⒹ	2 ⒶⒹ	3 ⒶⒹ	4 ⒶⒹ	5 ⒶⒹ	6 ⒶⒹ	7 ⒶⒹ	8 ⒶⒹ	9 ⒶⒹ
10 ⒶⒹ	11 ⒶⒹ	12 ⒶⒹ	13 ⒶⒹ	14 ⒶⒹ	15 ⒶⒹ	16 ⒶⒹ	17 ⒶⒹ	
18 ⒶⒹ	19 ⒶⒹ	20 ⒶⒹ	21 ⒶⒹ	22 ⒶⒹ	23 ⒶⒹ	24 ⒶⒹ	25 ⒶⒹ	
26 ⒶⒹ	27 ⒶⒹ	28 ⒶⒹ	29 ⒶⒹ	30 ⒶⒹ	31 ⒶⒹ	32 ⒶⒹ	33 ⒶⒹ	
34 ⒶⒹ	35 ⒶⒹ	36 ⒶⒹ	37 ⒶⒹ	38 ⒶⒹ	39 ⒶⒹ	40 ⒶⒹ	41 ⒶⒹ	
42 ⒶⒹ	43 ⒶⒹ	44 ⒶⒹ	45 ⒶⒹ	46 ⒶⒹ	47 ⒶⒹ	48 ⒶⒹ	49 ⒶⒹ	
50 ⒶⒹ	51 ⒶⒹ	52 ⒶⒹ	53 ⒶⒹ	54 ⒶⒹ	55 ⒶⒹ	56 ⒶⒹ	57 ⒶⒹ	
58 ⒶⒹ	59 ⒶⒹ	60 ⒶⒹ	61 ⒶⒹ	62 ⒶⒹ	63 ⒶⒹ	64 ⒶⒹ	65 ⒶⒹ	
66 ⒶⒹ	67 ⒶⒹ	68 ⒶⒹ	69 ⒶⒹ	70 ⒶⒹ	71 ⒶⒹ	72 ⒶⒹ	73 ⒶⒹ	
74 ⒶⒹ	75 ⒶⒹ	76 ⒶⒹ	77 ⒶⒹ	78 ⒶⒹ	79 ⒶⒹ	80 ⒶⒹ	81 ⒶⒹ	
82 ⒶⒹ	83 ⒶⒹ	84 ⒶⒹ	85 ⒶⒹ	86 ⒶⒹ	87 ⒶⒹ	88 ⒶⒹ	89 ⒶⒹ	
90 ⒶⒹ	91 ⒶⒹ	92 ⒶⒹ	93 ⒶⒹ	94 ⒶⒹ	95 ⒶⒹ			

TIME:

DRILL 2

1 Ⓐ Ⓓ	2 Ⓐ Ⓓ	3 Ⓐ Ⓓ	4 Ⓐ Ⓓ	5 Ⓐ Ⓓ	6 Ⓐ Ⓓ	7 Ⓐ Ⓓ	8 Ⓐ Ⓓ	9 Ⓐ Ⓓ
10 Ⓐ Ⓓ	11 Ⓐ Ⓓ	12 Ⓐ Ⓓ	13 Ⓐ Ⓓ	14 Ⓐ Ⓓ	15 Ⓐ Ⓓ	16 Ⓐ Ⓓ	17 Ⓐ Ⓓ	
18 Ⓐ Ⓓ	19 Ⓐ Ⓓ	20 Ⓐ Ⓓ	21 Ⓐ Ⓓ	22 Ⓐ Ⓓ	23 Ⓐ Ⓓ	24 Ⓐ Ⓓ	25 Ⓐ Ⓓ	
26 Ⓐ Ⓓ	27 Ⓐ Ⓓ	28 Ⓐ Ⓓ	29 Ⓐ Ⓓ	30 Ⓐ Ⓓ	31 Ⓐ Ⓓ	32 Ⓐ Ⓓ	33 Ⓐ Ⓓ	
34 Ⓐ Ⓓ	35 Ⓐ Ⓓ	36 Ⓐ Ⓓ	37 Ⓐ Ⓓ	38 Ⓐ Ⓓ	39 Ⓐ Ⓓ	40 Ⓐ Ⓓ	41 Ⓐ Ⓓ	
42 Ⓐ Ⓓ	43 Ⓐ Ⓓ	44 Ⓐ Ⓓ	45 Ⓐ Ⓓ	46 Ⓐ Ⓓ	47 Ⓐ Ⓓ	48 Ⓐ Ⓓ	49 Ⓐ Ⓓ	
50 Ⓐ Ⓓ	51 Ⓐ Ⓓ	52 Ⓐ Ⓓ	53 Ⓐ Ⓓ	54 Ⓐ Ⓓ	55 Ⓐ Ⓓ	56 Ⓐ Ⓓ	57 Ⓐ Ⓓ	
58 Ⓐ Ⓓ	59 Ⓐ Ⓓ	60 Ⓐ Ⓓ	61 Ⓐ Ⓓ	62 Ⓐ Ⓓ	63 Ⓐ Ⓓ	64 Ⓐ Ⓓ	65 Ⓐ Ⓓ	
66 Ⓐ Ⓓ	67 Ⓐ Ⓓ	68 Ⓐ Ⓓ	69 Ⓐ Ⓓ	70 Ⓐ Ⓓ	71 Ⓐ Ⓓ	72 Ⓐ Ⓓ	73 Ⓐ Ⓓ	
74 Ⓐ Ⓓ	75 Ⓐ Ⓓ	76 Ⓐ Ⓓ	77 Ⓐ Ⓓ	78 Ⓐ Ⓓ	79 Ⓐ Ⓓ	80 Ⓐ Ⓓ	81 Ⓐ Ⓓ	
82 Ⓐ Ⓓ	83 Ⓐ Ⓓ	84 Ⓐ Ⓓ	85 Ⓐ Ⓓ	86 Ⓐ Ⓓ	87 Ⓐ Ⓓ	88 Ⓐ Ⓓ	89 Ⓐ Ⓓ	
90 Ⓐ Ⓓ	91 Ⓐ Ⓓ	92 Ⓐ Ⓓ	93 Ⓐ Ⓓ	94 Ⓐ Ⓓ	95 Ⓐ Ⓓ			

TIME:

DRILL 3

1 Ⓐ Ⓓ	2 Ⓐ Ⓓ	3 Ⓐ Ⓓ	4 Ⓐ Ⓓ	5 Ⓐ Ⓓ	6 Ⓐ Ⓓ	7 Ⓐ Ⓓ	8 Ⓐ Ⓓ	9 Ⓐ Ⓓ
10 Ⓐ Ⓓ	11 Ⓐ Ⓓ	12 Ⓐ Ⓓ	13 Ⓐ Ⓓ	14 Ⓐ Ⓓ	15 Ⓐ Ⓓ	16 Ⓐ Ⓓ	17 Ⓐ Ⓓ	
18 Ⓐ Ⓓ	19 Ⓐ Ⓓ	20 Ⓐ Ⓓ	21 Ⓐ Ⓓ	22 Ⓐ Ⓓ	23 Ⓐ Ⓓ	24 Ⓐ Ⓓ	25 Ⓐ Ⓓ	
26 Ⓐ Ⓓ	27 Ⓐ Ⓓ	28 Ⓐ Ⓓ	29 Ⓐ Ⓓ	30 Ⓐ Ⓓ	31 Ⓐ Ⓓ	32 Ⓐ Ⓓ	33 Ⓐ Ⓓ	
34 Ⓐ Ⓓ	35 Ⓐ Ⓓ	36 Ⓐ Ⓓ	37 Ⓐ Ⓓ	38 Ⓐ Ⓓ	39 Ⓐ Ⓓ	40 Ⓐ Ⓓ	41 Ⓐ Ⓓ	
42 Ⓐ Ⓓ	43 Ⓐ Ⓓ	44 Ⓐ Ⓓ	45 Ⓐ Ⓓ	46 Ⓐ Ⓓ	47 Ⓐ Ⓓ	48 Ⓐ Ⓓ	49 Ⓐ Ⓓ	
50 Ⓐ Ⓓ	51 Ⓐ Ⓓ	52 Ⓐ Ⓓ	53 Ⓐ Ⓓ	54 Ⓐ Ⓓ	55 Ⓐ Ⓓ	56 Ⓐ Ⓓ	57 Ⓐ Ⓓ	
58 Ⓐ Ⓓ	59 Ⓐ Ⓓ	60 Ⓐ Ⓓ	61 Ⓐ Ⓓ	62 Ⓐ Ⓓ	63 Ⓐ Ⓓ	64 Ⓐ Ⓓ	65 Ⓐ Ⓓ	
66 Ⓐ Ⓓ	67 Ⓐ Ⓓ	68 Ⓐ Ⓓ	69 Ⓐ Ⓓ	70 Ⓐ Ⓓ	71 Ⓐ Ⓓ	72 Ⓐ Ⓓ	73 Ⓐ Ⓓ	
74 Ⓐ Ⓓ	75 Ⓐ Ⓓ	76 Ⓐ Ⓓ	77 Ⓐ Ⓓ	78 Ⓐ Ⓓ	79 Ⓐ Ⓓ	80 Ⓐ Ⓓ	81 Ⓐ Ⓓ	
82 Ⓐ Ⓓ	83 Ⓐ Ⓓ	84 Ⓐ Ⓓ	85 Ⓐ Ⓓ	86 Ⓐ Ⓓ	87 Ⓐ Ⓓ	88 Ⓐ Ⓓ	89 Ⓐ Ⓓ	
90 Ⓐ Ⓓ	91 Ⓐ Ⓓ	92 Ⓐ Ⓓ	93 Ⓐ Ⓓ	94 Ⓐ Ⓓ	95 Ⓐ Ⓓ			

TIME:

DRILL 4

1 Ⓐ Ⓓ	2 Ⓐ Ⓓ	3 Ⓐ Ⓓ	4 Ⓐ Ⓓ	5 Ⓐ Ⓓ	6 Ⓐ Ⓓ	7 Ⓐ Ⓓ	8 Ⓐ Ⓓ	9 Ⓐ Ⓓ
10 Ⓐ Ⓓ	11 Ⓐ Ⓓ	12 Ⓐ Ⓓ	13 Ⓐ Ⓓ	14 Ⓐ Ⓓ	15 Ⓐ Ⓓ	16 Ⓐ Ⓓ	17 Ⓐ Ⓓ	
18 Ⓐ Ⓓ	19 Ⓐ Ⓓ	20 Ⓐ Ⓓ	21 Ⓐ Ⓓ	22 Ⓐ Ⓓ	23 Ⓐ Ⓓ	24 Ⓐ Ⓓ	25 Ⓐ Ⓓ	
26 Ⓐ Ⓓ	27 Ⓐ Ⓓ	28 Ⓐ Ⓓ	29 Ⓐ Ⓓ	30 Ⓐ Ⓓ	31 Ⓐ Ⓓ	32 Ⓐ Ⓓ	33 Ⓐ Ⓓ	
34 Ⓐ Ⓓ	35 Ⓐ Ⓓ	36 Ⓐ Ⓓ	37 Ⓐ Ⓓ	38 Ⓐ Ⓓ	39 Ⓐ Ⓓ	40 Ⓐ Ⓓ	41 Ⓐ Ⓓ	
42 Ⓐ Ⓓ	43 Ⓐ Ⓓ	44 Ⓐ Ⓓ	45 Ⓐ Ⓓ	46 Ⓐ Ⓓ	47 Ⓐ Ⓓ	48 Ⓐ Ⓓ	49 Ⓐ Ⓓ	
50 Ⓐ Ⓓ	51 Ⓐ Ⓓ	52 Ⓐ Ⓓ	53 Ⓐ Ⓓ	54 Ⓐ Ⓓ	55 Ⓐ Ⓓ	56 Ⓐ Ⓓ	57 Ⓐ Ⓓ	
58 Ⓐ Ⓓ	59 Ⓐ Ⓓ	60 Ⓐ Ⓓ	61 Ⓐ Ⓓ	62 Ⓐ Ⓓ	63 Ⓐ Ⓓ	64 Ⓐ Ⓓ	65 Ⓐ Ⓓ	
66 Ⓐ Ⓓ	67 Ⓐ Ⓓ	68 Ⓐ Ⓓ	69 Ⓐ Ⓓ	70 Ⓐ Ⓓ	71 Ⓐ Ⓓ	72 Ⓐ Ⓓ	73 Ⓐ Ⓓ	
74 Ⓐ Ⓓ	75 Ⓐ Ⓓ	76 Ⓐ Ⓓ	77 Ⓐ Ⓓ	78 Ⓐ Ⓓ	79 Ⓐ Ⓓ	80 Ⓐ Ⓓ	81 Ⓐ Ⓓ	
82 Ⓐ Ⓓ	83 Ⓐ Ⓓ	84 Ⓐ Ⓓ	85 Ⓐ Ⓓ	86 Ⓐ Ⓓ	87 Ⓐ Ⓓ	88 Ⓐ Ⓓ	89 Ⓐ Ⓓ	
90 Ⓐ Ⓓ	91 Ⓐ Ⓓ	92 Ⓐ Ⓓ	93 Ⓐ Ⓓ	94 Ⓐ Ⓓ	95 Ⓐ Ⓓ			

TIME:

DRILL 5

1 Ⓐ Ⓓ	49 Ⓐ Ⓓ
2 Ⓐ Ⓓ	50 Ⓐ Ⓓ
3 Ⓐ Ⓓ	51 Ⓐ Ⓓ
4 Ⓐ Ⓓ	52 Ⓐ Ⓓ
5 Ⓐ Ⓓ	53 Ⓐ Ⓓ
6 Ⓐ Ⓓ	54 Ⓐ Ⓓ
7 Ⓐ Ⓓ	55 Ⓐ Ⓓ
8 Ⓐ Ⓓ	56 Ⓐ Ⓓ
9 Ⓐ Ⓓ	57 Ⓐ Ⓓ
10 Ⓐ Ⓓ	58 Ⓐ Ⓓ
11 Ⓐ Ⓓ	59 Ⓐ Ⓓ
12 Ⓐ Ⓓ	60 Ⓐ Ⓓ
13 Ⓐ Ⓓ	61 Ⓐ Ⓓ
14 Ⓐ Ⓓ	62 Ⓐ Ⓓ
15 Ⓐ Ⓓ	63 Ⓐ Ⓓ
16 Ⓐ Ⓓ	64 Ⓐ Ⓓ
17 Ⓐ Ⓓ	65 Ⓐ Ⓓ
18 Ⓐ Ⓓ	66 Ⓐ Ⓓ
19 Ⓐ Ⓓ	67 Ⓐ Ⓓ
20 Ⓐ Ⓓ	68 Ⓐ Ⓓ
21 Ⓐ Ⓓ	69 Ⓐ Ⓓ
22 Ⓐ Ⓓ	70 Ⓐ Ⓓ
23 Ⓐ Ⓓ	71 Ⓐ Ⓓ
24 Ⓐ Ⓓ	72 Ⓐ Ⓓ
25 Ⓐ Ⓓ	73 Ⓐ Ⓓ
26 Ⓐ Ⓓ	74 Ⓐ Ⓓ
27 Ⓐ Ⓓ	75 Ⓐ Ⓓ
28 Ⓐ Ⓓ	76 Ⓐ Ⓓ
29 Ⓐ Ⓓ	77 Ⓐ Ⓓ
30 Ⓐ Ⓓ	78 Ⓐ Ⓓ
31 Ⓐ Ⓓ	79 Ⓐ Ⓓ
32 Ⓐ Ⓓ	80 Ⓐ Ⓓ
33 Ⓐ Ⓓ	81 Ⓐ Ⓓ
34 Ⓐ Ⓓ	82 Ⓐ Ⓓ
35 Ⓐ Ⓓ	83 Ⓐ Ⓓ
36 Ⓐ Ⓓ	84 Ⓐ Ⓓ
37 Ⓐ Ⓓ	85 Ⓐ Ⓓ
38 Ⓐ Ⓓ	86 Ⓐ Ⓓ
39 Ⓐ Ⓓ	87 Ⓐ Ⓓ
40 Ⓐ Ⓓ	88 Ⓐ Ⓓ
41 Ⓐ Ⓓ	89 Ⓐ Ⓓ
42 Ⓐ Ⓓ	90 Ⓐ Ⓓ
43 Ⓐ Ⓓ	91 Ⓐ Ⓓ
44 Ⓐ Ⓓ	92 Ⓐ Ⓓ
45 Ⓐ Ⓓ	93 Ⓐ Ⓓ
46 Ⓐ Ⓓ	94 Ⓐ Ⓓ
47 Ⓐ Ⓓ	95 Ⓐ Ⓓ
48 Ⓐ Ⓓ	

TIME:

DRILL 6

1 Ⓐ Ⓓ	49 Ⓐ Ⓓ
2 Ⓐ Ⓓ	50 Ⓐ Ⓓ
3 Ⓐ Ⓓ	51 Ⓐ Ⓓ
4 Ⓐ Ⓓ	52 Ⓐ Ⓓ
5 Ⓐ Ⓓ	53 Ⓐ Ⓓ
6 Ⓐ Ⓓ	54 Ⓐ Ⓓ
7 Ⓐ Ⓓ	85 Ⓐ Ⓓ
8 Ⓐ Ⓓ	56 Ⓐ Ⓓ
9 Ⓐ Ⓓ	57 Ⓐ Ⓓ
10 Ⓐ Ⓓ	58 Ⓐ Ⓓ
11 Ⓐ Ⓓ	59 Ⓐ Ⓓ
12 Ⓐ Ⓓ	60 Ⓐ Ⓓ
13 Ⓐ Ⓓ	61 Ⓐ Ⓓ
14 Ⓐ Ⓓ	62 Ⓐ Ⓓ
15 Ⓐ Ⓓ	63 Ⓐ Ⓓ
16 Ⓐ Ⓓ	64 Ⓐ Ⓓ
17 Ⓐ Ⓓ	65 Ⓐ Ⓓ
18 Ⓐ Ⓓ	66 Ⓐ Ⓓ
19 Ⓐ Ⓓ	67 Ⓐ Ⓓ
20 Ⓐ Ⓓ	68 Ⓐ Ⓓ
21 Ⓐ Ⓓ	69 Ⓐ Ⓓ
22 Ⓐ Ⓓ	70 Ⓐ Ⓓ
23 Ⓐ Ⓓ	71 Ⓐ Ⓓ
24 Ⓐ Ⓓ	72 Ⓐ Ⓓ
25 Ⓐ Ⓓ	73 Ⓐ Ⓓ
26 Ⓐ Ⓓ	74 Ⓐ Ⓓ
27 Ⓐ Ⓓ	75 Ⓐ Ⓓ
28 Ⓐ Ⓓ	76 Ⓐ Ⓓ
29 Ⓐ Ⓓ	77 Ⓐ Ⓓ
30 Ⓐ Ⓓ	78 Ⓐ Ⓓ
31 Ⓐ Ⓓ	79 Ⓐ Ⓓ
32 Ⓐ Ⓓ	80 Ⓐ Ⓓ
33 Ⓐ Ⓓ	81 Ⓐ Ⓓ
34 Ⓐ Ⓓ	82 Ⓐ Ⓓ
35 Ⓐ Ⓓ	83 Ⓐ Ⓓ
36 Ⓐ Ⓓ	84 Ⓐ Ⓓ
37 Ⓐ Ⓓ	85 Ⓐ Ⓓ
38 Ⓐ Ⓓ	86 Ⓐ Ⓓ
39 Ⓐ Ⓓ	87 Ⓐ Ⓓ
40 Ⓐ Ⓓ	88 Ⓐ Ⓓ
41 Ⓐ Ⓓ	89 Ⓐ Ⓓ
42 Ⓐ Ⓓ	90 Ⓐ Ⓓ
43 Ⓐ Ⓓ	91 Ⓐ Ⓓ
44 Ⓐ Ⓓ	92 Ⓐ Ⓓ
45 Ⓐ Ⓓ	93 Ⓐ Ⓓ
46 Ⓐ Ⓓ	94 Ⓐ Ⓓ
47 Ⓐ Ⓓ	95 Ⓐ Ⓓ
48 Ⓐ Ⓓ	

TIME:

DRILL 7

1 Ⓐ Ⓓ	49 Ⓐ Ⓓ
2 Ⓐ Ⓓ	50 Ⓐ Ⓓ
3 Ⓐ Ⓓ	51 Ⓐ Ⓓ
4 Ⓐ Ⓓ	52 Ⓐ Ⓓ
5 Ⓐ Ⓓ	53 Ⓐ Ⓓ
6 Ⓐ Ⓓ	54 Ⓐ Ⓓ
7 Ⓐ Ⓓ	55 Ⓐ Ⓓ
8 Ⓐ Ⓓ	56 Ⓐ Ⓓ
9 Ⓐ Ⓓ	57 Ⓐ Ⓓ
10 Ⓐ Ⓓ	58 Ⓐ Ⓓ
11 Ⓐ Ⓓ	59 Ⓐ Ⓓ
12 Ⓐ Ⓓ	60 Ⓐ Ⓓ
13 Ⓐ Ⓓ	61 Ⓐ Ⓓ
14 Ⓐ Ⓓ	62 Ⓐ Ⓓ
15 Ⓐ Ⓓ	63 Ⓐ Ⓓ
16 Ⓐ Ⓓ	64 Ⓐ Ⓓ
17 Ⓐ Ⓓ	65 Ⓐ Ⓓ
18 Ⓐ Ⓓ	66 Ⓐ Ⓓ
19 Ⓐ Ⓓ	67 Ⓐ Ⓓ
20 Ⓐ Ⓓ	68 Ⓐ Ⓓ
21 Ⓐ Ⓓ	69 Ⓐ Ⓓ
22 Ⓐ Ⓓ	70 Ⓐ Ⓓ
23 Ⓐ Ⓓ	71 Ⓐ Ⓓ
24 Ⓐ Ⓓ	72 Ⓐ Ⓓ
25 Ⓐ Ⓓ	73 Ⓐ Ⓓ
26 Ⓐ Ⓓ	74 Ⓐ Ⓓ
27 Ⓐ Ⓓ	75 Ⓐ Ⓓ
28 Ⓐ Ⓓ	76 Ⓐ Ⓓ
29 Ⓐ Ⓓ	77 Ⓐ Ⓓ
30 Ⓐ Ⓓ	78 Ⓐ Ⓓ
31 Ⓐ Ⓓ	79 Ⓐ Ⓓ
32 Ⓐ Ⓓ	80 Ⓐ Ⓓ
33 Ⓐ Ⓓ	81 Ⓐ Ⓓ
34 Ⓐ Ⓓ	82 Ⓐ Ⓓ
35 Ⓐ Ⓓ	83 Ⓐ Ⓓ
36 Ⓐ Ⓓ	84 Ⓐ Ⓓ
37 Ⓐ Ⓓ	85 Ⓐ Ⓓ
38 Ⓐ Ⓓ	86 Ⓐ Ⓓ
39 Ⓐ Ⓓ	87 Ⓐ Ⓓ
40 Ⓐ Ⓓ	88 Ⓐ Ⓓ
41 Ⓐ Ⓓ	89 Ⓐ Ⓓ
42 Ⓐ Ⓓ	90 Ⓐ Ⓓ
43 Ⓐ Ⓓ	91 Ⓐ Ⓓ
44 Ⓐ Ⓓ	92 Ⓐ Ⓓ
45 Ⓐ Ⓓ	93 Ⓐ Ⓓ
46 Ⓐ Ⓓ	94 Ⓐ Ⓓ
47 Ⓐ Ⓓ	95 Ⓐ Ⓓ
48 Ⓐ Ⓓ	

TIME:

DRILL 8

1 Ⓐ Ⓓ	49 Ⓐ Ⓓ
2 Ⓐ Ⓓ	50 Ⓐ Ⓓ
3 Ⓐ Ⓓ	51 Ⓐ Ⓓ
4 Ⓐ Ⓓ	52 Ⓐ Ⓓ
5 Ⓐ Ⓓ	53 Ⓐ Ⓓ
6 Ⓐ Ⓓ	54 Ⓐ Ⓓ
7 Ⓐ Ⓓ	55 Ⓐ Ⓓ
8 Ⓐ Ⓓ	56 Ⓐ Ⓓ
9 Ⓐ Ⓓ	57 Ⓐ Ⓓ
10 Ⓐ Ⓓ	58 Ⓐ Ⓓ
11 Ⓐ Ⓓ	59 Ⓐ Ⓓ
12 Ⓐ Ⓓ	60 Ⓐ Ⓓ
13 Ⓐ Ⓓ	61 Ⓐ Ⓓ
14 Ⓐ Ⓓ	62 Ⓐ Ⓓ
15 Ⓐ Ⓓ	63 Ⓐ Ⓓ
16 Ⓐ Ⓓ	64 Ⓐ Ⓓ
17 Ⓐ Ⓓ	65 Ⓐ Ⓓ
18 Ⓐ Ⓓ	66 Ⓐ Ⓓ
19 Ⓐ Ⓓ	67 Ⓐ Ⓓ
20 Ⓐ Ⓓ	68 Ⓐ Ⓓ
21 Ⓐ Ⓓ	69 Ⓐ Ⓓ
22 Ⓐ Ⓓ	70 Ⓐ Ⓓ
23 Ⓐ Ⓓ	71 Ⓐ Ⓓ
24 Ⓐ Ⓓ	72 Ⓐ Ⓓ
25 Ⓐ Ⓓ	73 Ⓐ Ⓓ
26 Ⓐ Ⓓ	74 Ⓐ Ⓓ
27 Ⓐ Ⓓ	75 Ⓐ Ⓓ
28 Ⓐ Ⓓ	76 Ⓐ Ⓓ
29 Ⓐ Ⓓ	77 Ⓐ Ⓓ
30 Ⓐ Ⓓ	78 Ⓐ Ⓓ
31 Ⓐ Ⓓ	79 Ⓐ Ⓓ
32 Ⓐ Ⓓ	80 Ⓐ Ⓓ
33 Ⓐ Ⓓ	81 Ⓐ Ⓓ
34 Ⓐ Ⓓ	82 Ⓐ Ⓓ
35 Ⓐ Ⓓ	83 Ⓐ Ⓓ
36 Ⓐ Ⓓ	84 Ⓐ Ⓓ
37 Ⓐ Ⓓ	85 Ⓐ Ⓓ
38 Ⓐ Ⓓ	86 Ⓐ Ⓓ
39 Ⓐ Ⓓ	87 Ⓐ Ⓓ
40 Ⓐ Ⓓ	88 Ⓐ Ⓓ
41 Ⓐ Ⓓ	89 Ⓐ Ⓓ
42 Ⓐ Ⓓ	90 Ⓐ Ⓓ
43 Ⓐ Ⓓ	91 Ⓐ Ⓓ
44 Ⓐ Ⓓ	92 Ⓐ Ⓓ
45 Ⓐ Ⓓ	93 Ⓐ Ⓓ
46 Ⓐ Ⓓ	94 Ⓐ Ⓓ
47 Ⓐ Ⓓ	95 Ⓐ Ⓓ
48 Ⓐ Ⓓ	

TIME:

DRILL 9

1 Ⓐ Ⓓ	49 Ⓐ Ⓓ
2 Ⓐ Ⓓ	50 Ⓐ Ⓓ
3 Ⓐ Ⓓ	51 Ⓐ Ⓓ
4 Ⓐ Ⓓ	52 Ⓐ Ⓓ
5 Ⓐ Ⓓ	53 Ⓐ Ⓓ
6 Ⓐ Ⓓ	54 Ⓐ Ⓓ
7 Ⓐ Ⓓ	55 Ⓐ Ⓓ
8 Ⓐ Ⓓ	56 Ⓐ Ⓓ
9 Ⓐ Ⓓ	57 Ⓐ Ⓓ
10 Ⓐ Ⓓ	58 Ⓐ Ⓓ
11 Ⓐ Ⓓ	59 Ⓐ Ⓓ
12 Ⓐ Ⓓ	60 Ⓐ Ⓓ
13 Ⓐ Ⓓ	61 Ⓐ Ⓓ
14 Ⓐ Ⓓ	62 Ⓐ Ⓓ
15 Ⓐ Ⓓ	63 Ⓐ Ⓓ
16 Ⓐ Ⓓ	64 Ⓐ Ⓓ
17 Ⓐ Ⓓ	65 Ⓐ Ⓓ
18 Ⓐ Ⓓ	66 Ⓐ Ⓓ
19 Ⓐ Ⓓ	67 Ⓐ Ⓓ
20 Ⓐ Ⓓ	68 Ⓐ Ⓓ
21 Ⓐ Ⓓ	69 Ⓐ Ⓓ
22 Ⓐ Ⓓ	70 Ⓐ Ⓓ
23 Ⓐ Ⓓ	71 Ⓐ Ⓓ
24 Ⓐ Ⓓ	72 Ⓐ Ⓓ
25 Ⓐ Ⓓ	73 Ⓐ Ⓓ
26 Ⓐ Ⓓ	74 Ⓐ Ⓓ
27 Ⓐ Ⓓ	75 Ⓐ Ⓓ
28 Ⓐ Ⓓ	76 Ⓐ Ⓓ
29 Ⓐ Ⓓ	77 Ⓐ Ⓓ
30 Ⓐ Ⓓ	78 Ⓐ Ⓓ
31 Ⓐ Ⓓ	79 Ⓐ Ⓓ
32 Ⓐ Ⓓ	80 Ⓐ Ⓓ
33 Ⓐ Ⓓ	81 Ⓐ Ⓓ
34 Ⓐ Ⓓ	82 Ⓐ Ⓓ
35 Ⓐ Ⓓ	83 Ⓐ Ⓓ
36 Ⓐ Ⓓ	84 Ⓐ Ⓓ
37 Ⓐ Ⓓ	85 Ⓐ Ⓓ
38 Ⓐ Ⓓ	86 Ⓐ Ⓓ
39 Ⓐ Ⓓ	87 Ⓐ Ⓓ
40 Ⓐ Ⓓ	88 Ⓐ Ⓓ
41 Ⓐ Ⓓ	89 Ⓐ Ⓓ
42 Ⓐ Ⓓ	90 Ⓐ Ⓓ
43 Ⓐ Ⓓ	91 Ⓐ Ⓓ
44 Ⓐ Ⓓ	92 Ⓐ Ⓓ
45 Ⓐ Ⓓ	93 Ⓐ Ⓓ
46 Ⓐ Ⓓ	94 Ⓐ Ⓓ
47 Ⓐ Ⓓ	95 Ⓐ Ⓓ
48 Ⓐ Ⓓ	

TIME:

OVERCOMING REVERSAL ERRORS

The following table shows errors made when individual letters, groups of letters, or entire words are somehow reversed in our perception. Check the questions you had wrong on the Address Checking portion of the Diagnostic Practice Test. Pick out any errors showing this kind of reversal mistake.

SOME COMMON PERCEPTION ERRORS MADE IN READING

Letters	Letter Groups	Words
b – d	ton – town	on – no
p – d	ville – view	top – pot
q – d	lawn – land	cite – ten
p – q	man – mon	never – ever
u – n	la – al	not – ton
u – v	le – el	pat – tap
n – m	ry – rey	saw – was
m – w	berg – burg	own – won
a – e	mont – mount	mar – arm
a – o	ham – heim	mint – tin

The three drills explained below may be used to remedy this situation. We've assumed, for the sake of illustration, that you are confusing *b* and *d*.

DRILL 10

Write the letters *b* and *d* side by side.

b–d

1. _____   3. _____   5. _____   7. _____   9. _____

2. _____   4. _____   6. _____   8. _____   10. _____

Reverse their order and write them again.

d—b

1. _____   3. _____   5. _____   7. _____   9. _____

2. _____   4. _____   6. _____   8. _____   10. _____

Immediately after you write each pair, look away and picture the letters mentally. Write each pair ten times at each drill. Do this with other reversals with which you are having a problem.

DRILL 11

On one side of a 3″ × 5″ card, write the letter *b* about one inch high. Write *d* on the other side. You have just made a flash card. Have a friend (or do it yourself) flash one side before you for the briefest instant. Call out what you see. Jot it down. Either side should be flashed at random. Each drill need last only 1 or 2 minutes. Do this with other reversals with which you are having a problem.

DRILL 12

Take 3 seconds to check the line below to see how many *b*'s there are. Now check it for the number of *d*'s. Jot down the figures (the answer is at the end of this chapter).

b   b   d   b   d   d   d   b   d   d

Number of *b*'s	Number of *d*'s
___	___

You or a friend can prepare similar lines consisting of the letters or groups of letters causing difficulty. Make certain that the number of items on each line varies. Drill several different lines each time.

DEVELOPING SPEED AND ACCURACY WITH NAMES

A word or name is presented in Column 1. This word is not always a real one. Look at it once and then compare it to the words in Column 2. As your eyes sweep along these words, pick out the ones that are *exactly* the same as the one in Column 1. In the answer column, jot down the number of times you saw the original word repeated.

SAMPLE		
Column 1	*Column 2*	*Answers*
heater	heaten—heated—heater—beater—heater—heated	2

Do the following drills. The answer column has space for you to repeat each drill three times. (Cover the line of answers you have already done so they do not influence you.) Keep a record in the space below each drill of the time it took (in seconds) and the number of correct answers. The object is to build speed and accuracy. Do at least one drill a day. The answers to these drills are on page 71. Mark your progress on the Personal Progress Chart on page 233.

DRILL 13

Column 1	Column 2	Trials	3	2	1
1. Hobart	Habart Hobard Habort Hobart Habort Hobart Habart				
2. Mainly	Mainley Mainly Manley Mairly Manly Mainly				
3. Pinelawn	Pinalawn Pinlawn Pinelaun Pineland				
4. Wood	Wood Wode Wood Wood Mood Woode				
5. Purton	Purtem Purdom Pumtom Partom Purdam				
6. Dumont	Dumont Dumomt Dumount Dummon Dumuumt Dumont				
7. Clover	Clover Claver Clovar Glover Clever				
8. Dunville	Duval Dunville Deville Duville Duvalle				
9. Logan	Logan Logan Locan Logan Locan Logam				
10. Mounte	Momte Montey Mounty Monte Mounte Mounty				

Number Right
Time

DRILL 14

	Column 1	Column 2	Trials	3	2	1
			Answers			
1.	Hammond	Hammon Hammand Hammont Hammon Hamnond				
2.	Iceburg	Iceberg Iceburg Iceburg Iceberg Iceburg				
3.	Forge	Force Farce Fogge Forge				
4.	Minnow	Minnow Minnow Minmow Nimmow Minow Minnou				
5.	Fieldson	Fielson Feldson Fekdson Fiestone Fellson				
6.	Never	Nevem Nevel Levem Ever Evers				
7.	Pomona	Ponoma Panoma Pomona Pomana Ponoma				
8.	Lafayette	Lafayette Lafayitte Lafayete Lefayette Lafayute				
9.	Hanger	Hunger Hanker Hancer Hangar Hangar				
10.	Sierra	Seirra Siera Sierra Aerra Sierra Sierra				
		Number Right				
		Time				

DRILL 15

	Column 1	Column 2	Trials	3	2	1
			Answers			
1.	Soundport	Soundpoint Soomdport Somdport Southport Southpert				
2.	Eggnog	Eccnog Eccnoc Eggnog Eggnag Egnog Egmog				
3.	Fullawn	Fulland Fullamn Fulawn Fillawn				
4.	Windfall	Wimdfall Wimdfall Windfall Windfall Windfall				
5.	Jaspar	Jasper Jaspar Jasper Jaspar Jasquar Jasdar				
6.	Yucca	Yucco Yucce Yucca Yucca Yugga Yucca				
7.	Germantown	Germentown Germanton Germanton Germentown Germantown				
8.	Levine	Lavine Levine Lewine Lavine Levin Lavine				
9.	La Jolie	La Jolia Le Jolie La Jalie La Jolie La Jolee				
10.	Crescent	Cressent Crescent Crescent Crescant Crescent Crescent				
		Number Right				
		Time				

DRILL 16

	Column 1	Column 2	Trials	3	2	1
			Answers			
1.	Narrowsburg	Narrowsberg Narowsburg Narromburg Narrowsberg				
2.	Trenton	Trenton Trentin Trenton Trentan Trenton Trenton				
3.	Vinton	Windon Vintom Vindon Vanton Winton Vimton				
4.	Alberta	Elberta Alberta Alperta Alberta Elberta Alburto				
5.	Sawridge	Sawbridge Sawridge Sawridge Samridge				
6.	Zanocca	Zanocca Zannocca Zanoca Zamocca Zawocca				
7.	Boca Raton	Boca Raton Baca Raton Boca Ratan Bocca Raton				
8.	Realsboro	Reelsboro Realboro Realborough Realsboro Realsboro				
9.	Catnap	Catnip Gatnap Catmap Catnap Catnip Catnap				
10.	Kaspar	Kaspar Kaspar Kastar Kasper Kaspar Kasdar Kasper				
		Number Right				
		Time				

DRILL 17

Column 1	Column 2	Trials	3	2	1
1. Fishkill	Fishkill Dishkill Fisskill Fishkill Fishkill				
2. Ankava	Ankava Ankara Ankaqe Ankare Ankara Emkara Ankara				
3. Ellville	Ellvile Ellvalle Elville Ellview Elville Ellville				
4. Shepherd	Shepherd Shepherd Sheepherd Shepard Shepherd Shephard				
5. Seminary	Seminary Seminary Suminary Seminary Seminary				
6. Wallaby	Wallaby Wallbye Wallabey Wallaby Wallaby Wallaby				
7. Palmtry	Palmtree Palmitry Palmtry Palmtrey Palmtry Palmtry				
8. Overview	Overview Ovarview Ovarview Overville				
9. Lansdale	Lawnsdale Lansdale Landale Landsdale Lamdale				
10. Rottal	Rottal Rottel Rottal Rottel Rattal Rattle				

Number Right / Time

DEVELOPING SPEED AND ACCURACY WITH NUMBERS

A number is printed in Column 1. Look at it once and then compare it to the numbers in Column 2. As your eyes sweep along these numbers pick out the ones that are *exactly* the same as the one in Column 1. In the answer column jot down the number of times you saw the original number repeated.

SAMPLE		
Column 1	Column 2	Answers
11240	11240 12140 12104 11240 11240 21240 11204	3

Do the four drills on these pages. The answer column has space for you to repeat each drill three times. (Cover the line of answers you have already done so they do not influence you.) Keep a record in the space below each drill of the time it took (in seconds) and the number of correct answers. The object is speed and accuracy. Do one drill a day. See page 71 for the answers.

DRILL 18

Column 1	Column 2	Trials	3	2	1
1. 142	142 142 241 214 124 142 412 142				
2. 361	316 361 361 631 613 136 361 316 316				
3. 519	591 591 159 519 159 519				
4. 890	890 980 890 809 809 980 890 890				
5. 378	387 738 873 378 378				
6. 233	323 332 233 323 233 233 323 233 323				
7. 980	980 980 890 980 890 908 908				
8. 442	424 442 244 424 442 424 442 442 442				
9. 257	527 527 257 257 275 275 257 257				
10. 693	693 639 643 639 693 396 963 963				

Number Right / Time

DRILL 19

	Column 1	Column 2									Trials	3	2	1
1.	2280	2280	2230	2820	2208	2280	2276							
2.	8193	8913	8913	8193	8182	8139								
3.	7455	7455	7545	7455	7455	7454								
4.	1010	1010	1100	1100	1010	1010	1100	1001						
5.	9648	9648	9643	9648	9468	9968	9648							
6.	1412	1412	1412	1421	1241	1421	1412	1412	1421	1422				
7.	3359	3359	3859	3395	3395	3359	3395	3395						
8.	7276	7276	7277	7267	7262	7276	7726	7276						
9.	1340	1304	1390	1840	1304	1304	1304	1034						
10.	2645	2645	2645	2645	2645	2644	2645	2645	2645					

Answers

Number Right

Time

DRILL 20

	Column 1	Column 2								Trials	3	2	1
1.	46342	46342	46324	46224	46342	46324	46342	43642					
2.	96114	96141	91614	96114	96141	96114							
3.	97423	79423	97432	97243	97433	97723	94732						
4.	59340	59304	59344	59840	95840	95340	95430						
5.	39045	30945	39044	39045	39054	39045	39044						
6.	42566	42566	42565	45266	46256	42666	42555						
7.	28683	28683	28688	28683	23683	23683	23688	28683					
8.	98337	97833	98373	98387	98337	68337	98333	98331					
9.	04567	04567	04568	04561	40516	4061	04576	04596					
10.	70634	70634	70634	70634	79634	70684	70674						

Answers

Number Right

Time

DRILL 21

	Column 1	Column 2								Trials	3	2	1
1.	50401	54010	50901	50401	50410	50410	50410	50140					
2.	28013	28031	82013	28113	28018	28310							
3.	90551	95051	90551	90515	90551	99551	90515	90551					
4.	52045	52045	52545	25452	50245	52095							
5.	75923	79523	75923	75923	75924	75932	75932						
6.	10458	14058	10458	10458	10485	10458	10458	10458	10458				
7.	11762	17162	11726	17162	11726	11762	11762						
8.	41097	41097	41097	40197	41097	41079	41094	41097					
9.	23819	32819	23819	28819	28819	23819	28819	28819					
10.	55710	57510	55710	55701	55701	55710	55107	55017	55017				

Answers

Number Right

Time

INCREASING EYE SPAN

Here are several methods to increase eye span. All of them work, but for the sake of variety you may wish to alternate their use from day to day.

Method A: The Pyramid

Twenty-five addresses and parts of addresses are printed on separate lines below. They form a pyramid as the lines get successively wider toward the bottom of the page. Try to read each line with one fixation at its midpoint. The midpoint is indicated by a dot immediately above the line. Use your peripheral vision to make out the letters at the beginning and end of each line. Do not shift or slide your eyes. It may be unfamiliar at first, but with practice you will be able to grasp (perceive) larger and larger pieces of each address. The width of each line is measured by the number of type units it includes: letters, numbers, and spaces in-between. That number is printed near the right margin. Drill daily until you can span at least 15 units at one fixation. This amount will enable you to check half of any address that you are likely to encounter on the test. Eventually, you can develop your eye span to take in a *long* address (22–25 type units) at one fixation.

Two full-scale drills are on the next two pages. Before you work on them, try this little drill. Do it before each of your practice sessions.

•
I
•
am
•
sure
•
to see
•
increases
•
in my span
•
if I practice
•
keeping my eyes
•
focused on the spot
•
at the middle of the line

DRILL 22

	Type Units
St	2
929	3
Bank	4
02446	5
Westom	6
Captree	7
91 Fifth	8
364 Birch	9
1278 Apple	10
Cedar Mount	11
820 W Fourth	12
Grand View CA	13
W Palm Springs	14
Brookline 02108	15
2203 West End Ave	16
3491 Draper Dr SE	17
Walland Tenn 37886	18
4102 Georgia Ave NW	19
2293 Montgomery Lane	20
1904 John Marshall Dr	21
5 West End Av NY 10062	22
1401 Eastern Blvd Bklyn	23
6 Columbia Heights Rd La	24
93 Missouri St Tenn 47121	25

DRILL 23

	Type Units
46	2
NYC	3
Ohio	4
37142	5
Oak St	6
W Drive	7
276 Pear	8
El Centro	9
Paducah KY	10
394 E Apple	11
10 Orange Dr	12
Beaverkill NY	13
1004 Pitkim Av	14
795 N Jefferson	15
2 Brentwood Lane	16
Creelling Av W VA	17
98 S 132 Dr Joliet	18
4 Haring Zemba Kans	19
West Philadelphia PA	20
Jameville Calif 96114	21
5504 Caroline St Miami	22
Small Point Maine 04567	23
East Falmouth Mass 02536	24
158 St Massapequa Park NY	25

Method B: Using the Eye Span Selector

Two Eye Span Selectors are imprinted on page 227 of the Appendix. These Selectors have been designed to help you gradually develop a greater eye span. Together, the Selectors have twelve slot windows ranging in size from 4 to 26 type units. The greater the number of type units, the wider the eye span you will need to see them all at one fixation. The middle slots on both cards are 32 type units wide, enabling you to see even the longest address at one glance. Use the Selectors to check the address pairs in Drills 24 through 29.

Sample Eye Span Selector

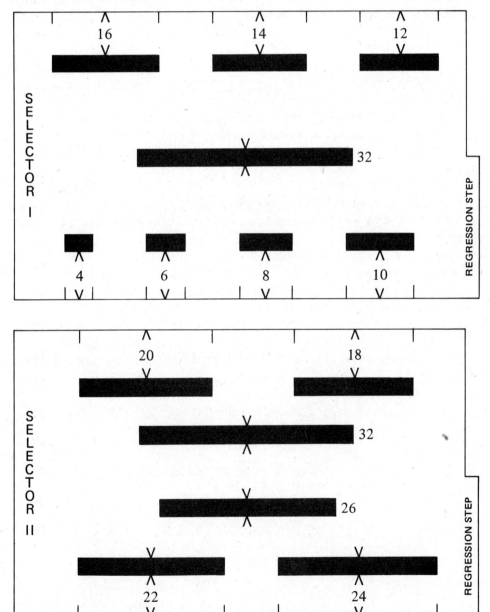

How to Use This Selector in the Following Drills

1. Select one of the twelve slot windows with a width that just about matches your present eye span, or is even a trifle wider.
2. Place the window over the first address line so that the beginning of the address and the left edge of the slot line up.
3. You should now see part of the address framed in the slot. Notice that there is a small arrow that indicates the middle of the slot.
4. Quickly scan the part of the address you see. Use your peripheral vision to see the beginning and end letters or numbers. Remember, your task is to compare whatever you see with the line below.
5. Make the comparison of the address either by (a) moving the Selector back and forth from the top line to the one below until you have scanned the entire address, or (b) moving the Selector horizontally along each part of the entire address and *then* checking what you saw against each part of the line below.
6. In either case, write in your answer choice, Ⓐ alike or Ⓓ different, in the spaces available. (Cover the line of answers you have already completed so that they do not influence you on your second and third trials.)
7. If you wish, you may use the "guidelines" scribed along the edge of the Selectors. The space between each pair of lines exactly corresponds in width to the slot adjoining it. The center of each width is indicated by an arrow. The "guidelines" may be used for exactly the same purpose as the window slots. It is strictly a matter of preference in deciding which method to use. Incidentally, the Selectors may be used for practice when you are reading *any* printed matter—your favorite newspaper, magazine or book.
8. The important thing is to keep drilling until you've mastered a certain width. Then move on to the next larger size. Keep increasing the size of the slots until you reach one that brings you consistently good results. You will, therefore, progress from Selector I to Selector II.
9. Do away with the Selector as soon as you can. It is only a tool designed to help develop new habits. At every opportunity drill for awhile *without* it. Soon, you will find your new skills are a really natural part of the way you read.

DRILL 24

Follow the directions for using the Eye Span Selector, on page 58, to complete this exercise.

		Trials	3	2	1
1.	Mobile Al 36608 Mobile Al 36608				
2.	399 Powell Av NE 399 Powell Av NW				
3.	6241 Daly Rd 6242 Dely Rd				
4.	19 Washington Av SW 19 Washington Av SW				
5.	Cambridge Springs PA 16043 Cambridge Springs PA 16043				
6.	200 Peter Smith W 300 Peter Smith W				
7.	2762 Airport S Acres 2762 Airport S Acres				
8.	12 W Normandy Dr 12 W Normandy Dr				
9.	3204 Princess Court Ln E 3204 Princess Court Ln W				
10.	Bethleyville PA 15314 Bethleyview PA 15314				
11.	4902 Briarcliff Cir NE 4902 Briarcliff Cir SE				
12.	143 Park Av S 103 Park Av S				
13.	7671 Claremont Av N 7671 Claremont Rd N				
14.	634 Rocky Fork Blvd SW 643 Rocky Fork Blvd SW				
15.	Ridgedale Drive Columbus OH Ridgefield Drive Columbus OH				
16.	1943 S Overhill Rd 1943 S Overdale Rd				
17.	4001 Harvard Av E 4010 Harvard Av E				
18.	123 Bellefontaine Dr 223 Bellefontaine Dr				
19.	561 E 145 St 561 E 145 Ct				
20.	1466 S Findlay Av 1466 S Findly Av				
	Number Right				
	Time				

DRILL 25

Follow the directions for using the Eye Span Selector, on page 58, to complete this exercise.

Follow the directions for using the Eye Span Selector, on page 58, to complete this exercise.

Answers

	Trials	3	2	1
1. 54631 Amagansett Court NW 54631 Amagansitt Court NW				
2. Sumter GA 31709 Sumtre GA 31709				
3. 8732 E Farmers Dr 8732 E Farmers Dr				
4. Morrisville VT 05657 Morristown VT 05657				
5. 1015 El Rancho Way West 1015 Le Rancho Way West				
6. 13 Long Lake Dr SE 13 Long Lake Dr SE				
7. 87-34 84 Av Howard Beach 87-34 84 Av Howard Beach				
8. 2204 Jibstav Ct SE 2024 Jibstay Ct SE				
9. Berkeley West Va 25420 Barkeley West Va 25420				
10. 4114 W Momongalia St 4114 W Momomgalia St				
11. 1032 Aldus St Bx 10485 1032 Aldus St Bx 10485				
12. 243 1st Av Paterson 234 1st Av Paterson				
13. 10 Alexander Hamilton Pkwy 10 Alexander Hamilton Pkwy				
14. 14013 NW Knollwood Ct 14013 NW Knollwood Ct				
15. Vermilion La 70510 Vermilion La 70510				
16. 98 N Winding Way Rd 89 N Winding Way Rd				
17. 2401 Sterling Terrace E 2401 Sterling Terrace W				
18. Saint James La 70052 Saint James La 70052				
19. 4910 Queens Blvd SW 4910 Queens Blvd NW				
20. Massapequa Park NY 11762 Massapequa Park NJ 11762				
	Number Right			
	Time			

DRILL 26

Follow the directions for using the Eye Span Selector, on page 58, to complete this exercise.

		Answers		
	Trials	3	2	1

1.   1401 Apricale Ln
     1401 Apricale Pl

2.   2894 Cremona Ave E
     2984 Cremona Ave E

3.   6401 Downdale Pl W
     6401 Downdale Pl W

4.   4561 Griffing Blvd
     4561 Griffith Blvd

5.   1095 S Westlawn Rd
     1095 S Westlawn Rd

6.   3798 NW 62nd Pl
     3798 NE 62nd Pl

7.   Naples FL 33940
     Naples FL 33940

8.   17094 Rosemond Ct S
     17094 Rosemond Ct S

9.   676 Willow Point Ter
     676 Willow Point Pkwy

10. 8281 Van Born Ct
     8181 Van Boren Ct

11. 3938 E Parkingham St
     3938 E Parkingham St

12. Bethesda MD 21046
     Bethesda ME 21046

13. 1601 E 224 Rd
     1601 E 229 Rd

14. 6204 Dahlonega Dr SE
     6204 Dahlonega Dr NE

15. Rockford IL 61108
     Rockport IL 61108

16. 4409 Stanton Lane S
     4490 Stanton Lane S

17. 9118 Kettering Rd W
     9118 Kettering Rd W

18. 4532 N Sterling Way
     4532 N Starling Way

19. 2004 E Stonehedge Ter
     2004 E Stonehedge Ter

20. 6571 N Salisbury Blvd
     6571 N Salisburg Blvd

Number Right
Time

DRILL 27

Follow the directions for using the Eye Span Selector, on page 58, to complete this exercise.

	Trials	3	2	1
	Answers			

1. 6789 Rutherglen Ave S
   6798 Rutherglen Ave S

2. 7307 Sunnymeade Path
   7037 Synnymeade Path

3. 2781 E Rapadan Ln
   2781 E Ramadan Ln

4. 3898 N 14th Ave
   3898 N 14th Ave

5. Huntsville AL 35805
   Huntsville AR 35805

6. 3803 W Abercorn St
   3803 W Abercorn St

7. 4947 Braxfield Dr NE
   4947 Braxfield Dr NE

8. 6412 N Parkchester Blvd
   6419 N Parkchester Blvd

9. 1681 Quincy Ct S
   1681 Quince Ct S

10. 17094 Highway North Ext
    17094 Highway North Ext

11. Jackson MI 49203
    Jackson ME 49203

12. 1514 Grand Gorge Pkwy
    1514 Grand Groge Pkwy

13. 252 S Andrea Rd
    252 S Angrea Rd

14. 7603 S Garahime Ave
    7603 S Garaheim Ave

15. 8124 E Hickory Dr
    8124 E Hickory Dr

16. Camino CA 95709
    Camina CA 95709

17. 2504 S 114th Pl
    2504 S 114th Pl

18. 5288 Riverview Walk SW
    5288 Riverview Walk SW

19. 50 Buena Vista Trailer Ct
    50 Buena Vista Trailer Ct

20. Jeffersonville NY 12748
    Jeffersonville NY 12747

Number Right
Time

DRILL 28

Follow the directions for using the Eye Span Selector, on page 58, to complete this exercise.

(Eye Span Selector, on page 58)

		Answers		
	Trials	3	2	1
1. 9664 W Oahu Ave 9664 W Oahu Ave				
2. 7793 S Glastonbury Ave 7793 S Glastonbury Ave				
3. Burbank CA 91505 Burbank CO 91505				
4. 6167 E 217th Ter 6167 E 216th Ter				
5. 1514 Sewickley Way SE 1514 Sweickley Way SE				
6. 29418 W Main St 29418 W Main St				
7. 3712 E Jewell Ave 3712 E Jewett Ave				
8. 6036 W Yolande St 6036 W Yolande Ct				
9. Scottsdale AZ 85257 Scottsdale AZ 85257				
10. Rhoadesville VA 22542 Rhoadesville VA 22542				
11. 7453 E Athlone Ave 7453 E Athbone Ave				
12. 3816 McCollough Ct NW 3816 McCullough Ct NW				
13. Marengo IN 47140 Marango IN 47140				
14. 1614 S 161st Pl 1614 S 161st Pl				
15. 1705 Forest Isle Ct W 1705 Forest Isle Ct W				
16. 8067 N Trimbach Ln 8067 N Trimback Ln				
17. 4134 Nottingham Park Pl 4143 Nottingham Park Pl				
18. Woodbridge VA Woodridge VA				
19. 6491 S Burntwood Cir 6491 N Burntwood Cir				
20. 4849 Summitville View Walk 4849 Summitville View Walk				
	Number Right			
	Time			

DRILL 29

Follow the directions for using the Eye Span Selector, on page 58, to complete this exercise.

on page 58

			Answers		
	Trials	3	2	1	

1. 4198 109th Ave NE
   4198 109th Ave NE

2. 5771 S Newell St
   5771 S Nevell St

3. Glendale AZ 85304
   Glendale AZ 85304

4. 7061 S 20th Cir
   7061 S 20th Ct

5. 1352 Johanna Ave SW
   1352 Johanna Ave SE

6. 20739 Back River Neck Rd
   20739 Back River Neck Rd

7. 86 Fair Meadows Pl
   86 Fair Meadows Pl

8. 1440 W Platten Dr
   1440 W Platte Dr

9. 282 McDuffie Ln S
   282 MacDuffie Ln S

10. 5753 Oakcrest Pl
    5735 Oakcrest Pl

11. 9367 E Pohick Ln
    9367 E Potick Ln

12. 135 San Carlos Ct
    135 San Carlas Ct

13. 2031 Spotted Jack Loop
    2031 Spotted Jack Loop

14. 8043 Shasta Blvd S
    8043 Shanta Blvd S

15. Port Neches TX 77651
    Port Neches TX 77651

16. 6457 N Penelope Cir
    6457 N Penelope Cir

17. 89 S Mescolero Dr
    89 S Mescolera Dr

18. 4172 E Compere Blvd
    4171 E Compere Blvd

19. 100 La Salle Ridge Rd
    100 La Salle Ridge Rd

20. 5307 W 104th St
    5307 W 104th St

Number Right
Time

PREVENTING REGRESSION

There are several methods to use to help break yourself of the habit of re-reading the address.

1. Use the top edge of the Eye Span Selector or of any small index card to block off each line after you have checked it. In that way you won't be able to look back even if you want to. Keep moving the card down the page, line-by-line, as rapidly as you can. This method may be used with any of the practice tests or drills in this book.
2. You may find that you are looking back at *parts* of an address instead of moving ahead to scan the rest of the line. The Eye Span Selector has a simple, yet effective design feature to help overcome that practice. Use it to check the addresses on the next drills. (See the figure below and on the next page on ''Using the Selector for Regressions'' and the following instructions.)

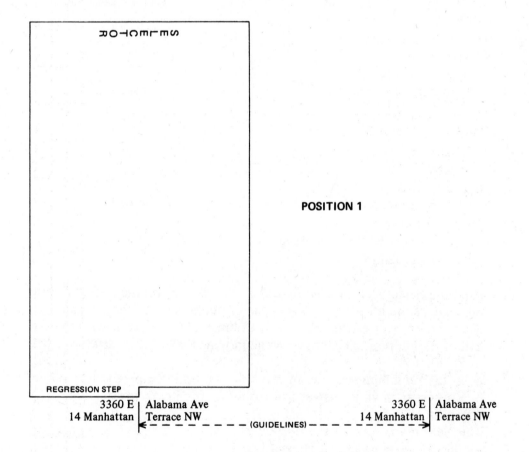

Using the Selector for Regressions

(position 2 continued on next page)

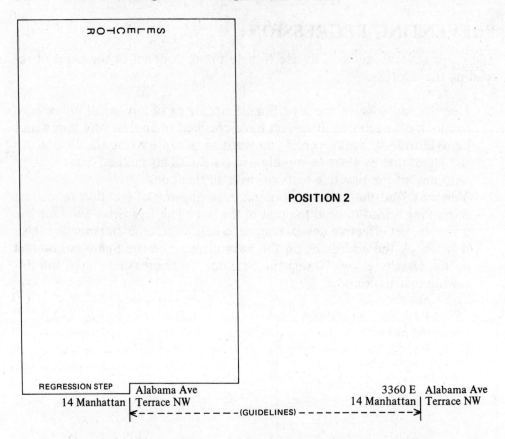

Using the Selector for Regressions

How to Use the Selector to Prevent Regression in the Following Drills

Assuming that you will be checking each address using two fixations, use the following procedure.

1. Hold the Selector *above the first line of addresses* on the page. Line up the edge of the little "STEP" with the dotted guide line (see Position 1). Scan the left half of the address in Column 1. Compare it with the left half of the address in Column 2 while moving the Selector down one line to Position 2.
2. Scan the *remaining portion of the address*, and compare it to Column 2. Now write in your answer as to whether the items are Ⓐ alike, or Ⓓ different.
3. The Selector is now in the correct position for you to begin checking the *next line*. Now repeat steps 1 and 2 above.

DRILL 30

Follow the directions for using the Eye Span Selector, on page 66, to complete this exercise.

			Answers		
			Trials	3	2	1

#		
1.	9382 Ivaloo Ct NW	9382 Ivaloo Ct SW
2.	437 Stonehorse Towers Ct	437 Stonehouse Towers Ct
3.	3606 W Gisella Dr	3606 W Gisella Dr
4.	5992 Winnebago Blvd N	5992 Winnebago Blvd N
5.	7514 Yaruba Pl	7514 Yaruda Pl
6.	7614 Navarro Walk	7614 Navarro Walk
7.	74 Green Valley Heights Rd	74 Green Valley Heights Rd
8.	132 Pleasant Valley Way	132 Pleasant Valley Way
9.	204 E Fauquer Cres	204 E Fauquer Cres
10.	5711 Freeman St SE	5711 Freeman St SE
11.	3754 La Mesa Del Sol Ln	3754 La Mesa Del Sol Ln
12.	North Canton Ct 06059	North Canton Ct 06059
13.	87140 Montauk Highway E	87140 Montauk Highway E
14.	7501 E Pinehurst Ln	7501 E Pinehorse Ln
15.	1830 W Avenue M	1830 W Avenue N
16.	6341 S Mohegan Path	6341 S Mohegan Path
17.	4949 Grand Ter	4949 Grand Ter
18.	4166 E Barclay Ave	4166 E Barclay Ave
19.	Moravia Ia 52571	Moravia Ia 52571
20.	19914 Southold Pkwy	19914 Southold Pkwy
21.	9405 Val de Mere Ave	9405 Val de Mere Ave
22.	2114 Eckhart Hill Ct	2114 Eckhard Hill Ct
23.	4308 S Trumbull Ave	4308 N Trumbull Ave
24.	583 Natrona Ave W	583 Natrona Ave W
25.	314 Virgilina Cir	314 Virgilina Cir
26.	8784 S Oscalosa St	8874 S Oscalosa St
27.	Boscobel WI	Boscobel WI
28.	5171 Shady Point Canal Rd	5117 Schady Point Canal Rd
29.	3347 E 207 St	3347 E 270 St
30.	Westfield NJ 07066	Westfield NJ 07006
31.	2741 Vaughan Ave	2741 Vaughan Ave
32.	4189 S Montserrado Pl	4189 S Montserrato Pl
33.	6004 El Florencia Ave	6004 El Florencia Ave
34.	2834 E Bentwood	2834 E Brentwood Ct
35.	80-17 150th Dr	80-17 160th Dr
36.	5076 Nottingham Ln E	5076 Nottingham Ln E
37.	West Falmouth MA	West Falmouth ME
38.	1012 Saint Mihiel Ave	1012 Saint Mihiel Ave
39.	6499 El Campo Grande Ave	6499 El Campo Grande Ave
40.	Sarcoxie MO 64862	Sarcoxie MO 64852
41.	Nassawadox VA 23413	Nassawadox VA 23143
42.	4908 Decoty Blvd N	4908 Degoty Blvd N
43.	109 E 148th Pl	109 E 148th Pl

44.	Woodbine MD 21797	Woodbone MD 21797		
45.	2457 N Guerida St	2457 N Guerita Pl		
46.	1156 Seneca Trl W	1156 Seneca Trl W		
47.	8756 Rosemond Path NE	8756 Rosemond Path NW		
48.	3847 W Woodbridge Cir	3847 W Woodbridge Cir		
49.	1423 Luddington Rd NW	1423 Luddingtown Rd NW		
50.	968 Deepdene Rd	968 Deepdene Rd		
51.	6943 Merchant Blvd	6943 Merchant Blvd		
52.	3617 S Chimney Rock Ln	3617 S Chimney Rock Ln		
53.	27045 Rockview Rd	27045 Rockview Rd		
54.	9450 Remsen Ave	9540 Remsen Ave		
55.	6257 Villalobos Park Cir	6257 Villalobos Park Cir		
56.	947 Petaluma Blvd	947 Petalumo Blvd		
57.	6061 Okendorfer Ct	6061 Okendorfer Ct		
58.	1843 Janof Pl	1843 Janof Pl		
59.	8108 Helsley Ave	8108 Hemsley Ave		
60.	2843 Tappahonnock Blvd SE	2834 Tappahonnock Blvd SE		

Number Right

Time

DRILL 31

Follow the directions for using the Eye Span Selector, on page 66, to complete this exercise.

Answers

			Trials	3	2	1
1.	1913 Via Las Cumbres	1913 Via Las Combres				
2.	3731 Temescal Ter	3731 Tenescal Ter				
3.	8108 Rutland Dr	8108 Rutland Dr				
4.	6761 Powhattan Ln	6761 Powhattan Ln				
5.	324 S Miramar St	324 S Mirimar St				
6.	1534 S 112 Pl	1534 E 112 Pl				
7.	9413 S Blazewood Pl	9413 S Blakewood Pl				
8.	Holladay Vt 84117	Holliday Vt 84117				
9.	200 E Angelucci Way	200 E Andelucci Way				
10.	734 Quantico Ave S	734 Quantico Ave S				
11.	7748 Quesada Path S	7748 Quesada Path S				
12.	7008 Yuerba Buena Rd	7008 Yuerba Buena Rd				
13.	6281 Point Loma Ct NE	6281 Point Loma Ct NE				
14.	Arlington Heights IL 60004	Arlington Heights IL 60004				
15.	3650 Baccus Ct	3650 Baccus Ct				
16.	5936 Frobisher Cir	5936 Frobisher Cir				
17.	2870 Stockton Pl E	2870 Stockton Pl E				
18.	4473 Viewbridge Pl	4473 Viewridge Pl				
19.	17 Kandace Villa Ln	17 Kandace Villa Pl				
20.	West Ossipee NH 03890	West Ossipee NH 03890				
21.	17981 Ashford Ave	17931 Ashford Ave				

		647 West Portal St	647 West Portol St	
22.		647 West Portal St	647 West Portol St	
23.		7200 Hempstead Cir S	7200 Hempstead Cir S	
24.		8483 Isleta Ave	8483 Isleta Cir	
25.		Vestaburg PA 15368	Vestaburg PA 15368	
26.		6011 N Gabarda Rd	6011 S Gabarda Rd	
27.		2587 Leicester Way NW	2587 Leicester Way SW	
28.		17045 Kelloch Ave NE	17405 Kelloch Ave NE	
29.		1617 Alta Vista Way	1617 Alta Vista Way	
30.		4025 Urbano Dr	4025 Urbano Dr	
31.		Kenosha WI 53142	Kenosha WI 53132	
32.		9724 Junipero Serra Blvd	9724 Jupitero Serra Blvd	
33.		8293 N Idora Ave	8293 N Idopa Ave	
34.		8039 S Revelstoke Ter	8039 S Bevelstore Ter	
35.		5732 O'Farrell St SE	5732 O'Farrell St SE	
36.		7012 W Hamerton Ave	7012 W Hammerton Ave	
37.		4712 Fratessa Ct S	4712 Fratessa Ct S	
38.		2751 Triton Blvd	2751 Triton Blvd	
39.		Sturdivant MO 64782	Sturdivant MO 63782	
40.		9658 South Van Ness Ave	9658 South Van Ness Ave	
41.		Alvaton KY 42122	Alvaton KS 42122	
42.		481 Bernal Heights Blvd	481 Bernal Heights Blvd	
43.		Cecilton MD 21913	Cecilton MD 21913	
44.		Wynantkill NY 12198	Wynantrill NY 12198	
45.		5908 W Wayland Ave	5908 W Wayland Ave	
46.		4360 New Salem Ter	4360 New Salem Ter	
47.		4289 Cale Nobleza	4289 Cale Nobleza	
48.		5527 El Mirasol	5572 El Mirasol Pl	
49.		6349 Grand View Ter	6349 Grand View Trl	
50.		9112 Jocatal St	9112 Jocatal St	
51.		Yacima WA 98902	Yakima WA 98902	
52.		3712 Upshur St W	3712 Upshur St E	
53.		3597 Mariposa St	3597 Mariposo St	
54.		5051 Orleck Pl	5015 Orleck Pl	
55.		2580 W 234 Dr	2580 W 234 Dr	
56.		4745 Nob Hill Cir	4745 Knob Hill Cir	
57.		9401 Sabina Rd	9401 Sabrina Rd	
58.		85 Zircon Ln SW	85 Zircon Ln SW	
59.		5053 Zagala Ln	5053 Zacala Ln	
60.		3089 E Codman Pl	3089 E Cadman Pl	

Number Right

Time

MISCELLANEOUS DRILL

DRILL 32

There are opportunities all around you for practicing address checking skills. When walking down the street, quickly scan license plates, street signs and posters. Look away and attempt to repeat them. Try to read the quickly moving screen credits shown on television and in the movies. Practice using the Eye Span Selector and guide card on the books, newspapers and magazines you normally read. Use wider and wider slots to increase your eye span.

Also, have a friend help you play the following game. Your friend should checkmark, at random, a few names, telephone numbers or addresses on different pages of an old phone book or catalog, making notes of the page numbers. You are to turn to each of these pages, scan the checkmarked item as fast as you can and jot it down immediately. Then compare it with the book to see how accurate you are.

Or, have someone (or do it yourself) prepare 3″ × 5″ flash cards (see page 49), with the same address on either side. Make some exactly the same—Ⓐ, and others different—Ⓓ. After you have a stack of twenty or more cards, shuffle them and flash each side of each card before your eyes as quickly as you can. See how well you pick out the Ⓐ's and Ⓓ's.

The possibilities for practice are endless. Just use your imagination.

ANSWER KEY TO DRILLS

Drills 1–11, not applicable

Drill 12, page 50

4 *b*'s
6 *d*'s

Drill 13, page 50

1.	2	4.	3	7.	1	10.	1
2.	2	5.	0	8.	1		
3.	0	6.	2	9.	3		

Drill 14, page 51

1.	0	4.	2	7.	1	10.	3
2.	3	5.	0	8.	1		
3.	1	6.	0	9.	0		

Drill 15, page 51

1.	0	4.	3	7.	1	10.	4
2.	1	5.	2	8.	1		
3.	0	6.	3	9.	1		

Drill 16, page 51

1.	0	4.	2	7.	1	10.	3
2.	4	5.	2	8.	2		
3.	0	6.	1	9.	2		

Drill 17, page 52

1.	3	4.	3	7.	3	10.	2
2.	1	5.	4	8.	1		
3.	2	6.	4	9.	1		

Drill 18, page 52

1.	4	4.	4	7.	3	10.	2
2.	3	5.	2	8.	5		
3.	2	6.	4	9.	4		

Drill 19, page 53

1.	2	4.	3	7.	2	10.	7
2.	1	5.	3	8.	3		
3.	3	6.	4	9.	0		

Drill 20, page 53

1.	3	4.	0	7.	3	10.	3
2.	1	5.	2	8.	1		
3.	0	6.	1	9.	1		

Drill 21, page 53

1.	1	4.	1	7.	2	10. 2
2.	0	5.	2	8.	5	
3.	3	6.	7	9.	2	

Drills 22, 23, not applicable

Drill 24, page 59

1.	A	6.	D	11.	D	16.	D
2.	D	7.	A	12.	D	17.	D
3.	D	8.	A	13.	D	18.	D
4.	A	9.	D	14.	D	19.	D
5.	A	10.	D	15.	D	20.	D

Drill 25, page 60

1.	D	6.	A	11.	A	16.	D
2.	D	7.	A	12.	D	17.	D
3.	A	8.	D	13.	A	18.	A
4.	D	9.	D	14.	A	19.	D
5.	D	10.	D	15.	A	20.	D

Drill 26, page 61

1.	D	6.	D	11.	A	16.	D
2.	D	7.	A	12.	D	17.	A
3.	A	8.	A	13.	D	18.	D
4.	D	9.	D	14.	D	19.	A
5.	A	10.	D	15.	D	20.	D

Drill 27, page 62

1.	D	6.	A	11.	D	16.	D
2.	D	7.	A	12.	D	17.	A
3.	D	8.	D	13.	D	18.	A
4.	A	9.	D	14.	D	19.	A
5.	D	10.	A	15.	A	20.	D

Drill 28, page 63

1.	A	6.	A	11.	D	16.	D
2.	A	7.	D	12.	D	17.	D
3.	D	8.	D	13.	D	18.	D
4.	D	9.	A	14.	A	19.	D
5.	D	10.	A	15.	A	20.	A

Drill 29, page 64

1.	A	6.	A	11.	D	16.	A
2.	D	7.	A	12.	D	17.	D
3.	A	8.	D	13.	A	18.	D
4.	D	9.	D	14.	D	19.	A
5.	D	10.	D	15.	A	20.	A

Drill 30, page 67

1.	D	16.	A	31.	A	46.	A
2.	D	17.	A	32.	D	47.	D
3.	A	18.	A	33.	A	48.	A
4.	A	19.	A	34.	D	49.	D
5.	D	20.	A	35.	D	50.	A
6.	A	21.	A	36.	A	51.	A
7.	A	22.	D	37.	D	52.	A
8.	A	23.	D	38.	A	53.	A
9.	A	24.	A	39.	A	54.	D
10.	A	25.	A	40.	D	55.	A
11.	A	26.	D	41.	D	56.	D
12.	A	27.	A	42.	D	57.	A
13.	A	28.	D	43.	A	58.	A
14.	D	29.	D	44.	D	59.	D
15.	D	30.	D	45.	D	60.	D

Drill 31, page 68

1.	D	16.	A	31.	D	46.	A
2.	D	17.	A	32.	D	47.	A
3.	A	18.	D	33.	D	48.	D
4.	A	19.	D	34.	D	49.	D
5.	D	20.	A	35.	A	50.	A
6.	D	21.	D	36.	D	51.	D
7.	D	22.	D	37.	A	52.	D
8.	D	23.	A	38.	A	53.	D
9.	D	24.	D	39.	D	54.	D
10.	A	25.	A	40.	A	55.	A
11.	A	26.	D	41.	D	56.	D
12.	A	27.	D	42.	A	57.	D
13.	A	28.	D	43.	A	58.	A
14.	A	29.	A	44.	D	59.	D
15.	A	30.	A	45.	A	60.	D

Drill 32, not applicable

Memory for *Direct* Addresses—How to Improve Your Score

TEST STRATEGY

You have seen how important good test strategy is in taking the Address Checking tests. You will be even more impressed by what an effective strategy can mean to your score on the Memory for Addresses tests. We have three major suggestions for you to consider.

USE SOME PRACTICE TIME FOR STUDYING

On the actual test, you will be given a preliminary period of time to review the test directions and to do some sample questions. The purpose is to make certain that the test takers understand what the exam is all about—what is wanted, and where and how to mark down the answers. *But you already know all of that.* The Diagnostic Practice Test you took used most of the same format that has appeared on prior examinations. Furthermore, if there should be any change in the type of question or in the format, you will know about it ahead of time. All test candidates receive, prior to the test, a description of the test and several sample questions. So, why spend time re-reading the same directions and doing samples? *Instead, use this time to memorize the addresses in the boxes.*

After reviewing the directions and the sample questions, you will be given several trial tests, preceded by brief study periods. On some of these tests you must answer the questions from memory. You must follow the official monitor's instructions. But for the other trial tests, the boxes with the addresses will be in view as you answer the questions. You may then proceed to answer the questions from memory in the regular way. On the other hand, you may decide to spend the allotted time *studying* the addresses in the boxes instead. We believe that, for most people, time is better spent studying the boxes rather than answering the sample questions or the questions on List 1. It is true that there is a benefit in answering the questions by memory and then discovering what you don't know. On the other hand, comparatively little *new* learning takes place. The majority of our students report far better results by spending almost all the available time studying and remembering the addresses.

In the past, the time *designated* for study totaled 8 minutes. If a test candidate had followed the suggestions above, and had taken advantage of all the time *available* for study, he or she might easily have doubled that amount. In this book, we have tried to be conservative by estimating that a total of 14 minutes will be available for study. It is better not to be overly optimistic but rather to be trained and ready to meet stricter standards. In any case, you will have a distinct advantage over your competitors!

ELIMINATE THE LAST BOX

If you learn the memory techniques explained in the following pages, you won't need to employ this strategy. We believe that, with practice, you will be able to remember all 25 items. But if you can't quite remember all 25, consider skipping Box E either entirely or in part. *Then, when you take the test, you can mark Box E for any name or number that you don't recognize. And you'll be correct!*

TO GUESS OR NOT TO GUESS

What if you come across an address which you are not sure about? Should you guess? *The answer is YES.* Mathematically, even for a completely blind guess, you won't lose anything if you guess. Here's why. For each question, there are five choices, Box A, B, C, D, or E. One of these five has to be correct. That means that you have one chance out of 5 (20%) of getting the correct answer, even if you guess. For example, if you took a test that had 100 questions and you guessed the answers to all of them, you would be likely to answer 20 correctly (20% of 100) and get the other 80 wrong. For *any* number of questions the odds are still the same. Let us see how this fact affects your actual score. Assume you guessed the answers to five of the memory questions instead of leaving them blank. If you got only what the odds dictated you would end up with 1 answer correct and 4 wrong.

Calculations: Number Right 1
Number Wrong 4
¼ × 4 .... −1
YOUR SCORE = 1 − 1 = 0

In this case, you have not lost anything, but you have not gained anything either.

However, you won't be making a *completely* blind guess on most questions you are not sure of. More likely, you will have a glimmer of recognition and will be unsure as to which one of two or three boxes to choose. If you then guess at one of them, you are going to come out ahead in the long run.

The odds are such that when you are guessing at one out of two or three choices, you will get enough questions right to more than make up for the ones you get wrong.

To summarize, you now know about three vital test strategies. Decide how to use them after you have gained some experience doing the practice tests.

IMPROVING YOUR MEMORY

Science has yet to discover exactly how the human brain works. It knows enough to tell us that the brain is an awesomely complex structure that makes the most advanced computer look crude. We also know that it has enormous untapped potential. One commonly cited bit of knowledge has it that the average person uses only about ten percent of his ten billion brain cells. If he were able to tap the unused powers of his mind, he might be able to accomplish wondrous things. Studies that have been made of individuals with just such extraordinary mental abilities bear out the supposition.

One famous case that was extensively documented is that of Mr. S. He was an obscure Russian who had a fantastic memory. He was able to memorize a list of 18 six-digit numbers in 3 minutes. He retained it so well that he could repeat the list in any order, even reciting each number in reverse! Amazingly, he was able to repeat these feats years later, even though he had not seen the list in the interim! Extraordinary displays of memory also are given by professional entertainers, the so-called memory experts who can recall the names and addresses of dozens of members of an audience they have never met before. In addition, we all have heard stories about famous generals, hostesses, and politicians who never forget a name or a place.

Intensive studies of people with "super-memories" have helped psychologists understand how those of us with ordinary memories, may improve them. The methods outlined below are based on such studies and on *demonstrated improvements* made by students who have used them to prepare for the Postal Service exam.

The study plan that was used for these students will be followed now as we look at various memory techniques. First, we will review the techniques applicable to remembering the names of "direct" addresses. In the next chapter, we will study techniques to remember the "numbered" addresses. We strongly recommend that you begin your memory improvement program with the *direct* addresses. Experience shows that the techniques for remembering direct addresses will bring you quick, encouraging results. The confidence you gain will help when you undertake the more difficult task of remembering numbered addresses.

TECHNIQUES FOR REMEMBERING THE DIRECT ADDRESSES

ASSOCIATION AND IMAGERY

If you are like most people, you will find it easier to remember names than numbers. This is because names bring forth a meaningful association with something familiar. They may remind us of a place, a thing, or a word we know about. Even better, the address name may bring a vivid picture to mind. For example, take the word *ice*. As soon as we see or hear this word, we may form an association with the words *cream* or *snow*. We may also associate *ice* with ideas or feelings such as *cold* and *chilly*. In our mind's eye, the image of an *iceberg* or an *ice cube* may form without conscious effort.

When we see a name that carries a meaningful association and presents an image, the name will probably stick in our memory. Two key memorization techniques to use, therefore, are *association* and *imagery*. Here is an illustration of the power and practicality of these techniques applied to the Memory for Addresses portion of the Diagnostic Practice Test. (For the sake of clarity, only direct names have been reproduced.)

A	B	C	D	E
Ceres Natoma	Cedar Foster	Niles Dexter	Cicero Pearl	Dehli Magnet

In Box A, *Ceres* looks and sounds like . . . sure, like *Cereal* or *Series*. You may also have associated Ceres with something out of a fairy tale (Ceres happens to be the name of the ancient Italian goddess of agriculture). What about *Natoma*? It looks almost like the word *atom*. Remember what was discussed about associations and images? If we can form a single picture associating both names, they will stay in our memory even better. Can you picture a bowl of breakfast cereal (Ceres) with little atoms (Natoma) floating about in it? It may seem absurd, but in a way that's the point! Authorities on memory techniques say that the more vivid, colorful and startling the image is, the better you'll remember it.

Nevertheless, we are not done yet. How about Box A? After all, on the test we are required to remember in which box each address belongs. A useful technique to employ now is to make up a little story. It can be weird or silly, as long as it helps to connect the box with the names. Let's assume, for example, that an *Apple* stands for *Box A*. Now the associations are complete. You have got a mental picture of little Apples (Box A) and Atoms (Natoma) floating in a bowl of Cereal (Ceres). You will never forget that.

What if you made a quick association between Ceres and Series? That brings to mind the World Series with its two opposing teams, the American (Box A) and National (Natoma). Remember, the association you make does not have to fit and spell exactly right. As long as *you* make the connection, that's all that counts. You might even have imagined an *Ace* (Box A) pitching the World Series (Ceres) for the National (Natoma) League. This image is vivid, and forms a good association among the two words and Box A. *You won't forget it on the test.*

Actually, Box A illustrates one of the more difficult associations you will have to make because the names Ceres and Natoma are off-beat. If you now feel confident of your ability to remember them, you will find remembering Box B even easier. Start associating the names in the box.

> *Cedar* brings to mind . . . a tree, a storage chest, wood, shingles, etc.

> *Foster* brings to mind . . . a forest; child; the actor, Foster Brooks; etc.

That's it!

> . . . see the Cedar (Cedar) tree standing in the Forest (Foster),

> . . . see Foster (Foster) Brooks, slightly stewed, leaning against a Cedar (Cedar) tree.

How about the connection to *Box B*?

> . . . Make the tree a *B*lue Cedar (which is a common type). If you like, hang a hundred *B*ananas on it or a *B*eehive

> . . . See Foster Brooks *B*urping.

And so it goes. The possibilities for imagery and extended associations are great in Box B. Although everyone may do it a little differently, everyone *can* do it. Just practice this technique on the tests in this book, letting your imagination run free. Start now by trying your hand with the names in Boxes C, D, and E.

THE "LOCI" TECHNIQUE

Mr. S., the Russian with the fabulous memory, partially explained it by telling about a system of "places" he used. (*Loci* is a Greek word meaning "places.") He said that he remembered long lists of objects by mentally putting each object in a particular place that was familiar to him. By remembering the place, he could "see" the object. For example, assume that Mr. S. were given a list of objects to remember such as a hat, cane, dog, violin, etc. He would assign each of them to a particular place in a certain scene. A scene that he sometimes used was a street near his home. He knew every inch of it because he walked it daily. To remember the list of objects, he merely imagined himself walking down the street. On his imaginary walk, he put the *hat* on a lamp post, leaned the *cane* against the side of a shop, saw the *dog* near a tree across the road, put the *violin* in a pawnshop window, etc. He could recall each object by mentally retracing his path down the street. So, when he saw the tree, he saw the dog, too! Each of the other objects on his list was recalled in the same way.

Performers, politicians, students and others from all walks of life have been using the loci system, or a variation on it, down through the ages. It will work for you, too, provided you do two things:

1. Decide on your personal system of places, or loci.
2. Become so familiar with your loci that you can immediately "see" every one of the places.

You might choose a street on the way to work, your shop or office, a room in your house. The objects can range from your kitchen shelf to your desk drawer. Make the scene as detailed as you wish. The more "places" it has in it, the more items you will be able to remember.

Using the Loci Technique on the Test

The system or scene that you set up needs to have only five places. Each one has to correspond with one of the five boxes—A, B, C, D, and E. For example, a good system to use is the layout of rooms in your home. One student followed the room layout in her house like this:

A	B	C	D	E
Kitchen	Bathroom	Dining Room	Living Room	Workroom

In her mind's eye she was able to build these pictures, using the boxes on page 21 as a basis.

```
Box A—Kitchen
I'm sitting in my kitchen
eating a bowl of Cereal (Ceres)
with little Atoms (Natoma)
floating in it.
```

Note that she did not have to think of an association with Box A (like Apple) because Box A is the kitchen.

```
Box B—Bathroom
I'm giving my Foster
child a bath and rubbing
his Chest (Cedar) with
soap.
```

If you like her system, see if you can use it to remember the addresses in Boxes C, D, and E. Do it now—the more you practice the art of imagery, the faster you will learn to do it. If you prefer to use your own system of places, remember to use the guidelines above.

REDUCTION CODING

This, the third of our memory tools, has become the favorite of many students in our classes. It means that we cut down, or *reduce*, the amount we have to remember and then put what remains into a special, easy-to-remember form. Here are some simple examples:

SAMPLE

We can remember the order in which the colors of the rainbow appear (<u>r</u>ed, <u>o</u>range, <u>y</u>ellow, <u>g</u>reen, <u>b</u>lue, <u>i</u>ndigo, <u>v</u>iolet) by using their initials, ROYGBIV.

SAMPLE

If you want to remember the names of the Great Lakes, just remember the word HOMES:

<u>H</u>uron
<u>O</u>ntario
<u>M</u>ichigan
<u>E</u>rie
<u>S</u>uperior

In each case, *one* word replaces many words.

One more example. This time it is a word frequently used by those preparing for a test to select managers. (That might be you after you enter the Postal Service.)

SAMPLE

The word is POSDCORB, and it stands for the seven basic duties of every manager:

<u>P</u>lanning
<u>O</u>rganizing
<u>S</u>taffing
<u>D</u>irecting
<u>C</u>
<u>O</u>} ordinating
<u>R</u>eporting
<u>B</u>udgeting

Seven different words made into one! Although POSDCORB, as a word, doesn't mean anything, it can be *sounded out* and seen in the mind's eye very easily. In this way, it will be remembered far longer and better than by drilling on the original seven.

Let's see how this method works on another sample test question.

A	B	C	D	E
1800-2299 Peach Frechett 3100-3299 Kerry Benson 1500-1999 Martin	2400-2999 Peach Stokes 4500-4999 Kerry Yalta 2000-2199 Martin	1200-1799 Peach Hyberg 3600-4499 Kerry Island 2700-3499 Martin	3000-3699 Peach Graybar 3300-3599 Kerry Otiak 4100-4499 Martin	2300-2399 Peach Lorry 5000-5899 Kerry Upville 3500-4099 Martin

To remember the ten direct (name) addresses with these boxes using *reduction coding*, you have your choice of three approaches.

Method A

Step 1

Make an image. Use the first letter of each of the five direct addresses in the second row, going from left to right, to set up your first new word.

> FSHGL . . . See it in your mind's eye.
> Make an image.

Do the same thing with the five direct addresses in the fourth row.

> BYIOU . . . See it in your mind's eye.
> Make an image.

Step 2

Sound out the word. If your mind can retain the special sound or quality of the new "word" even though it has no meaning, then you have the battle more than half won. You will now have a fine substitute for the five original words *in the same order* in which they appear in each of the five boxes. Thereafter, whenever you see the address name Lorry, you will associate it with the last box—E, because the *l* sound comes last in the word FSHGL. Likewise, you can use the sound of FSHGL to correctly place each of the words on line 2 of each of the boxes: *F*rechett, *S*tokes, *H*yberg, *G*raybar and *L*orry. You will be able to mentally see each of these words in their correct order.

You now have two of your senses working for you—sound and sight. You will have no need to attempt any of the usual memorization and repetitious drilling which yield far less satisfactory results.

Step 3

Does the new word have any meaning? Although it was pointed out that the new "word" need not have any meaning, sometimes it does. Or, it may be associated with a word that does mean something. (It need not be an English word. A word in Spanish, German, Hindi, or any other language you know will do.) Once you have attached a meaning to the word, remembering it will become still easier.

Let's go back to FSHGL. What do these five letters sound like when you try to pronounce them? Of course! It sounds like FISH GILL, the breathing agent of a fish. I don't think there is any chance that you will easily forget the vivid picture associated with this word. Once this picture flashes into your awareness (which should take only a brief second), you can work confidently on the rest of the addresses in the five boxes.

What about the five remaining direct addresses on the fourth line? They formed our second new word—BYIOU. Suppose you now use these two new words to see how well you can employ the methods we've just discussed.

DRILL 1

Below are twenty addresses contained in the sample five boxes on page 81. Study only the direct name addresses and their locations in the sample five boxes for *1 minute*, using the two new words FSHGL and BYIOU. Then, from memory, enter the correct box location (A–E) for each. (You may wish to take this exercise more than once.)

	Answers Trials	3	2	1			Answers Trials	3	2	1
1. Frechett					11. Hyberg				
2. Lorry					12. Stokes				
3. Benson					13. Otiak				
4. Stokes					14. Upville				
5. Island					15. Frechett				
6. Otiak					16. Otiak				
7. Graybar					17. Island				
8. Lorry					18. Lorry				
9. Yalta					19. Graybar				
10. Benson					20. Hyberg				
					Number Right				
					Time				

Did you use BYIOU successfully? Did you sound it? It has a musical, easy-to-remember sound. You probably noticed immediately that BYIOU sounds exactly like the word *bayou* (from the song "Blue Bayou"). Does it have any meaning? Sure it does. It is a body of water, an arm of a lake or river. Now you have formed a vivid, mental image. With the triple combination of *sound, meaning* and *imagery* that BYIOU conjures up, you cannot help but remember those five addresses.

Step 4

Make up a story. Use each of the five letters as the initial letters of a five-word story, slogan, or phrase. The more vivid and breezy it is, the better.

SAMPLE

FSHGL   Feel So Happy Go Lucky.
            Few Sleepy Heads Get Lively.
            Father Saw His Green Lawn.

SAMPLE

BYIOU   Buy Yourself! IOU.
            Bananas are Yellow, Inside, Outside and Underneath.
            Baby is Young and Innocent, not Old and Ugly.

The trick is to be able to create the story freely and quickly. With a little practice, you can develop the knack. When you have it, you can remember any five letter combination even if you cannot sound it (Step 2) or find any meaning (Step 3).

Method B

For a variety of reasons which we shall discuss later, you may decide to memorize all the addresses within each of the boxes A, B, C, D, and E, separately. If so, you may still employ reduction coding.

Step 1

Make an image. Select the first letter of each of the two direct addresses in each box plus the letter above the box itself.

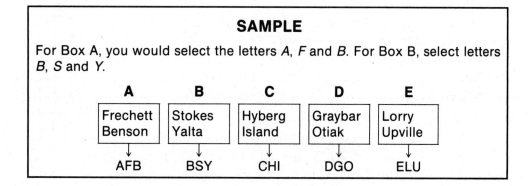

SAMPLE

For Box A, you would select the letters *A*, *F* and *B*. For Box B, select letters *B*, *S* and *Y*.

A	B	C	D	E
Frechett Benson	Stokes Yalta	Hyberg Island	Graybar Otiak	Lorry Upville
↓	↓	↓	↓	↓
AFB	BSY	CHI	DGO	ELU

Step 2

Sound out the word. We don't get anything too useful with AFB, but we get immediate results with Box B. When you sound BSY you get—BUSY! Notice that the *B* in "Busy" immediately gives you the box location.

Step 3

*Does it have **meaning**?* When we discussed using associations, we said that many of the best associations are strictly personal and exist only for you.

This means that some of the three-letter words may be an abbreviation of a person, place or thing with which only *you* are familiar. If so, you will immediately make the association and store it for future use. For example, in Box A, AFB might be the initials of your best friend, A̲lfred F̲rederick B̲ates, or, in military terms, A̲ir F̲orce B̲ase. In Box B, CHI might be the letters of your old fraternity, or the C̲ity of H̲Ī̲cago, where you once lived.

But let's go further. We will learn how to use those three-letter combinations in other ways, if Steps 2 and 3 don't produce immediate results.

Step 4

Move the letters around. If the three letters do not produce a meaningful sound or word, play mental Scrabble. For instance, move just one letter of DGO and you've got DOG, man's best friend; DOG has the key letter *D*, which gives you the box location on which you peg the *O* and *G*. These letters stand, of course, for O̲TIAK and G̲RAYBAR. The only problem that can arise is when you are given five boxes that contain 2 or more addresses with the same first letter. This problem, however, can be readily solved by Method C.

DRILL 2

Transpose the initial letters of the direct addresses in Boxes A and C on page 81. In each case you will be able to come up with meaningful words.

1. Box A _____

2. Box C _____

Step 5

Make Up a Story. Use exactly the same technique as explained in Method A, page 82. You will find it even easier because your story needs only three words instead of five.

Method C

Sometimes you may wish to combine Methods A and B. In our sample question you may have felt very confident about remembering BYIOU, but not about FSHGL (Method A). You might then use a few of the three-letter words developed in Method B to reinforce your memory for the remaining addresses.

Let us try to visualize what might be going on in your mind's eye by drawing a simple "mental diagram."

A Mind's Eye View

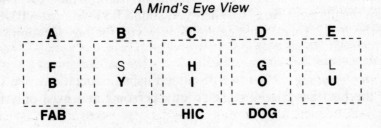

Here, the three-letter words FAB, HIC and DOG plus the word BYIOU stand out clearly. They give you eight of the ten direct addresses without any of the ordinary rote memorization on your part. They also give you cues on the two missing address names. By memorizing only *one* of them, you can ensure knowing all ten well enough to attain a perfect score!

EIDETIC (PHOTOGRAPHIC) MEMORY

All of us can form mental pictures which we are able to review whenever we want to remember something. Methods A, B, and C all employ this ability to some extent.

There are a few people who have "picture taking" ability far beyond the capabilities of most of us. They can reproduce the pictures they have taken in such great detail that it is as though they literally were looking at a photograph. They can even see the picture in color and keep it stored for a long time.

Needless to say, those who were born with an eidetic memory have an enormous advantage on this test. The rest of us, although we cannot hope to develop such a memory, can learn, through practice, to intensify and retain longer the mental pictures we make. In any case, you now have an arsenal of techniques which do away with the need for special or hard-to-achieve powers. You can practice them now on some of the practice tests or wait until you have read the next chapter which will teach you how to deal with the numbered addresses.

SPECIAL EXERCISES FOR BUILDING MEMORY FOR *DIRECT* ADDRESSES

DRILLS FOR ASSOCIATION

Do Drills 3 through 6 to get the feel of associating words and images freely and quickly. They are fun to do and you can do them by yourself or, if you prefer, with a friend.

Directions for Drills 3 through 6

Each drill consists of a list of 20 names. Cover the list with your hand or a piece of paper so that you can uncover the names one at a time as you move it down the list. If a friend is helping you, just hand him/her the list and ask him/her to call out each name when you are ready to begin.

As soon as you hear or see the name, call out the images and the words that come into your mind. Be free and spontaneous. Don't be concerned or embarrassed if your associations seem weird or foolish. The thing that *is* important is that the images come to you quickly and naturally. That is why there is no answer key to these drills. The only right answers are what *you* supply.

Take no more than 8 to 10 seconds per name on the average. In succeeding drills you will become able to make associations more rapidly. If you blank out on a particular name, skip over it and continue the drill until you complete all twenty names. These drills may be repeated as often as you like.

DRILL 3

1. Ballin	8. Youngsgap	15. Hopkins
2. Tulip	9. Peter	16. Barnes
3. Parsons	10. Oak	17. Fairview
4. Foster	11. Dorchester	18. Main
5. Truebridge	12. Westlake	19. Crescent
6. Chester	13. Marlboro	20. Pearson
7. Buckley	14. Shaster	

DRILL 4

1. Charles	8. Downing	15. Welk
2. Daley	9. Mall	16. Newly
3. Exeter	10. Oxford	17. Quinones
4. Bair	11. Laurel	18. Pear
5. Willow	12. Rippon	19. Logandell
6. Central	13. Levering	20. Townsend
7. Lott	14. Cliff	

DRILL 5

1. Shipwright	8. Seacrest	15. Sutton
2. Bridge	9. Partridge	16. Able
3. Ashley	10. Austin	17. Sunnyside
4. Niles	11. Portland	18. York
5. Reese	12. Baton	19. Astor
6. Fruitland	13. Sampson	20. Calvary
7. Coral	14. Zerba	

DRILL 6

1. Dumont	8. Victor	15. Lakeside
2. Grafton	9. Barbarossa	16. Pompona
3. Newberry	10. Church	17. Kissel
4. Malta	11. Lever	18. Marshal
5. Fox	12. Paris	19. Varick
6. Kismet	13. Edison	20. Post
7. Yule	14. Cherry	

DRILLS USING ASSOCIATION AND IMAGERY

The next two drills (7 and 8) will be especially helpful to those who intend to rely primarily on forming associations and images to remember the direct name addresses. (The numbered addresses have been left out for the sake of clarity.) For a full discussion on this method, see pages 77 to 78.

Here are some guidelines.

1. As you examine each address name, make your associations and see the images each brings forth.
2. Associate the images in each box with their corresponding box letter (A, B, C, D, or E) by means of a mental picture story.
3. Drill on the names that you were not able to incorporate in your picture stories.

DRILL 7

Study the ten address names and memorize in which box (A, B, C, D, or E) each belongs. *Take exactly 5 minutes to study these names and their locations.* When the study time is over, cover the boxes and answer as many of the 40 questions as you can in *two minutes*. For each question, mark the answer space next to it to show the letter of the box in which the address belongs. (Cover the line of answers you have already completed so that they do not influence you on your second and third trials.)

A	B	C	D	E
Branch Tiffany	Highview Archer	Chestnut Henry	Vine Stein	Masters Green

Answers

Trials | 3 | 2 | 1

1. Archer
2. Stein
3. Chestnut
4. Henry
5. Highview
6. Tiffany
7. Green
8. Branch
9. Masters
10. Archer
11. Tiffany
12. Green
13. Henry
14. Tiffany
15. Stein
16. Masters
17. Vine
18. Stein
19. Henry
20. Highview

Answers

Trials | 3 | 2 | 1

21. Chestnut
22. Branch
23. Green
24. Masters
25. Vine
26. Highview
27. Tiffany
28. Branch
29. Archer
30. Vine
31. Masters
32. Highview
33. Tiffany
34. Stein
35. Branch
36. Henry
37. Green
38. Archer
39. Vine
40. Stein

Number Right
Time

DRILL 8

Study the ten address names and memorize in which box (A, B, C, D, or E) each belongs. *Take exactly 5 minutes to study these names and their locations.* When the study time is over, cover the boxes and answer as many of the 40 questions as you can in *two minutes*. For each question, mark the answer space next to it to show the letter of the box in which the address belongs. (Cover the line of answers you have already completed so that they do not influence you on your second and third trials.)

A	B	C	D	E
Beacon Sterling	Akron Fuller	Grande Cove	Fields South	Harvard Worth

	Answers						Answers			
	Trials	3	2	1			Trials	3	2	1
1. Grande						21. Harvard				
2. Sterling						22. Sterling				
3. Fuller						23. South				
4. Harvard						24. Fuller				
5. South						25. Fields				
6. Worth						26. Cove				
7. Akron						27. Worth				
8. Beacon						28. Akron				
9. Fields						29. Fuller				
10. South						30. Beacon				
11. Cove						31. Cove				
12. Harvard						32. South				
13. Grande						33. Fields				
14. Fuller						34. Beacon				
15. Beacon						35. Worth				
16. Sterling						36. Cove				
17. Harvard						37. Sterling				
18. Worth						38. South				
19. Grande						39. Fuller				
20. Akron						40. Fields				
						Number Right				
						Time				

DRILLS USING THE LOCI SYSTEM

You may have decided that you like the Loci System*, in conjunction with associations and imagery, for remembering the direct name addresses. If so, do Drills 9 and 10 with these guidelines in mind:

---

* NOTE: Those who are not using the loci system, but who are relying on regular associations, may use these drills in the same way as for Drills 7 and 8.

1. Make sure that your loci system is at your command. You should be able to visualize instantly which box each place in your system represents.
2. Form your association with the two direct names in each box in the regular way to come up with a vivid object picture for each name.
3. Place each of these object pictures in the place representing the box in your system. Make up a little story or slogan if it helps to strengthen the association.

DRILL 9

Study the ten address names and memorize in which box (A, B, C, D, or E) each belongs. *Take exactly 5 minutes to study these names and their locations.* When the study time is over, cover the boxes and answer as many of the 40 questions as you can in *two minutes*. For each question, mark the answer space next to it to show the letter of the box in which the address belongs. (Cover the line of answers you have already completed so that they do not influence you on your second and third trials.)

A	B	C	D	E
Barber	Kings	Pine	Fleet	Wood
Ajax	North	Crane	Mason	Chopin

Answers — Trials 3 2 1

1. Chopin
2. North
3. Barber
4. Wood
5. Ajax
6. Kings
7. Pine
8. Mason
9. Crane
10. Fleet
11. Ajax
12. Wood
13. Mason
14. Chopin
15. Pine
16. Kings
17. North
18. Chopin
19. Ajax
20. Barber

21. Mason
22. Crane
23. Fleet
24. Mason
25. Kings
26. Ajax
27. North
28. Barber
29. Pine
30. Ajax
31. Chopin
32. Wood
33. Kings
34. Crane
35. Fleet
36. Wood
37. Barber
38. Chopin
39. North
40. Pine

Number Right
Time

DRILL 10

Study the ten address names and memorize in which box (A, B, C, D, or E) each belongs. *Take exactly 5 minutes to study these names and their locations.* When the study time is over, cover the boxes and answer as many of the 40 questions as you can in *two minutes*. For each question, mark the answer space next to it to show the letter of the box in which the address belongs. (Cover the line of answers you have already completed so that they do not influence you on your second and third trials.)

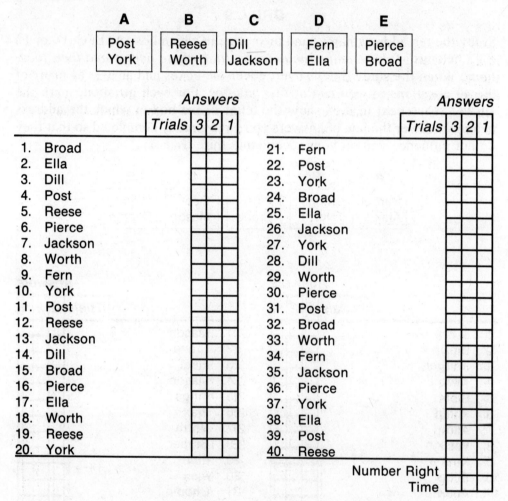

A	B	C	D	E
Post York	Reese Worth	Dill Jackson	Fern Ella	Pierce Broad

Answers   *Answers*

	Trials	3	2	1			Trials	3	2	1
1. Broad					21. Fern				
2. Ella					22. Post				
3. Dill					23. York				
4. Post					24. Broad				
5. Reese					25. Ella				
6. Pierce					26. Jackson				
7. Jackson					27. York				
8. Worth					28. Dill				
9. Fern					29. Worth				
10. York					30. Pierce				
11. Post					31. Post				
12. Reese					32. Broad				
13. Jackson					33. Worth				
14. Dill					34. Fern				
15. Broad					35. Jackson				
16. Pierce					36. Pierce				
17. Ella					37. York				
18. Worth					38. Ella				
19. Reese					39. Post				
20. York					40. Reese				
					Number Right Time				

DRILLS USING REDUCTION CODING (METHOD A)

Drills 11 and 12 give you an opportunity to practice the Reduction Coding system for memorizing the direct name addresses (see pages 80 to 85 for the complete discussion). Below is a summary of the steps to follow if you are going to use *horizontal* coding (Method A).

1.   Use the first letter of each of the five name addresses on the top row to make a five-letter word. Visualize it.

2. Sound the word mentally. Is it catchy and easy to remember?
3. Does the word have any meaning or evoke a picture?
4. Make up a little story or slogan using the five letters. (Step 4 is optional. You need not use it if you are able to remember the new "word" after completing Steps 1 to 3.)
5. Repeat Steps 1 to 4 above for the second row of five direct name addresses.

DRILL 11

Study the ten address names and memorize in which box (A, B, C, D, or E) each belongs. *Take exactly 5 minutes to study these names and their locations.* When the study time is over, cover the boxes and answer as many of the 40 questions as you can in *two minutes*. For each question, mark the answer space next to it, to show the letter of the box in which the address belongs. (Cover the line of answers you have already completed so that they do not influence you on your second and third trials.)

A	B	C	D	E
Slote Philip	Ladd Echo	Acorn Baily	Vestry Tress	Rail Neel

Answers

Trials | 3 | 2 | 1

1. Ladd
2. Baily
3. Rail
4. Tress
5. Slote
6. Philip
7. Acorn
8. Vestry
9. Neel
10. Echo
11. Acorn
12. Neel
13. Baily
14. Slote
15. Philip
16. Rail
17. Neel
18. Vestry
19. Echo
20. Tress

Answers

Trials | 3 | 2 | 1

21. Baily
22. Acorn
23. Slote
24. Rail
25. Philip
26. Tress
27. Vestry
28. Ladd
29. Neel
30. Echo
31. Acorn
32. Vestry
33. Echo
34. Ladd
35. Baily
36. Acorn
37. Philip
38. Vestry
39. Neel
40. Rail

Number Right
Time

DRILLS USING REDUCTION CODING (METHOD B)

In this method, you employ the same basic idea as Method A except that you memorize the *individual* box letters as you memorize the addresses in each. Here is a summary of the steps.

1. For each individual box (A, B, C, D, and E), use the first letter of the two direct name addresses and the box letter itself to make up a three-letter word.
2. Sound the "word" mentally. Is it catchy and easy to remember?
3. Does the "word" have any meaning or evoke a picture?
4. Transpose the letters if it helps produce a better "word."
5. Make up a little story or slogan using the three letters. (Step 5 is optional. You need not use it if you are able to remember the new "word" after completing Step 4.)
6. Repeat Steps 1 to 5 for each box in turn.

DRILL 12

Study the ten address names and memorize in which box (A, B, C, D, or E) each belongs. *Take exactly 5 minutes to study these names and their locations.* When the study time is over, cover the boxes and answer as many of the 40 questions as you can in *two minutes.* For each question, mark the answer space next to it to show the letter of the box in which the address belongs. (Cover the line of answers you have already completed so that they do not influence you on your second and third trials.)

A	B	C	D	E
Western Gary	Cross Able	Oxford Brook	Ridge Iris	Nestor Turner

Answers   *Answers*

#	Name	Trials 3 2 1		#	Name	Trials 3 2 1
1.	Turner			21.	Able	
2.	Ridge			22.	Cross	
3.	Gary			23.	Ridge	
4.	Cross			24.	Iris	
5.	Able			25.	Gary	
6.	Iris			26.	Turner	
7.	Nestor			27.	Western	
8.	Brook			28.	Gary	
9.	Western			29.	Oxford	
10.	Oxford			30.	Nestor	
11.	Nestor			31.	Turner	
12.	Turner			32.	Able	
13.	Iris			33.	Brook	
14.	Oxford			34.	Cross	
15.	Cross			35.	Brook	
16.	Gary			36.	Iris	
17.	Able			37.	Oxford	
18.	Western			38.	Nestor	
19.	Ridge			39.	Turner	
20.	Brook			40.	Able	

Number Right
Time

DRILLS FOR MAKING UP STORIES AND SLOGANS

A little story or slogan that connects the address names with each other and with the box letters can be very useful for strengthening associations. They are particularly helpful if you use reduction coding and want to make sure of some hard-to-remember initials (read pages 80 to 85 for a complete discussion). Here are some brief guidelines to follow.

Your task is to use five initials (Method A) or three initials (Method B) to make up the words forming a brief story or slogan. For example, if you had to deal with the initials FSTAB, you might come up with "Five Sailors Took A Boat" or "Feed Salami To A Baby." Three letters such as CTB could stand for "Cock-eyed Teddy Bears" or "Chocolate Tastes Best." Anything goes. The more humorous, colorful and vivid the story/slogan is, the better.

Do Drills 13 to 22 to develop your facility and speed. Drills 13 to 17 each have five, 3-letter combinations. Drills 18 to 22 each consist of two lines of 5-letter combinations. Each drill, therefore, contains the equivalent of ten direct name addresses, the same as on the regular test.

Directions 13 through 22

Take 5 minutes to study each drill. Make up your story/slogan as you examine each group of three or five letters. When the 5 minutes are up, cover the letter groups and jot down the initials, *in the same order as originally given*, on the answer line for that group. *Take 30 seconds to do this.* (Cover the line of answers you have already completed so that they do not influence you on your second and third trials.)

DRILL 13

Answers

	Trials	3	2	1
1. BCN				
2. AFR				
3. SEW				
4. MBO				
5. DAG				
	Number Right			
	Time			

DRILL 15

Answers

	Trials	3	2	1
1. HOD				
2. UCA				
3. EFT				
4. BRX				
5. LID				
	Number Right			
	Time			

DRILL 14

Answers

	Trials	3	2	1
1. PFE				
2. YAR				
3. ZUD				
4. EBP				
5. CSG				
	Number Right			
	Time			

DRILL 16

Answers

	Trials	3	2	1
1. TLC				
2. NAT				
3. RBW				
4. VES				
5. SDD				
	Number Right			
	Time			

DRILL 17

		Answers		
	Trials	3	2	1
1. CPO				
2. ADB				
3. GEL				
4. RCF				
5. BHS				
	Number Right			
	Time			

DRILL 20

		Answers		
	Trials	3	2	1
1. CBTUP				
2. ERDNS				
	Number Right			
	Time			

DRILL 18

		Answers		
	Trials	3	2	1
1. MOPLT				
2. RSEND				
	Number Right			
	Time			

DRILL 21

		Answers		
	Trials	3	2	1
1. TVEKA				
2. MCSOD				
	Number Right			
	Time			

DRILL 19

		Answers		
	Trials	3	2	1
1. NBITG				
2. AHFSM				
	Number Right			
	Time			

DRILL 22

		Answers		
	Trials	3	2	1
1. OZWSL				
2. CNBIJ				
	Number Right			
	Time			

ANSWER KEY TO DRILLS

Drill 1, page 82

1.	A	6.	D	11.	C	16.	D
2.	E	7.	D	12.	B	17.	C
3.	A	8.	E	13.	D	18.	E
4.	B	9.	B	14.	E	19.	D
5.	C	10.	A	15.	A	20.	C

Drill 2, page 84

1. Box *A* plus *F* and *B* gives—*FAB*, the laundry detergent.
2. Box *C* plus *H* and *I* gives—*CHI*, slang for CHICAGO.
                           —*HIC*, as in HICCUP.

Drills 3–6, not applicable

Drill 7, page 87

1.	B	11.	A	21.	C	31.	E
2.	D	12.	E	22.	A	32.	B
3.	C	13.	C	23.	E	33.	A
4.	C	14.	A	24.	E	34.	D
5.	B	15.	D	25.	D	35.	A
6.	A	16.	E	26.	B	36.	C
7.	E	17.	D	27.	A	37.	E
8.	A	18.	D	28.	A	38.	B
9.	E	19.	C	29.	B	39.	D
10.	B	20.	B	30.	D	40.	D

Drill 8, page 88

1.	C	11.	C	21.	E	31.	C
2.	A	12.	E	22.	A	32.	D
3.	B	13.	C	23.	D	33.	D
4.	E	14.	B	24.	B	34.	A
5.	D	15.	A	25.	D	35.	E
6.	E	16.	A	26.	C	36.	C
7.	B	17.	E	27.	E	37.	A
8.	A	18.	E	28.	B	38.	D
9.	D	19.	C	29.	B	39.	B
10.	D	20.	B	30.	A	40.	D

Drill 9, page 89

1.	E	7.	C	13.	D	19.	A
2.	B	8.	D	14.	E	20.	A
3.	A	9.	C	15.	C	21.	D
4.	E	10.	D	16.	B	22.	C
5.	A	11.	A	17.	B	23.	D
6.	B	12.	E	18.	E	24.	D

25. B	29. C	33. B	37. A
26. A	30. A	34. C	38. E
27. B	31. E	35. D	39. B
28. A	32. E	36. E	40. C

Drill 10, page 90

1. E	11. A	21. D	31. A
2. D	12. B	22. A	32. E
3. C	13. C	23. A	33. B
4. A	14. C	24. E	34. D
5. B	15. E	25. D	35. C
6. E	16. E	26. C	36. E
7. C	17. D	27. A	37. A
8. B	18. B	28. C	38. D
9. D	19. B	29. B	39. A
10. A	20. A	30. E	40. B

Drill 11, page 91

1. B	11. C	21. C	31. C
2. C	12. E	22. C	32. D
3. E	13. C	23. A	33. B
4. D	14. A	24. E	34. B
5. A	15. A	25. A	35. C
6. A	16. E	26. D	36. C
7. C	17. E	27. D	37. A
8. D	18. D	28. B	38. D
9. E	19. B	29. E	39. E
10. B	20. D	30. B	40. E

Drill 12, page 92

1. E	11. E	21. B	31. E
2. D	12. E	22. B	32. B
3. A	13. D	23. D	33. C
4. B	14. C	24. D	34. B
5. B	15. B	25. A	35. C
6. D	16. A	26. E	36. D
7. E	17. B	27. A	37. C
8. C	18. A	28. A	38. E
9. A	19. D	29. C	39. E
10. C	20. C	30. E	40. B

Drills 13–22, not applicable

Memory for *Numbered* Addresses—How to Improve Your Score

If you have been studying and practicing as recommended, you should feel quite good about what you have accomplished. You probably are able to remember most of the direct (name) addresses in the practice tests without trouble. If you can, you will earn a respectable score without answering a single question on the numbered addresses. (If half of the 88 questions are direct names, and you get all of them right, your score will be a good 44.) But don't be satisfied with 44! By pushing on and learning how to remember the numbered addresses, your score will easily rise to the sixties, seventies, and beyond.

TEST STRATEGY

In addition to the three memory strategies described in Chapter 4, pages 77 through 85, there is another strategy applicable only to the numbered addresses, which we will call "Reduce the Number."

REDUCE THE NUMBER

The sample boxes in the Diagnostic Test can serve as an illustration of this. (For the sake of clarity, only the numbered addresses have been reproduced.)

A	B	C	D	E
2100-2799 Mall	3900-4399 Mall	4400-4599 Mall	3400-3899 Mall	2800-3399 Mall
4800-4999 Cliff	4000-4299 Cliff	3300-3999 Cliff	4500-4799 Cliff	4300-4499 Cliff
1900-2299 Laurel	2300-2999 Laurel	3200-3799 Laurel	3000-3199 Laurel	1500-1899 Laurel

Original Numbered Addresses

We can reduce all of the above to a far simpler and easier-to-remember form. The boxes below illustrate how few items you actually need to remember.

A	B	C	D	E
21	39	44	34	28
48	40	33	45	43
19	23	32	30	15

Simplified Numbered Addresses

Now See Why

1. *The addresses on each horizontal line follow each other in consecutive order.* This can be seen for the "Mall" line when we rearrange the five addresses:

A	E	D	B	C
2100–2799	2800–3399	3400–3899	3900–4399	4400–4599

Where one address ends, the other begins. For example, Box A covers 2100–2799 Mall; Box E begins with 2800. There are no gaps. Therefore, the last half of the address, 2799, need not be remembered. All addresses beginning with 2100 Mall must be in Box A.

2. *The questions on the text are always about the same ranges of numbers.* For example, there are no questions about single numbers in the middle of a range of numbers, such as 2345 Mall or 2697 Mall. Neither are there questions about other ranges, such as 2200–2400 Mall. You need only focus on the numbers shown, such as 2100 Mall.

3. *The last two digits of every address number are either "00" or "99."* So, why bother remembering them? It is easier to keep 21 in mind than 2100.

To sum up, each of the address ranges is fully represented by the first two digits. Why take on the task of memorizing eight? Using this simple technique, the alert test candidate can reduce the original total of 30 four-digit numbers to 15 two-digit numbers!

An additional way to make the test easier involves the names—Mall, Cliff, Laurel. You probably don't have to remember them at all. That's because the two-digit numbers themselves pinpoint the box. You don't need to remember the name Mall to place the 21 in Box A except in the unlikely event that 21 is used to start *another* address in some *other* box.

DRILL 1

Answer the questions below to get the feel of our discussion. Look only at the first two digits in each address to determine whether the materials would be found in Box A, B, C, D, or E of the set of boxes found on page 97. (You may wish to do this exercise more than once.)

		Answers		
	Trials	3	2	1
1. 3400–3899 Mall				
2. 1900–2299 Laurel				
3. 3300–3999 Cliff				
4. 2300–2999 Laurel				
5. 2800–3399 Mall				
	Number Right			
	Time			

TECHNIQUES FOR REMEMBERING THE NUMBERED ADDRESSES

CHUNK THE NUMBER

SAMPLE

Try this experiment. Get a pencil and a blank sheet of paper. Next, study line 1 below for 5 seconds. Then look away and write, in order, the numbers you saw.

Line 1: 7 4 3 0 1 9 4 1 1 8 6 5

That was not easy. Try it once more using line 2 below. Study it for 5 seconds, look away, and write the numbers from memory.

Line 2: 7430   1941   1865

It was much easier to do the second time, wasn't it? Although the numbers were identical, the fact that they were organized into "chunks" made all the difference. Here is why.

The way our mind works, most of us cannot retain more than seven or eight pieces of information presented to us separately. The way the numbers were displayed on line 1, you were required to remember *twelve* separate items. On line 2, the same numbers were gathered into chunks of four numbers each. Each of these chunks, believe it or not, is as difficult (or easy) to remember as just *one* of the original digits. In effect, a chunk counts as a single piece of information. This is particularly true when the chunks have a meaningful association. In the example above, most of us will associate 1941 with Pearl Harbor, and 1865 with the end of the Civil War or President Lincoln's assassination. The chunking technique will make it far easier to remember the numbers in the boxes. Chunk them like this:

A	B	C	D	E
21 →	2139 ← 39	44 →	4434 ← 34	28
48 →	4840 ← 40	33 →	3345 ← 45	43
19 →	1923 ← 23	32 →	3230 ← 30	15

At this point, the original job of remembering 30 four-digit numbers has been cut down to 6! This assumes that you are omitting Box E in accordance with "Eliminate the Last Box," the strategy discussed on page 75.

Now, use your powers of visualization. Help your memory by forming a mental screen like the one above, on which you see each 4-number chunk in its place. In that way, you will be able to identify in which box each part belongs. For example, when you picture 2139 between Box A and Box B on the top line in the figure, you are automatically putting 21 in Box A and 39 in Box B. Similarly, see how 4434 can be used for Box C and Box D. Chunking across each line in this way has other advantages. It guarantees that you will get the right box for this address—2800–3399 Mall. That is, you will get the correct answer if you visualize "chunks" 2139 and 4434 "floating" on the top line of your screen (the "Mall" line). The only possible answer to an unfamiliar address with "Mall" in it, *has* to be Box E. (This fits in with the strategy of not trying to remember the last box.)

DRILL 2

Project the image below on your mental screen. It shows only what is necessary to score a perfect mark on the numbered address. Study it for 5 minutes.

```
┌ ─ ─ ─ ─ ─ ─ ─ ─ ─ ┐
│   2139    4434    │
│                   │
│   4840    3345    │
│                   │
│   1923    3230    │
└ ─ ─ ─ ─ ─ ─ ─ ─ ─ ┘
```

Now cover the above boxes from view and write in as many chunks as you can remember in the empty numbered boxes below. After writing each chunk, split it into (2) two-digit numbers and place each in the appropriate space below the boxes.

A	B	C	D	E
1.		4.		
2.		5.		
3.		6.		

A B   C D
1. ____ – ____   4. ____ – ____
2. ____ – ____   5. ____ – ____
3. ____ – ____   6. ____ – ____

After you have used this technique on several practice tests, you may feel that you are able to remember a chunk of 6 numbers. If you can, the number of chunks you need to remember to attain a perfect score will come down to *4*. The figure below shows how this works.

A	B	C	D	E
㉑	39	44	34	28
㊽	40	33	45	43
⑲	23	32	30	15
214819	394023	443332	344530	

If you are good at remembering telephone numbers, you might use that talent on these chunks. For Box A, substitute A21-4819. For Box B, use B39-4023, etc.

Additional Drills Using Chunking

Drills 3 through 17 will help you to develop your ability to organize and remember four-digit number chunks (see pages 99 to 100 for a full discussion and explanation). The two-digit numbers from which the chunks are to be formed have been printed in four adjoining columns marked A, B, C, and D. The space between the four columns is about the same as that between the numbers if they were in boxes. (The direct name addresses have been omitted for clarity.) This has been done to give you practice in organizing the chunks, as well as in remembering them.

Directions for Drills 3 through 17

1. Combine mentally the numbers in Columns A and B so that they become a single four-digit number. Do the same with the numbers in Columns C and D.
2. Visualize each chunk as though it were in its place between two boxes. (See the diagram on page 100.)
3. Study the drills using the time posted next to each as a guide. These times represent goals toward which you should be working. Because individuals vary in their experience and ability on this kind of memorization, you may find you need to increase the time allowance for particular drills. If that is the case, by all means, do so. Your starting point for all the drills is the point at which you achieve good results with a fair amount of effort. With that as a beginning, use the drills regularly to push yourself to gradually develop your capacity and speed.
4. For each question, mark the letter on the answer sheet to show the column in which each address belongs. (Cover the line of answers you have already completed so that they do not influence you on your second and third trials.) *Take three minutes to answer the questions in each drill.*

Study Time _____

DRILLS 3 TO 5—1 minute

	A	B	C	D
DRILL 3	25	18	21	14
DRILL 4	49	51	57	42
DRILL 5	12	19	27	17

DRILLS 6 TO 8—3 minutes

	A	B	C	D
DRILL 6	38 41	32 39	16 —	26 —
DRILL 7	57 12	55 20	61 —	69 —
DRILL 8	97 71	91 68	83 —	85 —

DRILLS 9 TO 11—5 minutes

	A	B	C	D
DRILL 9	30 17	26 34	43 22	21 27
DRILL 10	41 19	58 11	49 21	55 25
DRILL 11	36 80	42 74	33 85	39 77

DRILLS 12 TO 14—8 minutes

	A	B	C	D
DRILL 12	15 37 55	18 42 60	29 48 —	26 31 —
DRILL 13	92 71 14	88 85 25	86 77 —	95 74 —
DRILL 14	68 47 83	64 11 74	58 16 —	53 37 —

Study Time

DRILLS 15 TO 17—9 minutes

DRILL 15	10	18	23	30
	39	27	34	24
	57	62	53	59
DRILL 16	19	11	21	17
	33	42	36	47
	69	61	73	78
DRILL 17	42	49	55	59
	31	27	24	33
	23	30	18	34

Questions

DRILL 3

Answers

Trials	3	2	1
1. 18			
2. 25			
3. 14			
4. 25			
5. 18			
6. 21			
7. 14			
8. 14			
9. 25			
10. 21			
11. 18			
12. 21			
13. 14			
14. 25			
15. 18			
16. 21			
17. 14			
18. 21			
19. 18			
20. 25			
21. 18			
22. 14			
23. 18			
24. 21			
25. 25			
26. 18			
27. 14			
28. 21			
29. 18			
30. 25			
31. 18			
32. 14			
33. 21			
34. 21			
35. 18			
36. 25			
37. 25			
38. 18			
39. 14			
40. 21			
41. 14			
42. 18			
43. 21			
44. 25			
Number Right			
Time			

DRILL 4

Answers

Trials	3	2	1
1. 49			
2. 51			
3. 57			
4. 42			
5. 57			
6. 51			
7. 49			
8. 42			
9. 51			
10. 57			
11. 42			
12. 49			
13. 51			
14. 57			
15. 42			
16. 51			
17. 57			
18. 57			
19. 49			
20. 49			
21. 51			
22. 57			
23. 49			
24. 51			
25. 57			
26. 42			
27. 51			
28. 49			
29. 57			
30. 42			
31. 42			
32. 51			
33. 57			
34. 49			
35. 51			
36. 42			
37. 57			
38. 49			
39. 57			
40. 51			
41. 42			
42. 49			
43. 51			
44. 57			
Number Right			
Time			

Questions

DRILL 5

Answers

Trials	3	2	1
1. 27			
2. 17			
3. 12			
4. 19			
5. 27			
6. 12			
7. 19			
8. 17			
9. 17			
10. 27			
11. 12			
12. 19			
13. 27			
14. 17			
15. 12			
16. 27			
17. 17			
18. 19			
19. 27			
20. 17			
21. 12			
22. 12			
23. 19			
24. 12			
25. 27			
26. 17			
27. 19			
28. 12			
29. 19			
30. 27			
31. 17			
32. 27			
33. 19			
34. 12			
35. 19			
36. 27			
37. 17			
38. 12			
39. 12			
40. 17			
41. 27			
42. 17			
43. 12			
44. 19			
Number Right			
Time			

DRILL 6

Answers

Trials	3	2	1
1. 16			
2. 26			
3. 41			
4. 39			
5. 38			
6. 32			
7. 39			
8. 16			
9. 41			
10. 26			
11. 32			
12. 38			
13. 16			
14. 32			
15. 38			
16. 32			
17. 41			
18. 39			
19. 16			
20. 26			
21. 38			
22. 39			
23. 41			
24. 32			
25. 16			
26. 26			
27. 38			
28. 32			
29. 41			
30. 39			
31. 26			
32. 16			
33. 32			
34. 38			
35. 41			
36. 16			
37. 26			
38. 32			
39. 39			
40. 38			
41. 41			
42. 38			
43. 32			
44. 26			
Number Right			
Time			

Questions

DRILL 7

	Trials	3	2	1
	Answers			
1. 61				
2. 69				
3. 12				
4. 20				
5. 57				
6. 55				
7. 61				
8. 55				
9. 20				
10. 12				
11. 55				
12. 57				
13. 55				
14. 61				
15. 69				
16. 12				
17. 20				
18. 20				
19. 12				
20. 57				
21. 69				
22. 55				
23. 20				
24. 69				
25. 61				
26. 55				
27. 57				
28. 55				
29. 20				
30. 12				
31. 61				
32. 69				
33. 57				
34. 55				
35. 20				
36. 12				
37. 20				
38. 55				
39. 61				
40. 69				
41. 12				
42. 57				
43. 55				
44. 20				
Number Right				
Time				

DRILL 8

	Trials	3	2	1
	Answers			
1. 71				
2. 83				
3. 85				
4. 91				
5. 68				
6. 97				
7. 91				
8. 71				
9. 68				
10. 83				
11. 85				
12. 91				
13. 83				
14. 85				
15. 68				
16. 71				
17. 97				
18. 91				
19. 85				
20. 83				
21. 71				
22. 68				
23. 91				
24. 85				
25. 97				
26. 91				
27. 71				
28. 85				
29. 83				
30. 68				
31. 71				
32. 68				
33. 97				
34. 91				
35. 83				
36. 85				
37. 91				
38. 85				
39. 71				
40. 68				
41. 97				
42. 85				
43. 83				
44. 68				
Number Right				
Time				

Questions _____

DRILL 9

Answers

	Trials	3	2	1
1. 17				
2. 34				
3. 43				
4. 21				
5. 30				
6. 26				
7. 22				
8. 27				
9. 34				
10. 30				
11. 21				
12. 34				
13. 43				
14. 21				
15. 30				
16. 17				
17. 34				
18. 26				
19. 27				
20. 21				
21. 17				
22. 34				
23. 43				
24. 22				
25. 27				
26. 26				
27. 30				
28. 26				
29. 34				
30. 17				
31. 34				
32. 21				
33. 22				
34. 27				
35. 43				
36. 26				
37. 22				
38. 27				
39. 43				
40. 21				
41. 30				
42. 26				
43. 17				
44. 34				
Number Right				
Time				

DRILL 10

Answers

	Trials	3	2	1
1. 21				
2. 25				
3. 58				
4. 49				
5. 55				
6. 11				
7. 21				
8. 25				
9. 19				
10. 11				
11. 49				
12. 58				
13. 41				
14. 58				
15. 19				
16. 21				
17. 25				
18. 55				
19. 58				
20. 49				
21. 55				
22. 19				
23. 11				
24. 41				
25. 21				
26. 58				
27. 25				
28. 41				
29. 58				
30. 49				
31. 55				
32. 11				
33. 21				
34. 19				
35. 11				
36. 25				
37. 41				
38. 58				
39. 11				
40. 49				
41. 55				
42. 21				
43. 25				
44. 41				
Number Right				
Time				

Questions

DRILL 11

Answers

Trials	3	2	1
1. 80			
2. 74			
3. 33			
4. 39			
5. 85			
6. 77			
7. 36			
8. 42			
9. 74			
10. 85			
11. 33			
12. 42			
13. 39			
14. 77			
15. 80			
16. 36			
17. 42			
18. 85			
19. 77			
20. 80			
21. 74			
22. 85			
23. 77			
24. 42			
25. 33			
26. 39			
27. 36			
28. 74			
29. 33			
30. 39			
31. 85			
32. 77			
33. 36			
34. 42			
35. 33			
36. 80			
37. 77			
38. 74			
39. 33			
40. 39			
41. 42			
42. 74			
43. 85			
44. 77			
Number Right			
Time			

DRILL 12

Answers

Trials	3	2	1
1. 55			
2. 60			
3. 48			
4. 31			
5. 26			
6. 29			
7. 26			
8. 15			
9. 18			
10. 42			
11. 60			
12. 48			
13. 31			
14. 18			
15. 37			
16. 42			
17. 29			
18. 26			
19. 60			
20. 48			
21. 15			
22. 18			
23. 60			
24. 37			
25. 42			
26. 31			
27. 29			
28. 26			
29. 18			
30. 55			
31. 60			
32. 31			
33. 15			
34. 18			
35. 60			
36. 29			
37. 26			
38. 48			
39. 31			
40. 37			
41. 18			
42. 60			
43. 29			
44. 26			
Number Right			
Time			

Questions

DRILL 13

Answers

	Trials	3	2	1
1.	77			
2.	95			
3.	88			
4.	86			
5.	25			
6.	92			
7.	88			
8.	71			
9.	85			
10.	86			
11.	14			
12.	25			
13.	95			
14.	74			
15.	71			
16.	85			
17.	14			
18.	25			
19.	86			
20.	95			
21.	77			
22.	71			
23.	85			
24.	74			
25.	92			
26.	86			
27.	95			
28.	71			
29.	85			
30.	25			
31.	88			
32.	86			
33.	77			
34.	74			
35.	71			
36.	92			
37.	88			
38.	14			
39.	25			
40.	71			
41.	85			
42.	86			
43.	95			
44.	74			
Number Right				
Time				

DRILL 14

Answers

	Trials	3	2	1
1.	47			
2.	11			
3.	74			
4.	16			
5.	37			
6.	58			
7.	53			
8.	68			
9.	64			
10.	83			
11.	74			
12.	16			
13.	58			
14.	47			
15.	11			
16.	83			
17.	53			
18.	37			
19.	47			
20.	11			
21.	68			
22.	64			
23.	74			
24.	16			
25.	37			
26.	58			
27.	53			
28.	68			
29.	83			
30.	74			
31.	16			
32.	37			
33.	64			
34.	58			
35.	53			
36.	83			
37.	74			
38.	64			
39.	11			
40.	16			
41.	37			
42.	68			
43.	64			
44.	47			
Number Right				
Time				

Questions

DRILL 15

Answers

Trials	3	2	1
1. 39			
2. 27			
3. 53			
4. 59			
5. 23			
6. 30			
7. 57			
8. 62			
9. 39			
10. 53			
11. 59			
12. 24			
13. 10			
14. 18			
15. 53			
16. 57			
17. 62			
18. 27			
19. 34			
20. 24			
21. 59			
22. 18			
23. 23			
24. 30			
25. 57			
26. 59			
27. 34			
28. 30			
29. 23			
30. 30			
31. 18			
32. 39			
33. 27			
34. 10			
35. 62			
36. 57			
37. 62			
38. 24			
39. 39			
40. 34			
41. 53			
42. 59			
43. 10			
44. 18			
Number Right			
Time			

DRILL 16

Answers

Trials	3	2	1
1. 11			
2. 21			
3. 17			
4. 69			
5. 61			
6. 11			
7. 19			
8. 11			
9. 73			
10. 78			
11. 36			
12. 47			
13. 42			
14. 33			
15. 21			
16. 36			
17. 47			
18. 73			
19. 78			
20. 33			
21. 61			
22. 73			
23. 69			
24. 61			
25. 73			
26. 78			
27. 33			
28. 21			
29. 36			
30. 47			
31. 19			
32. 11			
33. 69			
34. 73			
35. 33			
36. 42			
37. 78			
38. 21			
39. 17			
40. 47			
41. 69			
42. 61			
43. 42			
44. 21			
Number Right			
Time			

Questions _____

DRILL 17

	Answers		
	Trials	3	2	1
1. 18				
2. 34				
3. 31				
4. 27				
5. 55				
6. 59				
7. 23				
8. 30				
9. 27				
10. 42				
11. 49				
12. 30				
13. 18				
14. 23				
15. 55				
16. 59				
17. 24				
18. 33				
19. 18				
20. 34				
21. 31				
22. 49				

	Answers		
	Trials	3	2	1
23. 42				
24. 49				
25. 23				
26. 30				
27. 33				
28. 18				
29. 34				
30. 27				
31. 59				
32. 55				
33. 59				
34. 49				
35. 30				
36. 42				
37. 49				
38. 55				
39. 33				
40. 34				
41. 31				
42. 27				
43. 24				
44. 33				
Number Right				
Time				

USE ASSOCIATIONS

Using associations to remember the address names was discussed in Chapter 4. It worked quickly and easily, with many of the names, i.e., *Pearl*—Bailey, necklace; *Magnet*—pull, iron; *Cedar*—tree, chest, red; *Niles*—river, Cleopatra.

Numbers may be remembered in the same way.

Now See Why

1. *There are numbers which hold immediate associations for almost everyone.*

With 4 digits

1492—Columbus, Discovery of America
1776—Declaration of Independence, Revolutionary War
1914—Outbreak of World War I
1929—Stock Market Crash

With 2 digits

12—dozen eggs, midnight, lunch, noon
13—bad luck, Bar Mitzvah
16—sweet sixteen
21—voting age, adulthood
40—life begins, etc.

(Only illustrations of 2-digit and 4-digit numbers are shown because these are the kinds of numbers you need to remember for the test.)

Now see the figure below.

A	B	C	D	E
21 → 2139 ← 39		44 → 4434 ← 34		28
48 → 4840 ← 40		33 → 3345 ← 45		43
19 → 1923 ← 23		32 → 3230 ← 30		15

Note the number 2139. Imagine 21 as an *Adult* in Box *A*. What was the name of the famous comedian who always claimed he was 39 years old? Right—*Benny* in Box *B*.

Note the number 4840. What do you associate with 40? That's when life *Begins* (Box *B*).

2. *Some numbers hold personal associations.* The chances are that most of us can make an immediate connection with all or part of some of the following items.

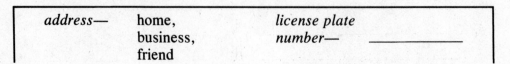

| *address*— | home, business, friend | *license plate number*— | _____ |

age—	yours, wife, child	*anniversary—*	wedding, job, retirement
telephone number—	home, job, friend	*birthdate—*	yours, loved one's
Social Security number—	_____	*credit card number—*	_____

Study the chunks and the 2-digit numbers for one minute. Does anything connect for you? Was anyone that you know born in 1923? If so, you can get the right answer to every question asking for the location of *1900–2299* Laurel and *2300–2999* Laurel. Do you wear an undergarment sized *40B, 32C* or *34D*? Then you are in luck. Jot down any personal associations you make that will assist you in remembering the numbers in the box above.

Associate Numbers with Your "Loci"

If you have a system of "loci" (see Chapter 4, pages 78 and 79), it may be used to "place" some numbers. For example, using the same layout used on page 79, you might see your hi-fi set in the living room (Box D) playing a *45* r.p.m. record. Nearby, in the dining room (Box C) a stack of *33* r.p.m. L.P.'s sits on the table to be played next.

DRILL 18

See the list of numbers from 1 to 99 below. Next to each, write the word, name or idea that immediately comes to mind.

Sample

10—Bowling
11—Seven Eleven food stores
12—Dozen eggs
13—Bar Mitzvah, bad luck

If nothing comes to mind for a particular number, examine some of the numbers in your life (see page 112 for suggestions). See if any of these numbers, or any part of them, evokes a word or name. Extend your list every day by ten numbers until you reach item 99. The more complete your list is, the better the odds are in your favor of making a quick number-word association on the test.

1. _____
2. _____
3. _____
4. _____
5. _____

6. _____
7. _____
8. _____
9. _____
10. _____

11. _____   44. _____
12. _____   45. _____
13. _____   46. _____
14. _____   47. _____
15. _____   48. _____
16. _____   49. _____
17. _____   50. _____
18. _____   51. _____
19. _____   52. _____
20. _____   53. _____
21. _____   54. _____
22. _____   55. _____
23. _____   56. _____
24. _____   57. _____
25. _____   58. _____
26. _____   59. _____
27. _____   60. _____
28. _____   61. _____
29. _____   62. _____
30. _____   63. _____
31. _____   64. _____
32. _____   65. _____
33. _____   66. _____
34. _____   67. _____
35. _____   68. _____
36. _____   69. _____
37. _____   70. _____
38. _____   71. _____
39. _____   72. _____
40. _____   73. _____
41. _____   74. _____
42. _____   75. _____
43. _____   76. _____

77. _____	89. _____
78. _____	90. _____
79. _____	91. _____
80. _____	92. _____
81. _____	93. _____
82. _____	94. _____
83. _____	95. _____
84. _____	96. _____
85. _____	97. _____
86. _____	98. _____
87. _____	99. _____
88. _____	

LOOK FOR ONE-OF-A-KIND NUMBERS AND NUMBER POSITIONS

After you have reduced the numbers, chunked them, and tried to associate them with their boxes, examine them quickly to see if any of them are "one-of-a-kind"! Also, look to see if any of the numbers fall into easy-to-remember positions. See the figure below.

A	B	C	D	E
21 →	2139 ← 39	44 →	4434 ← 34	28
48 →	4840 ← 40	33 →	3345 ← 45	43
19 →	1923 ← 23	32 →	3230 ← 30	15

1. Out of the twelve 2-digit numbers, only one is in the teens, i.e., 19 in Box A. Just realizing that makes it easier to remember. *Whenever the boxes contain only one number in a category* (the 10's, 20's, 30's, etc.) *or even two, those number(s) take on a special association with the box in which they are located.*
2. *Notice numerical relationships.*
   a. The highest "chunk"—4840—is located directly above the lowest one—1923.
   b. The only two chunks starting with two repeating digits—4434 and 3345—lie one above the other.
   c. The numbers on the top line—21, 39, 44, 34, 28—increase gradually from Box A to Box C and then decrease gradually to Box E.
   d. Exactly the same thing happens on the bottom line—19, 23, 32, 30, 15. In both cases, the highest number is in the middle.

When you train your eye to quickly pick up relationships like these, you are embedding those numbers more firmly in your mind. It is far easier to remember a pattern than a group of numbers at random.

USE A RHYMING CODE

This memory system is designed especially for remembering numbers. In it, each of the numbers from 1 to 20 is associated with one or more designated words with which it rhymes. (See table below.) You memorize a number by translating it into a word picture or story, using the rhyming code words. Make the story picture as unusual, funny, and active as you can. Later, when you wish to recall the numbers, just bring that story picture back to mind. The words in it should automatically bring back the numbers too.

For example, if this method were used to remember the 6-digit number in Box A—214819, the story would go like this:

I found a shoe that had a *bun* in it and took it to the *door* and *ate* it. That *bun* was so hard it felt like swallowing a fish *spine*.

RHYMING TABLE FOR NUMBERS

Number	Word(s)	Number	Word(s)
1	Bun, Won	11	Eleven (as in football), Enliven
2	Shoe, Flew	12	Delve, Shelve
3	Tree, See	13	Flirting, Thirsting
4	Door, Score	14	Courting, Sorting
5	Hive, Strive	15	Lifting, Drifting
6	Sticks, Picks	16	Fixing, Sicking (as in dog)
7	Heaven, Leaven	17	Leavening, Leveling
8	Gate, Ate	18	Mating, Grating
9	Spine, Dine	19	Pining
10	Hen, Pen	*20	Plenty

*Although this table is sufficient for you to encode all possible number combinations, it will help if you add some key words:

0	hero, zero	60	sickly, sexy
30	dirty, thirsty	70	TNT, sentry
40	naughty, haughty	80	lately, Haiti
50	nifty, swiftly	90	Numbly, pine tree

If you had a command of the extra code words and numbers shown at the bottom of the table, you also could have used this story for the same number.

I saw *plenty* of *buns* (21) on the wedding table. I jumped on the table and *haughtly ate* (48) them because I was *pining* (19) away.

The story is ridiculous, but it is vivid. It can be made up quickly and recollected just as easily. With practice, stories like these can be made up in 15 to 20 seconds. See if you have the knack for doing it. First, memorize the above table. Then, try to make up stories for Boxes B, C, and D.

You will increase the flexibility and power of this system if you incorporate some of your favorite personal associations with it. (See pages 112–115). The fact that they may not rhyme is not important, as long as they give you a key for additional numbers. For example, to remember the number 72 in a box, you may prefer to use an image of your father (if he is 72) instead of an image of a *sentry* without *shoes* (72).

Drills Using Six-Digit Chunks

Drills 19 through 33 are to be used if you intend to memorize the three separate address numbers in each box as a *single* six-digit number (see page 101). The three separate two-digit address numbers have been printed one above the other in boxes, similar to the way in which they would appear on the regular test. (The direct name addresses have been omitted, for clarity.)

Directions for Drills 19 through 33

1. Mentally, combine the three numbers, one after the other, starting with the top number in each box. You now have formed a single, six-digit chunk.
2. Visualize and drill this chunk using the time specified above each drill as a guide.*
3. When the study period has ended, try to recall each six-digit number. Mentally, separate each into its three constituent addresses. Take one minute to put each of the original two-digit addresses into its correct place in the boxes provided on the special answer sheet for these drills.

Study Time _____

DRILL 19

32
41
28

1 minute

DRILL 21

73
29
48

1 minute

DRILL 20

47
55
72

1 minute

DRILL 22

22	16
38	44
61	86

3 minutes

---

* NOTE: Drills 31, 32, and 33 require you to memorize all five of the six-digit addresses. Although it is entirely possible to get a perfect score by remembering only four (see **page** 101), all five have been included for those desiring the practice.

DRILL 23

20	42
62	76
83	97

3 minutes

DRILL 24

91	75
52	37
10	20

3 minutes

DRILL 25

65	49	33
19	31	15
28	39	46

5 minutes

DRILL 26

87	72	83
18	16	11
39	53	42

5 minutes

DRILL 27

15	27	21
66	78	59
87	82	76

5 minutes

DRILL 28

79	94	83	87
29	14	17	20
11	18	24	30

8 minutes

DRILL 29

35	21	29	42
81	79	64	70
46	22	31	38

8 minutes

DRILL 30

27	13	17	25
34	32	44	50
77	84	71	88

8 minutes

DRILL 31

14	10	19	23	27
28	38	42	30	45
89	93	95	81	84

9 minutes

DRILL 32

61	57	43	52	48
20	17	25	29	30
74	66	79	82	69

9 minutes

DRILL 33

59	45	35	40	52
49	36	33	47	39
10	18	13	21	15

9 minutes

Answer Sheet _____

_____ **Trial 1** _____

DRILL 19

DRILL 26

DRILL 20

DRILL 27

DRILL 21

DRILL 28

DRILL 22

DRILL 29

DRILL 23

DRILL 30

DRILL 24

DRILL 31

DRILL 25

DRILL 32

Answer Sheet _____

DRILL 33

Trial 2 _____

DRILL 19

DRILL 25

DRILL 20

DRILL 26

DRILL 21

DRILL 27

DRILL 22

DRILL 28

DRILL 23

DRILL 29

DRILL 24

DRILL 30

Answer Sheet

DRILL 31

☐ ☐ ☐ ☐ ☐

DRILL 33

☐ ☐ ☐ ☐ ☐

DRILL 32

☐ ☐ ☐ ☐ ☐

Trial 3

DRILL 19
☐

DRILL 20
☐

DRILL 21
☐

DRILL 22
☐ ☐

DRILL 23
☐ ☐

DRILL 24
☐ ☐

DRILL 25
☐ ☐ ☐

DRILL 26
☐ ☐ ☐

DRILL 27
☐ ☐ ☐

DRILL 28
☐ ☐ ☐ ☐

Answer Sheet _____

DRILL 29

☐ ☐ ☐ ☐

DRILL 32

☐ ☐ ☐ ☐ ☐

DRILL 30

☐ ☐ ☐ ☐

DRILL 33

☐ ☐ ☐ ☐ ☐

DRILL 31

☐ ☐ ☐ ☐ ☐

ANSWER KEY TO DRILLS

Drill 1, page 98

1. D
2. A
3. C
4. B
5. E

Drill 2, not applicable

Drill 3, page 104

1.	B	12.	C	23.	B	34.	C
2.	A	13.	D	24.	C	35.	B
3.	D	14.	A	25.	A	36.	A
4.	A	15.	B	26.	B	37.	A
5.	B	16.	C	27.	D	38.	B
6.	C	17.	D	28.	C	39.	D
7.	D	18.	C	29.	B	40.	C
8.	D	19.	B	30.	A	41.	D
9.	A	20.	A	31.	B	42.	B
10.	C	21.	B	32.	D	43.	C
11.	B	22.	D	33.	C	44.	A

Drill 4, page 104

1.	A	12.	A	23.	A	34.	A
2.	B	13.	B	24.	B	35.	B
3.	C	14.	C	25.	C	36.	D
4.	D	15.	D	26.	D	37.	C
5.	C	16.	B	27.	B	38.	A
6.	B	17.	C	28.	A	39.	C
7.	A	18.	C	29.	C	40.	B
8.	D	19.	A	30.	D	41.	D
9.	B	20.	A	31.	D	42.	A
10.	C	21.	B	32.	B	43.	B
11.	D	22.	C	33.	C	44.	C

Drill 5, page 105

1.	C	12.	B	23.	B	34.	A
2.	D	13.	C	24.	A	35.	B
3.	A	14.	D	25.	C	36.	C
4.	B	15.	A	26.	D	37.	D
5.	C	16.	C	27.	B	38.	A
6.	A	17.	D	28.	A	39.	A
7.	B	18.	B	29.	B	40.	D
8.	D	19.	C	30.	C	41.	C
9.	D	20.	D	31.	D	42.	D
10.	C	21.	A	32.	C	43.	A
11.	A	22.	A	33.	B	44.	B

Drill 6, page 105

1.	C	12.	A	23.	A	34.	A
2.	D	13.	C	24.	B	35.	A
3.	A	14.	B	25.	C	36.	C
4.	B	15.	A	26.	D	37.	D
5.	A	16.	B	27.	A	38.	B
6.	B	17.	A	28.	B	39.	B
7.	B	18.	B	29.	A	40.	A
8.	C	19.	C	30.	B	41.	A
9.	A	20.	D	31.	D	42.	A
10.	D	21.	A	32.	C	43.	B
11.	B	22.	B	33.	B	44.	D

Drill 7, page 106

1.	C	12.	A	23.	B	34.	B
2.	D	13.	B	24.	D	35.	B
3.	A	14.	C	25.	C	36.	A
4.	B	15.	D	26.	B	37.	B
5.	A	16.	A	27.	A	38.	B
6.	B	17.	B	28.	B	39.	C
7.	C	18.	B	29.	B	40.	D
8.	B	19.	A	30.	A	41.	A
9.	B	20.	A	31.	C	42.	A
10.	A	21.	D	32.	D	43.	B
11.	B	22.	B	33.	A	44.	B

Drill 8, page 106

1.	A	12.	B	23.	B	34.	B
2.	C	13.	C	24.	D	35.	C
3.	D	14.	D	25.	A	36.	D
4.	B	15.	B	26.	B	37.	B
5.	B	16.	A	27.	A	38.	D
6.	A	17.	A	28.	D	39.	A
7.	B	18.	B	29.	C	40.	B
8.	A	19.	D	30.	B	41.	A
9.	B	20.	C	31.	A	42.	D
10.	C	21.	A	32.	B	43.	C
11.	D	22.	B	33.	A	44.	B

Drill 9, page 107

1.	A	12.	B	23.	C	34.	D
2.	B	13.	C	24.	C	35.	C
3.	C	14.	D	25.	D	36.	B
4.	D	15.	A	26.	B	37.	C
5.	A	16.	A	27.	A	38.	D
6.	B	17.	B	28.	B	39.	C
7.	C	18.	B	29.	B	40.	D
8.	D	19.	D	30.	A	41.	A
9.	B	20.	D	31.	B	42.	B
10.	A	21.	A	32.	D	43.	A
11.	D	22.	B	33.	C	44.	B

Drill 10, page 107

1.	C	12.	B	23.	B	34.	A
2.	D	13.	A	24.	A	35.	B
3.	B	14.	B	25.	C	36.	D
4.	C	15.	A	26.	B	37.	A
5.	D	16.	C	27.	D	38.	B
6.	B	17.	D	28.	A	39.	B
7.	C	18.	D	29.	B	40.	C
8.	D	19.	B	30.	C	41.	D
9.	A	20.	C	31.	D	42.	C
10.	B	21.	D	32.	B	43.	D
11.	C	22.	A	33.	C	44.	A

Drill 11, page 108

1.	A	12.	B	23.	D	34.	B
2.	B	13.	D	24.	B	35.	C
3.	C	14.	D	25.	C	36.	A
4.	D	15.	A	26.	D	37.	D
5.	C	16.	A	27.	A	38.	B
6.	D	17.	B	28.	B	39.	C
7.	A	18.	C	29.	C	40.	D
8.	B	19.	D	30.	D	41.	B
9.	B	20.	A	31.	C	42.	B
10.	C	21.	B	32.	D	43.	C
11.	C	22.	C	33.	A	44.	D

Drill 12, page 108

1.	A	12.	C	23.	B	34.	B
2.	B	13.	D	24.	A	35.	B
3.	C	14.	B	25.	B	36.	C
4.	D	15.	A	26.	D	37.	D
5.	D	16.	B	27.	C	38.	C
6.	C	17.	C	28.	D	39.	D
7.	D	18.	D	29.	B	40.	A
8.	A	19.	B	30.	A	41.	B
9.	B	20.	C	31.	B	42.	B
10.	B	21.	A	32.	D	43.	C
11.	B	22.	B	33.	A	44.	D

Drill 13, page 109

1.	C	12.	B	23.	B	34.	D
2.	D	13.	D	24.	D	35.	A
3.	B	14.	D	25.	A	36.	A
4.	C	15.	A	26.	C	37.	B
5.	B	16.	B	27.	D	38.	A
6.	A	17.	A	28.	A	39.	B
7.	B	18.	B	29.	B	40.	A
8.	A	19.	C	30.	B	41.	B
9.	B	20.	D	31.	B	42.	C
10.	C	21.	C	32.	C	43.	D
11.	A	22.	A	33.	C	44.	D

Drill 14, page 109

1.	A	12.	C	23.	B	34.	C
2.	B	13.	C	24.	C	35.	D
3.	B	14.	A	25.	D	36.	A
4.	C	15.	B	26.	C	37.	B
5.	D	16.	A	27.	D	38.	B
6.	C	17.	D	28.	A	39.	B
7.	D	18.	D	29.	A	40.	C
8.	A	19.	A	30.	B	41.	D
9.	B	20.	B	31.	C	42.	A
10.	A	21.	A	32.	D	43.	B
11.	B	22.	B	33.	B	44.	A

Drill 15, page 110

1.	A	12.	D	23.	C	34.	A
2.	B	13.	A	24.	D	35.	B
3.	C	14.	B	25.	A	36.	A
4.	D	15.	C	26.	D	37.	B
5.	C	16.	A	27.	C	38.	D
6.	D	17.	B	28.	D	39.	A
7.	A	18.	B	29.	C	40.	C
8.	B	19.	C	30.	D	41.	C
9.	A	20.	D	31.	B	42.	D
10.	C	21.	D	32.	A	43.	A
11.	D	22.	B	33.	B	44.	B

Drill 16, page 110

1.	B	12.	D	23.	A	34.	C
2.	C	13.	B	24.	B	35.	A
3.	D	14.	A	25.	C	36.	B
4.	A	15.	C	26.	D	37.	D
5.	B	16.	C	27.	A	38.	C
6.	B	17.	D	28.	C	39.	D
7.	A	18.	C	29.	C	40.	D
8.	B	19.	D	30.	D	41.	A
9.	C	20.	A	31.	A	42.	B
10.	D	21.	B	32.	B	43.	B
11.	C	22.	C	33.	A	44.	C

Drill 17, page 111

1.	C	12.	B	23.	A	34.	B
2.	D	13.	C	24.	B	35.	B
3.	A	14.	A	25.	A	36.	A
4.	B	15.	C	26.	B	37.	B
5.	C	16.	D	27.	D	38.	C
6.	D	17.	C	28.	C	39.	D
7.	A	18.	D	29.	D	40.	D
8.	B	19.	C	30.	B	41.	A
9.	B	20.	D	31.	D	42.	B
10.	A	21.	A	32.	C	43.	C
11.	B	22.	B	33.	D	44.	D

Drills 18–33, not applicable

A
Final
Review

ANSWER SHEET—PRACTICE TEST 1

PART A—ADDRESS CHECKING   DATE _____

1 Ⓐ Ⓓ	25 Ⓐ Ⓓ	49 Ⓐ Ⓓ	73 Ⓐ Ⓓ
2 Ⓐ Ⓓ	26 Ⓐ Ⓓ	50 Ⓐ Ⓓ	74 Ⓐ Ⓓ
3 Ⓐ Ⓓ	27 Ⓐ Ⓓ	51 Ⓐ Ⓓ	75 Ⓐ Ⓓ
4 Ⓐ Ⓓ	28 Ⓐ Ⓓ	52 Ⓐ Ⓓ	76 Ⓐ Ⓓ
5 Ⓐ Ⓓ	29 Ⓐ Ⓓ	53 Ⓐ Ⓓ	77 Ⓐ Ⓓ
6 Ⓐ Ⓓ	30 Ⓐ Ⓓ	54 Ⓐ Ⓓ	78 Ⓐ Ⓓ
7 Ⓐ Ⓓ	31 Ⓐ Ⓓ	55 Ⓐ Ⓓ	79 Ⓐ Ⓓ
8 Ⓐ Ⓓ	32 Ⓐ Ⓓ	56 Ⓐ Ⓓ	80 Ⓐ Ⓓ
9 Ⓐ Ⓓ	33 Ⓐ Ⓓ	57 Ⓐ Ⓓ	81 Ⓐ Ⓓ
10 Ⓐ Ⓓ	34 Ⓐ Ⓓ	58 Ⓐ Ⓓ	82 Ⓐ Ⓓ
11 Ⓐ Ⓓ	35 Ⓐ Ⓓ	59 Ⓐ Ⓓ	83 Ⓐ Ⓓ
12 Ⓐ Ⓓ	36 Ⓐ Ⓓ	60 Ⓐ Ⓓ	84 Ⓐ Ⓓ
13 Ⓐ Ⓓ	37 Ⓐ Ⓓ	61 Ⓐ Ⓓ	85 Ⓐ Ⓓ
14 Ⓐ Ⓓ	38 Ⓐ Ⓓ	62 Ⓐ Ⓓ	86 Ⓐ Ⓓ
15 Ⓐ Ⓓ	39 Ⓐ Ⓓ	63 Ⓐ Ⓓ	87 Ⓐ Ⓓ
16 Ⓐ Ⓓ	40 Ⓐ Ⓓ	64 Ⓐ Ⓓ	88 Ⓐ Ⓓ
17 Ⓐ Ⓓ	41 Ⓐ Ⓓ	65 Ⓐ Ⓓ	89 Ⓐ Ⓓ
18 Ⓐ Ⓓ	42 Ⓐ Ⓓ	66 Ⓐ Ⓓ	90 Ⓐ Ⓓ
19 Ⓐ Ⓓ	43 Ⓐ Ⓓ	67 Ⓐ Ⓓ	91 Ⓐ Ⓓ
20 Ⓐ Ⓓ	44 Ⓐ Ⓓ	68 Ⓐ Ⓓ	92 Ⓐ Ⓓ
21 Ⓐ Ⓓ	45 Ⓐ Ⓓ	69 Ⓐ Ⓓ	93 Ⓐ Ⓓ
22 Ⓐ Ⓓ	46 Ⓐ Ⓓ	70 Ⓐ Ⓓ	94 Ⓐ Ⓓ
23 Ⓐ Ⓓ	47 Ⓐ Ⓓ	71 Ⓐ Ⓓ	95 Ⓐ Ⓓ
24 Ⓐ Ⓓ	48 Ⓐ Ⓓ	72 Ⓐ Ⓓ	

ANSWER SHEET—PRACTICE TEST 1

PART B—MEMORY FOR ADDRESSES
LIST 1   DATE _____

1 Ⓐ Ⓑ Ⓒ Ⓓ Ⓔ   31 Ⓐ Ⓑ Ⓒ Ⓓ Ⓔ   61 Ⓐ Ⓑ Ⓒ Ⓓ Ⓔ
2 Ⓐ Ⓑ Ⓒ Ⓓ Ⓔ   32 Ⓐ Ⓑ Ⓒ Ⓓ Ⓔ   62 Ⓐ Ⓑ Ⓒ Ⓓ Ⓔ
3 Ⓐ Ⓑ Ⓒ Ⓓ Ⓔ   33 Ⓐ Ⓑ Ⓒ Ⓓ Ⓔ   63 Ⓐ Ⓑ Ⓒ Ⓓ Ⓔ
4 Ⓐ Ⓑ Ⓒ Ⓓ Ⓔ   34 Ⓐ Ⓑ Ⓒ Ⓓ Ⓔ   64 Ⓐ Ⓑ Ⓒ Ⓓ Ⓔ
5 Ⓐ Ⓑ Ⓒ Ⓓ Ⓔ   35 Ⓐ Ⓑ Ⓒ Ⓓ Ⓔ   65 Ⓐ Ⓑ Ⓒ Ⓓ Ⓔ
6 Ⓐ Ⓑ Ⓒ Ⓓ Ⓔ   36 Ⓐ Ⓑ Ⓒ Ⓓ Ⓔ   66 Ⓐ Ⓑ Ⓒ Ⓓ Ⓔ
7 Ⓐ Ⓑ Ⓒ Ⓓ Ⓔ   37 Ⓐ Ⓑ Ⓒ Ⓓ Ⓔ   67 Ⓐ Ⓑ Ⓒ Ⓓ Ⓔ
8 Ⓐ Ⓑ Ⓒ Ⓓ Ⓔ   38 Ⓐ Ⓑ Ⓒ Ⓓ Ⓔ   68 Ⓐ Ⓑ Ⓒ Ⓓ Ⓔ
9 Ⓐ Ⓑ Ⓒ Ⓓ Ⓔ   39 Ⓐ Ⓑ Ⓒ Ⓓ Ⓔ   69 Ⓐ Ⓑ Ⓒ Ⓓ Ⓔ
10 Ⓐ Ⓑ Ⓒ Ⓓ Ⓔ   40 Ⓐ Ⓑ Ⓒ Ⓓ Ⓔ   70 Ⓐ Ⓑ Ⓒ Ⓓ Ⓔ
11 Ⓐ Ⓑ Ⓒ Ⓓ Ⓔ   41 Ⓐ Ⓑ Ⓒ Ⓓ Ⓔ   71 Ⓐ Ⓑ Ⓒ Ⓓ Ⓔ
12 Ⓐ Ⓑ Ⓒ Ⓓ Ⓔ   42 Ⓐ Ⓑ Ⓒ Ⓓ Ⓔ   72 Ⓐ Ⓑ Ⓒ Ⓓ Ⓔ
13 Ⓐ Ⓑ Ⓒ Ⓓ Ⓔ   43 Ⓐ Ⓑ Ⓒ Ⓓ Ⓔ   73 Ⓐ Ⓑ Ⓒ Ⓓ Ⓔ
14 Ⓐ Ⓑ Ⓒ Ⓓ Ⓔ   44 Ⓐ Ⓑ Ⓒ Ⓓ Ⓔ   74 Ⓐ Ⓑ Ⓒ Ⓓ Ⓔ
15 Ⓐ Ⓑ Ⓒ Ⓓ Ⓔ   45 Ⓐ Ⓑ Ⓒ Ⓓ Ⓔ   75 Ⓐ Ⓑ Ⓒ Ⓓ Ⓔ
16 Ⓐ Ⓑ Ⓒ Ⓓ Ⓔ   46 Ⓐ Ⓑ Ⓒ Ⓓ Ⓔ   76 Ⓐ Ⓑ Ⓒ Ⓓ Ⓔ
17 Ⓐ Ⓑ Ⓒ Ⓓ Ⓔ   47 Ⓐ Ⓑ Ⓒ Ⓓ Ⓔ   77 Ⓐ Ⓑ Ⓒ Ⓓ Ⓔ
18 Ⓐ Ⓑ Ⓒ Ⓓ Ⓔ   48 Ⓐ Ⓑ Ⓒ Ⓓ Ⓔ   78 Ⓐ Ⓑ Ⓒ Ⓓ Ⓔ
19 Ⓐ Ⓑ Ⓒ Ⓓ Ⓔ   49 Ⓐ Ⓑ Ⓒ Ⓓ Ⓔ   79 Ⓐ Ⓑ Ⓒ Ⓓ Ⓔ
20 Ⓐ Ⓑ Ⓒ Ⓓ Ⓔ   50 Ⓐ Ⓑ Ⓒ Ⓓ Ⓔ   80 Ⓐ Ⓑ Ⓒ Ⓓ Ⓔ
21 Ⓐ Ⓑ Ⓒ Ⓓ Ⓔ   51 Ⓐ Ⓑ Ⓒ Ⓓ Ⓔ   81 Ⓐ Ⓑ Ⓒ Ⓓ Ⓔ
22 Ⓐ Ⓑ Ⓒ Ⓓ Ⓔ   52 Ⓐ Ⓑ Ⓒ Ⓓ Ⓔ   82 Ⓐ Ⓑ Ⓒ Ⓓ Ⓔ
23 Ⓐ Ⓑ Ⓒ Ⓓ Ⓔ   53 Ⓐ Ⓑ Ⓒ Ⓓ Ⓔ   83 Ⓐ Ⓑ Ⓒ Ⓓ Ⓔ
24 Ⓐ Ⓑ Ⓒ Ⓓ Ⓔ   54 Ⓐ Ⓑ Ⓒ Ⓓ Ⓔ   84 Ⓐ Ⓑ Ⓒ Ⓓ Ⓔ
25 Ⓐ Ⓑ Ⓒ Ⓓ Ⓔ   55 Ⓐ Ⓑ Ⓒ Ⓓ Ⓔ   85 Ⓐ Ⓑ Ⓒ Ⓓ Ⓔ
26 Ⓐ Ⓑ Ⓒ Ⓓ Ⓔ   56 Ⓐ Ⓑ Ⓒ Ⓓ Ⓔ   86 Ⓐ Ⓑ Ⓒ Ⓓ Ⓔ
27 Ⓐ Ⓑ Ⓒ Ⓓ Ⓔ   57 Ⓐ Ⓑ Ⓒ Ⓓ Ⓔ   87 Ⓐ Ⓑ Ⓒ Ⓓ Ⓔ
28 Ⓐ Ⓑ Ⓒ Ⓓ Ⓔ   58 Ⓐ Ⓑ Ⓒ Ⓓ Ⓔ   88 Ⓐ Ⓑ Ⓒ Ⓓ Ⓔ
29 Ⓐ Ⓑ Ⓒ Ⓓ Ⓔ   59 Ⓐ Ⓑ Ⓒ Ⓓ Ⓔ
30 Ⓐ Ⓑ Ⓒ Ⓓ Ⓔ   60 Ⓐ Ⓑ Ⓒ Ⓓ Ⓔ

ANSWER SHEET—PRACTICE TEST 1
PART B—MEMORY FOR ADDRESSES
LIST 2   DATE _____

1 Ⓐ Ⓑ Ⓒ Ⓓ Ⓔ	31 Ⓐ Ⓑ Ⓒ Ⓓ Ⓔ	61 Ⓐ Ⓑ Ⓒ Ⓓ Ⓔ
2 Ⓐ Ⓑ Ⓒ Ⓓ Ⓔ	32 Ⓐ Ⓑ Ⓒ Ⓓ Ⓔ	62 Ⓐ Ⓑ Ⓒ Ⓓ Ⓔ
3 Ⓐ Ⓑ Ⓒ Ⓓ Ⓔ	33 Ⓐ Ⓑ Ⓒ Ⓓ Ⓔ	63 Ⓐ Ⓑ Ⓒ Ⓓ Ⓔ
4 Ⓐ Ⓑ Ⓒ Ⓓ Ⓔ	34 Ⓐ Ⓑ Ⓒ Ⓓ Ⓔ	64 Ⓐ Ⓑ Ⓒ Ⓓ Ⓔ
5 Ⓐ Ⓑ Ⓒ Ⓓ Ⓔ	35 Ⓐ Ⓑ Ⓒ Ⓓ Ⓔ	65 Ⓐ Ⓑ Ⓒ Ⓓ Ⓔ
6 Ⓐ Ⓑ Ⓒ Ⓓ Ⓔ	36 Ⓐ Ⓑ Ⓒ Ⓓ Ⓔ	66 Ⓐ Ⓑ Ⓒ Ⓓ Ⓔ
7 Ⓐ Ⓑ Ⓒ Ⓓ Ⓔ	37 Ⓐ Ⓑ Ⓒ Ⓓ Ⓔ	67 Ⓐ Ⓑ Ⓒ Ⓓ Ⓔ
8 Ⓐ Ⓑ Ⓒ Ⓓ Ⓔ	38 Ⓐ Ⓑ Ⓒ Ⓓ Ⓔ	68 Ⓐ Ⓑ Ⓒ Ⓓ Ⓔ
9 Ⓐ Ⓑ Ⓒ Ⓓ Ⓔ	39 Ⓐ Ⓑ Ⓒ Ⓓ Ⓔ	69 Ⓐ Ⓑ Ⓒ Ⓓ Ⓔ
10 Ⓐ Ⓑ Ⓒ Ⓓ Ⓔ	40 Ⓐ Ⓑ Ⓒ Ⓓ Ⓔ	70 Ⓐ Ⓑ Ⓒ Ⓓ Ⓔ
11 Ⓐ Ⓑ Ⓒ Ⓓ Ⓔ	41 Ⓐ Ⓑ Ⓒ Ⓓ Ⓔ	71 Ⓐ Ⓑ Ⓒ Ⓓ Ⓔ
12 Ⓐ Ⓑ Ⓒ Ⓓ Ⓔ	42 Ⓐ Ⓑ Ⓒ Ⓓ Ⓔ	72 Ⓐ Ⓑ Ⓒ Ⓓ Ⓔ
13 Ⓐ Ⓑ Ⓒ Ⓓ Ⓔ	43 Ⓐ Ⓑ Ⓒ Ⓓ Ⓔ	73 Ⓐ Ⓑ Ⓒ Ⓓ Ⓔ
14 Ⓐ Ⓑ Ⓒ Ⓓ Ⓔ	44 Ⓐ Ⓑ Ⓒ Ⓓ Ⓔ	74 Ⓐ Ⓑ Ⓒ Ⓓ Ⓔ
15 Ⓐ Ⓑ Ⓒ Ⓓ Ⓔ	45 Ⓐ Ⓑ Ⓒ Ⓓ Ⓔ	75 Ⓐ Ⓑ Ⓒ Ⓓ Ⓔ
16 Ⓐ Ⓑ Ⓒ Ⓓ Ⓔ	46 Ⓐ Ⓑ Ⓒ Ⓓ Ⓔ	76 Ⓐ Ⓑ Ⓒ Ⓓ Ⓔ
17 Ⓐ Ⓑ Ⓒ Ⓓ Ⓔ	47 Ⓐ Ⓑ Ⓒ Ⓓ Ⓔ	77 Ⓐ Ⓑ Ⓒ Ⓓ Ⓔ
18 Ⓐ Ⓑ Ⓒ Ⓓ Ⓔ	48 Ⓐ Ⓑ Ⓒ Ⓓ Ⓔ	78 Ⓐ Ⓑ Ⓒ Ⓓ Ⓔ
19 Ⓐ Ⓑ Ⓒ Ⓓ Ⓔ	49 Ⓐ Ⓑ Ⓒ Ⓓ Ⓔ	79 Ⓐ Ⓑ Ⓒ Ⓓ Ⓔ
20 Ⓐ Ⓑ Ⓒ Ⓓ Ⓔ	50 Ⓐ Ⓑ Ⓒ Ⓓ Ⓔ	80 Ⓐ Ⓑ Ⓒ Ⓓ Ⓔ
21 Ⓐ Ⓑ Ⓒ Ⓓ Ⓔ	51 Ⓐ Ⓑ Ⓒ Ⓓ Ⓔ	81 Ⓐ Ⓑ Ⓒ Ⓓ Ⓔ
22 Ⓐ Ⓑ Ⓒ Ⓓ Ⓔ	52 Ⓐ Ⓑ Ⓒ Ⓓ Ⓔ	82 Ⓐ Ⓑ Ⓒ Ⓓ Ⓔ
23 Ⓐ Ⓑ Ⓒ Ⓓ Ⓔ	53 Ⓐ Ⓑ Ⓒ Ⓓ Ⓔ	83 Ⓐ Ⓑ Ⓒ Ⓓ Ⓔ
24 Ⓐ Ⓑ Ⓒ Ⓓ Ⓔ	54 Ⓐ Ⓑ Ⓒ Ⓓ Ⓔ	84 Ⓐ Ⓑ Ⓒ Ⓓ Ⓔ
25 Ⓐ Ⓑ Ⓒ Ⓓ Ⓔ	55 Ⓐ Ⓑ Ⓒ Ⓓ Ⓔ	85 Ⓐ Ⓑ Ⓒ Ⓓ Ⓔ
26 Ⓐ Ⓑ Ⓒ Ⓓ Ⓔ	56 Ⓐ Ⓑ Ⓒ Ⓓ Ⓔ	86 Ⓐ Ⓑ Ⓒ Ⓓ Ⓔ
27 Ⓐ Ⓑ Ⓒ Ⓓ Ⓔ	57 Ⓐ Ⓑ Ⓒ Ⓓ Ⓔ	87 Ⓐ Ⓑ Ⓒ Ⓓ Ⓔ
28 Ⓐ Ⓑ Ⓒ Ⓓ Ⓔ	58 Ⓐ Ⓑ Ⓒ Ⓓ Ⓔ	88 Ⓐ Ⓑ Ⓒ Ⓓ Ⓔ
29 Ⓐ Ⓑ Ⓒ Ⓓ Ⓔ	59 Ⓐ Ⓑ Ⓒ Ⓓ Ⓔ	
30 Ⓐ Ⓑ Ⓒ Ⓓ Ⓔ	60 Ⓐ Ⓑ Ⓒ Ⓓ Ⓔ	

Practice Test 1

Five complete practice tests are contained in this book. The first section of each test is called Part A and has 95 questions on Address Checking. The second section of each test, called Part B, has 88 questions testing your Memory for Addresses. Part B has, of course, questions on both *direct name* addresses and *numbered* addresses. This point is important for you to consider before doing any of the practice tests.

Up until now, the discussion on memory has separated questions on direct names from questions on numbered addresses. This was done to help you become thoroughly familiar with the special techniques for each and with the techniques common to both. Now, we will help you put together everything you have learned so that you achieve the highest possible score on the real test, where you must handle both direct name and numbered addresses.

FINAL GUIDELINES

Here are some points to consider before taking Practice Tests 1 and 2.

1. *How to divide your study time between the direct and numbered addresses?* If you are like most people who find it easier to memorize the direct name addresses, we suggest that you start out by allowing one-third of your study time (about 5 minutes) to the direct names, and two-thirds of your study time (about 9 minutes) to the numbers. (We are estimating that there will be a *total* of at least 14 minutes that can be used for studying.)
2. *What method to use for memorization?* Use any of the memorization methods, or combination of methods, that work best for you. See the list of these methods on page 135 for a quick review. As you do more of the practice tests, you will be in a good position to make a final decision

on how to proceed on the real test. Make this decision by the time you complete all of the practice tests in this book and, definitely, *before* you take the actual exam. For example, if you have been getting good scores on the practice tests by the use of Reduction Coding, stick to it. For memorizing numbers, you may be doing very well remembering Number Associations. Others will have found they are good at Chunking and should immediately use that technique on the test.

3. *How much to go for?* After sufficient practice, you will know more or less what your memory achievement level is. For example, you will know whether or not you can remember four, five, or six chunks. If you find that you have no problem with five, then you have to decide whether to concentrate on those five or whether to go for six. Don't bite off more than you can chew.

4. *How to make the best use of test time?* We recommend taking each question in order, and answering each to the best of your ability. Some people feel they might do better by answering all of the direct names first, and then going back to work on the numbers. Do this *only* if you cannot remember any numbers at all. This is extremely unlikely. Even if you can remember only a few numbered addresses, answer every question in turn, guessing when you must. (Refer to Chapter 4 for the full explanation of ''Guessing.'')

The timing and directions for taking Practice Tests 1 through 5 are exactly the same as those for the Diagnostic Practice Test. These directions are reprinted at the beginning of each part of each test.

A REVIEW OF TEST STRATEGIES
AND TECHNIQUES

ADDRESS CHECKING

1. *Balance*. Find *your* best combination of speed and accuracy.
2. *Score*. Percentages do not count. It is okay to make some errors. Your final score is what counts.
3. *Guess?* Do *not* guess wildly. Your score will suffer in the long run.
4. *Use Your Hands Properly*. Do not lose time or your place because of waste motion.
5. *Make Your Mark*. Make it neat, dark, and *fast* . . . but *not* perfect.
6. *Do NOT Read for Comprehension*. Your job is to perceive *differences* between addresses, not to study and interpret them.
7. *Do NOT Sound Out Addresses*. This will waste time. No one is listening, anyway.
8. *Widen Your Eye Span*. If you see *more* at a glance, your checking speed will increase. Never read word-for-word.
9. *Work with Rhythm*. Maintain a smooth, even pace as you work. You will get more done.
10. *Practice—Practice—Practice*.

MEMORY FOR ADDRESSES

1. *Use Some Practice Time for Studying.* Check the test directions on the actual examination. Once that is done, you are better off studying the addresses than answering the practice questions. The more you study and remember, the better you will be able to answer the questions that *count*.
2. *Eliminate the Last Box.* If you have memorized all addresses in four out of the five boxes, you know automatically that an unfamiliar address belongs in the fifth box.
3. *Guessing.* Yes, you should guess. You have more to gain than to lose. Enter an answer for every question.

Direct Addresses

1. *Association and Imagery.* Attach a vivid, colorful, or active image to the address; and it comes alive and is easier to remember. For example, Grand with Canyon, Crescent with Moon, Carpenter with Swinging a Hammer.
2. *Loci.* Decide on a familiar setting and imagine each of the five boxes—A, B, C, D, and E—to be parts of that scene. For example, the setting could be my office, with Box A standing for my desk; Box B, for the filing cabinet; Box C, as the window, etc. Assume that, on a test the actual address names in Box A were Gruyer and French. The picture I could come up with would show a big, smelly piece of cheese (Gruyer) between two slices of bread (French) lying on top of my desk—Box A.
3. *Reduction Coding.* NATO is easier to remember than North Atlantic Treaty Organization. U.I.B., FBI, UNICEF are other examples of how lengthy words and phrases may be easily remembered by using their initials to form a new word. On the test you can use this principle to remember each box individually with its two direct name addresses. For example, Box B has Newton and Fresco. Reduce this to BNF. The same idea is employed if you take five names on a line that includes all the boxes.
   A. *Check the Sound.* The three- or five-initial words may have a distinctive sound, like "BUZ" or "CRUMP."
   B. *Check For Meaning.* The new word may mean something like the one formed by the initials of these five address names.
      GANTT   RAMAPO   OTIS   WEST   SHORE
   C. *Make Up a Story/Slogan.* Use the initials to make up a story or slogan. For example, if the five letters are TRMAB you could think of The Red Monkey Ate Bananas. The three initials above, BNF, might be used for the slogan "broiled, not fried."

Numbered Addresses

1. *Reduce Numbers.* An address like 2200–2799 Barnes can be replaced by the number 22. You don't need more than that.

2. *Chunk the Number*. Combine two adjoining address numbers, like 22 in Box A and 57 in Box B to become 2257. It is far easier to remember the single four-digit number as *one* chunk rather than the *two* separate addresses. This principle can be applied to three separate, two-digit addresses replaced by a single six-digit number.

3. *Association*. Numbers can evoke associations, just as names can. Look for numbered addresses that mean something to you, like your birthday, your address, your height, your weight.

4. *Rhymes and Codes*. Numbers can be associated with a word with which they rhyme. For example, 1 with "won," 2 with "shoe," 10 with "hen." With practice, you can make up a story or picture using two-, four- or six-digit chunks.

5. *Loci*. The technique explained for letters can also be applied to numbers.

6. *Practice—Practice—Practice*.

PRACTICE TEST 1

PART A—ADDRESS CHECKING

WORK—*6 minutes*

In this test you are to decide whether two addresses are alike or different. If the two addresses are *exactly alike in every way*, darken space Ⓐ. If they are *different in any way*, darken space Ⓓ.

Mark your answers on the Answer Sheet for Address Checking at the beginning of this chapter. Tear it out, put today's date on it, and place it next to the questions.

Allow yourself *exactly 6 minutes* to do as many of the 95 questions as you can. If you finish before the time is up, re-check your answers.

1.	403 Americana Blvd SW	403 Amerigana Blvd SW
2.	2704 Kingsbury Rd	2704 Kingsbury Rd
3.	1121 Acom Dr	1121 Agom Dr
4.	Aaronsburg PA	Aaronsburg PA
5.	5405 Xavier St	5540 Xavier St
6.	1187 W Brompton Ave	1178 W Brompton Ave
7.	2066 W Lockerbie Dr	2066 W Lockerdie Dr
8.	3622 S Stanley St	3622 S Stanley Ct
9.	96 Willow St	96 Willow St
10.	6612 Conover Ave SW	6612 Connover Ave SW
11.	8282 Gardiner Rock Ln	8282 Garpiner Rock Ln
12.	5450 Sawgrass Rd	5450 Sawgrass Rd
13.	984 S York St	984 S York Pl
14.	2665 Ida St	2665 Ida St
15.	5 Keswick Dr NW	5 Keswick Dr NW
16.	4999 Whippoorwill Ct SE	4999 Whippoorvill Ct SE
17.	Hardee FL 33834	Hardee FL 33834
18.	1189 6th St NE	1189 6th Pl NE
19.	119 E Guerad Dr	119 W Guerad Dr
20.	1764 Pamakani Pl NE	1764 Pamakani Pl NE
21.	3327 Campbell Rd	3327 Campbell Rd
22.	2123 Cregier Ave	2123 Cregeir Ave
23.	1804 Gills Mill Ct	1804 Gills Mill Ct
24.	64 North Point Cir Dr	64 North Point Cir Dr
25.	7449 E 220 St	4749 E 220 St
26.	Duluth MN 55812	Duluth MN 58512
27.	9545 Buckwalter Rd NW	9545 Buckwalter Rd NW
28.	8305 Iglehart Ct	8305 Iglehert Ct
29.	1184 E Casteel Ct	1184 W Casteel Ct
30.	9767 Jonquil Ter	9767 Jonquil Ter
31.	McKessport PA 15132	Mackessport PA 15132

32.	735 Delmar Ct SE	735 Denar Ct SE
33.	4010 Narcissus Ave SW	4010 Narccissus Ave SW
34.	10 Quincy Dr	10 Quincy Rd
35.	7164 Malabar Dr NE	7164 Malabar Dr NE
36.	842 18th Pl SE	842 18th St SE
37.	57 Oakwood Trail South Dr	57 Oakwood Trail South Dr
38.	6319 Loch Lomond Trl	3619 Loch Lomond Trl
39.	6398 Greenleaf Ave	6398 Greenleaf St
40.	2216 N Dubuque Ave	2216 N Dubuque Ave
41.	139 Hammock Rd	139 Hammond Rd
42.	3123 Ivy Pky NE	3123 Ivy Pky NW
43.	7489 Ella St	7489 Ello St
44.	8701 Holokahana Ln W	8701 Holokahana Ln W
45.	4601 N Palmetto Ct	4601 N Palmetto Ct
46.	1553 Kreutzinger Ln E	1553 Kreutzinger Ln S
47.	303 S Wellington Ave	303 S Wellington Ave
48.	3876 E Edmunds Ave	3786 E Edmunds Ave
49.	6231 Martin Luther King Dr	6213 Martin Luther King Dr
50.	489 W 5th St	489 W 5th St
51.	Orocovis Pr	Ocorovis Pr
52.	240 Halcyon Dr	240 Halcyon Dr
53.	5924 S Breeze Ln	5924 S Breeze Ln
54.	2204 Youngs Ridge Ct	2204 Youngs Ridge Ct
55.	1698 Railroad Ave	1689 Railroad Ave
56.	Union Traction Blvd IN	Union Traction Blvd IN
57.	7589 Wrightwood Ave W	7589 Wrightwood Ave W
58.	7004 Flintridge Sq S	7004 Flintridge Sq S
59.	7820 Hamilton St	7820 Hamilton St
60.	989 S Poplar St	989 N Poplar St
61.	6745 E 9nd St	6745 E 92nd St
62.	198 Gideons Dr SW	198 Gideons Dr SW
63.	1021 S Port O'Manaco Ter	1021 S Port O'Manaco Ter
64.	2909 Pennsylvania Ave	2909 Pennsylvania Ave
65.	943 Gaspar Cir E	943 Gaspar Cir E
66.	655 E Vermillion Ave	655 E Vermillion Ave
67.	9623 Fort Rapadan Heights Ln	9623 Fort Ramadan Heights Ln
68.	82 East Handy Dr NW	82 West Handy Dr NW
69.	5992 N Upland Ave	5992 N Udland Ave
70.	9002 Fortingale Dr	9002 Fortindale Dr
71.	6069 El Paso Blvd	6069 El Peso Blvd
72.	7368 Eggleston Ave S	7368 Eggleston Ave S
73.	Shreveport LA 71109	Shreveport LA 71109
74.	83 Rue Le Ray	83 Rue La Ray
75.	865 S 3rd St	865 S 3rd St
76.	217 Intervale Rd	217 Interile Rd
77.	4003 Jonathon St	4003 Jonathan St

78.	Elyria OH 44039	Elyrio OH 44039
79.	3894 W. Diversey Blvd	3894 E. Diversey Blvd
80.	4045 Twin Willow Dr	4045 Twin Willow Dr
81.	1152 East Hickory Landing Way	1152 East Hickory Landing Way
82.	4232 Yale Rd	4232 Yale Rd
83.	High Point NC 27609	High Point NC 27609
84.	Pawtucket RI 02941	Pawtucket RI 02941
85.	5606 Fournoy St	5606 Fournoy St
86.	998 N Alta Vista Ter	998 N Alta Viste Ter
87.	San Mateo CA 94020	San Mateo CA 94020
88.	Owyhee NV	Omyhee NV
89.	8118 Fairfield Pl	8118 Fairfield Pl
90.	3773 Valley Brook Dr	3773 Valley Brood Dr
91.	Grande Ronde OR	Grande Ronde OH
92.	9225 Shelbyville Rd N	9225 Shelbyville Rd N
93.	7218 Queensbridge Commons Ct	7218 Queensbridge Commons Ct
94.	4621 Jackson Ave	4612 Jackson Ave
95.	4071 Cartwright Blvd	4017 Cartwright Blvd

STOP.

**If you finish before the time is up, go back
and check the questions in this section of the
test only.**

PART B—MEMORY FOR ADDRESSES

In this test you will have five boxes labeled A, B, C, D, and E. Each box contains five addresses. Three of the five are groups of street addresses, like 2500–3199 Clinton, 4000–4299 Singer, and 6100–6699 Tully; and two are names of places. They are different in each box.

You will also be given two lists of addresses. You will have to decide in which box each address belongs. When you are working on the first list, you will have the boxes with the addresses *in front* of you. It's a kind of warm-up trial test. When you are working on the second list, you will *not* be able to look at the boxes. The second list is the *real* test.

SAMPLES

A	B	C	D	E
1900-2299 Clinton Barber 4000-4299 Singer Miles 6700-7299 Tully	3200-3699 Clinton Aiden 2800-3299 Singer Timpot 5400-5699 Tully	3700-4499 Clinton Gallow 4800-5199 Singer Orange 6100-6699 Tully	2500-3199 Clinton Renwick 3300-3999 Singer Longson 5700-6099 Tully	2300-2499 Clinton Empire 4300-4799 Singer Wren 7300-7599 Tully

Questions 1 through 7 show the way the questions look. You have to decide in which lettered box (A, B, C, D, or E) the address belongs and then mark that answer in the answer grid.

1.	5400–5699 Tully	1 Ⓐ Ⓑ Ⓒ Ⓓ Ⓔ
2.	Empire	2 Ⓐ Ⓑ Ⓒ Ⓤ Ⓔ
3.	2800–3299 Singer	3 Ⓐ Ⓑ Ⓒ Ⓓ Ⓔ
4.	Orange	4 Ⓐ Ⓑ Ⓒ Ⓓ Ⓔ
5.	3200–3699 Clinton	5 Ⓐ Ⓑ Ⓒ Ⓓ Ⓔ
6.	Miles	6 Ⓐ Ⓑ Ⓒ Ⓓ Ⓔ
7.	2500–3199 Clinton	7 Ⓐ Ⓑ Ⓒ Ⓓ Ⓔ

Answers

1. B	3. B	5. B	7. D
2. E	4. C	6. A	

STUDY—*3 minutes*

You will now have *3 minutes to spend memorizing the addresses in the boxes.* These are the addresses that will be on the test. Try to learn as many as you can. When the three minutes are up, go to page 141 to begin your practice test.

List 1

WORK—*3 minutes*

Tear out the Answer Sheet for this section of the test. For each question, mark the answer sheet to show the letter of the box in which the address belongs. Try to remember the location of as many addresses as you can. *You will now have 3 minutes to complete List 1.* If you are not sure of an answer, you should guess.

A	B	C	D	E
1900-2299 Clinton Barber 4000-4299 Singer Miles 6700-7299 Tully	3200-3699 Clinton Aiden 2800-3299 Singer Timpot 5400-5699 Tully	3700-4499 Clinton Gallow 4800-5199 Singer Orange 6100-6699 Tully	2500-3199 Clinton Renwick 3300-3999 Singer Longson 5700-6099 Tully	2300-2499 Clinton Empire 4300-4799 Singer Wren 7300-7599 Tully

1. Barber
2. 4000–4299 Singer
3. 1900–2299 Clinton
4. Longson
5. Empire
6. 4800–5199 Singer
7. 7300–7599 Tully
8. 3700–4499 Clinton
9. Miles
10. 4300–4799 Singer
11. Wren
12. 5400–5699 Tully
13. 2300–2499 Clinton
14. Renwick
15. 6700–7299 Tully
16. 3200–3699 Clinton
17. 5700–6099 Tully
18. 3300–3999 Singer
19. Orange
20. 1900–2299 Clinton
21. 2500–3199 Clinton
22. 2800–3299 Singer
23. Timpot
24. Wren
25. 6100–6699 Tully
26. Aiden
27. Gallow
28. Orange
29. 4800–5199 Singer
30. 5700–6099 Tully

31. 3700–4499 Clinton
32. Renwick
33. 7300–7599 Tully
34. 2800–3299 Singer
35. Orange
36. 2800–3299 Singer
37. Barber
38. 6100–6699 Tully
39. 4000–4299 Singer
40. Aiden
41. Renwick
42. Timpot
43. 1900–2299 Clinton
44. Aiden
45. 5400–5699 Tully
46. 2500–3199 Clinton
47. 3200–3699 Clinton
48. Timpot
49. Longson
50. 3200–3699 Clinton
51. Gallow
52. 3700–4499 Clinton
53. 7300–7599 Tully
54. 2500–3199 Clinton
55. 3300–3999 Singer
56. Empire
57. Aiden
58. Miles
59. 2800–3299 Singer
60. Barber

61. 2300–2499 Clinton
62. Wren
63. 6700–7299 Tully
64. Miles
65. Orange
66. 5400–5699 Tully
67. 2300–2499 Clinton
68. Gallow
69. 6700–7299 Tully
70. 4300–4799 Singer
71. Renwick
72. 5700–6099 Tully
73. Barber
74. 4300–4799 Singer
75. 2300–2499 Clinton
76. Longson
77. 2500–3199 Clinton
78. 3300–3999 Singer
79. Wren
80. 6700–7299 Tully
81. Empire
82. 1900–2299 Clinton
83. Timpot
84. 4800–5199 Singer
85. 6100–6699 Tully
86. 4300–4799 Singer
87. Renwick
88. 4000–4299 Singer

STOP.

If you finish before the time is up, go back and check the questions in this section of the test only.

List 2

STUDY—*5 minutes*

You are now about to take the test using List 2. *(This is the test that counts!)*

Turn back to the first page of Part B of this test and study the boxes again. You have *5 minutes to restudy the addresses*. When the time is up, tear out the Answer Sheet for List 2. Use it for this test.

WORK—*5 minutes*

For each question, mark the Answer Sheet to show the letter of the box in which the address belongs. You will have *exactly 5 minutes to do the test*. During the 5 minutes, do *not* turn to any other page.

1. 1900–2299 Clinton	31. Timpot	61. 4000–4299 Singer
2. Renwick	32. Orange	62. 2300–2499 Clinton
3. Timpot	33. 3700–4499 Clinton	63. 3700–4499 Clinton
4. Empire	34. 2500–3199 Clinton	64. Gallow
5. 6700–7299 Tully	35. 6700–7299 Tully	65. 4000–4299 Singer
6. 2800–3299 Singer	36. 4300–4799 Singer	66. 5400–5699 Tully
7. Wren	37. Longson	67. Renwick
8. 2300–2499 Clinton	38. 3300–3999 Singer	68. 1900–2299 Clinton
9. 6100–6699 Tully	39. Barber	69. Aiden
10. 4300–4799 Singer	40. 2300–2499 Clinton	70. Empire
11. Orange	41. 7300–7599 Tully	71. 3300–3999 Singer
12. 5700–6099 Tully	42. Wren	72. 1900–2299 Clinton
13. Longson	43. Aiden	73. 5700–6099 Tully
14. Timpot	44. 4300–4799 Singer	74. 2800–3299 Singer
15. 4300–4799 Singer	45. 7300–7599 Tully	75. Timpot
16. 7300–7599 Tully	46. 4800–5199 Singer	76. 6700–7299 Tully
17. 1900–2299 Clinton	47. Wren	77. Miles
18. 6100–6699 Tully	48. Gallow	78. 4000–4299 Singer
19. 2500–3199 Clinton	49. 3300–3999 Singer	79. 2500–3199 Clinton
20. 6700–7299 Tully	50. Renwick	80. Miles
21. Aiden	51. 5400–5699 Tully	81. Renwick
22. Orange	52. Barber	82. 3700–4499 Clinton
23. 3200–3699 Clinton	53. Empire	83. Gallow
24. Wren	54. 2800–3299 Singer	84. 2500–3199 Clinton
25. 6100–6699 Tully	55. Orange	85. 5400–5699 Tully
26. Miles	56. Longson	86. 2300–2499 Clinton
27. 5700–6099 Tully	57. 3200–3899 Clinton	87. Orange
28. 3200–3699 Clinton	58. Barber	88. 4800–5199 Singer
29. 2800–3299 Singer	59. 4800–5199 Singer	
30. Barber	60. Aiden	

END OF EXAMINATION.

**If you finish before the time is up, go back
and check the questions in this section of the
test only.**

ANSWER KEY

PART A—ADDRESS CHECKING

1.	D	25.	D	49.	D	73.	A
2.	A	26.	D	50.	A	74.	D
3.	D	27.	A	51.	D	75.	A
4.	A	28.	D	52.	A	76.	D
5.	D	29.	D	53.	A	77.	D
6.	D	30.	A	54.	A	78.	D
7.	D	31.	D	55.	D	79.	D
8.	D	32.	D	56.	A	80.	A
9.	A	33.	D	57.	A	81.	A
10.	D	34.	D	58.	A	82.	A
11.	D	35.	A	59.	A	83.	A
12.	A	36.	D	60.	D	84.	A
13.	D	37.	A	61.	D	85.	A
14.	A	38.	D	62.	A	86.	D
15.	A	39.	D	63.	A	87.	A
16.	D	40.	A	64.	A	88.	D
17.	A	41.	D	65.	A	89.	A
18.	D	42.	D	66.	A	90.	D
19.	D	43.	D	67.	D	91.	D
20.	A	44.	A	68.	D	92.	A
21.	A	45.	A	69.	D	93.	A
22.	D	46.	D	70.	D	94.	D
23.	A	47.	A	71.	D	95.	D
24.	A	48.	D	72.	A		

PART B—MEMORY FOR ADDRESSES

List 1

1.	A	17.	D	33.	E	49.	D
2.	A	18.	D	34.	B	50.	B
3.	A	19.	C	35.	C	51.	C
4.	D	20.	A	36.	B	52.	C
5.	E	21.	D	37.	A	53.	E
6.	C	22.	B	38.	C	54.	D
7.	E	23.	B	39.	A	55.	D
8.	C	24.	E	40.	B	56.	E
9.	A	25.	C	41.	D	57.	B
10.	E	26.	B	42.	B	58.	A
11.	E	27.	C	43.	A	59.	B
12.	B	28.	C	44.	B	60.	A
13.	E	29.	C	45.	B	61.	E
14.	D	30.	D	46.	D	62.	E
15.	A	31.	C	47.	B	63.	A
16.	B	32.	D	48.	B	64.	A

65.	C	71.	D	77.	D	83.	B
66.	B	72.	D	78.	D	84.	C
67.	E	73.	A	79.	E	85.	C
68.	C	74.	E	80.	A	86.	E
69.	A	75.	E	81.	E	87.	D
70.	E	76.	D	82.	A	88.	A

List 2

1.	A	23.	B	45.	E	67.	D
2.	D	24.	E	46.	C	68.	A
3.	B	25.	C	47.	E	69.	B
4.	E	26.	A	48.	C	70.	E
5.	A	27.	D	49.	D	71.	D
6.	B	28.	B	50.	D	72.	A
7.	E	29.	B	51.	B	73.	D
8.	E	30.	A	52.	A	74.	B
9.	C	31.	B	53.	E	75.	B
10.	E	32.	C	54.	B	76.	A
11.	C	33.	C	55.	C	77.	A
12.	D	34.	D	56.	D	78.	A
13.	D	35.	A	57.	B	79.	D
14.	B	36.	E	58.	A	80.	A
15.	E	37.	D	59.	C	81.	D
16.	E	38.	D	60.	B	82.	C
17.	A	39.	A	61.	A	83.	C
18.	C	40.	E	62.	E	84.	D
19.	D	41.	E	63.	C	85.	B
20.	A	42.	E	64.	C	86.	E
21.	B	43.	B	65.	A	87.	C
22.	C	44.	E	66.	B	88.	C

EVALUATING YOUR PROGRESS

PART A

Computing Your Score

Check your answers against the Answer Key. Score yourself by using this formula:

Number right
<u>− Number wrong</u>
YOUR SCORE

For example, if you completed 52 questions and got 8 wrong,

Number right 44
<u>− Number wrong ..... − 8</u>
YOUR SCORE = 36

Notice that you do *not* figure in the questions you did not answer.

Guidelines

How good is the score you just made?

52 or higher .... Good
Between 32 and 52 ...... Fair
Below 32 .... You need to improve

These are commonly accepted figures. We believe, however, that you should not be satisfied with anything *less* than 52. Our experience in training many people to prepare for this test shows that most serious test candidates who use the preparation program described in this book will be able to raise their score to the upper sixties and seventies.

Personal Progress Record

As was mentioned before, one of the most satisfying things that can happen while you are working toward a goal is to see signs of progress. The improvement you make on Address Checking can readily be seen by examining the scores you make on the practice tests and exercises in this book. We think that keeping track of your growing skill is so important that a Personal Progress Record has been furnished for your use on page 231.

A sample of this Personal Progress Record may be found on the next page in order to familiarize you with it. The entries on this sample are based on the example above.

Personal Progress Record—Sample

		Initial Tests				Repeated Tests			
		ADDRESS CHECKING							
Date	Test	Number Completed	Number Correct −	Number Wrong	= Score	Date	Score	Date	Score
5/15	Diagnostic Practice Test	52	44 −	8	= 36				
5/16	Practice Test 1	64	54 −	10	= 44				
5/18	Practice Test 2	66	57 −	9	= 48				
5/20	Practice Test 3	70	60 −	10	= 50				
	Practice Test 4		−		=				
	Practice Test 5		−		=				

Now turn to page 231. Look at the table entitled "Personal Progress Record—Address Checking." Make the proper entries on the line for Practice Test 1 which you just took. Review the special techniques in Chapter 3 on Address Checking before taking Practice Test 2. After taking the additional practice tests, enter the results immediately. Keep this record. It will help you record your progress.

PART B

Computing Your Score

Check the answers on your answer sheet against the Answer Key. Calculate your score by using these four steps:

1. Enter the number of answers you got right ....—————
2. Enter the number of answers you got wrong ....—————
3. Divide the number wrong by 4 (or multiply by ¼)........... −—————
4. Subtract Line 3 from Line 1....................YOUR SCORE =—————

Follow this example to make sure that you have figured your score correctly. We will assume that you completed 32 questions, of which you got 24 right and 8 wrong.

Line 1.......Number right................... 24
Line 2.......Number wrong.............. 8
Line 3.......¼ of line 2 = ¼ × 8... $\frac{-2}{}$
Line 4.......24 − 2....YOUR SCORE = $\overline{22}$

Notice that just as for Address Checking, questions that are not answered are *not* taken into account.

Guidelines

How good is the score you just made?

44 or more ....Good
26 to 43 ....Fair
25 or less ....You need to improve

If your score on this test was low, don't be discouraged. Nevertheless, you may wish to review the chapters offering special techniques for handling "Memory for Addresses" before taking Practice Test 2.

Personal Progress Record

Turn to page 231. Look at the table entitled "Personal Progress—Memory for Addresses." Keep a permanent record of your scores on the practice tests, as you have been doing. A sample is printed below to familiarize you with it. The entries are based on the preceding example.

Personal Progress Record—Sample

		MEMORY FOR ADDRESSES										
		Initial Tests								Repeated Tests		
Date	Test	Number Completed	Number Correct A	Number Wrong	$\times$ ¼ $=$		Points off B	Score (A − B)	Date	Score	Date	Score
5/15	Diagnostic Practice Test	32	24	8	$\times$ ¼ $=$		2	22				
5/16	Practice Test 1	46	38	8	$\times$ ¼ $=$		2	36				
5/18	Practice Test 2	58	52	6	$\times$ ¼ $=$		1½	50½				
5/20	Practice Test 3	64	60	4	$\times$ ¼ $=$		1	59				
	Practice Test 4				$\times$ ¼ $=$							
	Practice Test 5				$\times$ ¼ $=$							

Make the proper entries on the record for Practice Test 1 that you just took. Use it to keep a record of the additional practice tests you take. You should be pleasantly surprised at how much higher your next entry on this card will be.

DIAGNOSTIC CHART

PART A—ADDRESS CHECKING

Type of Difference	"D" Questions	Number of "D" Questions Wrong		
		TRIAL 1	TRIAL 2	TRIAL 3
Numbers: transposed	5, 6, 25, 26, 38, 48, 49, 55, 94, 95			
changed	61			
omitted				
Directions	19, 29, 42, 46, 60, 79			
Abbreviations: streets, roads, avenues, etc.	8, 13, 18, 34, 36, 39			
states	91			
Spelling: single letters	1, 3, 7, 10, 11, 16, 22, 28, 31, 32, 33, 43, 51, 67, 69, 70, 71, 78, 86, 88, 90			
groups of letters	41, 68, 74, 76, 77			
Total Number of Each Type	50			
	Use the columns on the right to enter the question numbers of those "A" you marked "D"			

This chart will help you to pinpoint the kinds of errors you have made on this Practice Test. Use it as directed below after you have taken and marked the test.

The first column on the left, "Type of Difference," contains the same categories whereby addresses may differ shown on page 30 in Chapter 2. On the same line across, the second column gives the number of the questions that fall within each category. In the third column, you are to enter the number of the questions you had wrong. Do not include those you did not do. Use the space indicated in this column to list the number of any "A" questions you answered as "D." Checking these addresses may reveal a problem on which you will want to work.

After you have made all the entries, you will be able to see the areas in which you need to improve. Then turn to the appropriate part of Chapter 3,

Address Checking: How to Improve Your Score, and re-read it. Then repeat those drills that can help. For example, if you find you have been making too many errors picking out number differences, read pages 38 to 40 and do Drills 18 through 21. If you have a problem with single letters because of reversals like *b* and *d*, or if you have been overlooking the difference between *a*, *e*, and *o*, read pages 38 to 40. Examine the table on page 49 and work on Drills 10 and 11 if the problem persists.

Remember that this chart is designed for diagnostic purposes and guidance on further practice. It has been drawn so that you can enter the results each time you retake a Practice Test. In this way you will be able to see how you are progressing. It is not necessary to try to score it. That is best done by using the Personal Progress Record Card.

PART B—MEMORY FOR ADDRESSES

Kind of Address		Number of Questions	Number Wrong		
			TRIAL 1	TRIAL 2	TRIAL 3
Direct:					
	list 1	40			
	list 2	38			
Numbered:					
	list 1	48			
	list 2	50			

The purpose of this chart is to help you evaluate your performance on the two kinds of memory questions that appear in the Practice Test—the questions on the direct (name) addresses and the questions on the numbered addresses. Use it as directed below after you have taken and marked the entire test.

The first column on the left, "Kind of Address," is divided by category into "Direct Address" versus "Numbered Address." The second column gives the number of questions in each category. Use the third column to enter the total number of questions in each category that you answered incorrectly. There is room for you to make additional entries if you take the Practice Test more than once.

At a glance, you will be able to see which area you need to concentrate on and how well you are progressing as you take repeat trials. Use Chapter 4 and the drills in it to improve your memory for the direct addresses. Use Chapter 5 for the numbered addresses.

Remember to use the Personal Progress Record Card (Memory for Addresses) to keep track of your actual scores as you keep studying and practicing.

ANSWER SHEET—PRACTICE TEST 2

PART A—ADDRESS CHECKING   DATE _____

1 Ⓐ Ⓓ	25 Ⓐ Ⓓ	49 Ⓐ Ⓓ	73 Ⓐ Ⓓ
2 Ⓐ Ⓓ	26 Ⓐ Ⓓ	50 Ⓐ Ⓓ	74 Ⓐ Ⓓ
3 Ⓐ Ⓓ	27 Ⓐ Ⓓ	51 Ⓐ Ⓓ	75 Ⓐ Ⓓ
4 Ⓐ Ⓓ	28 Ⓐ Ⓓ	52 Ⓐ Ⓓ	76 Ⓐ Ⓓ
5 Ⓐ Ⓓ	29 Ⓐ Ⓓ	53 Ⓐ Ⓓ	77 Ⓐ Ⓓ
6 Ⓐ Ⓓ	30 Ⓐ Ⓓ	54 Ⓐ Ⓓ	78 Ⓐ Ⓓ
7 Ⓐ Ⓓ	31 Ⓐ Ⓓ	55 Ⓐ Ⓓ	79 Ⓐ Ⓓ
8 Ⓐ Ⓓ	32 Ⓐ Ⓓ	56 Ⓐ Ⓓ	80 Ⓐ Ⓓ
9 Ⓐ Ⓓ	33 Ⓐ Ⓓ	57 Ⓐ Ⓓ	81 Ⓐ Ⓓ
10 Ⓐ Ⓓ	34 Ⓐ Ⓓ	58 Ⓐ Ⓓ	82 Ⓐ Ⓓ
11 Ⓐ Ⓓ	35 Ⓐ Ⓓ	59 Ⓐ Ⓓ	83 Ⓐ Ⓓ
12 Ⓐ Ⓓ	36 Ⓐ Ⓓ	60 Ⓐ Ⓓ	84 Ⓐ Ⓓ
13 Ⓐ Ⓓ	37 Ⓐ Ⓓ	61 Ⓐ Ⓓ	85 Ⓐ Ⓓ
14 Ⓐ Ⓓ	38 Ⓐ Ⓓ	62 Ⓐ Ⓓ	86 Ⓐ Ⓓ
15 Ⓐ Ⓓ	39 Ⓐ Ⓓ	63 Ⓐ Ⓓ	87 Ⓐ Ⓓ
16 Ⓐ Ⓓ	40 Ⓐ Ⓓ	64 Ⓐ Ⓓ	88 Ⓐ Ⓓ
17 Ⓐ Ⓓ	41 Ⓐ Ⓓ	65 Ⓐ Ⓓ	89 Ⓐ Ⓓ
18 Ⓐ Ⓓ	42 Ⓐ Ⓓ	66 Ⓐ Ⓓ	90 Ⓐ Ⓓ
19 Ⓐ Ⓓ	43 Ⓐ Ⓓ	67 Ⓐ Ⓓ	91 Ⓐ Ⓓ
20 Ⓐ Ⓓ	44 Ⓐ Ⓓ	68 Ⓐ Ⓓ	92 Ⓐ Ⓓ
21 Ⓐ Ⓓ	45 Ⓐ Ⓓ	69 Ⓐ Ⓓ	93 Ⓐ Ⓓ
22 Ⓐ Ⓓ	46 Ⓐ Ⓓ	70 Ⓐ Ⓓ	94 Ⓐ Ⓓ
23 Ⓐ Ⓓ	47 Ⓐ Ⓓ	71 Ⓐ Ⓓ	95 Ⓐ Ⓓ
24 Ⓐ Ⓓ	48 Ⓐ Ⓓ	72 Ⓐ Ⓓ	

ANSWER SHEET—PRACTICE TEST 2

PART B—MEMORY FOR ADDRESSES
LIST 1　　　　　　　　DATE _____

1 Ⓐ Ⓑ Ⓒ Ⓓ Ⓔ	31 Ⓐ Ⓑ Ⓒ Ⓓ Ⓔ	61 Ⓐ Ⓑ Ⓒ Ⓓ Ⓔ
2 Ⓐ Ⓑ Ⓒ Ⓓ Ⓔ	32 Ⓐ Ⓑ Ⓒ Ⓓ Ⓔ	62 Ⓐ Ⓑ Ⓒ Ⓓ Ⓔ
3 Ⓐ Ⓑ Ⓒ Ⓓ Ⓔ	33 Ⓐ Ⓑ Ⓒ Ⓓ Ⓔ	63 Ⓐ Ⓑ Ⓒ Ⓓ Ⓔ
4 Ⓐ Ⓑ Ⓒ Ⓓ Ⓔ	34 Ⓐ Ⓑ Ⓒ Ⓓ Ⓔ	64 Ⓐ Ⓑ Ⓒ Ⓓ Ⓔ
5 Ⓐ Ⓑ Ⓒ Ⓓ Ⓔ	35 Ⓐ Ⓑ Ⓒ Ⓓ Ⓔ	65 Ⓐ Ⓑ Ⓒ Ⓓ Ⓔ
6 Ⓐ Ⓑ Ⓒ Ⓓ Ⓔ	36 Ⓐ Ⓑ Ⓒ Ⓓ Ⓔ	66 Ⓐ Ⓑ Ⓒ Ⓓ Ⓔ
7 Ⓐ Ⓑ Ⓒ Ⓓ Ⓔ	37 Ⓐ Ⓑ Ⓒ Ⓓ Ⓔ	67 Ⓐ Ⓑ Ⓒ Ⓓ Ⓔ
8 Ⓐ Ⓑ Ⓒ Ⓓ Ⓔ	38 Ⓐ Ⓑ Ⓒ Ⓓ Ⓔ	68 Ⓐ Ⓑ Ⓒ Ⓓ Ⓔ
9 Ⓐ Ⓑ Ⓒ Ⓓ Ⓔ	39 Ⓐ Ⓑ Ⓒ Ⓓ Ⓔ	69 Ⓐ Ⓑ Ⓒ Ⓓ Ⓔ
10 Ⓐ Ⓑ Ⓒ Ⓓ Ⓔ	40 Ⓐ Ⓑ Ⓒ Ⓓ Ⓔ	70 Ⓐ Ⓑ Ⓒ Ⓓ Ⓔ
11 Ⓐ Ⓑ Ⓒ Ⓓ Ⓔ	41 Ⓐ Ⓑ Ⓒ Ⓓ Ⓔ	71 Ⓐ Ⓑ Ⓒ Ⓓ Ⓔ
12 Ⓐ Ⓑ Ⓒ Ⓓ Ⓔ	42 Ⓐ Ⓑ Ⓒ Ⓓ Ⓔ	72 Ⓐ Ⓑ Ⓒ Ⓓ Ⓔ
13 Ⓐ Ⓑ Ⓒ Ⓓ Ⓔ	43 Ⓐ Ⓑ Ⓒ Ⓓ Ⓔ	73 Ⓐ Ⓑ Ⓒ Ⓓ Ⓔ
14 Ⓐ Ⓑ Ⓒ Ⓓ Ⓔ	44 Ⓐ Ⓑ Ⓒ Ⓓ Ⓔ	74 Ⓐ Ⓑ Ⓒ Ⓓ Ⓔ
15 Ⓐ Ⓑ Ⓒ Ⓓ Ⓔ	45 Ⓐ Ⓑ Ⓒ Ⓓ Ⓔ	75 Ⓐ Ⓑ Ⓒ Ⓓ Ⓔ
16 Ⓐ Ⓑ Ⓒ Ⓓ Ⓔ	46 Ⓐ Ⓑ Ⓒ Ⓓ Ⓔ	76 Ⓐ Ⓑ Ⓒ Ⓓ Ⓔ
17 Ⓐ Ⓑ Ⓒ Ⓓ Ⓔ	47 Ⓐ Ⓑ Ⓒ Ⓓ Ⓔ	77 Ⓐ Ⓑ Ⓒ Ⓓ Ⓔ
18 Ⓐ Ⓑ Ⓒ Ⓓ Ⓔ	48 Ⓐ Ⓑ Ⓒ Ⓓ Ⓔ	78 Ⓐ Ⓑ Ⓒ Ⓓ Ⓔ
19 Ⓐ Ⓑ Ⓒ Ⓓ Ⓔ	49 Ⓐ Ⓑ Ⓒ Ⓓ Ⓔ	79 Ⓐ Ⓑ Ⓒ Ⓓ Ⓔ
20 Ⓐ Ⓑ Ⓒ Ⓓ Ⓔ	50 Ⓐ Ⓑ Ⓒ Ⓓ Ⓔ	80 Ⓐ Ⓑ Ⓒ Ⓓ Ⓔ
21 Ⓐ Ⓑ Ⓒ Ⓓ Ⓔ	51 Ⓐ Ⓑ Ⓒ Ⓓ Ⓔ	81 Ⓐ Ⓑ Ⓒ Ⓓ Ⓔ
22 Ⓐ Ⓑ Ⓒ Ⓓ Ⓔ	52 Ⓐ Ⓑ Ⓒ Ⓓ Ⓔ	82 Ⓐ Ⓑ Ⓒ Ⓓ Ⓔ
23 Ⓐ Ⓑ Ⓒ Ⓓ Ⓔ	53 Ⓐ Ⓑ Ⓒ Ⓓ Ⓔ	83 Ⓐ Ⓑ Ⓒ Ⓓ Ⓔ
24 Ⓐ Ⓑ Ⓒ Ⓓ Ⓔ	54 Ⓐ Ⓑ Ⓒ Ⓓ Ⓔ	84 Ⓐ Ⓑ Ⓒ Ⓓ Ⓔ
25 Ⓐ Ⓑ Ⓒ Ⓓ Ⓔ	55 Ⓐ Ⓑ Ⓒ Ⓓ Ⓔ	85 Ⓐ Ⓑ Ⓒ Ⓓ Ⓔ
26 Ⓐ Ⓑ Ⓒ Ⓓ Ⓔ	56 Ⓐ Ⓑ Ⓒ Ⓓ Ⓔ	86 Ⓐ Ⓑ Ⓒ Ⓓ Ⓔ
27 Ⓐ Ⓑ Ⓒ Ⓓ Ⓔ	57 Ⓐ Ⓑ Ⓒ Ⓓ Ⓔ	87 Ⓐ Ⓑ Ⓒ Ⓓ Ⓔ
28 Ⓐ Ⓑ Ⓒ Ⓓ Ⓔ	58 Ⓐ Ⓑ Ⓒ Ⓓ Ⓔ	88 Ⓐ Ⓑ Ⓒ Ⓓ Ⓔ
29 Ⓐ Ⓑ Ⓒ Ⓓ Ⓔ	59 Ⓐ Ⓑ Ⓒ Ⓓ Ⓔ	
30 Ⓐ Ⓑ Ⓒ Ⓓ Ⓔ	60 Ⓐ Ⓑ Ⓒ Ⓓ Ⓔ	

ANSWER SHEET—PRACTICE TEST 2

PART B—MEMORY FOR ADDRESSES
LIST 2   DATE _____

1 Ⓐ Ⓑ Ⓒ Ⓓ Ⓔ   31 Ⓐ Ⓑ Ⓒ Ⓓ Ⓔ   61 Ⓐ Ⓑ Ⓒ Ⓓ Ⓔ
2 Ⓐ Ⓑ Ⓒ Ⓓ Ⓔ   32 Ⓐ Ⓑ Ⓒ Ⓓ Ⓔ   62 Ⓐ Ⓑ Ⓒ Ⓓ Ⓔ
3 Ⓐ Ⓑ Ⓒ Ⓓ Ⓔ   33 Ⓐ Ⓑ Ⓒ Ⓓ Ⓔ   63 Ⓐ Ⓑ Ⓒ Ⓓ Ⓔ
4 Ⓐ Ⓑ Ⓒ Ⓓ Ⓔ   34 Ⓐ Ⓑ Ⓒ Ⓓ Ⓔ   64 Ⓐ Ⓑ Ⓒ Ⓓ Ⓔ
5 Ⓐ Ⓑ Ⓒ Ⓓ Ⓔ   35 Ⓐ Ⓑ Ⓒ Ⓓ Ⓔ   65 Ⓐ Ⓑ Ⓒ Ⓓ Ⓔ
6 Ⓐ Ⓑ Ⓒ Ⓓ Ⓔ   36 Ⓐ Ⓑ Ⓒ Ⓓ Ⓔ   66 Ⓐ Ⓑ Ⓒ Ⓓ Ⓔ
7 Ⓐ Ⓑ Ⓒ Ⓓ Ⓔ   37 Ⓐ Ⓑ Ⓒ Ⓓ Ⓔ   67 Ⓐ Ⓑ Ⓒ Ⓓ Ⓔ
8 Ⓐ Ⓑ Ⓒ Ⓓ Ⓔ   38 Ⓐ Ⓑ Ⓒ Ⓓ Ⓔ   68 Ⓐ Ⓑ Ⓒ Ⓓ Ⓔ
9 Ⓐ Ⓑ Ⓒ Ⓓ Ⓔ   39 Ⓐ Ⓑ Ⓒ Ⓓ Ⓔ   69 Ⓐ Ⓑ Ⓒ Ⓓ Ⓔ
10 Ⓐ Ⓑ Ⓒ Ⓓ Ⓔ   40 Ⓐ Ⓑ Ⓒ Ⓓ Ⓔ   70 Ⓐ Ⓑ Ⓒ Ⓓ Ⓔ
11 Ⓐ Ⓑ Ⓒ Ⓓ Ⓔ   41 Ⓐ Ⓑ Ⓒ Ⓓ Ⓔ   71 Ⓐ Ⓑ Ⓒ Ⓓ Ⓔ
12 Ⓐ Ⓑ Ⓒ Ⓓ Ⓔ   42 Ⓐ Ⓑ Ⓒ Ⓓ Ⓔ   72 Ⓐ Ⓑ Ⓒ Ⓓ Ⓔ
13 Ⓐ Ⓑ Ⓒ Ⓓ Ⓔ   43 Ⓐ Ⓑ Ⓒ Ⓓ Ⓔ   73 Ⓐ Ⓑ Ⓒ Ⓓ Ⓔ
14 Ⓐ Ⓑ Ⓒ Ⓓ Ⓔ   44 Ⓐ Ⓑ Ⓒ Ⓓ Ⓔ   74 Ⓐ Ⓑ Ⓒ Ⓓ Ⓔ
15 Ⓐ Ⓑ Ⓒ Ⓓ Ⓔ   45 Ⓐ Ⓑ Ⓒ Ⓓ Ⓔ   75 Ⓐ Ⓑ Ⓒ Ⓓ Ⓔ
16 Ⓐ Ⓑ Ⓒ Ⓓ Ⓔ   46 Ⓐ Ⓑ Ⓒ Ⓓ Ⓔ   76 Ⓐ Ⓑ Ⓒ Ⓓ Ⓔ
17 Ⓐ Ⓑ Ⓒ Ⓓ Ⓔ   47 Ⓐ Ⓑ Ⓒ Ⓓ Ⓔ   77 Ⓐ Ⓑ Ⓒ Ⓓ Ⓔ
18 Ⓐ Ⓑ Ⓒ Ⓓ Ⓔ   48 Ⓐ Ⓑ Ⓒ Ⓓ Ⓔ   78 Ⓐ Ⓑ Ⓒ Ⓓ Ⓔ
19 Ⓐ Ⓑ Ⓒ Ⓓ Ⓔ   49 Ⓐ Ⓑ Ⓒ Ⓓ Ⓔ   79 Ⓐ Ⓑ Ⓒ Ⓓ Ⓔ
20 Ⓐ Ⓑ Ⓒ Ⓓ Ⓔ   50 Ⓐ Ⓑ Ⓒ Ⓓ Ⓔ   80 Ⓐ Ⓑ Ⓒ Ⓓ Ⓔ
21 Ⓐ Ⓑ Ⓒ Ⓓ Ⓔ   51 Ⓐ Ⓑ Ⓒ Ⓓ Ⓔ   81 Ⓐ Ⓑ Ⓒ Ⓓ Ⓔ
22 Ⓐ Ⓑ Ⓒ Ⓓ Ⓔ   52 Ⓐ Ⓑ Ⓒ Ⓓ Ⓔ   82 Ⓐ Ⓑ Ⓒ Ⓓ Ⓔ
23 Ⓐ Ⓑ Ⓒ Ⓓ Ⓔ   53 Ⓐ Ⓑ Ⓒ Ⓓ Ⓔ   83 Ⓐ Ⓑ Ⓒ Ⓓ Ⓔ
24 Ⓐ Ⓑ Ⓒ Ⓓ Ⓔ   54 Ⓐ Ⓑ Ⓒ Ⓓ Ⓔ   84 Ⓐ Ⓑ Ⓒ Ⓓ Ⓔ
25 Ⓐ Ⓑ Ⓒ Ⓓ Ⓔ   55 Ⓐ Ⓑ Ⓒ Ⓓ Ⓔ   85 Ⓐ Ⓑ Ⓒ Ⓓ Ⓔ
26 Ⓐ Ⓑ Ⓒ Ⓓ Ⓔ   56 Ⓐ Ⓑ Ⓒ Ⓓ Ⓔ   86 Ⓐ Ⓑ Ⓒ Ⓓ Ⓔ
27 Ⓐ Ⓑ Ⓒ Ⓓ Ⓔ   57 Ⓐ Ⓑ Ⓒ Ⓓ Ⓔ   87 Ⓐ Ⓑ Ⓒ Ⓓ Ⓔ
28 Ⓐ Ⓑ Ⓒ Ⓓ Ⓔ   58 Ⓐ Ⓑ Ⓒ Ⓓ Ⓔ   88 Ⓐ Ⓑ Ⓒ Ⓓ Ⓔ
29 Ⓐ Ⓑ Ⓒ Ⓓ Ⓔ   59 Ⓐ Ⓑ Ⓒ Ⓓ Ⓔ
30 Ⓐ Ⓑ Ⓒ Ⓓ Ⓔ   60 Ⓐ Ⓑ Ⓒ Ⓓ Ⓔ

Practice Test 2

PART A—ADDRESS CHECKING

WORK—*6 minutes*

In this test you are to decide whether two addresses are alike or different. If the two addresses are *exactly alike*, in every way, darken space Ⓐ. If they are *different in any way*, darken space Ⓓ.

Mark your answers on the Answer Sheet for Address Checking at the beginning of this chapter. Tear it out, put today's date on it, and place it next to the questions.

Allow yourself *exactly 6 minutes* to do as many of the 95 questions as you can. If you finish before the time is up, re-check your answers.

1.	96 Malapai Dr	96 Malapai Dr
2.	298 Kappa Ave S	298 Kappa St S
3.	627 N Doneny Dr	627 N Doneny Dr
4.	Belleville IL 62225	Belleview IL 62225
5.	9614 Manzanita Dr W	9614 Manzanida Dr W
6.	84 Mills	84 Mills
7.	4312 La Cienega Blvd S	4312 La Cienega Blvd S
8.	9921 Franciville Coal Mine Rd	9921 Franciville Coal Mine Rd
9.	62 Mac Arthur Pl	62 Mac Arthur Pl
10.	942 Park Lake Dr	942 Park Lawn Dr
11.	1656 Qualla Ct	1656 Quaila Ct
12.	4299 Grandview Rd	4299 Grandview Rd
13.	5457 Racquet Ct N	5457 Racquet Ct N
14.	913 Oak Ln	913 Oak Ln
15.	48 Toluca Lake Ave	48 Toluca Lake Ave
16.	264 Panatela Pky	264 Patanela Pky
17.	3617 Yorkton Dr NW	3617 Yorktown Dr NW
18.	9203 S University Ave	9230 S University Ave
19.	257 S Wakefield Dr	257 Wakefield Dr

20.	3032 Heather Ln	3032 Heather Ln
21.	3901 Alanda Pl NE	3901 Alanda Pl NW
22.	Rockville MD 20850	Rockville MT 20850
23.	1445 London Village Pky NW	1445 London Village Pky NW
24.	55 Maytor Pl	55 Maytor Pl
25.	9704 E 1st Pl	9704 E 1st Ct
26.	131 Lord Baranof Dr	131 Lord Baronof Dr
27.	3449 Lee Rd	3449 Lea Rd
28.	1489 79 Ave N	1487 79 Ave E
29.	2216 Finley Blvd	2216 Finley Blvd
30.	93 Goldcrest Way SW	93 Goldcrest Way SW
31.	3751 S Zeigler Ln	3751 S Zeigler Ln
32.	674 Saint James Ct	674 Saint Janes Ct
33.	784 El Roble Ln	784 El Ruble Ln
34.	Yerington NV	Yerington NV
35.	9 S Jokake St	9 S Jokake St
36.	8312 Olive St S	8312 Olive St S
37.	3134 Cedar Ave SW	3134 Cedar Ave SW
38.	5696 E Hazelwood St	5696 E Hazelton St
39.	Worcester MA 01608	Worcester MA 01608
40.	16893 North Dakota Dr E	16839 North Dakota Dr E
41.	132 Highland Gorge Dr	132 Highland Gorge Dr
42.	6041 E Talladega Dr	6041 E Talladega Dr
43.	578 Cielo Dr	578 Cielo Pl
44.	814 Tally-Ho Trl	814 Tally-Ho Ave
45.	2774 Bar X Rd	2774 Bar X Rd
46.	Missoula MT 59803	Missoula MT 59903
47.	5742 31st St SW	5742 31st Ln SW
48.	818 N Van Buren St	818 N Van Buren St
49.	Pierce GA 31518	Pierce CA 31518
50.	704 Valley View Crest	704 Valley View Crest
51.	3403 N San Fernando Blvd	3403 N San Fernando Blvd
52.	47 Englisa Knoll St	47 Englisa Knoll St
53.	7935 Nebrina Pl	7935 Nedrina Pl
54.	69 McCarrey St	69 McGarrey St
55.	842 N Reese Pl	842 N Reise Pl
56.	9350 Wollaston Rd S	9350 Wolliston Rd S
57.	9781 8th Ave E	9781 8th Ave W
58.	1012 Verbena Dr W	1072 Verbena Dr W
59.	89 Ferrari Dr W	89 Ferrari Dr W
60.	545 Indian Springs Ln	545 Indian Springs Ln
61.	83 E Allen	83 E Allen
62.	3462 Queens Ct	3462 Queens Ct
63.	5942 Dartmoor Rd N	5942 Dartmouth Rd N
64.	843 Olson St	843 Olson St
65.	4142 Beeson Dr	4142 Beeson Dr

66.	Drewsey OR	Drevsey OR
67.	328 Flower Cir N	328 Flower Cir N
68.	42 Canyon Crest Cir	42 Canyon Crest Cir
69.	3524 Johan St SW	3524 Johana St SW
70.	Covington KY 41018	Covington KY 41081
71.	12414 S Kosh	12414 S Kosh
72.	4339 Buena Terra Way E	4339 Buena Terra Way E
73.	163 38th Ave E	163 38th Ave E
74.	6589 Chesterfield Pl NW	6588 Chesterfield Pl NW
75.	649 Damon Cir	649 Damon Ct
76.	84 South Calusa Club Dr	84 South Caluso Club Dr
77.	702 Norman St Ext	702 Morman St Ext
78.	6649 Uclan Dr W	6639 Uclan Dr W
79.	8989 Olympic Blvd	8989 Olympia Blvd
80.	7172 Upper Pike Creek Rd	7172 Upper Pike Creek Ct
81.	5901 Stough Park Rd	5901 Stough Park Rd
82.	Saint Paul MN 55116	Saint Paul MI 55116
83.	Elkhart IN 46517	Elkhart IN 46517
84.	Lake Charles LA 70701	Lake Charles LA 70601
85.	5052 Lake Shore Ter	5052 Lake Shore Trl
86.	4010 Brentwood Dr	4010 Brentwood Dr
87.	2324 Eugie Ave W	2432 Eugie Ave W
88.	126 Abemarle Dr	126 Abemarle Dr
89.	Chickensaw MD	Chickensaw MA
90.	Maricopa AZ	Maricopa AL
91.	9234 Gloaming Way NE	9234 Gloawing Way NE
92.	5693 John Wesley Cir	6593 John Wesley Cir
93.	815 Via Rimini	815 Via Romini
94.	97 Old Muldoon Rd	97 Old Nuldoon Rd
95.	3203 Iredell Ave SE	3203 Irebell Ave SE

STOP.

**If you finish before the time is up, go back
and check the questions in this section of the
test only.**

PART B—MEMORY FOR ADDRESSES

In this test you will have five boxes labeled A, B, C, D, and E. Each box contains five addresses. Three of the five are groups of street addresses, like 5400–6199 Finch, 2700–2999 Spooner, and 2900–3299 Lyle; and two are names of places. They are different in each box.

You will also be given two lists of addresses. You will have to decide in which box each address belongs. When you are working on the first list, you will have the boxes with the addresses *in front* of you. (It's a kind of warm-up trial test.) When you are working on the second list, you will *not* be able to look at the boxes. (The second list is the *real* test.)

SAMPLES

A	B	C	D	E
4600-4799 Finch	6200-6599 Finch	5400-6199 Finch	4800-5399 Finch	6600-6899 Finch
Drexel	Custer	Overton	Wheeler	Haven
1800-2699 Spooner	3000-3399 Spooner	3400-3799 Spooner	2700-2999 Spooner	3800-4199 Spooner
Estes	Scully	Negrin	India	Cole
2200-2599 Lyle	2900-3299 Lyle	2600-2899 Lyle	4100-4799 Lyle	3300-4099 Lyle

Questions 1 through 7 show the way the questions look. You have to decide in which lettered box (A, B, C, D, or E) the address belongs and then mark that answer grid.

1. 1800–2699 Spooner   1 Ⓐ Ⓑ Ⓒ Ⓓ Ⓔ
2. Wheeler   2 Ⓐ Ⓑ Ⓒ Ⓓ Ⓔ
3. 3000–3399 Spooner   3 Ⓐ Ⓑ Ⓒ Ⓓ Ⓔ
4. India   4 Ⓐ Ⓑ Ⓒ Ⓓ Ⓔ
5. 5400–6199 Finch   5 Ⓐ Ⓑ Ⓒ Ⓓ Ⓔ
6. Haven   6 Ⓐ Ⓑ Ⓒ Ⓓ Ⓔ
7. 2200–2599 Lyle   7 Ⓐ Ⓑ Ⓒ Ⓓ Ⓔ

Answers

1. A   3. B   5. C   7. A
2. D   4. D   6. E

STUDY—*3 minutes*

You will now have *3 minutes to spend memorizing the addresses in the boxes.* These are the addresses that will be on the test. Try to learn as many as you can. When the 3 minutes are up, go to page 159 to begin your practice test.

List 1

WORK—*3 minutes*

Tear out the Answer Sheet for this section of the test. For each question, mark the answer sheet to show the letter of the box in which the address belongs. Try to remember the location of as many addresses as you can. *You will now have 3 minutes to complete List 1*. If you are not sure of an answer, you should guess.

A	B	C	D	E
4600-4799 Finch Drexel 1800-2699 Spooner Estes 2200-2599 Lyle	6200-6599 Finch Custer 3000-3399 Spooner Scully 2900-3299 Lyle	5400-6199 Finch Overton 3400-3799 Spooner Negrin 2600-2899 Lyle	4800-5399 Finch Wheeler 2700-2999 Spooner India 4100-4799 Lyle	6600-6899 Finch Haven 3800-4199 Spooner Cole 3300-4099 Lyle

1. 2900–3299 Lyle
2. Cole
3. 4600–4799 Finch
4. 4100–4799 Lyle
5. 2700–2999 Spooner
6. Scully
7. 4800–5399 Finch
8. Wheeler
9. 5400–6199 Finch
10. Estes
11. 2600–2899 Lyle
12. India
13. Drexel
14. 3400–3799 Spooner
15. Overton
16. 2200–2599 Lyle
17. 1800–2699 Spooner
18. 5400–6199 Finch
19. Negrin
20. Haven
21. 3300–4099 Lyle
22. Custer
23. 3300–4099 Lyle
24. Wheeler
25. 1800–2699 Spooner
26. Overton
27. 6600–6899 Finch
28. 2200–2599 Lyle
29. Haven
30. 2600–2899 Lyle

31. Estes
32. 5400–6199 Finch
33. 2700–2999 Spooner
34. Overton
35. 4100–4799 Lyle
36. 4800–5399 Finch
37. 3800–4199 Spooner
38. Drexel
39. 2200–2599 Lyle
40. 6200–6599 Finch
41. India
42. 2900–3299 Lyle
43. 4800–5399 Finch
44. Scully
45. 3000–3399 Spooner
46. 3300–4099 Lyle
47. 4800–5399 Finch
48. Wheeler
49. 4100–4799 Lyle
50. 1800–2699 Spooner
51. 2600–2899 Lyle
52. Custer
53. 3400–3799 Spooner
54. 6200–6599 Finch
55. Drexel
56. 2900–3299 Lyle
57. Negrin
58. 6600–6899 Finch
59. 3800–4199 Spooner
60. Estes

61. Cole
62. 3000–3399 Spooner
63. Haven
64. 1800–2699 Spooner
65. India
66. 6600–6899 Finch
67. Wheeler
68. 3400–3799 Spooner
69. 4600–4799 Finch
70. 3000–3399 Spooner
71. Overton
72. Negrin
73. 6200–6599 Finch
74. India
75. 2700–2999 Spooner
76. Cole
77. Custer
78. 2200–2599 Lyle
79. 3800–4199 Spooner
80. Drexel
81. Custer
82. 4100–4799 Lyle
83. Negrin
84. 3400–3799 Spooner
85. 4600–4799 Finch
86. 2700–2999 Spooner
87. Scully
88. 4600–4799 Finch

STOP.

If you finish before the time is up, go back and check the questions in this section of the test only.

List 2

STUDY—5 minutes

You are now about to take the test using List 2. (*This is the test that counts!*)
    Turn back to the first page of Part B of this test and study the boxes again. You have *5 minutes to restudy the addresses*. When the time is up, tear out the Answer Sheet for List 2. Use it for this test.

WORK—5 minutes

For each question, mark the Answer Sheet to show the letter of the box in which the address belongs. You will have *exactly 5 minutes to do the test*. During the 5 minutes, do *not* turn to any other page.

1. Estes
2. 2900–3299 Lyle
3. 4800–5399 Finch
4. 2700–2999 Spooner
5. Haven
6. 4600–4799 Finch
7. Scully
8. 6200–6599 Finch
9. Negrin
10. 3800–4199 Spooner
11. Overton
12. Drexel
13. 5400–6199 Finch
14. 3300–4099 Lyle
15. 1800–2699 Spooner
16. 4100–4799 Lyle
17. India
18. Custer
19. 6600–6899 Finch
20. 3000–3399 Spooner
21. 4600–4799 Finch
22. Cole
23. 2600–2899 Lyle
24. 3800–4199 Spooner
25. Custer
26. India
27. 1800–2699 Spooner
28. Wheeler
29. 4100–4799 Lyle
30. 3400–3799 Spooner
31. 2200–2599 Lyle
32. 1800–2699 Spooner
33. Overton
34. 2200–2599 Lyle
35. Scully
36. Drexel
37. 2700–2999 Spooner
38. Haven
39. 6600–6899 Finch
40. 3000–3399 Spooner
41. India
42. 6600–6899 Finch
43. 3400–3799 Spooner
44. Scully
45. 5400–6199 Finch
46. 1800–2699 Spooner
47. Negrin
48. Drexel
49. Cole
50. 3300–4099 Lyle
51. India
52. 2700–2999 Spooner
53. Wheeler
54. 2600–2899 Lyle
55. 4600–4799 Finch
56. Overton
57. 3000–3399 Spooner
58. 4800–5399 Finch
59. 2900–3299 Lyle
60. Cole
61. 4600–4799 Finch
62. 4100–4799 Lyle
63. 4800–5399 Finch
64. Wheeler
65. Custer
66. 2200–2599 Lyle
67. Overton
68. Estes
69. 3300–4099 Lyle
70. Haven
71. 5400–6199 Finch
72. Negrin
73. 2200–2599 Lyle
74. 6200–6599 Finch
75. Custer
76. Cole
77. 3800–4199 Spooner
78. Wheeler
79. 4800–5399 Finch
80. Negrin
81. 2900–3299 Lyle
82. Drexel
83. 6200–6599 Finch
84. Wheeler
85. 3400–3799 Spooner
86. 2600–2899 Lyle
87. 2700–2999 Spooner
88. Estes

END OF EXAMINATION.

**If you finish before the time is up, go back
and check the questions in this section of the
test only.**

ANSWER KEY

PART A—ADDRESS CHECKING

1.	A	25.	D	49.	D	73.	A
2.	D	26.	A	50.	A	74.	D
3.	A	27.	D	51.	A	75.	D
4.	D	28.	D	52.	A	76.	D
5.	D	29.	A	53.	D	77.	D
6.	A	30.	A	54.	D	78.	D
7.	A	31.	A	55.	D	79.	D
8.	A	32.	D	56.	D	80.	D
9.	A	33.	D	57.	D	81.	A
10.	D	34.	A	58.	D	82.	D
11.	D	35.	A	59.	A	83.	A
12.	A	36.	A	60.	A	84.	D
13.	A	37.	A	61.	A	85.	D
14.	A	38.	D	62.	A	86.	A
15.	A	39.	A	63.	D	87.	D
16.	D	40.	D	64.	A	88.	A
17.	D	41.	A	65.	A	89.	D
18.	D	42.	A	66.	D	90.	D
19.	D	43.	D	67.	A	91.	D
20.	A	44.	D	68.	A	92.	D
21.	D	45.	A	69.	D	93.	D
22.	D	46.	D	70.	D	94.	D
23.	A	47.	D	71.	A	95.	D
24.	A	48.	A	72.	A		

PART B—MEMORY FOR ADDRESSES

List 1

1.	B	17.	A	33.	D	49.	D
2.	E	18.	C	34.	C	50.	A
3.	A	19.	C	35.	D	51.	C
4.	D	20.	E	36.	D	52.	B
5.	D	21.	E	37.	E	53.	C
6.	B	22.	B	38.	A	54.	B
7.	D	23.	E	39.	A	55.	A
8.	D	24.	D	40.	B	56.	B
9.	C	25.	A	41.	D	57.	C
10.	A	26.	C	42.	B	58.	E
11.	C	27.	E	43.	D	59.	E
12.	D	28.	A	44.	B	60.	A
13.	A	29.	E	45.	B	61.	E
14.	C	30.	C	46.	E	62.	B
15.	C	31.	A	47.	D	63.	E
16.	A	32.	C	48.	D	64.	A

65.	D	71.	C	77.	B	83.	C
66.	E	72.	C	78.	A	84.	C
67.	D	73.	B	79.	E	85.	A
68.	C	74.	D	80.	A	86.	D
69.	A	75.	D	81.	B	87.	B
70.	B	76.	E	82.	D	88.	A

List 2

1.	A	23.	C	45.	C	67.	C
2.	B	24.	E	46.	A	68.	A
3.	D	25.	B	47.	C	69.	E
4.	D	26.	D	48.	A	70.	E
5.	E	27.	A	49.	E	71.	C
6.	A	28.	D	50.	E	72.	C
7.	B	29.	D	51.	D	73.	A
8.	B	30.	C	52.	D	74.	B
9.	C	31.	A	53.	D	75.	B
10.	E	32.	A	54.	C	76.	E
11.	C	33.	C	55.	A	77.	E
12.	A	34.	A	56.	C	78.	D
13.	C	35.	B	57.	B	79.	D
14.	E	36.	A	58.	D	80.	C
15.	A	37.	D	59.	B	81.	B
16.	D	38.	E	60.	E	82.	A
17.	D	39.	E	61.	A	83.	B
18.	B	40.	B	62.	D	84.	D
19.	E	41.	D	63.	D	85.	C
20.	B	42.	E	64.	D	86.	C
21.	A	43.	C	65.	B	87.	D
22.	E	44.	B	66.	A	88.	A

EVALUATING YOUR PROGRESS

PART A

Computing Your Score

Check your answers against the Answer Key. Score yourself by using this formula:

Number right
− Number wrong
YOUR SCORE

For example, if you completed 52 questions and got 8 wrong,

Number right 44
− Number wrong ..... − 8
YOUR SCORE = 36

Notice that you do *not* figure in the questions that you did not answer.

Guidelines

How good is the score you just made?

52 or higher .... Good
Between 32 and 52 ...... Fair
Below 32 .... You need to improve

These are commonly accepted figures. We believe, however, that you should not be satisfied with anything *less* than 52. Our experience in training many people to prepare for this test shows that most serious test candidates who use the preparation program described in this book will be able to raise their score to the upper sixties and seventies.

Personal Progress Record

As was mentioned before, one of the most satisfying things that can happen while you are working toward a goal is to see signs of progress. The improvement you make on Address Checking can readily be seen by examining the scores you make on the practice tests and exercises in this book. We think that keeping track of your growing skill is so important that a Personal Progress Record has been furnished for your use on page 231.

A sample of this Personal Progress Record may be found on the next page in order to familiarize you with it. The entries on this sample are based on the example above.

Personal Progress Record—Sample

ADDRESS CHECKING										
		Initial Tests					Repeated Tests			
Date	Test	Number Completed	Number Correct	−	Number Wrong	= Score	Date	Score	Date	Score
5/15	Diagnostic Practice Test	52	44	−	8	= 36				
5/16	Practice Test 1	64	54	−	10	= 44				
5/18	Practice Test 2	66	57	−	9	= 48				
5/20	Practice Test 3	70	60	−	10	= 50				
	Practice Test 4			−		=				
	Practice Test 5			−		=				

Now turn to page 231. Look at the table entitled "Personal Progress Record—Address Checking." Make the proper entries on the line for Practice Test 2 which you just took. Review the special techniques in Chapter 3 on Address Checking before taking Practice Test 3. After taking the additional practice tests, enter the results immediately. Keep this record. It will help you record your progress.

PART B

Computing Your Score

Check the answers on your answer sheet against the Answer Key. Calculate your score by using these four steps:

1. Enter the number of answers you got right ...._____
2. Enter the number of answers you got wrong ...._____
3. Divide the number wrong by 4 (or multiply by ¼) .... −_____
4. Subtract Line 3 from Line 1....................YOUR SCORE =_____

Follow this example to make sure that you have figured your score correctly. We will assume that you completed 32 questions, of which you got 24 right and 8 wrong.

Line 1.......Number right................... 24
Line 2.......Number wrong.............. 8
Line 3.......¼ of line 2 = ¼ × 8... −2
Line 4.......24 − 2....YOUR SCORE = 22

Notice that just as for Address Checking, questions that are not answered are *not* taken into account.

Guidelines

How good is the score you just made?

> 44 or more ....Good
> 26 to 43 ....Fair
> 25 or less ....You need to improve

If your score on this test was low, don't be discouraged. Nevertheless, you may wish to review the chapters offering special techniques for handling "Memory for Addresses" before taking Practice Test 3.

Personal Progress Record

Turn to page 231. Look at the table entitled "Personal Progress—Memory for Addresses." Keep a permanent record of your scores on the practice tests, as you have been doing. A sample is printed below to familiarize you with it. The entries are based on the preceding example.

Personal Progress Record—Sample

		Initial Tests							Repeated Tests			
					MEMORY FOR ADDRESSES							
Date	Test	Number Completed	Number Correct **A**	Number Wrong	$\times$ ¼ $=$	Points off **B**	Score **(A − B)**		Date	Score	Date	Score
5/15	Diagnostic Practice Test	32	24	8	$\times$ ¼ $=$	2	22					
5/16	Practice Test 1	46	38	8	$\times$ ¼ $=$	2	36					
5/18	Practice Test 2	58	52	6	$\times$ ¼ $=$	1½	50½					
5/20	Practice Test 3	64	60	4	$\times$ ¼ $=$	1	59					
	Practice Test 4				$\times$ ¼ $=$							
	Practice Test 5				$\times$ ¼ $=$							

Make the proper entries on the record for Practice Test 2 that you just took. Use it to keep a record of the additional practice tests you take. You should be pleasantly surprised at how much higher your next entry on this card will be.

DIAGNOSTIC CHART

PART A—ADDRESS CHECKING

Type of Difference	"D" Questions	"D" Questions Wrong		
		TRIAL 1	TRIAL 2	TRIAL 3
Numbers: transposed	18, 40, 84, 87, 92			
changed	28, 46, 58, 70, 74, 78			
omitted				
Directions	19, 21, 57			
Abbreviations: streets, roads, avenues, etc.	2, 25, 43, 44, 47, 75, 80, 85			
states	22, 49, 82, 89, 90			
Spelling: single letters	5, 11, 27, 32, 33, 53, 54, 55, 56, 66, 69, 76, 77, 79, 91, 93, 94, 95			
groups of letters	4, 10, 16, 17, 38, 63			
Total Number of Each Type	51			
	Use the columns on the right to enter the question numbers of those "A" you marked "D"			

This chart will help you to pinpoint the kinds of errors you have made on this Practice Test. Use it as directed below after you have taken and marked the test.

The first column on the left, "Type of Difference," contains the same categories whereby addresses may differ shown on page 30 in Chapter 2. On the same line across, the second column gives the number of the questions that fall within each category. In the third column, you are to enter the number of the questions you had wrong. Do not include those you did not do. Use the space indicated in this column to list the number of any "A" questions you answered as "D." Checking these addresses may reveal a problem on which you will want to work.

After you have made all the entries, you will be able to see the areas in which you need to improve. Then turn to the appropriate part of Chapter 3,

Address Checking: How to Improve Your Score, and re-read it. Then repeat those drills that can help. For example, if you find you have been making too many errors picking out number differences, read pages 38 to 40 and do Drills 18 through 21. If you have a problem with single letters because of reversals like *b* and *d*, or if you have been overlooking the difference between *a*, *e*, and *o*, read pages 38 to 40. Examine the table on page 49 and work on Drills 10 and 11 if the problem persists.

Remember that this chart is designed for diagnostic purposes and guidance on further practice. It has been drawn so that you can enter the results each time you retake a Practice Test. In this way you will be able to see how you are progressing. It is not necessary to try to score it. That is best done by using the Personal Progress Record Card.

PART B—MEMORY FOR ADDRESSES

Kind of Address		Number of Questions	Number Wrong		
			TRIAL 1	TRIAL 2	TRIAL 3
Direct:					
	list 1	40			
	list 2	40			
Numbered:					
	list 1	48			
	list 2	48			

The purpose of this chart is to help you evaluate your performance on the two kinds of memory questions that appear in the Practice Test—the questions on the direct (name) addresses and the questions on the numbered addresses. Use it as directed below after you have taken and marked the entire test.

The first column on the left, "Kind of Address," is divided by category into "Direct Address" versus "Numbered Address." The second column gives the number of questions in each category. Use the third column to enter the total number of questions in each category that you answered incorrectly. There is room for you to make additional entries if you take the Practice Test more than once.

At a glance, you will be able to see which area you need to concentrate on and how well you are progressing as you take repeat trials. Use Chapter 4 and the drills in it to improve your memory for the direct addresses. Use Chapter 5 for the numbered addresses.

Remember to use the Personal Progress Record Card (Memory for Addresses) to keep track of your actual scores as you keep studying and practicing.

ANSWER SHEET—PRACTICE TEST 3

PART A—ADDRESS CHECKING   DATE _____

1 Ⓐ Ⓓ	25 Ⓐ Ⓓ	49 Ⓐ Ⓓ	73 Ⓐ Ⓓ
2 Ⓐ Ⓓ	26 Ⓐ Ⓓ	50 Ⓐ Ⓓ	74 Ⓐ Ⓓ
3 Ⓐ Ⓓ	27 Ⓐ Ⓓ	51 Ⓐ Ⓓ	75 Ⓐ Ⓓ
4 Ⓐ Ⓓ	28 Ⓐ Ⓓ	52 Ⓐ Ⓓ	76 Ⓐ Ⓓ
5 Ⓐ Ⓓ	29 Ⓐ Ⓓ	53 Ⓐ Ⓓ	77 Ⓐ Ⓓ
6 Ⓐ Ⓓ	30 Ⓐ Ⓓ	54 Ⓐ Ⓓ	78 Ⓐ Ⓓ
7 Ⓐ Ⓓ	31 Ⓐ Ⓓ	55 Ⓐ Ⓓ	79 Ⓐ Ⓓ
8 Ⓐ Ⓓ	32 Ⓐ Ⓓ	56 Ⓐ Ⓓ	80 Ⓐ Ⓓ
9 Ⓐ Ⓓ	33 Ⓐ Ⓓ	57 Ⓐ Ⓓ	81 Ⓐ Ⓓ
10 Ⓐ Ⓓ	34 Ⓐ Ⓓ	58 Ⓐ Ⓓ	82 Ⓐ Ⓓ
11 Ⓐ Ⓓ	35 Ⓐ Ⓓ	59 Ⓐ Ⓓ	83 Ⓐ Ⓓ
12 Ⓐ Ⓓ	36 Ⓐ Ⓓ	60 Ⓐ Ⓓ	84 Ⓐ Ⓓ
13 Ⓐ Ⓓ	37 Ⓐ Ⓓ	61 Ⓐ Ⓓ	85 Ⓐ Ⓓ
14 Ⓐ Ⓓ	38 Ⓐ Ⓓ	62 Ⓐ Ⓓ	86 Ⓐ Ⓓ
15 Ⓐ Ⓓ	39 Ⓐ Ⓓ	63 Ⓐ Ⓓ	87 Ⓐ Ⓓ
16 Ⓐ Ⓓ	40 Ⓐ Ⓓ	64 Ⓐ Ⓓ	88 Ⓐ Ⓓ
17 Ⓐ Ⓓ	41 Ⓐ Ⓓ	65 Ⓐ Ⓓ	89 Ⓐ Ⓓ
18 Ⓐ Ⓓ	42 Ⓐ Ⓓ	66 Ⓐ Ⓓ	90 Ⓐ Ⓓ
19 Ⓐ Ⓓ	43 Ⓐ Ⓓ	67 Ⓐ Ⓓ	91 Ⓐ Ⓓ
20 Ⓐ Ⓓ	44 Ⓐ Ⓓ	68 Ⓐ Ⓓ	92 Ⓐ Ⓓ
21 Ⓐ Ⓓ	45 Ⓐ Ⓓ	69 Ⓐ Ⓓ	93 Ⓐ Ⓓ
22 Ⓐ Ⓓ	46 Ⓐ Ⓓ	70 Ⓐ Ⓓ	94 Ⓐ Ⓓ
23 Ⓐ Ⓓ	47 Ⓐ Ⓓ	71 Ⓐ Ⓓ	95 Ⓐ Ⓓ
24 Ⓐ Ⓓ	48 Ⓐ Ⓓ	72 Ⓐ Ⓓ	

ANSWER SHEET—PRACTICE TEST 3

PART B—MEMORY FOR ADDRESSES
LIST 1   DATE _____

1 Ⓐ Ⓑ Ⓒ Ⓓ Ⓔ	31 Ⓐ Ⓑ Ⓒ Ⓓ Ⓔ	61 Ⓐ Ⓑ Ⓒ Ⓓ Ⓔ
2 Ⓐ Ⓑ Ⓒ Ⓓ Ⓔ	32 Ⓐ Ⓑ Ⓒ Ⓓ Ⓔ	62 Ⓐ Ⓑ Ⓒ Ⓓ Ⓔ
3 Ⓐ Ⓑ Ⓒ Ⓓ Ⓔ	33 Ⓐ Ⓑ Ⓒ Ⓓ Ⓔ	63 Ⓐ Ⓑ Ⓒ Ⓓ Ⓔ
4 Ⓐ Ⓑ Ⓒ Ⓓ Ⓔ	34 Ⓐ Ⓑ Ⓒ Ⓓ Ⓔ	64 Ⓐ Ⓑ Ⓒ Ⓓ Ⓔ
5 Ⓐ Ⓑ Ⓒ Ⓓ Ⓔ	35 Ⓐ Ⓑ Ⓒ Ⓓ Ⓔ	65 Ⓐ Ⓑ Ⓒ Ⓓ Ⓔ
6 Ⓐ Ⓑ Ⓒ Ⓓ Ⓔ	36 Ⓐ Ⓑ Ⓒ Ⓓ Ⓔ	66 Ⓐ Ⓑ Ⓒ Ⓓ Ⓔ
7 Ⓐ Ⓑ Ⓒ Ⓓ Ⓔ	37 Ⓐ Ⓑ Ⓒ Ⓓ Ⓔ	67 Ⓐ Ⓑ Ⓒ Ⓓ Ⓔ
8 Ⓐ Ⓑ Ⓒ Ⓓ Ⓔ	38 Ⓐ Ⓑ Ⓒ Ⓓ Ⓔ	68 Ⓐ Ⓑ Ⓒ Ⓓ Ⓔ
9 Ⓐ Ⓑ Ⓒ Ⓓ Ⓔ	39 Ⓐ Ⓑ Ⓒ Ⓓ Ⓔ	69 Ⓐ Ⓑ Ⓒ Ⓓ Ⓔ
10 Ⓐ Ⓑ Ⓒ Ⓓ Ⓔ	40 Ⓐ Ⓑ Ⓒ Ⓓ Ⓔ	70 Ⓐ Ⓑ Ⓒ Ⓓ Ⓔ
11 Ⓐ Ⓑ Ⓒ Ⓓ Ⓔ	41 Ⓐ Ⓑ Ⓒ Ⓓ Ⓔ	71 Ⓐ Ⓑ Ⓒ Ⓓ Ⓔ
12 Ⓐ Ⓑ Ⓒ Ⓓ Ⓔ	42 Ⓐ Ⓑ Ⓒ Ⓓ Ⓔ	72 Ⓐ Ⓑ Ⓒ Ⓓ Ⓔ
13 Ⓐ Ⓑ Ⓒ Ⓓ Ⓔ	43 Ⓐ Ⓑ Ⓒ Ⓓ Ⓔ	73 Ⓐ Ⓑ Ⓒ Ⓓ Ⓔ
14 Ⓐ Ⓑ Ⓒ Ⓓ Ⓔ	44 Ⓐ Ⓑ Ⓒ Ⓓ Ⓔ	74 Ⓐ Ⓑ Ⓒ Ⓓ Ⓔ
15 Ⓐ Ⓑ Ⓒ Ⓓ Ⓔ	45 Ⓐ Ⓑ Ⓒ Ⓓ Ⓔ	75 Ⓐ Ⓑ Ⓒ Ⓓ Ⓔ
16 Ⓐ Ⓑ Ⓒ Ⓓ Ⓔ	46 Ⓐ Ⓑ Ⓒ Ⓓ Ⓔ	76 Ⓐ Ⓑ Ⓒ Ⓓ Ⓔ
17 Ⓐ Ⓑ Ⓒ Ⓓ Ⓔ	47 Ⓐ Ⓑ Ⓒ Ⓓ Ⓔ	77 Ⓐ Ⓑ Ⓒ Ⓓ Ⓔ
18 Ⓐ Ⓑ Ⓒ Ⓓ Ⓔ	48 Ⓐ Ⓑ Ⓒ Ⓓ Ⓔ	78 Ⓐ Ⓑ Ⓒ Ⓓ Ⓔ
19 Ⓐ Ⓑ Ⓒ Ⓓ Ⓔ	49 Ⓐ Ⓑ Ⓒ Ⓓ Ⓔ	79 Ⓐ Ⓑ Ⓒ Ⓓ Ⓔ
20 Ⓐ Ⓑ Ⓒ Ⓓ Ⓔ	50 Ⓐ Ⓑ Ⓒ Ⓓ Ⓔ	80 Ⓐ Ⓑ Ⓒ Ⓓ Ⓔ
21 Ⓐ Ⓑ Ⓒ Ⓓ Ⓔ	51 Ⓐ Ⓑ Ⓒ Ⓓ Ⓔ	81 Ⓐ Ⓑ Ⓒ Ⓓ Ⓔ
22 Ⓐ Ⓑ Ⓒ Ⓓ Ⓔ	52 Ⓐ Ⓑ Ⓒ Ⓓ Ⓔ	82 Ⓐ Ⓑ Ⓒ Ⓓ Ⓔ
23 Ⓐ Ⓑ Ⓒ Ⓓ Ⓔ	53 Ⓐ Ⓑ Ⓒ Ⓓ Ⓔ	83 Ⓐ Ⓑ Ⓒ Ⓓ Ⓔ
24 Ⓐ Ⓑ Ⓒ Ⓓ Ⓔ	54 Ⓐ Ⓑ Ⓒ Ⓓ Ⓔ	84 Ⓐ Ⓑ Ⓒ Ⓓ Ⓔ
25 Ⓐ Ⓑ Ⓒ Ⓓ Ⓔ	55 Ⓐ Ⓑ Ⓒ Ⓓ Ⓔ	85 Ⓐ Ⓑ Ⓒ Ⓓ Ⓔ
26 Ⓐ Ⓑ Ⓒ Ⓓ Ⓔ	56 Ⓐ Ⓑ Ⓒ Ⓓ Ⓔ	86 Ⓐ Ⓑ Ⓒ Ⓓ Ⓔ
27 Ⓐ Ⓑ Ⓒ Ⓓ Ⓔ	57 Ⓐ Ⓑ Ⓒ Ⓓ Ⓔ	87 Ⓐ Ⓑ Ⓒ Ⓓ Ⓔ
28 Ⓐ Ⓑ Ⓒ Ⓓ Ⓔ	58 Ⓐ Ⓑ Ⓒ Ⓓ Ⓔ	88 Ⓐ Ⓑ Ⓒ Ⓓ Ⓔ
29 Ⓐ Ⓑ Ⓒ Ⓓ Ⓔ	59 Ⓐ Ⓑ Ⓒ Ⓓ Ⓔ	
30 Ⓐ Ⓑ Ⓒ Ⓓ Ⓔ	60 Ⓐ Ⓑ Ⓒ Ⓓ Ⓔ	

ANSWER SHEET—PRACTICE TEST 3

PART B—MEMORY FOR ADDRESSES
LIST 2   DATE _____

1 Ⓐ Ⓑ Ⓒ Ⓓ Ⓔ	31 Ⓐ Ⓑ Ⓒ Ⓓ Ⓔ	61 Ⓐ Ⓑ Ⓒ Ⓓ Ⓔ
2 Ⓐ Ⓑ Ⓒ Ⓓ Ⓔ	32 Ⓐ Ⓑ Ⓒ Ⓓ Ⓔ	62 Ⓐ Ⓑ Ⓒ Ⓓ Ⓔ
3 Ⓐ Ⓑ Ⓒ Ⓓ Ⓔ	33 Ⓐ Ⓑ Ⓒ Ⓓ Ⓔ	63 Ⓐ Ⓑ Ⓒ Ⓓ Ⓔ
4 Ⓐ Ⓑ Ⓒ Ⓓ Ⓔ	34 Ⓐ Ⓑ Ⓒ Ⓓ Ⓔ	64 Ⓐ Ⓑ Ⓒ Ⓓ Ⓔ
5 Ⓐ Ⓑ Ⓒ Ⓓ Ⓔ	35 Ⓐ Ⓑ Ⓒ Ⓓ Ⓔ	65 Ⓐ Ⓑ Ⓒ Ⓓ Ⓔ
6 Ⓐ Ⓑ Ⓒ Ⓓ Ⓔ	36 Ⓐ Ⓑ Ⓒ Ⓓ Ⓔ	66 Ⓐ Ⓑ Ⓒ Ⓓ Ⓔ
7 Ⓐ Ⓑ Ⓒ Ⓓ Ⓔ	37 Ⓐ Ⓑ Ⓒ Ⓓ Ⓔ	67 Ⓐ Ⓑ Ⓒ Ⓓ Ⓔ
8 Ⓐ Ⓑ Ⓒ Ⓓ Ⓔ	38 Ⓐ Ⓑ Ⓒ Ⓓ Ⓔ	68 Ⓐ Ⓑ Ⓒ Ⓓ Ⓔ
9 Ⓐ Ⓑ Ⓒ Ⓓ Ⓔ	39 Ⓐ Ⓑ Ⓒ Ⓓ Ⓔ	69 Ⓐ Ⓑ Ⓒ Ⓓ Ⓔ
10 Ⓐ Ⓑ Ⓒ Ⓓ Ⓔ	40 Ⓐ Ⓑ Ⓒ Ⓓ Ⓔ	70 Ⓐ Ⓑ Ⓒ Ⓓ Ⓔ
11 Ⓐ Ⓑ Ⓒ Ⓓ Ⓔ	41 Ⓐ Ⓑ Ⓒ Ⓓ Ⓔ	71 Ⓐ Ⓑ Ⓒ Ⓓ Ⓔ
12 Ⓐ Ⓑ Ⓒ Ⓓ Ⓔ	42 Ⓐ Ⓑ Ⓒ Ⓓ Ⓔ	72 Ⓐ Ⓑ Ⓒ Ⓓ Ⓔ
13 Ⓐ Ⓑ Ⓒ Ⓓ Ⓔ	43 Ⓐ Ⓑ Ⓒ Ⓓ Ⓔ	73 Ⓐ Ⓑ Ⓒ Ⓓ Ⓔ
14 Ⓐ Ⓑ Ⓒ Ⓓ Ⓔ	44 Ⓐ Ⓑ Ⓒ Ⓓ Ⓔ	74 Ⓐ Ⓑ Ⓒ Ⓓ Ⓔ
15 Ⓐ Ⓑ Ⓒ Ⓓ Ⓔ	45 Ⓐ Ⓑ Ⓒ Ⓓ Ⓔ	75 Ⓐ Ⓑ Ⓒ Ⓓ Ⓔ
16 Ⓐ Ⓑ Ⓒ Ⓓ Ⓔ	46 Ⓐ Ⓑ Ⓒ Ⓓ Ⓔ	76 Ⓐ Ⓑ Ⓒ Ⓓ Ⓔ
17 Ⓐ Ⓑ Ⓒ Ⓓ Ⓔ	47 Ⓐ Ⓑ Ⓒ Ⓓ Ⓔ	77 Ⓐ Ⓑ Ⓒ Ⓓ Ⓔ
18 Ⓐ Ⓑ Ⓒ Ⓓ Ⓔ	48 Ⓐ Ⓑ Ⓒ Ⓓ Ⓔ	78 Ⓐ Ⓑ Ⓒ Ⓓ Ⓔ
19 Ⓐ Ⓑ Ⓒ Ⓓ Ⓔ	49 Ⓐ Ⓑ Ⓒ Ⓓ Ⓔ	79 Ⓐ Ⓑ Ⓒ Ⓓ Ⓔ
20 Ⓐ Ⓑ Ⓒ Ⓓ Ⓔ	50 Ⓐ Ⓑ Ⓒ Ⓓ Ⓔ	80 Ⓐ Ⓑ Ⓒ Ⓓ Ⓔ
21 Ⓐ Ⓑ Ⓒ Ⓓ Ⓔ	51 Ⓐ Ⓑ Ⓒ Ⓓ Ⓔ	81 Ⓐ Ⓑ Ⓒ Ⓓ Ⓔ
22 Ⓐ Ⓑ Ⓒ Ⓓ Ⓔ	52 Ⓐ Ⓑ Ⓒ Ⓓ Ⓔ	82 Ⓐ Ⓑ Ⓒ Ⓓ Ⓔ
23 Ⓐ Ⓑ Ⓒ Ⓓ Ⓔ	53 Ⓐ Ⓑ Ⓒ Ⓓ Ⓔ	83 Ⓐ Ⓑ Ⓒ Ⓓ Ⓔ
24 Ⓐ Ⓑ Ⓒ Ⓓ Ⓔ	54 Ⓐ Ⓑ Ⓒ Ⓓ Ⓔ	84 Ⓐ Ⓑ Ⓒ Ⓓ Ⓔ
25 Ⓐ Ⓑ Ⓒ Ⓓ Ⓔ	55 Ⓐ Ⓑ Ⓒ Ⓓ Ⓔ	85 Ⓐ Ⓑ Ⓒ Ⓓ Ⓔ
26 Ⓐ Ⓑ Ⓒ Ⓓ Ⓔ	56 Ⓐ Ⓑ Ⓒ Ⓓ Ⓔ	86 Ⓐ Ⓑ Ⓒ Ⓓ Ⓔ
27 Ⓐ Ⓑ Ⓒ Ⓓ Ⓔ	57 Ⓐ Ⓑ Ⓒ Ⓓ Ⓔ	87 Ⓐ Ⓑ Ⓒ Ⓓ Ⓔ
28 Ⓐ Ⓑ Ⓒ Ⓓ Ⓔ	58 Ⓐ Ⓑ Ⓒ Ⓓ Ⓔ	88 Ⓐ Ⓑ Ⓒ Ⓓ Ⓔ
29 Ⓐ Ⓑ Ⓒ Ⓓ Ⓔ	59 Ⓐ Ⓑ Ⓒ Ⓓ Ⓔ	
30 Ⓐ Ⓑ Ⓒ Ⓓ Ⓔ	60 Ⓐ Ⓑ Ⓒ Ⓓ Ⓔ	

Practice Test 3

THE LAST WORD

You now know that score improvements are possible and that the means to attain them lie in your hands. The study techniques for address checking and memorization of addresses are yours. You know they work. You have completed drills and practice tests to sharpen your skills. You have also completed special drills to help correct any areas of weakness, such as narrow eye span, regression, perception problems, etc. The strategies to use to make the most of your technique and skill have been prepared for you.

Also, by now you should be on your way to answering the test-taking questions posed in this book that are strictly personal:

- How fast should you go on the address checking questions to strike the balance between speed and accuracy that will yield the highest score?

- How should you divide your study time between the names and numbers?

- What method or combination of methods should you use to memorize the addresses in the boxes?

- How many addresses is it realistic for you to try to remember? Should you go for all 25, or are you better off concentrating on 16, 18, or 20?

As was noted before, it is important to come to the real test with your mind made up on these points.

There are three more full-scale practice tests to help you continue your exam preparation program. You may take them each more than once if you choose. Remember that the keys to skills improvement are knowledge and practice. Use the tests in this book to forge ahead. There is a good job waiting.

PRACTICE TEST 3

PART A—ADDRESS CHECKING

WORK—*6 minutes*

In this test you are to decide whether two addresses are alike or different. If the two addresses are *exactly alike in every way*, darken space Ⓐ. If they are *different in any way*, darken space Ⓓ.

Mark your answers on the Answer Sheet for Address Checking at the beginning of this chapter. Tear it out, put today's date on it, and place it next to the questions.

Allow yourself *exactly 6 minutes* to do as many of the 95 questions as you can. If you finish before the time is up, re-check your answers.

1.	Riverside CA	Riverside CO
2.	9006 Gage Center Cir	9060 Cage Center Cir
3.	3403 Lakeside Rd NW	3403 Lakeside Rd NW
4.	1734 E Alexandrine St	1734 E Alexandrine St
5.	2607 Maple Rd SE	2607 Mable Rd SE
6.	2323 18th St NE	2323 13th St NE
7.	7074 North Western Pky	7047 North Western Pky
8.	970 Harvard Sq	970 Harvard Ct
9.	6980 Montwood Ln	6890 Montwood Ln
10.	Sunflower MS 38778	Sunflower MS 38778
11.	515 Edmar Rd	515 Admar Rd
12.	3727 Imperial Woods Dr SW	3727 Imperial Woods Rd SW
13.	941 Rolf Ave	941 Rolf Ct
14.	3905 Renate Rd	3905 Renate Rd
15.	4600 Oak Lawn Rd	4600 Oak Lawn Rd
16.	Portland ME 04108	Portland ME 04018
17.	8612 Old Shepherdsville Rd	8612 Old Shepherdsville Rd
18.	95 Prentice St E	95 Prentice St E
19.	7432 Caffin Ave S	7432 Coffin Ave S
20.	2002 Grand Bayou Ln	2002 Grand Bayou Ln
21.	3715 Adams St SE	3715 Adams St NE
22.	6963 Fullerdale Ave	6963 Fullerdale Ave
23.	5837 White Oak Dr	5837 White Oak Dr
24.	10289 Hammond St	10289 Hammond St
25.	Whitesboro OK	Whitesboro OH
26.	4883 Bloomsbury St	4883 Bloomsburg St
27.	Wichita KS 67203	Wichita KS 67203
28.	57 Sheila Dr	57 Skeila Dr
29.	8409 Deckbar Ave NE	8409 Deckrab Ave NE
30.	4942 Woodward Hts E	4924 Woodward Hts E
31.	209 Valley Fair Way	209 Varley Fair Way
32.	7314 Edgewood Dr NE	7314 Edgeworth Dr NE
33.	3506 N Claireview St	3506 N Claireville St

34.	Rushsylvania OH 43347	Rushsylvania OH 43847
35.	8023 Sea Cove Rd	8023 Sea Cove Rd
36.	948 Washington St SE	948 Washington St SE
37.	42 Maplebrook Pky N	42 Maplebrook Pky N
38.	Saint Paul MN 55113	Saint Paul NM 55113
39.	5675 Zircon St	5765 Zircon St
40.	5998 Lakecrest Path N	5998 Lakecrest Path N
41.	8264 Queen Ct	8264 Queen St
42.	1412 Ingleside Ave SW	1412 Ingleside Ave SW
43.	7409 Parkdale Dr	7409 Parkdale Dr
44.	565 Zender Ln	565 Zender Ln
45.	3662 Westview St	3662 Westwood St
46.	Baton Rouge LA 70807	Baton Rouge LA 70870
47.	2794 Beacon Hill Rd	2794 Beacon Hill Rd
48.	98 Wainwright Cir E	98 Wainwright Cir W
49.	5999 Nevada Ave N	5999 Nevada Ave N
50.	Marquette NE	Marquette NH
51.	2401 Knollwood Dr NE	2401 Knollwood Dr NE
52.	174 W Lee St	174 W Lee Dr
53.	3019 Wentworth Dr	3109 Wentworth Dr
54.	Louisville KY 40504	Louisville KY 40504
55.	3039 Kearney Rd W	3039 Kearney Rd W
56.	9038 N Kossuth St	9038 E Kossuth St
57.	Forestdale PA	Forestdale PA
58.	Champaign IL	Champaign IN
59.	4417 Daniels Ave	4417 Daniels Ave
60.	15299 Highway K4 SW	15299 Highway P4 SW
61.	Litchfield Ct	Litchfield Ct
62.	7610 Russell St	7610 Russett St
63.	8768 E Ormond Ct	8768 E Ormont Ct
64.	5100 E Madeline St	5100 E Madeline St
65.	Gathersburg MD 20879	Gathersburg MD 20879
66.	4001 Virginia Ave	4001 Virginia Ave
67.	2104 Illinois Ave	2014 Illinois Ave
68.	1899 7 Mile Rd W	1899 7 Mile Rd W
69.	5713 Eastlawn St	5713 Eastland St
70.	16473 Fiarfield St	16493 Fairfield St
71.	7465 Navarre Pl	7465 Navarro Pl
72.	4817 W Yupon St	4817 W Yupon St
73.	4010 Saint Charles Ln	4010 Saint Charles Rd
74.	2908 Jane Rd	2908 Janet Rd
75.	6453 Twin Hill Rd	6543 Twin Hill Rd
76.	642 Quebec Pl	642 Quebec Pl
77.	5927 Carnahan Pl	5927 Caravan Pl
78.	1447 James Ave S	1474 James Ave S
79.	6203 North Riverview Ln	6203 North Riverview Ln

80.	6686 Dancaster Rd SW	6686 Dancaster Rd SW
81.	4019 King Oak Ter	4019 King Oak Ter
82.	17046 U.S. Highway 60	17046 U.S. Highway 60
83.	9431 Elysian Fields Ave	9431 Elysian Fields Ave
84.	6213 E Barrington Dr	6213 W Barrington Dr
85.	3491 New Island Ave	3491 New Island Ave
86.	94 N 9th Ave W	94 N 9th Ave W
87.	1740 Gray Haven Ct	1749 Gray Haven Ct
88.	4427 Normandale Highlands Dr	4427 Normandale Highlands Dr
89.	8904 N Hampson St	8904 N Hampton St
90.	3008 S Catherine St	3080 S Catherine St
91.	Venetia PA 15481	Vanetia PA 15481
92.	Lowell MA 01850	Lowell MO 01850
93.	5294 Pamela Ter	5294 Pamela Trl
94.	3734 Upper Darby Rd	3734 Upper Darby Rd
95.	1043 N Abington Ave	1043 N Apington Ave

STOP.

**If you finish before the time is up, go back
and check the questions in this section of the
test only.**

PART B—MEMORY FOR ADDRESSES

In this test you will have five boxes labeled A, B, C, D, and E. Each box contains five addresses. Three of the five are groups of street addresses, like 2700–2999 Park, 7600–7899 Canton, and 5900–6599 Dell; and two are names of places. They are different in each box.

You will also be given two lists of addresses. You will have to decide in which box each address belongs. When you are working on the first list, you will have the boxes with the addresses *in front* of you. It's a kind of warm-up trial test. When you are working on the second list, you will *not* be able to look at the boxes. The second list is the *real* test.

SAMPLES

A	B	C	D	E
2500-2699 Park Melba 7600-7899 Canton Weston 4000-4299 Dell	1600-2499 Park Angle 7000-7599 Canton Taylor 4300-4899 Dell	3000-3499 Park Boyd 5600-6199 Canton Ewing 4900-5699 Dell	3500-3899 Park Isabel 6200-6399 Canton Jiggetts 5900-6599 Dell	2700-2999 Park Laguna 6400-6999 Canton Spring 5700-5899 Dell

Questions 1 through 7 show the way the questions look. You have to decide in which lettered box (A, B, C, D, or E) the address belongs and then mark that answer in the answer grid.

1. 6200–6399 Canton   1 Ⓐ Ⓑ Ⓒ Ⓓ Ⓔ
2. Taylor   2 Ⓐ Ⓑ Ⓒ Ⓓ Ⓔ
3. 4000–4299 Dell   3 Ⓐ Ⓑ Ⓒ Ⓓ Ⓔ
4. Spring   4 Ⓐ Ⓑ Ⓒ Ⓓ Ⓔ
5. 2500–2699 Park   5 Ⓐ Ⓑ Ⓒ Ⓓ Ⓔ
6. Boyd   6 Ⓐ Ⓑ Ⓒ Ⓓ Ⓔ
7. 4300–4899 Dell   7 Ⓐ Ⓑ Ⓒ Ⓓ Ⓔ

Answers

1. D   3. A   5. A   7. B
2. B   4. E   6. C

STUDY—3 minutes

You will now have *3 minutes to spend memorizing the addresses in the boxes.* These are the addresses that will be on the test. Try to learn as many as you can. When the three minutes are up, turn to page 178 to begin your practice test.

List 1

WORK—*3 minutes*

Tear out the Answer Sheet for this section of the test. For each question, mark the answer sheet to show the letter of the box in which the address belongs. Try to remember the location of as many addresses as you can. *You will now have 3 minutes to complete List 1*. If you are not sure of an answer, you should guess.

A	B	C	D	E
2500-2699 Park Melba 7600-7899 Canton Weston 4000-4299 Dell	1600-2499 Park Angle 7000-7599 Canton Taylor 4300-4899 Dell	3000-3499 Park Boyd 5600-6199 Canton Ewing 4900-5699 Dell	3500-3899 Park Isabel 6200-6399 Canton Jiggetts 5900-6599 Dell	2700-2999 Park Laguna 6400-6999 Canton Spring 5700-5899 Dell

1. Weston
2. 5900–6599 Dell
3. Taylor
4. Angle
5. 4000–4299 Dell
6. 7600–7899 Canton
7. 2700–2999 Park
8. Spring
9. Isabel
10. 5700–5899 Dell
11. 7000–7599 Canton
12. 4300–4899 Dell
13. Ewing
14. 2500–2699 Park
15. 5900–6599 Dell
16. Taylor
17. 1600–2499 Park
18. Boyd
19. 5600–6199 Canton
20. Melba
21. 6200–6399 Canton
22. Laguna
23. 3500–3899 Park
24. Jiggetts
25. 7600–7899 Canton
26. 1600–2499 Park
27. Jiggetts
28. 4900–5699 Dell
29. Laguna
30. Boyd
31. Spring
32. Isabel
33. 7000–7599 Canton
34. Ewing
35. 5900–6599 Dell
36. 3500–3899 Park
37. Melba
38. Angle
39. 1600–2499 Park
40. Boyd
41. 3000–3499 Park
42. Isabel
43. 3000–3499 Park
44. 5700–5899 Dell
45. Boyd
46. 6200–6399 Canton
47. Weston
48. Ewing
49. Jiggetts
50. 6400–6999 Canton
51. Taylor
52. 1600–2499 Park
53. Angle
54. 2700–2999 Park

55. 7600–7899 Canton
56. Isabel
57. Melba
58. 5700–5899 Dell
59. 3500–3899 Park
60. Ewing
61. Laguna
62. 3000–3499 Park
63. 6200–6399 Canton
64. 4900–5600 Dell
65. Spring
66. 4300–4899 Dell
67. 2500–2699 Park
68. Weston
69. 7000–7599 Canton
70. 4000–4299 Dell
71. 6400–6999 Canton
72. Weston
73. Melba
74. Taylor
75. 4300–4899 Dell
76. 6200–6399 Canton
77. Laguna
78. Boyd
79. 4900–5600 Dell
80. Angle
81. 4900–5600 Dell
82. 5600–6199 Canton
83. Spring
84. 6400–6999 Canton
85. 2500–2699 Park
86. Jiggetts
87. 2700–2999 Park
88. 4000–4299 Dell

STOP.

**If you finish before the time is up, go back
and check the questions in this section of the
test only.**

180   **Practice Test 3**

List 2

STUDY—*5 minutes*

You are now about to take the test using List 2. (*This is the test that counts!*)

Turn back to the first page of Part B of this test and study the boxes again. You have *5 minutes to restudy the addresses*. When the time is up, tear out the Answer Sheet for List 2. Use it for this test.

WORK—*5 minutes*

For each question, mark the Answer Sheet to show the letter of the box in which the address belongs. You will have *exactly 5 minutes to do the test*. During the 5 minutes, do *not* turn to any other page.

1. Isabel	31. Melba	61. Ewing
2. 6200–6399 Canton	32. 6400–6999 Canton	62. 3500–3899 Park
3. Laguna	33. 2500–2699 Park	63. 4000–4299 Dell
4. 4900–5699 Dell	34. Isabel	64. Spring
5. 7000–7599 Canton	35. Boyd	65. 4300–4899 Dell
6. Jiggetts	36. 6400–6999 Canton	66. Weston
7. Weston	37. 2700–2999 Park	67. 7000–7599 Canton
8. 4000–4299 Dell	38. Spring	68. Melba
9. 1600–2499 Park	39. Jiggetts	69. 1600–2499 Park
10. Ewing	40. 4000–4299 Dell	70. 6400–6999 Canton
11. 3500–3899 Park	41. Isabel	71. 2500–2699 Park
12. Melba	42. Boyd	72. 4900–5699 Dell
13. Spring	43. 4900–5699 Dell	73. Weston
14. 7600–7899 Canton	44. 7000–7599 Canton	74. Boyd
15. 3000–3499 Park	45. Weston	75. 3000–3499 Park
16. Angle	46. Ewing	76. Taylor
17. Isabel	47. 1600–2499 Park	77. 6200–6399 Canton
18. 3500–3899 Park	48. 7600–7899 Canton	78. Isabel
19. 5700–5899 Dell	49. Taylor	79. Spring
20. 6400–6999 Canton	50. 5900–6599 Dell	80. 5700–5899 Dell
21. Boyd	51. 5600–6199 Canton	81. 1600–2499 Park
22. Taylor	52. Laguna	82. 7600–7899 Canton
23. Melba	53. Angle	83. 5600–6199 Canton
24. 2500–2699 Park	54. 3000–3499 Park	84. Jiggetts
25. Jiggetts	55. 6200–6399 Canton	85. Laguna
26. 5600–6199 Canton	56. Boyd	86. 3000–3499 Park
27. Laguna	57. 4300–4899 Dell	87. 5700–5899 Dell
28. 2700–2999 Park	58. Jiggetts	88. 4300–4899 Dell
29. 5900–6599 Dell	59. 2700–2999 Park	
30. Angle	60. 6200–6399 Canton	

END OF EXAMINATION.

**If you finish before the time is up, go back
and check the questions in this section of the
test only.**

ANSWER KEY

PART A—ADDRESS CHECKING

1.	D	25.	D	49.	A	73.	D
2.	D	26.	D	50.	D	74.	D
3.	A	27.	A	51.	A	75.	D
4.	A	28.	D	52.	D	76.	A
5.	D	29.	D	53.	D	77.	D
6.	D	30.	D	54.	A	78.	D
7.	D	31.	D	55.	A	79.	A
8.	D	32.	D	56.	D	80.	A
9.	D	33.	D	57.	A	81.	A
10.	A	34.	D	58.	D	82.	A
11.	D	35.	A	59.	A	83.	A
12.	D	36.	A	60.	D	84.	D
13.	D	37.	A	61.	A	85.	A
14.	A	38.	D	62.	D	86.	A
15.	A	39.	D	63.	D	87.	D
16.	D	40.	A	64.	A	88.	A
17.	A	41.	D	65.	A	89.	D
18.	A	42.	A	66.	A	90.	D
19.	D	43.	A	67.	D	91.	D
20.	A	44.	A	68.	A	92.	D
21.	D	45.	D	69.	D	93.	D
22.	A	46.	D	70.	D	94.	A
23.	A	47.	A	71.	D	95.	D
24.	A	48.	D	72.	A		

PART B—MEMORY FOR ADDRESSES

List 1

1.	A	17.	B	33.	B	49.	D
2.	D	18.	C	34.	C	50.	E
3.	B	19.	C	35.	D	51.	B
4.	B	20.	A	36.	D	52.	B
5.	A	21.	D	37.	A	53.	B
6.	A	22.	E	38.	B	54.	E
7.	E	23.	D	39.	B	55.	A
8.	E	24.	D	40.	C	56.	D
9.	D	25.	A	41.	C	57.	A
10.	E	26.	B	42.	D	58.	E
11.	B	27.	D	43.	C	59.	D
12.	B	28.	C	44.	E	60.	C
13.	C	29.	E	45.	C	61.	E
14.	A	30.	C	46.	D	62.	C
15.	D	31.	E	47.	A	63.	D
16.	B	32.	D	48.	C	64.	C

65.	E	71.	E	77.	E	83.	E
66.	B	72.	A	78.	C	84.	E
67.	A	73.	A	79.	C	85.	A
68.	A	74.	B	80.	B	86.	D
69.	B	75.	B	81.	C	87.	E
70.	A	76.	D	82.	C	88.	A

List 2

1.	D	23.	A	45.	A	67.	B
2.	D	24.	A	46.	C	68.	A
3.	E	25.	D	47.	B	69.	B
4.	C	26.	C	48.	A	70.	E
5.	B	27.	E	49.	B	71.	A
6.	D	28.	E	50.	D	72.	C
7.	A	29.	D	51.	C	73.	A
8.	A	30.	B	52.	E	74.	C
9.	B	31.	A	53.	B	75.	C
10.	C	32.	E	54.	C	76.	B
11.	D	33.	A	55.	D	77.	D
12.	A	34.	D	56.	C	78.	D
13.	E	35.	C	57.	B	79.	E
14.	A	36.	E	58.	D	80.	E
15.	C	37.	E	59.	E	81.	B
16.	B	38.	E	60.	D	82.	A
17.	D	39.	D	61.	C	83.	C
18.	D	40.	A	62.	D	84.	D
19.	E	41.	D	63.	A	85.	E
20.	E	42.	C	64.	E	86.	C
21.	C	43.	C	65.	B	87.	E
22.	B	44.	B	66.	A	88.	B

EVALUATING YOUR PROGRESS

PART A

Computing Your Score

Check your answers against the Answer Key. Score yourself by using this formula:

$$\begin{array}{r} \text{Number right} \\ \underline{-\text{ Number wrong}} \\ \text{YOUR SCORE} \end{array}$$

For example, if you completed 52 questions and got 8 wrong,

$$\begin{array}{rr} \text{Number right} \dots\dots & 44 \\ \underline{-\text{ Number wrong} \dots\dots -} & \underline{8} \\ \text{YOUR SCORE } = & 36 \end{array}$$

Notice that you do *not* figure in the questions you did not answer.

Guidelines

How good is the score you just made?

> 52 or higher...............Good
> Between 32 and 52 ......Fair
> Below 32 ....You need to improve

These are commonly accepted figures. We believe, however, that you should not be satisfied with anything *less* than 52. Our experience in training many people to prepare for this test shows that most serious test candidates who use the preparation program described in this book will be able to raise their score to the upper sixties and seventies.

Personal Progress Record

As was mentioned before, one of the most satisfying things that can happen while you are working toward a goal is to see signs of progress. The improvement you make on Address Checking can readily be seen by examining the scores you make on the practice tests and exercises in this book. We think that keeping track of your growing skill is so important that a Personal Progress Record has been furnished for your use on page 231.

A sample of this Personal Progress Record may be found on the next page in order to familiarize you with it. The entries on this sample are based on the example above.

Personal Progress Record—Sample

		ADDRESS CHECKING								
		Initial Tests					Repeated Tests			
Date	Test	Number Completed	Number Correct	− Number Wrong	= Score		Date	Score	Date	Score
5/15	Diagnostic Practice Test	52	44	− 8	= 36					
5/16	Practice Test 1	64	54	− 10	= 44					
5/18	Practice Test 2	66	57	− 9	= 48					
5/20	Practice Test 3	70	60	− 10	= 50					
	Practice Test 4			−	=					
	Practice Test 5			−	=					

Now turn to page 231. Look at the table entitled "Personal Progress Record—Address Checking." Make the proper entries on the line for Practice Test 3 which you just took. Review the special techniques in Chapter 3 on Address Checking before taking Practice Test 4. After taking the additional practice tests, enter the results immediately. Keep this record. It will help you record your progress.

PART B

Computing Your Score

Check the answers on your answer sheet against the Answer Key. Calculate your score by using these four steps:

1. Enter the number of answers you got right ...._____
2. Enter the number of answers you got wrong ...._____
3. Divide the number wrong by 4 (or multiply by ¼) .... −_____
4. Subtract Line 3 from Line 1....................YOUR SCORE =_____

Follow this example to make sure that you have figured your score correctly. We will assume that you completed 32 questions, of which you got 24 right and 8 wrong.

$$\text{Line 1.......Number right................... } 24$$
$$\text{Line 2.......Number wrong...............8}$$
$$\text{Line 3.......¼ of line 2 = ¼ × 8... } \underline{-2}$$
$$\text{Line 4.......24 − 2 ...YOUR SCORE = } \overline{22}$$

Notice that just as for Address Checking, questions that are not answered are *not* taken into account.

Guidelines

How good is the score you just made?

          44 or more ....Good
          26 to 43 ....Fair
          25 or less ....You need to improve

If your score on this test was low, don't be discouraged. Nevertheless, you may wish to review the chapters offering special techniques for handling "Memory for Addresses" before taking Practice Test 4.

Personal Progress Record

Turn to page 231. Look at the table entitled "Personal Progress—Memory for Addresses." Keep a permanent record of your scores on the practice tests, as you have been doing. A sample is printed below to familiarize you with it. The entries are based on the preceding example.

Personal Progress Record—Sample

		MEMORY FOR ADDRESSES										
		Initial Tests								Repeated Tests		
Date	Test	Number Completed	Number Correct *A*	Number Wrong	$\times$ ¼ $=$		Points off *B*	Score *(A − B)*	Date	Score	Date	Score
5/15	Diagnostic Practice Test	32	24	8	$\times$ ¼ $=$		2	22				
5/16	Practice Test 1	46	38	8	$\times$ ¼ $=$		2	36				
5/18	Practice Test 2	58	52	6	$\times$ ¼ $=$		1½	50½				
5/20	Practice Test 3	64	60	4	$\times$ ¼ $=$		1	59				
	Practice Test 4				$\times$ ¼ $=$							
	Practice Test 5				$\times$ ¼ $=$							

Make the proper entries on the record for Practice Test 3 that you just took. Use it to keep a record of the additional practice tests you take. You should be pleasantly surprised at how much higher your next entry on this card will be.

DIAGNOSTIC CHART

PART A—ADDRESS CHECKING

Type of Difference	"D" Questions	"D" Questions Wrong		
		TRIAL 1	TRIAL 2	TRIAL 3
Numbers: transposed	7, 9, 16, 30, 39, 46, 53, 75, 78, 90			
changed	6, 34, 70, 87			
omitted	2			
Directions	21, 41, 48, 56, 84			

Abbreviations:
    streets, roads,
        avenues, etc.
	8, 12, 13, 52, 73, 93			

states	1, 25, 38, 50, 58, 92			
Spelling: single letters	5, 11, 19, 28, 60, 63, 71, 74, 77, 89, 91, 95			
groups of letters	26, 29, 31, 32, 33, 45, 62, 69			
Total Number of Each Type	52			
	Use the columns on the right to enter the question numbers of those "A" you marked "D"			

This chart will help you to pinpoint the kinds of errors you have made on this Practice Test. Use it as directed below after you have taken and marked the test.

The first column on the left, "Type of Difference," contains the same categories whereby addresses may differ shown on page 30 in Chapter 2. On the same line across, the second column gives the number of the questions that fall within each category. In the third column, you are to enter the number of the questions you had wrong. Do not include those you did not do. Use the space indicated in this column to list the number of any "A" questions you answered as "D." Checking these addresses may reveal a problem on which you will want to work.

After you have made all the entries, you will be able to see the areas in which you need to improve. Then turn to the appropriate part of Chapter 3,

Address Checking: How to Improve Your Score, and re-read it. Then repeat those drills that can help. For example, if you find you have been making too many errors picking out number differences, read pages 38 to 40 and do Drills 18 through 21. If you have a problem with single letters because of reversals like *b* and *d*, or if you have been overlooking the difference between *a, e,* and *o,* read pages 38 to 40. Examine the table on page 49 and work on Drills 10 and 11 if the problem persists.

Remember that this chart is designed for diagnostic purposes and guidance on further practice. It has been drawn so that you can enter the results each time you retake a Practice Test. In this way you will be able to see how you are progressing. It is not necessary to try to score it. That is best done by using the Personal Progress Record Card.

PART B—MEMORY FOR ADDRESSES

Kind of Address		Number of Questions	Number Wrong		
			TRIAL 1	TRIAL 2	TRIAL 3
Direct:					
	list 1	41			
	list 2	40			
Numbered:					
	list 1	47			
	list 2	48			

The purpose of this chart is to help you evaluate your performance on the two kinds of memory questions that appear in the Practice Test—the questions on the direct (name) addresses and the questions on the numbered addresses. Use it as directed below after you have taken and marked the entire test.

The first column on the left, "Kind of Address," is divided by category into "Direct Address" versus "Numbered Address." The second column gives the number of questions in each category. Use the third column to enter the total number of questions in each category that you answered incorrectly. There is room for you to make additional entries if you take the Practice Test more than once.

At a glance, you will be able to see which area you need to concentrate on and how well you are progressing as you take repeat trials. Use Chapter 4 and the drills in it to improve your memory for the direct addresses. Use Chapter 5 for the numbered addresses.

Remember to use the Personal Progress Record Card (Memory for Addresses) to keep track of your actual scores as you keep studying and practicing.

ANSWER SHEET—PRACTICE TEST 4

PART A—ADDRESS CHECKING   DATE _____

1 Ⓐ Ⓓ	25 Ⓐ Ⓓ	49 Ⓐ Ⓓ	73 Ⓐ Ⓓ
2 Ⓐ Ⓓ	26 Ⓐ Ⓓ	50 Ⓐ Ⓓ	74 Ⓐ Ⓓ
3 Ⓐ Ⓓ	27 Ⓐ Ⓓ	51 Ⓐ Ⓓ	75 Ⓐ Ⓓ
4 Ⓐ Ⓓ	28 Ⓐ Ⓓ	52 Ⓐ Ⓓ	76 Ⓐ Ⓓ
5 Ⓐ Ⓓ	29 Ⓐ Ⓓ	53 Ⓐ Ⓓ	77 Ⓐ Ⓓ
6 Ⓐ Ⓓ	30 Ⓐ Ⓓ	54 Ⓐ Ⓓ	78 Ⓐ Ⓓ
7 Ⓐ Ⓓ	31 Ⓐ Ⓓ	55 Ⓐ Ⓓ	79 Ⓐ Ⓓ
8 Ⓐ Ⓓ	32 Ⓐ Ⓓ	56 Ⓐ Ⓓ	80 Ⓐ Ⓓ
9 Ⓐ Ⓓ	33 Ⓐ Ⓓ	57 Ⓐ Ⓓ	81 Ⓐ Ⓓ
10 Ⓐ Ⓓ	34 Ⓐ Ⓓ	58 Ⓐ Ⓓ	82 Ⓐ Ⓓ
11 Ⓐ Ⓓ	35 Ⓐ Ⓓ	59 Ⓐ Ⓓ	83 Ⓐ Ⓓ
12 Ⓐ Ⓓ	36 Ⓐ Ⓓ	60 Ⓐ Ⓓ	84 Ⓐ Ⓓ
13 Ⓐ Ⓓ	37 Ⓐ Ⓓ	61 Ⓐ Ⓓ	85 Ⓐ Ⓓ
14 Ⓐ Ⓓ	38 Ⓐ Ⓓ	62 Ⓐ Ⓓ	86 Ⓐ Ⓓ
15 Ⓐ Ⓓ	39 Ⓐ Ⓓ	63 Ⓐ Ⓓ	87 Ⓐ Ⓓ
16 Ⓐ Ⓓ	40 Ⓐ Ⓓ	64 Ⓐ Ⓓ	88 Ⓐ Ⓓ
17 Ⓐ Ⓓ	41 Ⓐ Ⓓ	65 Ⓐ Ⓓ	89 Ⓐ Ⓓ
18 Ⓐ Ⓓ	42 Ⓐ Ⓓ	66 Ⓐ Ⓓ	90 Ⓐ Ⓓ
19 Ⓐ Ⓓ	43 Ⓐ Ⓓ	67 Ⓐ Ⓓ	91 Ⓐ Ⓓ
20 Ⓐ Ⓓ	44 Ⓐ Ⓓ	68 Ⓐ Ⓓ	92 Ⓐ Ⓓ
21 Ⓐ Ⓓ	45 Ⓐ Ⓓ	69 Ⓐ Ⓓ	93 Ⓐ Ⓓ
22 Ⓐ Ⓓ	46 Ⓐ Ⓓ	70 Ⓐ Ⓓ	94 Ⓐ Ⓓ
23 Ⓐ Ⓓ	47 Ⓐ Ⓓ	71 Ⓐ Ⓓ	95 Ⓐ Ⓓ
24 Ⓐ Ⓓ	48 Ⓐ Ⓓ	72 Ⓐ Ⓓ	

ANSWER SHEET—PRACTICE TEST 4

PART B—MEMORY FOR ADDRESSES
LIST 1   DATE _____

1 Ⓐ Ⓑ Ⓒ Ⓓ Ⓔ	31 Ⓐ Ⓑ Ⓒ Ⓓ Ⓔ	61 Ⓐ Ⓑ Ⓒ Ⓓ Ⓔ
2 Ⓐ Ⓑ Ⓒ Ⓓ Ⓔ	32 Ⓐ Ⓑ Ⓒ Ⓓ Ⓔ	62 Ⓐ Ⓑ Ⓒ Ⓓ Ⓔ
3 Ⓐ Ⓑ Ⓒ Ⓓ Ⓔ	33 Ⓐ Ⓑ Ⓒ Ⓓ Ⓔ	63 Ⓐ Ⓑ Ⓒ Ⓓ Ⓔ
4 Ⓐ Ⓑ Ⓒ Ⓓ Ⓔ	34 Ⓐ Ⓑ Ⓒ Ⓓ Ⓔ	64 Ⓐ Ⓑ Ⓒ Ⓓ Ⓔ
5 Ⓐ Ⓑ Ⓒ Ⓓ Ⓔ	35 Ⓐ Ⓑ Ⓒ Ⓓ Ⓔ	65 Ⓐ Ⓑ Ⓒ Ⓓ Ⓔ
6 Ⓐ Ⓑ Ⓒ Ⓓ Ⓔ	36 Ⓐ Ⓑ Ⓒ Ⓓ Ⓔ	66 Ⓐ Ⓑ Ⓒ Ⓓ Ⓔ
7 Ⓐ Ⓑ Ⓒ Ⓓ Ⓔ	37 Ⓐ Ⓑ Ⓒ Ⓓ Ⓔ	67 Ⓐ Ⓑ Ⓒ Ⓓ Ⓔ
8 Ⓐ Ⓑ Ⓒ Ⓓ Ⓔ	38 Ⓐ Ⓑ Ⓒ Ⓓ Ⓔ	68 Ⓐ Ⓑ Ⓒ Ⓓ Ⓔ
9 Ⓐ Ⓑ Ⓒ Ⓓ Ⓔ	39 Ⓐ Ⓑ Ⓒ Ⓓ Ⓔ	69 Ⓐ Ⓑ Ⓒ Ⓓ Ⓔ
10 Ⓐ Ⓑ Ⓒ Ⓓ Ⓔ	40 Ⓐ Ⓑ Ⓒ Ⓓ Ⓔ	70 Ⓐ Ⓑ Ⓒ Ⓓ Ⓔ
11 Ⓐ Ⓑ Ⓒ Ⓓ Ⓔ	41 Ⓐ Ⓑ Ⓒ Ⓓ Ⓔ	71 Ⓐ Ⓑ Ⓒ Ⓓ Ⓔ
12 Ⓐ Ⓑ Ⓒ Ⓓ Ⓔ	42 Ⓐ Ⓑ Ⓒ Ⓓ Ⓔ	72 Ⓐ Ⓑ Ⓒ Ⓓ Ⓔ
13 Ⓐ Ⓑ Ⓒ Ⓓ Ⓔ	43 Ⓐ Ⓑ Ⓒ Ⓓ Ⓔ	73 Ⓐ Ⓑ Ⓒ Ⓓ Ⓔ
14 Ⓐ Ⓑ Ⓒ Ⓓ Ⓔ	44 Ⓐ Ⓑ Ⓒ Ⓓ Ⓔ	74 Ⓐ Ⓑ Ⓒ Ⓓ Ⓔ
15 Ⓐ Ⓑ Ⓒ Ⓓ Ⓔ	45 Ⓐ Ⓑ Ⓒ Ⓓ Ⓔ	75 Ⓐ Ⓑ Ⓒ Ⓓ Ⓔ
16 Ⓐ Ⓑ Ⓒ Ⓓ Ⓔ	46 Ⓐ Ⓑ Ⓒ Ⓓ Ⓔ	76 Ⓐ Ⓑ Ⓒ Ⓓ Ⓔ
17 Ⓐ Ⓑ Ⓒ Ⓓ Ⓔ	47 Ⓐ Ⓑ Ⓒ Ⓓ Ⓔ	77 Ⓐ Ⓑ Ⓒ Ⓓ Ⓔ
18 Ⓐ Ⓑ Ⓒ Ⓓ Ⓔ	48 Ⓐ Ⓑ Ⓒ Ⓓ Ⓔ	78 Ⓐ Ⓑ Ⓒ Ⓓ Ⓔ
19 Ⓐ Ⓑ Ⓒ Ⓓ Ⓔ	49 Ⓐ Ⓑ Ⓒ Ⓓ Ⓔ	79 Ⓐ Ⓑ Ⓒ Ⓓ Ⓔ
20 Ⓐ Ⓑ Ⓒ Ⓓ Ⓔ	50 Ⓐ Ⓑ Ⓒ Ⓓ Ⓔ	80 Ⓐ Ⓑ Ⓒ Ⓓ Ⓔ
21 Ⓐ Ⓑ Ⓒ Ⓓ Ⓔ	51 Ⓐ Ⓑ Ⓒ Ⓓ Ⓔ	81 Ⓐ Ⓑ Ⓒ Ⓓ Ⓔ
22 Ⓐ Ⓑ Ⓒ Ⓓ Ⓔ	52 Ⓐ Ⓑ Ⓒ Ⓓ Ⓔ	82 Ⓐ Ⓑ Ⓒ Ⓓ Ⓔ
23 Ⓐ Ⓑ Ⓒ Ⓓ Ⓔ	53 Ⓐ Ⓑ Ⓒ Ⓓ Ⓔ	83 Ⓐ Ⓑ Ⓒ Ⓓ Ⓔ
24 Ⓐ Ⓑ Ⓒ Ⓓ Ⓔ	54 Ⓐ Ⓑ Ⓒ Ⓓ Ⓔ	84 Ⓐ Ⓑ Ⓒ Ⓓ Ⓔ
25 Ⓐ Ⓑ Ⓒ Ⓓ Ⓔ	55 Ⓐ Ⓑ Ⓒ Ⓓ Ⓔ	85 Ⓐ Ⓑ Ⓒ Ⓓ Ⓔ
26 Ⓐ Ⓑ Ⓒ Ⓓ Ⓔ	56 Ⓐ Ⓑ Ⓒ Ⓓ Ⓔ	86 Ⓐ Ⓑ Ⓒ Ⓓ Ⓔ
27 Ⓐ Ⓑ Ⓒ Ⓓ Ⓔ	57 Ⓐ Ⓑ Ⓒ Ⓓ Ⓔ	87 Ⓐ Ⓑ Ⓒ Ⓓ Ⓔ
28 Ⓐ Ⓑ Ⓒ Ⓓ Ⓔ	58 Ⓐ Ⓑ Ⓒ Ⓓ Ⓔ	88 Ⓐ Ⓑ Ⓒ Ⓓ Ⓔ
29 Ⓐ Ⓑ Ⓒ Ⓓ Ⓔ	59 Ⓐ Ⓑ Ⓒ Ⓓ Ⓔ	
30 Ⓐ Ⓑ Ⓒ Ⓓ Ⓔ	60 Ⓐ Ⓑ Ⓒ Ⓓ Ⓔ	

ANSWER SHEET—PRACTICE TEST 4

PART B—MEMORY FOR ADDRESSES
LIST 2   DATE _____

1 Ⓐ Ⓑ Ⓒ Ⓓ Ⓔ   31 Ⓐ Ⓑ Ⓒ Ⓓ Ⓔ   61 Ⓐ Ⓑ Ⓒ Ⓓ Ⓔ
2 Ⓐ Ⓑ Ⓒ Ⓓ Ⓔ   32 Ⓐ Ⓑ Ⓒ Ⓓ Ⓔ   62 Ⓐ Ⓑ Ⓒ Ⓓ Ⓔ
3 Ⓐ Ⓑ Ⓒ Ⓓ Ⓔ   33 Ⓐ Ⓑ Ⓒ Ⓓ Ⓔ   63 Ⓐ Ⓑ Ⓒ Ⓓ Ⓔ
4 Ⓐ Ⓑ Ⓒ Ⓓ Ⓔ   34 Ⓐ Ⓑ Ⓒ Ⓓ Ⓔ   64 Ⓐ Ⓑ Ⓒ Ⓓ Ⓔ
5 Ⓐ Ⓑ Ⓒ Ⓓ Ⓔ   35 Ⓐ Ⓑ Ⓒ Ⓓ Ⓔ   65 Ⓐ Ⓑ Ⓒ Ⓓ Ⓔ
6 Ⓐ Ⓑ Ⓒ Ⓓ Ⓔ   36 Ⓐ Ⓑ Ⓒ Ⓓ Ⓔ   66 Ⓐ Ⓑ Ⓒ Ⓓ Ⓔ
7 Ⓐ Ⓑ Ⓒ Ⓓ Ⓔ   37 Ⓐ Ⓑ Ⓒ Ⓓ Ⓔ   67 Ⓐ Ⓑ Ⓒ Ⓓ Ⓔ
8 Ⓐ Ⓑ Ⓒ Ⓓ Ⓔ   38 Ⓐ Ⓑ Ⓒ Ⓓ Ⓔ   68 Ⓐ Ⓑ Ⓒ Ⓓ Ⓔ
9 Ⓐ Ⓑ Ⓒ Ⓓ Ⓔ   39 Ⓐ Ⓑ Ⓒ Ⓓ Ⓔ   69 Ⓐ Ⓑ Ⓒ Ⓓ Ⓔ
10 Ⓐ Ⓑ Ⓒ Ⓓ Ⓔ   40 Ⓐ Ⓑ Ⓒ Ⓓ Ⓔ   70 Ⓐ Ⓑ Ⓒ Ⓓ Ⓔ
11 Ⓐ Ⓑ Ⓒ Ⓓ Ⓔ   41 Ⓐ Ⓑ Ⓒ Ⓓ Ⓔ   71 Ⓐ Ⓑ Ⓒ Ⓓ Ⓔ
12 Ⓐ Ⓑ Ⓒ Ⓓ Ⓔ   42 Ⓐ Ⓑ Ⓒ Ⓓ Ⓔ   72 Ⓐ Ⓑ Ⓒ Ⓓ Ⓔ
13 Ⓐ Ⓑ Ⓒ Ⓓ Ⓔ   43 Ⓐ Ⓑ Ⓒ Ⓓ Ⓔ   73 Ⓐ Ⓑ Ⓒ Ⓓ Ⓔ
14 Ⓐ Ⓑ Ⓒ Ⓓ Ⓔ   44 Ⓐ Ⓑ Ⓒ Ⓓ Ⓔ   74 Ⓐ Ⓑ Ⓒ Ⓓ Ⓔ
15 Ⓐ Ⓑ Ⓒ Ⓓ Ⓔ   45 Ⓐ Ⓑ Ⓒ Ⓓ Ⓔ   75 Ⓐ Ⓑ Ⓒ Ⓓ Ⓔ
16 Ⓐ Ⓑ Ⓒ Ⓓ Ⓔ   46 Ⓐ Ⓑ Ⓒ Ⓓ Ⓔ   76 Ⓐ Ⓑ Ⓒ Ⓓ Ⓔ
17 Ⓐ Ⓑ Ⓒ Ⓓ Ⓔ   47 Ⓐ Ⓑ Ⓒ Ⓓ Ⓔ   77 Ⓐ Ⓑ Ⓒ Ⓓ Ⓔ
18 Ⓐ Ⓑ Ⓒ Ⓓ Ⓔ   48 Ⓐ Ⓑ Ⓒ Ⓓ Ⓔ   78 Ⓐ Ⓑ Ⓒ Ⓓ Ⓔ
19 Ⓐ Ⓑ Ⓒ Ⓓ Ⓔ   49 Ⓐ Ⓑ Ⓒ Ⓓ Ⓔ   79 Ⓐ Ⓑ Ⓒ Ⓓ Ⓔ
20 Ⓐ Ⓑ Ⓒ Ⓓ Ⓔ   50 Ⓐ Ⓑ Ⓒ Ⓓ Ⓔ   80 Ⓐ Ⓑ Ⓒ Ⓓ Ⓔ
21 Ⓐ Ⓑ Ⓒ Ⓓ Ⓔ   51 Ⓐ Ⓑ Ⓒ Ⓓ Ⓔ   81 Ⓐ Ⓑ Ⓒ Ⓓ Ⓔ
22 Ⓐ Ⓑ Ⓒ Ⓓ Ⓔ   52 Ⓐ Ⓑ Ⓒ Ⓓ Ⓔ   82 Ⓐ Ⓑ Ⓒ Ⓓ Ⓔ
23 Ⓐ Ⓑ Ⓒ Ⓓ Ⓔ   53 Ⓐ Ⓑ Ⓒ Ⓓ Ⓔ   83 Ⓐ Ⓑ Ⓒ Ⓓ Ⓔ
24 Ⓐ Ⓑ Ⓒ Ⓓ Ⓔ   54 Ⓐ Ⓑ Ⓒ Ⓓ Ⓔ   84 Ⓐ Ⓑ Ⓒ Ⓓ Ⓔ
25 Ⓐ Ⓑ Ⓒ Ⓓ Ⓔ   55 Ⓐ Ⓑ Ⓒ Ⓓ Ⓔ   85 Ⓐ Ⓑ Ⓒ Ⓓ Ⓔ
26 Ⓐ Ⓑ Ⓒ Ⓓ Ⓔ   56 Ⓐ Ⓑ Ⓒ Ⓓ Ⓔ   86 Ⓐ Ⓑ Ⓒ Ⓓ Ⓔ
27 Ⓐ Ⓑ Ⓒ Ⓓ Ⓔ   57 Ⓐ Ⓑ Ⓒ Ⓓ Ⓔ   87 Ⓐ Ⓑ Ⓒ Ⓓ Ⓔ
28 Ⓐ Ⓑ Ⓒ Ⓓ Ⓔ   58 Ⓐ Ⓑ Ⓒ Ⓓ Ⓔ   88 Ⓐ Ⓑ Ⓒ Ⓓ Ⓔ
29 Ⓐ Ⓑ Ⓒ Ⓓ Ⓔ   59 Ⓐ Ⓑ Ⓒ Ⓓ Ⓔ
30 Ⓐ Ⓑ Ⓒ Ⓓ Ⓔ   60 Ⓐ Ⓑ Ⓒ Ⓓ Ⓔ

Practice Test 4

PART A—ADDRESS CHECKING

WORK—*6 minutes*

In this test you are to decide whether two addresses are alike or different. If the two addresses are *exactly alike in every way*, darken space Ⓐ. If they are *different in any way*, darken space Ⓓ.

Mark your answers on the Answer Sheet for Address Checking at the beginning of this chapter. Tear it out, put today's date on it, and place it next to the questions.

Allow yourself *exactly 6 minutes* to do as many of the 95 questions as you can. If you finish before the time is up, re-check your answers.

1.	7004 W 214 St	7004 W 241 St
2.	8996 Harthlodge Dr W	8996 Harthlodge Dr W
3.	3064 10th Ave NE	3064 10th Ave SE
4.	9606 Itaska Dr SE	9606 Itaska Dr SE
5.	216 West Anawanda Dr	217 West Anawanda Dr
6.	Evensville TN	Evansville TN
7.	16049 E 229 St	19049 E 229 St
8.	6256 Wachusett Ave	6256 Wachusett St
9.	2884 Cavvy Rd	2884 Cavvy Rd
10.	Toledo OH 44483	Toledo OK 44483
11.	5690 Vespa Ln	5690 Vesda Ln
12.	9777 64th St E	9777 64th Rd E
13.	9412 Ingham Ave W	9412 Ingram Ave W
14.	5209 S Emilie Pl	5209 S Emilie Pl
15.	Provo UT	Provo UT
16.	5851 Marionette Ave	5815 Marionette Ave
17.	Cherry Hill NJ 07013	Cherry Hill NJ 07103
18.	75 Grosvenor Rd	75 Grosvenor Rd
19.	Warren MI	Warren MT

20.	5237 Vandaveer Ave SE	2537 Vandaveer Ave SE
21.	2408 W Bernath Dr	2408 W Bernath Dr
22.	9073 Hacienda Ave E	9078 Hacienda Ave E
23.	6130 Florister Dr N	6130 Florister Dr N
24.	Green Bay WI	Green Bay WI
25.	1316 Jachurst St SE	1316 Jachurst St SE
26.	4893 West Haven Ct	4893 West Haven Ct
27.	7692 Woodbine Ave	7629 Woodbine Ave
28.	383 Armijo Pl SW	383 Armija Pl SW
29.	Farmington GA	Farmington GU
30.	3047 E Charlotte Ave	3047 E Charlotte Ave
31.	3782 SE Kassabian Ave	3782 SE Kassabian Ave
32.	Glendale CA	Glendale CO
33.	1213 Provencher St	1231 Provencher St
34.	2704 S Winchester St	2704 S Westchester St
35.	3764 Disbrow Ct	3763 Disbrow Ct
36.	3006 Le Brun Ln	3006 Le Brun Ln
37.	8034 Hudson River Rd	8034 Hudson River Rd
38.	1981 E Rickman Way	1981 E Rickman Way
39.	9700 Alamosa Dr	9700 Amalosa Dr
40.	6883 E Wyandanch Ave	6883 W Wyandanch Ave
41.	601 Orange Blvd	601 Orange Blvd
42.	5723 Emaline Ave NW	5723 Evaline Ave NW
43.	2867 Kingshighway Blvd N	2867 Kingshighway Blvd N
44.	1390 E Dean St	1390 E Dean St
45.	2417 W Townsend Ave	2417 W Townsend Ter
46.	1103 W Sindelar Rd	1103 W Sindelar Rd
47.	8090 W Zeamer St	8090 W Zoamer St
48.	6083 Oso Grande Ct	6803 Oso Grande Ct
49.	3841 Tanglewood Cir W	3841 Tanglewood Cir W
50.	8004 Quimera Trl SE	8004 Guimera Trl SE
51.	4723 McDougal Dr	4723 McDougal Dr
52.	9170 Worthen Pl	9170 Worthen Pl
53.	7481 Prince Charles Ct	7481 Prince Charles St
54.	Arlington VA	Arlington WA
55.	1401 Abbott Dr	1401 Abbott Dr
56.	152 Nez Perce Lookout	152 Nez Perce Lookout
57.	Homestead FL 33034	Homestead FL 33034
58.	7470 Oakleigh St	7470 Oakland St
59.	94 Quimby Rd E	94 Quimby Rd E
60.	89140 Palmyra Ave	89104 Palmyra Ave
61.	8182 Stream Ct NW	8182 Stream Pl NW
62.	10 Burlington Ave	10 Burlingham Ave
63.	Gadsden AL 39503	Gapsdan AL 39503
64.	2647 E Pearsonville Rd	2647 E Pearsonville Rd
65.	6083 Featherstone Dr	6083 Featherstone Dr

66.	Wilkes-Barre, PA 17402	Wilkes-Barre, PE 17402
67.	714 Gapsch Ln	714 Gapsch Ln
68.	1033 Remillard Rd	1033 Remillard Rd
69.	Pawtucket RI 02861	Pawtucket RI 02851
70.	5148 Nemesia Pl NE	5148 Nemesia Pl NE
71.	1114 S Sycamore St	1114 E Sycamore St
72.	9276 Interpol Blvd NE	9276 Interpol Blvd NE
73.	4342 E Upstone St	4234 E Upstone St
74.	4101 Ludington St	4101 Ludington St
75.	8270 S Homestead Ave	8270 S Homestead Ave
76.	6398 S Oquendo Rd	6398 S Oquendo Rd
77.	141 Aberfeldy Ter	141 Abernathy Ter
78.	505 Fairfax St	505 Fairfax St
79.	3381 Claymont Path	3381 Claymont Path
80.	6814 Havelock Blvd	6814 Havelock Blvd
81.	7 Paso Del Puma NW	7 Paso Del Puma NE
82.	Corpus Christi TX 78410	Corpus Christi TX 78410
83.	5504 Wilmore Dr E	5504 Wilmont Dr E
84.	Fort Smith AR 72903	Fort Smith AR 72903
85.	Los Alamos CA 93440	Los Alamos CA 93440
86.	801 Xenia St	801 Xenia St
87.	8430 Quanta Ln SW	8430 Quanta Ln SW
88.	83 Grass Valley St	83 Green Valley St
89.	4799 SW Eastgate Cir	4789 SW Eastgate Cir
90.	3994 Vista Campo Blvd	3994 Vista Campo Blvd
91.	1809 N 236th Ave	1809 S 236th Ave
92.	2908 Sagamore Ave	2908 Sagamore Ter
93.	2403 Jamestown Way	2403 Jameston Way
94.	462 Los Poblanos Ranch Ln	462 Los Poblanos Ranch Pl
95.	4871 Dadebridge Ct	4871 Dadebridge Ct

STOP.

**If you finish before the time is up, go back
and check the questions in this section of the
test only.**

PART B—MEMORY FOR ADDRESSES

In this test you will have five boxes labeled A, B, C, D, and E. Each box contains five addresses. Three of the five are groups of street addresses, like 5500–5899 Jersey, 3100–3499 Grove, and 2800–3299 Beach; and two are names of places. They are different in each box.

You will also be given two lists of addresses. You will have to decide in which box each address belongs. When you are working on the first list, you will have the boxes with the addresses *in front* of you. It's a kind of warm-up trial test. When you are working on the second list, you will *not* be able to look at the boxes. The second list is the *real* test.

SAMPLES

A	B	C	D	E
5500-5899 Jersey Newell 1800-2099 Grove Updike 1100-1599 Beach	5900-6199 Jersey Victor 3500-3699 Grove Greco 3300-3999 Beach	3700-4199 Jersey Oriole 2700-3099 Grove Sears 2800-3299 Beach	4700-5499 Jersey Raines 2100-2699 Grove Hicks 2200-2799 Beach	4200-4699 Jersey Portal 3100-3499 Grove Avalon 1600-2199 Beach

Questions 1 through 7 show the way the questions look. You have to decide in which lettered box (A, B, C, D, or E) the address belongs and then mark that answer in the answer grid.

1. Newell   1 Ⓐ Ⓑ Ⓒ Ⓓ Ⓔ
2. 3700–4199 Jersey   2 Ⓐ Ⓑ Ⓒ Ⓓ Ⓔ
3. 3500–3699 Grove   3 Ⓐ Ⓑ Ⓒ Ⓓ Ⓔ
4. Sears   4 Ⓐ Ⓑ Ⓒ Ⓓ Ⓔ
5. 1600–2199 Beach   5 Ⓐ Ⓑ Ⓒ Ⓓ Ⓔ
6. Updike   6 Ⓐ Ⓑ Ⓒ Ⓓ Ⓔ
7. 5900–6199 Jersey   7 Ⓐ Ⓑ Ⓒ Ⓓ Ⓔ

Answers

1. A   3. B   5. E   7. B
2. C   4. C   6. A

STUDY—*3 minutes*

You will now have *3 minutes to spend memorizing the addresses in the boxes*. These are the addresses that will be on the test. Try to learn as many as you can. When the three minutes are up, go to page 197 to begin your practice test.

List 1

WORK—*3 minutes*

Tear out the Answer Sheet for this section of the test. For each question, mark the answer sheet to show the letter of the box in which the address belongs. Try to remember the location of as many addresses as you can. *You will now have 3 minutes to complete List 1.* If you are not sure of an answer, you should guess.

A	B	C	D	E
5500-5899 Jersey Newell 1800-2099 Grove Updike 1100-1599 Beach	5900-6199 Jersey Victor 3500-3699 Grove Greco 3300-3999 Beach	3700-4199 Jersey Oriole 2700-3099 Grove Sears 2800-3299 Beach	4700-5499 Jersey Raines 2100-2699 Grove Hicks 2200-2799 Beach	4200-4699 Jersey Portal 3100-3499 Grove Avalon 1600-2199 Beach

1. 3300–3999 Beach
2. Raines
3. 5500–5899 Jersey
4. Oriole
5. 1800–2099 Grove
6. Victor
7. 5900–6199 Jersey
8. 2200–2799 Beach
9. Greco
10. Newell
11. 2700–3099 Grove
12. 4700–5499 Jersey
13. Avalon
14. 2800–3299 Beach
15. 1100–1599 Beach
16. Hicks
17. Sears
18. 3700–4199 Jersey
19. Updike
20. 3500–3699 Grove
21. Victor
22. 4200–4699 Jersey
23. Oriole
24. Newell
25. 1600–2199 Beach
26. 4700–5499 Jersey
27. 3100–3499 Grove
28. 2100–2699 Grove
29. Portal
30. 3300–3999 Beach

31. Avalon
32. 2700–3099 Grove
33. Portal
34. Victor
35. Updike
36. 1100–1599 Beach
37. Greco
38. 2700–3099 Grove
39. 3500–3699 Grove
40. Raines
41. 5900–6199 Jersey
42. Updike
43. 1800–2099 Grove
44. Avalon
45. Oriole
46. 3700–4199 Jersey
47. 3100–3499 Grove
48. 4700–5499 Jersey
49. Raines
50. Newell
51. Sears
52. 1800–2099 Grove
53. Portal
54. Oriole
55. 5500–5899 Jersey
56. 3300–3999 Beach
57. Greco
58. 4200–4699 Jersey
59. Avalon
60. 2200–2799 Beach

61. Portal
62. 3700–4199 Jersey
63. Hicks
64. 1600–2199 Beach
65. Sears
66. 1800–2099 Grove
67. 5900–6199 Jersey
68. 1100–1599 Beach
69. Greco
70. Victor
71. 5500–5899 Jersey
72. 4200–4699 Jersey
73. Oriole
74. Hicks
75. 1600–2199 Beach
76. Newell
77. 3100–3499 Grove
78. Updike
79. 2800–3299 Beach
80. Hicks
81. Updike
82. 3500–3699 Grove
83. Raines
84. 2100–2699 Grove
85. Sears
86. 3100–3499 Grove
87. 4200–4699 Jersey
88. 2200–2799 Beach

STOP.

**If you finish before the time is up, go back
and check the questions in this section of the
test only.**

List 2

STUDY—5 minutes

You are now about to take the test using List 2. (*This is the test that counts!*)

Turn back to the first page of Part B of this test and study the boxes again. You have *5 minutes to restudy the addresses*. When the time is up, tear out the Answer Sheet for List 2. Use it for this test.

WORK—5 minutes

For each question, mark the Answer Sheet to show the letter of the box in which the address belongs. You will have *exactly 5 minutes to do the test*. During the 5 minutes, do *not* turn to any other page.

1. 5500–5899 Jersey	31. Updike	61. Avalon
2. Victor	32. 5500–5899 Jersey	62. 4200–4699 Jersey
3. 2200–2799 Beach	33. Raines	63. 2100–2699 Grove
4. Sears	34. Victor	64. Victor
5. Oriole	35. Avalon	65. Portal
6. 2100–2699 Grove	36. 2700–3099 Grove	66. 2200–2799 Beach
7. 3300–3999 Beach	37. 2200–2799 Beach	67. Victor
8. 3700–4199 Jersey	38. Hicks	68. 3500–3699 Grove
9. Portal	39. 4200–4699 Jersey	69. Hicks
10. 3500–3699 Grove	40. 1100–1599 Beach	70. Sears
11. Newell	41. Portal	71. 5900–6199 Jersey
12. 1100–1599 Beach	42. Updike	72. 3700–4199 Jersey
13. Avalon	43. Raines	73. Newell
14. 2800–3299 Beach	44. 1600–2199 Beach	74. 1600–2199 Beach
15. 3100–3499 Grove	45. 4700–5499 Jersey	75. Portal
16. Updike	46. 3700–4199 Jersey	76. 1800–2099 Grove
17. Greco	47. Avalon	77. Victor
18. Raines	48. 1800–2099 Grove	78. Greco
19. 1600–2199 Beach	49. Oriole	79. 2800–3299 Beach
20. Hicks	50. Newell	80. 3100–3499 Grove
21. 4700–5499 Jersey	51. 2800–3299 Beach	81. Newell
22. 1800–2099 Grove	52. Raines	82. Sears
23. Greco	53. 4700–5499 Jersey	83. 5900–6199 Jersey
24. 5900–6199 Jersey	54. 1800–2099 Grove	84. 1100–1599 Beach
25. 2700–3099 Grove	55. Updike	85. 3100–3499 Grove
26. Oriole	56. Greco	86. Raines
27. 4200–4699 Jersey	57. Sears	87. 3300–3999 Beach
28. 3500–3699 Grove	58. 2700–3099 Grove	88. 1800–2099 Grove
29. Hicks	59. Oriole	
30. 5500–5899 Jersey	60. 3300–3999 Beach	

END OF EXAMINATION.

If you finish before the time is up, go back and check the questions in this section of the test only.

ANSWER KEY

PART A—ADDRESS CHECKING

1.	D	25.	A	49.	A	73.	D
2.	A	26.	A	50.	D	74.	A
3.	D	27.	D	51.	A	75.	A
4.	A	28.	D	52.	A	76.	A
5.	D	29.	D	53.	D	77.	D
6.	D	30.	A	54.	D	78.	A
7.	D	31.	A	55.	A	79.	A
8.	D	32.	D	56.	A	80.	A
9.	A	33.	D	57.	A	81.	D
10.	D	34.	D	58.	D	82.	A
11.	D	35.	D	59.	A	83.	D
12.	D	36.	A	60.	D	84.	A
13.	D	37.	A	61.	D	85.	A
14.	A	38.	A	62.	D	86.	A
15.	A	39.	D	63.	D	87.	A
16.	D	40.	D	64.	A	88.	D
17.	D	41.	A	65.	A	89.	D
18.	A	42.	D	66.	D	90.	A
19.	D	43.	A	67.	A	91.	D
20.	A	44.	A	68.	A	92.	D
21.	A	45.	D	69.	D	93.	D
22.	D	46.	A	70.	A	94.	D
23.	A	47.	D	71.	D	95.	A
24.	A	48.	D	72.	A		

PART B—MEMORY FOR ADDRESSES

List 1

1.	B	17.	C	33.	E	49.	D
2.	D	18.	C	34.	B	50.	A
3.	A	19.	A	35.	A	51.	C
4.	C	20.	B	36.	A	52.	A
5.	A	21.	B	37.	B	53.	E
6.	B	22.	E	38.	C	54.	C
7.	B	23.	C	39.	B	55.	A
8.	D	24.	A	40.	D	56.	B
9.	B	25.	E	41.	B	57.	B
10.	A	26.	D	42.	A	58.	E
11.	C	27.	E	43.	A	59.	E
12.	D	28.	D	44.	E	60.	D
13.	E	29.	E	45.	C	61.	E
14.	C	30.	B	46.	C	62.	C
15.	A	31.	E	47.	E	63.	D
16.	D	32.	C	48.	D	64.	E

65.	C	71.	A	77.	E	83.	D
66.	A	72.	E	78.	A	84.	D
67.	B	73.	C	79.	C	85.	C
68.	A	74.	D	80.	D	86.	E
69.	B	75.	E	81.	A	87.	E
70.	B	76.	A	82.	B	88.	D

List 2

1.	A	23.	B	45.	D	67.	B
2.	B	24.	B	46.	C	68.	B
3.	D	25.	C	47.	E	69.	D
4.	C	26.	C	48.	A	70.	C
5.	C	27.	E	49.	C	71.	B
6.	D	28.	B	50.	A	72.	C
7.	B	29.	D	51.	C	73.	A
8.	C	30.	A	52.	D	74.	E
9.	E	31.	A	53.	D	75.	E
10.	B	32.	A	54.	A	76.	A
11.	A	33.	D	55.	A	77.	B
12.	A	34.	B	56.	B	78.	B
13.	E	35.	E	57.	C	79.	C
14.	C	36.	C	58.	C	80.	E
15.	E	37.	D	59.	C	81.	A
16.	A	38.	D	60.	B	82.	C
17.	B	39.	E	61.	E	83.	B
18.	D	40.	A	62.	E	84.	A
19.	E	41.	E	63.	D	85.	E
20.	D	42.	A	64.	B	86.	D
21.	D	43.	D	65.	E	87.	B
22.	A	44.	E	66.	D	88.	A

EVALUATING YOUR PROGRESS

PART A

Computing Your Score

Check your answers against the Answer Key. Score yourself by using this formula:

Number right
– Number wrong
YOUR SCORE

For example, if you completed 52 questions and got 8 wrong,

Number right 44
– Number wrong ..... – 8
YOUR SCORE = 36

Notice that you do *not* figure in the questions you did not answer.

Guidelines

How good is the score you just made?

52 or higher .... Good
Between 32 and 52 ...... Fair
Below 32 .... You need to improve

These are commonly accepted figures. We believe, however, that you should not be satisfied with anything *less* than 52. Our experience in training many people to prepare for this test shows that most serious test candidates who use the preparation program described in this book will be able to raise their score to the upper sixties and seventies.

Personal Progress Record

As was mentioned before, one of the most satisfying things that can happen while you are working toward a goal is to see signs of progress. The improvement you make on Address Checking can readily be seen by examining the scores you make on the practice tests and exercises in this book. We think that keeping track of your growing skill is so important that a Personal Progress Record has been furnished for your use on page 231.

A sample of this Personal Progress Record may be found on the next page in order to familiarize you with it. The entries on this sample are based on the example above.

Personal Progress Record—Sample

		ADDRESS CHECKING								
		Initial Tests					Repeated Tests			
Date	Test	Number Completed	Number Correct	− Number Wrong	= Score		Date	Score	Date	Score
5/15	Diagnostic Practice Test	52	44	− 8	= 36					
5/16	Practice Test 1	64	54	− 10	= 44					
5/18	Practice Test 2	66	57	− 9	= 48					
5/20	Practice Test 3	70	60	− 10	= 50					
	Practice Test 4			−	=					
	Practice Test 5			−	=					

Now turn to page 231. Look at the table entitled "Personal Progress Record—Address Checking." Make the proper entries on the line for Practice Test 4 which you just took. Review the special techniques in Chapter 3 on Address Checking before taking Practice Test 5. After taking the additional practice tests, enter the results immediately. Keep this record. It will help you record your progress.

PART B

Computing Your Score

Check the answers on your answer sheet against the Answer Key. Calculate your score by using these four steps:

1. Enter the number of answers you got right ...._____
2. Enter the number of answers you got wrong ...._____
3. Divide the number wrong by 4 (or multiply by ¼) .... −_____
4. Subtract Line 3 from Line 1....................YOUR SCORE =_____

Follow this example to make sure that you have figured your score correctly. We will assume that you completed 32 questions, of which you got 24 right and 8 wrong.

Line 1.......Number right................... 24
Line 2.......Number wrong.............. 8
Line 3.......¼ of line 2 = ¼ × 8... −2
Line 4.......24 − 2....YOUR SCORE = 22

Notice that just as for Address Checking, questions that are not answered are *not* taken into account.

Guidelines

How good is the score you just made?

  44 or more ....Good
  26 to 43 ....Fair
  25 or less ....You need to improve

If your score on this test was low, don't be discouraged. Nevertheless, you may wish to review the chapters offering special techniques for handling "Memory for Addresses" before taking Practice Test 5.

Personal Progress Record

Turn to page 231. Look at the table entitled "Personal Progress Card—Memory for Addresses." Keep a permanent record of your scores on the practice tests, as you have been doing. A sample is printed below to familiarize you with it. The entries are based on the preceding example.

Personal Progress Record—Sample

MEMORY FOR ADDRESSES													
Initial Tests										Repeated Tests		
Date	Test	Number Completed	Number Correct **A**	Number Wrong	× ¼ =	Points off **B**	Score **(A − B)**	Date	Score	Date	Score
5/15	Diagnostic Practice Test	32	24	8	× ¼ =	2	22				
5/16	Practice Test 1	46	38	8	× ¼ =	2	36				
5/18	Practice Test 2	58	52	6	× ¼ =	1½	50½				
5/20	Practice Test 3	64	60	4	× ¼ =	1	59				
	Practice Test 4				× ¼ =						
	Practice Test 5				× ¼ =						

Make the proper entries on the record for Practice Test 4 that you just took. Use it to keep a record of the additional practice test you take. You should be pleasantly surprised at how much higher your next entry on this card will be.

DIAGNOSTIC CHART

PART A—ADDRESS CHECKING

Type of Difference	"D" Questions	"D" Questions Wrong		
		TRIAL 1	TRIAL 2	TRIAL 3
Numbers: transposed	1, 16, 17, 27, 33, 48, 60			
changed	5, 7, 22, 35, 69, 73, 89			
omitted				
Directions	3, 40, 71, 81, 91			

Abbreviations:
    streets, roads,
       avenues, etc.
	8, 12, 45, 53, 61, 92, 95			

states	10, 19, 29, 32, 54, 66			
Spelling: single letters	6, 11, 13, 28, 42, 47, 50, 63			
groups of letters	34, 39, 58, 62, 77, 83, 88, 93			
Total Number of Each Type	48			
	Use the columns on the right to enter the question numbers of those "A" you marked "D"			

This chart will help you to pinpoint the kinds of errors you have made on this Practice Test. Use it as directed below after you have taken and marked the test.

The first column on the left, "Type of Difference," contains the same categories whereby addresses may differ shown on page 30 in Chapter 2. On the same line across, the second column gives the number of the questions that fall within each category. In the third column, you are to enter the number of the questions you had wrong. Do not include those you didn't do. Use the space indicated in this column to list the number of any "A" questions you answered as "D." Checking these addresses may reveal a problem on which you will want to work.

After you have made all the entries, you will be able to see the areas in which you need to improve. Then turn to the appropriate part of Chapter 3,

Address Checking: How to Improve Your Score, and re-read it. Then repeat those drills that can help. For example, if you find you have been making too many errors picking out number differences, read pages 38 to 40 and do Drills 18 through 21. If you have a problem with single letters because of reversals like *b* and *d*, or if you have been overlooking the difference between *a, e,* and *o,* read pages 38 to 40. Examine the table on page 49 and work on Drills 10 and 11 if the problem persists.

Remember that this chart is designed for diagnostic purposes and guidance on further practice. It has been drawn so that you can enter the results each time you retake a Practice Test. In this way you will be able to see how you are progressing. It is not necessary to try to score it. That is best done by using the Personal Progress Record Card.

PART B—MEMORY FOR ADDRESSES

Kind of Address		Number of Questions	Number Wrong		
			TRIAL 1	TRIAL 2	TRIAL 3
Direct:					
	list 1	42			
	list 2	42			
Numbered:					
	list 1	46			
	list 2	46			

The purpose of this chart is to help you evaluate your performance on the two kinds of memory questions that appear in the Practice Test—the questions on the direct (name) addresses and the questions on the numbered addresses. Use it as directed below after you have taken and marked the entire test.

The first column on the left, "Kind of Address," is divided by category into "Direct Address" versus "Numbered Address." The second column gives the number of questions in each category. Use the third column to enter the total number of questions in each category that you answered incorrectly. There is room for you to make additional entries if you take the Practice Test more than once.

At a glance, you will be able to see which area you need to concentrate on and how well you are progressing as you take repeat trials. Use Chapter 4 and the drills in it to improve your memory for the direct addresses. Use Chapter 5 for the numbered addresses.

Remember to use the Personal Progress Record Card (Memory for Addresses) to keep track of your actual scores as you keep studying and practicing.

ANSWER SHEET—PRACTICE TEST 5

PART A—ADDRESS CHECKING   DATE _____

1 Ⓐ Ⓓ	25 Ⓐ Ⓓ	49 Ⓐ Ⓓ	73 Ⓐ Ⓓ
2 Ⓐ Ⓓ	26 Ⓐ Ⓓ	50 Ⓐ Ⓓ	74 Ⓐ Ⓓ
3 Ⓐ Ⓓ	27 Ⓐ Ⓓ	51 Ⓐ Ⓓ	75 Ⓐ Ⓓ
4 Ⓐ Ⓓ	28 Ⓐ Ⓓ	52 Ⓐ Ⓓ	76 Ⓐ Ⓓ
5 Ⓐ Ⓓ	29 Ⓐ Ⓓ	53 Ⓐ Ⓓ	77 Ⓐ Ⓓ
6 Ⓐ Ⓓ	30 Ⓐ Ⓓ	54 Ⓐ Ⓓ	78 Ⓐ Ⓓ
7 Ⓐ Ⓓ	31 Ⓐ Ⓓ	55 Ⓐ Ⓓ	79 Ⓐ Ⓓ
8 Ⓐ Ⓓ	32 Ⓐ Ⓓ	56 Ⓐ Ⓓ	80 Ⓐ Ⓓ
9 Ⓐ Ⓓ	33 Ⓐ Ⓓ	57 Ⓐ Ⓓ	81 Ⓐ Ⓓ
10 Ⓐ Ⓓ	34 Ⓐ Ⓓ	58 Ⓐ Ⓓ	82 Ⓐ Ⓓ
11 Ⓐ Ⓓ	35 Ⓐ Ⓓ	59 Ⓐ Ⓓ	83 Ⓐ Ⓓ
12 Ⓐ Ⓓ	36 Ⓐ Ⓓ	60 Ⓐ Ⓓ	84 Ⓐ Ⓓ
13 Ⓐ Ⓓ	37 Ⓐ Ⓓ	61 Ⓐ Ⓓ	85 Ⓐ Ⓓ
14 Ⓐ Ⓓ	38 Ⓐ Ⓓ	62 Ⓐ Ⓓ	86 Ⓐ Ⓓ
15 Ⓐ Ⓓ	39 Ⓐ Ⓓ	63 Ⓐ Ⓓ	87 Ⓐ Ⓓ
16 Ⓐ Ⓓ	40 Ⓐ Ⓓ	64 Ⓐ Ⓓ	88 Ⓐ Ⓓ
17 Ⓐ Ⓓ	41 Ⓐ Ⓓ	65 Ⓐ Ⓓ	89 Ⓐ Ⓓ
18 Ⓐ Ⓓ	42 Ⓐ Ⓓ	66 Ⓐ Ⓓ	90 Ⓐ Ⓓ
19 Ⓐ Ⓓ	43 Ⓐ Ⓓ	67 Ⓐ Ⓓ	91 Ⓐ Ⓓ
20 Ⓐ Ⓓ	44 Ⓐ Ⓓ	68 Ⓐ Ⓓ	92 Ⓐ Ⓓ
21 Ⓐ Ⓓ	45 Ⓐ Ⓓ	69 Ⓐ Ⓓ	93 Ⓐ Ⓓ
22 Ⓐ Ⓓ	46 Ⓐ Ⓓ	70 Ⓐ Ⓓ	94 Ⓐ Ⓓ
23 Ⓐ Ⓓ	47 Ⓐ Ⓓ	71 Ⓐ Ⓓ	95 Ⓐ Ⓓ
24 Ⓐ Ⓓ	48 Ⓐ Ⓓ	72 Ⓐ Ⓓ	

ANSWER SHEET—PRACTICE TEST 5

PART B—MEMORY FOR ADDRESSES
LIST 1   DATE _____

1 Ⓐ Ⓑ Ⓒ Ⓓ Ⓔ	31 Ⓐ Ⓑ Ⓒ Ⓓ Ⓔ	61 Ⓐ Ⓑ Ⓒ Ⓓ Ⓔ
2 Ⓐ Ⓑ Ⓒ Ⓓ Ⓔ	32 Ⓐ Ⓑ Ⓒ Ⓓ Ⓔ	62 Ⓐ Ⓑ Ⓒ Ⓓ Ⓔ
3 Ⓐ Ⓑ Ⓒ Ⓓ Ⓔ	33 Ⓐ Ⓑ Ⓒ Ⓓ Ⓔ	63 Ⓐ Ⓑ Ⓒ Ⓓ Ⓔ
4 Ⓐ Ⓑ Ⓒ Ⓓ Ⓔ	34 Ⓐ Ⓑ Ⓒ Ⓓ Ⓔ	64 Ⓐ Ⓑ Ⓒ Ⓓ Ⓔ
5 Ⓐ Ⓑ Ⓒ Ⓓ Ⓔ	35 Ⓐ Ⓑ Ⓒ Ⓓ Ⓔ	65 Ⓐ Ⓑ Ⓒ Ⓓ Ⓔ
6 Ⓐ Ⓑ Ⓒ Ⓓ Ⓔ	36 Ⓐ Ⓑ Ⓒ Ⓓ Ⓔ	66 Ⓐ Ⓑ Ⓒ Ⓓ Ⓔ
7 Ⓐ Ⓑ Ⓒ Ⓓ Ⓔ	37 Ⓐ Ⓑ Ⓒ Ⓓ Ⓔ	67 Ⓐ Ⓑ Ⓒ Ⓓ Ⓔ
8 Ⓐ Ⓑ Ⓒ Ⓓ Ⓔ	38 Ⓐ Ⓑ Ⓒ Ⓓ Ⓔ	68 Ⓐ Ⓑ Ⓒ Ⓓ Ⓔ
9 Ⓐ Ⓑ Ⓒ Ⓓ Ⓔ	39 Ⓐ Ⓑ Ⓒ Ⓓ Ⓔ	69 Ⓐ Ⓑ Ⓒ Ⓓ Ⓔ
10 Ⓐ Ⓑ Ⓒ Ⓓ Ⓔ	40 Ⓐ Ⓑ Ⓒ Ⓓ Ⓔ	70 Ⓐ Ⓑ Ⓒ Ⓓ Ⓔ
11 Ⓐ Ⓑ Ⓒ Ⓓ Ⓔ	41 Ⓐ Ⓑ Ⓒ Ⓓ Ⓔ	71 Ⓐ Ⓑ Ⓒ Ⓓ Ⓔ
12 Ⓐ Ⓑ Ⓒ Ⓓ Ⓔ	42 Ⓐ Ⓑ Ⓒ Ⓓ Ⓔ	72 Ⓐ Ⓑ Ⓒ Ⓓ Ⓔ
13 Ⓐ Ⓑ Ⓒ Ⓓ Ⓔ	43 Ⓐ Ⓑ Ⓒ Ⓓ Ⓔ	73 Ⓐ Ⓑ Ⓒ Ⓓ Ⓔ
14 Ⓐ Ⓑ Ⓒ Ⓓ Ⓔ	44 Ⓐ Ⓑ Ⓒ Ⓓ Ⓔ	74 Ⓐ Ⓑ Ⓒ Ⓓ Ⓔ
15 Ⓐ Ⓑ Ⓒ Ⓓ Ⓔ	45 Ⓐ Ⓑ Ⓒ Ⓓ Ⓔ	75 Ⓐ Ⓑ Ⓒ Ⓓ Ⓔ
16 Ⓐ Ⓑ Ⓒ Ⓓ Ⓔ	46 Ⓐ Ⓑ Ⓒ Ⓓ Ⓔ	76 Ⓐ Ⓑ Ⓒ Ⓓ Ⓔ
17 Ⓐ Ⓑ Ⓒ Ⓓ Ⓔ	47 Ⓐ Ⓑ Ⓒ Ⓓ Ⓔ	77 Ⓐ Ⓑ Ⓒ Ⓓ Ⓔ
18 Ⓐ Ⓑ Ⓒ Ⓓ Ⓔ	48 Ⓐ Ⓑ Ⓒ Ⓓ Ⓔ	78 Ⓐ Ⓑ Ⓒ Ⓓ Ⓔ
19 Ⓐ Ⓑ Ⓒ Ⓓ Ⓔ	49 Ⓐ Ⓑ Ⓒ Ⓓ Ⓔ	79 Ⓐ Ⓑ Ⓒ Ⓓ Ⓔ
20 Ⓐ Ⓑ Ⓒ Ⓓ Ⓔ	50 Ⓐ Ⓑ Ⓒ Ⓓ Ⓔ	80 Ⓐ Ⓑ Ⓒ Ⓓ Ⓔ
21 Ⓐ Ⓑ Ⓒ Ⓓ Ⓔ	51 Ⓐ Ⓑ Ⓒ Ⓓ Ⓔ	81 Ⓐ Ⓑ Ⓒ Ⓓ Ⓔ
22 Ⓐ Ⓑ Ⓒ Ⓓ Ⓔ	52 Ⓐ Ⓑ Ⓒ Ⓓ Ⓔ	82 Ⓐ Ⓑ Ⓒ Ⓓ Ⓔ
23 Ⓐ Ⓑ Ⓒ Ⓓ Ⓔ	53 Ⓐ Ⓑ Ⓒ Ⓓ Ⓔ	83 Ⓐ Ⓑ Ⓒ Ⓓ Ⓔ
24 Ⓐ Ⓑ Ⓒ Ⓓ Ⓔ	54 Ⓐ Ⓑ Ⓒ Ⓓ Ⓔ	84 Ⓐ Ⓑ Ⓒ Ⓓ Ⓔ
25 Ⓐ Ⓑ Ⓒ Ⓓ Ⓔ	55 Ⓐ Ⓑ Ⓒ Ⓓ Ⓔ	85 Ⓐ Ⓑ Ⓒ Ⓓ Ⓔ
26 Ⓐ Ⓑ Ⓒ Ⓓ Ⓔ	56 Ⓐ Ⓑ Ⓒ Ⓓ Ⓔ	86 Ⓐ Ⓑ Ⓒ Ⓓ Ⓔ
27 Ⓐ Ⓑ Ⓒ Ⓓ Ⓔ	57 Ⓐ Ⓑ Ⓒ Ⓓ Ⓔ	87 Ⓐ Ⓑ Ⓒ Ⓓ Ⓔ
28 Ⓐ Ⓑ Ⓒ Ⓓ Ⓔ	58 Ⓐ Ⓑ Ⓒ Ⓓ Ⓔ	88 Ⓐ Ⓑ Ⓒ Ⓓ Ⓔ
29 Ⓐ Ⓑ Ⓒ Ⓓ Ⓔ	59 Ⓐ Ⓑ Ⓒ Ⓓ Ⓔ	
30 Ⓐ Ⓑ Ⓒ Ⓓ Ⓔ	60 Ⓐ Ⓑ Ⓒ Ⓓ Ⓔ	

ANSWER SHEET—PRACTICE TEST 5

PART B—MEMORY FOR ADDRESSES
LIST 2   DATE _____

1 Ⓐ Ⓑ Ⓒ Ⓓ Ⓔ	31 Ⓐ Ⓑ Ⓒ Ⓓ Ⓔ	61 Ⓐ Ⓑ Ⓒ Ⓓ Ⓔ
2 Ⓐ Ⓑ Ⓒ Ⓓ Ⓔ	32 Ⓐ Ⓑ Ⓒ Ⓓ Ⓔ	62 Ⓐ Ⓑ Ⓒ Ⓓ Ⓔ
3 Ⓐ Ⓑ Ⓒ Ⓓ Ⓔ	33 Ⓐ Ⓑ Ⓒ Ⓓ Ⓔ	63 Ⓐ Ⓑ Ⓒ Ⓓ Ⓔ
4 Ⓐ Ⓑ Ⓒ Ⓓ Ⓔ	34 Ⓐ Ⓑ Ⓒ Ⓓ Ⓔ	64 Ⓐ Ⓑ Ⓒ Ⓓ Ⓔ
5 Ⓐ Ⓑ Ⓒ Ⓓ Ⓔ	35 Ⓐ Ⓑ Ⓒ Ⓓ Ⓔ	65 Ⓐ Ⓑ Ⓒ Ⓓ Ⓔ
6 Ⓐ Ⓑ Ⓒ Ⓓ Ⓔ	36 Ⓐ Ⓑ Ⓒ Ⓓ Ⓔ	66 Ⓐ Ⓑ Ⓒ Ⓓ Ⓔ
7 Ⓐ Ⓑ Ⓒ Ⓓ Ⓔ	37 Ⓐ Ⓑ Ⓒ Ⓓ Ⓔ	67 Ⓐ Ⓑ Ⓒ Ⓓ Ⓔ
8 Ⓐ Ⓑ Ⓒ Ⓓ Ⓔ	38 Ⓐ Ⓑ Ⓒ Ⓓ Ⓔ	68 Ⓐ Ⓑ Ⓒ Ⓓ Ⓔ
9 Ⓐ Ⓑ Ⓒ Ⓓ Ⓔ	39 Ⓐ Ⓑ Ⓒ Ⓓ Ⓔ	69 Ⓐ Ⓑ Ⓒ Ⓓ Ⓔ
10 Ⓐ Ⓑ Ⓒ Ⓓ Ⓔ	40 Ⓐ Ⓑ Ⓒ Ⓓ Ⓔ	70 Ⓐ Ⓑ Ⓒ Ⓓ Ⓔ
11 Ⓐ Ⓑ Ⓒ Ⓓ Ⓔ	41 Ⓐ Ⓑ Ⓒ Ⓓ Ⓔ	71 Ⓐ Ⓑ Ⓒ Ⓓ Ⓔ
12 Ⓐ Ⓑ Ⓒ Ⓓ Ⓔ	42 Ⓐ Ⓑ Ⓒ Ⓓ Ⓔ	72 Ⓐ Ⓑ Ⓒ Ⓓ Ⓔ
13 Ⓐ Ⓑ Ⓒ Ⓓ Ⓔ	43 Ⓐ Ⓑ Ⓒ Ⓓ Ⓔ	73 Ⓐ Ⓑ Ⓒ Ⓓ Ⓔ
14 Ⓐ Ⓑ Ⓒ Ⓓ Ⓔ	44 Ⓐ Ⓑ Ⓒ Ⓓ Ⓔ	74 Ⓐ Ⓑ Ⓒ Ⓓ Ⓔ
15 Ⓐ Ⓑ Ⓒ Ⓓ Ⓔ	45 Ⓐ Ⓑ Ⓒ Ⓓ Ⓔ	75 Ⓐ Ⓑ Ⓒ Ⓓ Ⓔ
16 Ⓐ Ⓑ Ⓒ Ⓓ Ⓔ	46 Ⓐ Ⓑ Ⓒ Ⓓ Ⓔ	76 Ⓐ Ⓑ Ⓒ Ⓓ Ⓔ
17 Ⓐ Ⓑ Ⓒ Ⓓ Ⓔ	47 Ⓐ Ⓑ Ⓒ Ⓓ Ⓔ	77 Ⓐ Ⓑ Ⓒ Ⓓ Ⓔ
18 Ⓐ Ⓑ Ⓒ Ⓓ Ⓔ	48 Ⓐ Ⓑ Ⓒ Ⓓ Ⓔ	78 Ⓐ Ⓑ Ⓒ Ⓓ Ⓔ
19 Ⓐ Ⓑ Ⓒ Ⓓ Ⓔ	49 Ⓐ Ⓑ Ⓒ Ⓓ Ⓔ	79 Ⓐ Ⓑ Ⓒ Ⓓ Ⓔ
20 Ⓐ Ⓑ Ⓒ Ⓓ Ⓔ	50 Ⓐ Ⓑ Ⓒ Ⓓ Ⓔ	80 Ⓐ Ⓑ Ⓒ Ⓓ Ⓔ
21 Ⓐ Ⓑ Ⓒ Ⓓ Ⓔ	51 Ⓐ Ⓑ Ⓒ Ⓓ Ⓔ	81 Ⓐ Ⓑ Ⓒ Ⓓ Ⓔ
22 Ⓐ Ⓑ Ⓒ Ⓓ Ⓔ	52 Ⓐ Ⓑ Ⓒ Ⓓ Ⓔ	82 Ⓐ Ⓑ Ⓒ Ⓓ Ⓔ
23 Ⓐ Ⓑ Ⓒ Ⓓ Ⓔ	53 Ⓐ Ⓑ Ⓒ Ⓓ Ⓔ	83 Ⓐ Ⓑ Ⓒ Ⓓ Ⓔ
24 Ⓐ Ⓑ Ⓒ Ⓓ Ⓔ	54 Ⓐ Ⓑ Ⓒ Ⓓ Ⓔ	84 Ⓐ Ⓑ Ⓒ Ⓓ Ⓔ
25 Ⓐ Ⓑ Ⓒ Ⓓ Ⓔ	55 Ⓐ Ⓑ Ⓒ Ⓓ Ⓔ	85 Ⓐ Ⓑ Ⓒ Ⓓ Ⓔ
26 Ⓐ Ⓑ Ⓒ Ⓓ Ⓔ	56 Ⓐ Ⓑ Ⓒ Ⓓ Ⓔ	86 Ⓐ Ⓑ Ⓒ Ⓓ Ⓔ
27 Ⓐ Ⓑ Ⓒ Ⓓ Ⓔ	57 Ⓐ Ⓑ Ⓒ Ⓓ Ⓔ	87 Ⓐ Ⓑ Ⓒ Ⓓ Ⓔ
28 Ⓐ Ⓑ Ⓒ Ⓓ Ⓔ	58 Ⓐ Ⓑ Ⓒ Ⓓ Ⓔ	88 Ⓐ Ⓑ Ⓒ Ⓓ Ⓔ
29 Ⓐ Ⓑ Ⓒ Ⓓ Ⓔ	59 Ⓐ Ⓑ Ⓒ Ⓓ Ⓔ	
30 Ⓐ Ⓑ Ⓒ Ⓓ Ⓔ	60 Ⓐ Ⓑ Ⓒ Ⓓ Ⓔ	

Practice Test 5

PART A—ADDRESS CHECKING

WORK—*6 minutes*

In this test you are to decide whether two addresses are alike or different. If the two addresses are *exactly alike in every way*, darken space Ⓐ. If they are *different in any way*, darken space Ⓓ for the question.

Mark your answers on the Answer Sheet for Address Checking at the beginning of this chapter. Tear it out, put today's date on it, and place it next to the questions.

Allow yourself *exactly 6 minutes* to do as many of the 95 questions as you can. If you finish before the time is up, re-check your answers.

1.	8728 South Chelmsford Ave	8729 South Chelmsford Ave
2.	Wolcott IN 47995	Walcott IN 47995
3.	454 E Delgado Rd	454 E Delgado Rd
4.	4812 S Holmesburg Ave	4812 S Holmesbury Ave
5.	Colwich KS 67030	Colwich KS 67030
6.	4700 Mahopac Ln	4700 Mahopac Ln
7.	6304 Avalun Rd	6304 Avalun Rd
8.	5606 Quail Hollow Rd	5660 Quail Hollow Rd
9.	10472 Rolens Ave W	10472 Rolens Ave W
10.	8341 Quail Roost Rd N	8341 Quail Roost Rd N
11.	4811 E Yates St	4811 E Gates St
12.	5178 Indian Queen Ln	5178 Indian Queen Ln
13.	6118 Brushmore Ave NW	6118 Brushmore Ave NW
14.	3689 S Oxlow Ct	3689 S Oslow Ct
15.	2486 Zanfagna St NE	2486 Zanfagna St NE
16.	2001 Gorsten St	2001 Gorsten St
17.	362 Ortega Ct	362 Ortega Ct

18.	2037 Williamette Blvd	2037 Williamette Blvd
19.	Roselle IL 60172	Rosette IL 60172
20.	4401 Pickford Blvd N	4401 Pickford Ave N
21.	2140 S Magdalena Dr	1240 S Magdalena Dr
22.	4172 Ponagansett St	4172 Ponagansett St
23.	1012 Northwood Rd	1012 Northwalk Rd
24.	5116 Newell St	5116 Newall St
25.	2771 Onondago Trl	2771 Onondaga Trl
26.	Independence MO	Independence MO
27.	1501 SW 2nd Ave	1501 SW 2nd Ave
28.	178 El Camino Way	178 El Camino Way
29.	4401 11th Ave E	4401 11th Ave W
30.	Beaconsfield NY	Bakersfield NY
31.	4056 Yoncalla Ct	4056 Yoncalla Ct
32.	8630 Tim Dr	8630 Tin Dr
33.	290 Davisville River Rd	209 Davisville River Rd
34.	72 Peranna Path	72 Peranna Path
35.	3740 E Ellsworth Ave	3741 E Ellsworth Ave
36.	Norfolk VA 23505	Norwalk VA 23505
37.	6198 Juniata Cir	6198 Juniata Cir
38.	3008 N Graham St	3008 N Graham Ct
39.	9134 McTaggard Dr	9134 McTaggard Dr
40.	3431 W 65th Cir	3431 W 64th Cir
41.	7260 Aldawood Hill Dr	7260 Aldawood Mill Dr
42.	5836 S Inverness Rd	5836 S Inverness Rd
43.	6405 Worcester Blvd N	6405 Worcester Blvd N
44.	Medomak ME	Medomak MD
45.	923 Violet Memorial Pl	923 Violet Memorial Pl
46.	1045 East View Dr	1045 East View Dr
47.	Rochester NY 14625	Rochester NY 14625
48.	913 Manayunk Hill St	913 Manayunk Hill Ct
49.	1908 West Van Cortland Ave	1908 East Van Cortland Ave
50.	Tamassee SC 29686	Tamassee SC 29686
51.	1172 Jacobus St SE	1172 Jacobine St SE
52.	1137 N Woodstock Ave	1137 N Woodstock Ave
53.	14081 32 St NE	14081 32 St NE
54.	6962 Rolling Stone Rd	6632 Rolling Stone Rd
55.	1992 Verde Vista Ter NW	1992 Verde Vista Ter NW
56.	Davanport IA 52807	Davanport LA 52807
57.	431 Coddington Ave	431 Coddingtown Ave
58.	Kingshill VI	Kingshill VA
59.	Bowlus MN	Bowlus MN
60.	1415 Ave X S	1415 Ave Y S
61.	2445 Nemesio Canales Rd	2444 Nemesio Canales Rd
62.	8232 La Burnum Dr	8232 La Barnum Dr
63.	3400 Aspen St	3400 Aspen St

64.	2976 Barrington Square Ext	2976 Barrington Square Ext
65.	8456 W Lancaster Pike	845 W Lancaster Pike
66.	7149 E Berghammer Ln	7149 E Bernhander Ln
67.	617 Owen Blvd	671 Owen Blvd
68.	7405 Kennebec Ln	7405 Kennebec Ln
69.	Salkum WA	Saltum WA
70.	4713 Hurlburt Ave	4713 Hurlburt Ave
71.	2638 Kingsbridge Ter W	2683 Kingsbridge Ter W
72.	1046 N Wynmill Rd	1046 N Windmill Rd
73.	7048 Kingsessing St	7048 Kingsessing St
74.	3810 University Commercial Place	3810 University Commercial Place
75.	398 N Laurel Ave	398 N Laurel St
76.	9081 Dogwood Ter	9181 Dogwood Ter
77.	1808 Armand Pl	1808 Armond Pl
78.	164 E Firestone Blvd	164 E Firestone Blvd
79.	619 Fairmount Pl S	619 Fairmount Pl N
80.	718 Schofield View Cir	718 Schofield View Ter
81.	5054 Digney Ln	5504 Digney Ln
82.	91 Whispering Oak Canyon Trl	91 Whispering Oak Canyon Trl
83.	5968 Ziggarut Cir	5968 Ziggarut Cir
84.	2066 Timrod St NE	2066 Timrod St SE
85.	9789 E Rhone Ct	9789 E Rhine Ct
86.	984 Derry Dell Ct	984 Derry Dell Ct
87.	Springfield MA 01104	Springfield MA 01104
88.	8560 Tanglewood St	8506 Tanglewood St
89.	6809 Jenkintown Rd	6809 Jenkintown Rd
90.	Frametown WV 26623	Frametown WV 26623
91.	Warwick RI	Warwick RI
92.	2803 Flowering Tree Cir	2803 Flowering Tree Cir
93.	2709 Bailey Ave	2709 Baisley Ave
94.	8452 Caroline Ct	8452 Caroline St
95.	5054 W Quapah Pl	5054 W Quapah Pl

STOP.

**If you finish before the time is up, go back
and check the questions in this section of the
test only.**

PART B—MEMORY FOR ADDRESSES

In this test you will have five boxes labeled A, B, C, D, and E. Each box contains five addresses. Three of the five are groups of street addresses, like 2500–2999 Shell, 3700–4199 Bever, and 6400–6599 Martha; and two are names of places. They are different in each box.

You will also be given two lists of addresses. You will have to decide in which box each address belongs. When you are working on the first list, you will have the boxes with the addresses *in front* of you. It's a kind of warm-up trial test. When you are working on the second list, you will *not* be able to look at the boxes. The second list is the real test.

SAMPLES

A	B	C	D	E
2300-2499 Shell Cooney 4600-4999 Bever Butler 6400-6599 Martha	2500-2999 Shell Edwin 4200-4599 Bever Reales 7200-8099 Martha	3000-3799 Shell Stone 5700-6300 Bever Inwood 8100-8799 Martha	1600-2299 Shell Harmon 3700-4199 Bever Thorne 6600-6899 Martha	1200-1599 Shell Acre 5000-5699 Bever Mapes 6900-7199 Martha

Questions 1 through 7 show the way the questions look. You have to decide in which lettered box (A, B, C, D, or E) the address belongs and then mark that answer in the answer grid.

1. Acre   1 Ⓐ Ⓑ Ⓒ Ⓓ Ⓔ
2. 7200–8099 Martha   2 Ⓐ Ⓑ Ⓒ Ⓓ Ⓔ
3. Stone   3 Ⓐ Ⓑ Ⓒ Ⓓ Ⓔ
4. 4600–4999 Bever   4 Ⓐ Ⓑ Ⓒ Ⓓ Ⓔ
5. Harmon   5 Ⓐ Ⓑ Ⓒ Ⓓ Ⓔ
6. 3000–3799 Shell   6 Ⓐ Ⓑ Ⓒ Ⓓ Ⓔ
7. Edwin   7 Ⓐ Ⓑ Ⓒ Ⓓ Ⓔ

Answers

1. E   3. C   5. D   7. B
2. B   4. A   6. C

STUDY—*3 minutes*

You will now have *3 minutes to spend memorizing the addresses in the boxes.* These are the addresses that will be on the test. Try to learn as many as you can. When the 3 minutes are up, go to page 215 to begin your practice test.

List 1

WORK—*3 minutes*

Tear out the Answer Sheet for this section of the test. For each question, mark the answer sheet to show the letter of the box in which the address belongs. Try to remember the location of as many addresses as you can. *You will now have 3 minutes to complete List 1*. If you are not sure of an answer, you should guess.

A	B	C	D	E
2300-2499 Shell Cooney 4600-4999 Bever Butler 6400-6599 Martha	2500-2999 Shell Edwin 4200-4599 Bever Reales 7200-8099 Martha	3000-3799 Shell Stone 5700-6300 Bever Inwood 8100-8799 Martha	1600-2299 Shell Harmon 3700-4199 Bever Thorne 6600-6899 Martha	1200-1599 Shell Acre 5000-5699 Bever Mapes 6900-7199 Martha

1. Mapes
2. 3700–4199 Bever
3. 6900–7999 Martha
4. Harmon
5. Cooney
6. 4200–4599 Bever
7. 1200–1599 Shell
8. Inwood
9. Stone
10. 6600–6899 Martha
11. Edwin
12. 2300–2499 Shell
13. 6400–6599 Martha
14. Reales
15. 5000–5699 Bever
16. Acre
17. 1600–2299 Shell
18. 5700–6399 Bever
19. Thorne
20. Butler
21. 3000–3799 Shell
22. Harmon
23. 8100–8799 Martha
24. 2500–2999 Shell
25. Thorne
26. 7200–8099 Martha
27. 4200–4599 Bever
28. Mapes
29. Acre
30. 4600–4999 Bever

31. 6600–6899 Martha
32. Thorne
33. 2300–2499 Shell
34. 8100–8799 Martha
35. Butler
36. Cooney
37. 4200–4599 Bever
38. Edwin
39. 7200–8099 Martha
40. Acre
41. 3700–4199 Bever
42. Harmon
43. Stone
44. 3000–3799 Shell
45. 6400–6599 Martha
46. Reales
47. Inwood
48. 4600–4999 Bever
49. Stone
50. 5000–5699 Bever
51. Reales
52. 1600–2299 Shell
53. Cooney
54. 2300–2499 Shell
55. 6400–6599 Martha
56. 7200–8099 Martha
57. Acre
58. Inwood
59. Butler
60. 1200–1599 Shell

61. 8100–8799 Martha
62. Stone
63. Harmon
64. 5700–6399 Bever
65. Cooney
66. Thorne
67. 5700–6399 Bever
68. 2500–2999 Shell
69. Inwood
70. 6600–6899 Martha
71. 3000–3799 Shell
72. 6400–6599 Martha
73. Stone
74. Butler
75. 2300–2499 Shell
76. Inwood
77. 1600–2299 Shell
78. Thorne
79. Reales
80. 5000–5699 Bever
81. Edwin
82. 1200–1599 Shell
83. Mapes
84. 4600–4999 Bever
85. Acre
86. Mapes
87. 3700–4199 Bever
88. 2500–2999 Shell

STOP.

**If you finish before the time is up, go back
and check the questions in this section of the
test only.**

List 2

STUDY—5 *minutes*

You are now about to take the test using List 2. (*This is the test that counts!*)

Turn back to the first page of Part B of this test and study the boxes again. You have *5 minutes to restudy the addresses*. When the time is up, tear out the Answer Sheet for List 2. Use it for this test.

WORK—5 *minutes*

For each question, mark the Answer Sheet to show the letter of the box in which the address belongs. You will have *exactly 5 minutes to do the test*. During the 5 minutes, do *not* turn to any other page.

1. Thorne	31. Stone	61. Stone
2. 6400–6599 Martha	32. 1600–2299 Shell	62. 3700–4199 Bever
3. Harmon	33. Harmon	63. Inwood
4. 2300–2499 Shell	34. 7200–8099 Martha	64. 5700–6399 Bever
5. 4600–4999 Bever	35. 5700–6399 Bever	65. 8100–8799 Martha
6. Stone	36. Harmon	66. 1200–1599 Shell
7. Inwood	37. Acre	67. 6400–6599 Martha
8. 5700–6399 Bever	38. 8100–8799 Martha	68. Reales
9. 3000–3799 Shell	39. 2300–2499 Shell	69. Edwin
10. Butler	40. Cooney	70. 1200–1599 Shell
11. 5000–5699 Bever	41. 2500–2999 Shell	71. Harmon
12. 1600–2299 Shell	42. 5000–5699 Bever	72. 3000–3799 Shell
13. 6900–7199 Martha	43. 6900–7199 Martha	73. Butler
14. Acre	44. Thorne	74. Cooney
15. Cooney	45. Edwin	75. 4600–4999 Bever
16. Edwin	46. 7200–8099 Martha	76. Stone
17. 8100–8799 Martha	47. Mapes	77. 6400–6599 Martha
18. Stone	48. Reales	78. 3700–4199 Bever
19. Mapes	49. Butler	79. 4200–4599 Bever
20. 3700–4199 Bever	50. 2300–2499 Shell	80. Thorne
21. 6600–6899 Martha	51. 3000–3799 Shell	81. Mapes
22. 4200–4599 Bever	52. 5000–5699 Bever	82. 2500–2999 Shell
23. Reales	53. Mapes	83. Inwood
24. Edwin	54. Thorne	84. 1600–2299 Shell
25. 1200–1599 Shell	55. 4600–4999 Bever	85. Butler
26. Acre	56. 4200–4599 Bever	86. Thorne
27. 7200–8099 Martha	57. Inwood	87. 2300–2499 Shell
28. 2500–2999 Shell	58. 6600–6899 Martha	88. 6600–6899 Martha
29. Inwood	59. Reales	
30. Cooney	60. Acre	

END OF EXAMINATION.

**If you finish before the time is up, go back
and check the questions in this section of the
test only.**

ANSWER KEY

PART A—ADDRESS CHECKING

1.	D	25.	D	49.	D	73.	A
2.	D	26.	A	50.	A	74.	A
3.	A	27.	A	51.	D	75.	D
4.	D	28.	A	52.	A	76.	D
5.	A	29.	D	53.	A	77.	D
6.	A	30.	D	54.	D	78.	A
7.	A	31.	A	55.	A	79.	D
8.	D	32.	D	56.	D	80.	D
9.	A	33.	D	57.	D	81.	D
10.	A	34.	A	58.	D	82.	A
11.	D	35.	D	59.	A	83.	A
12.	A	36.	D	60.	D	84.	D
13.	A	37.	A	61.	D	85.	D
14.	D	38.	D	62.	D	86.	A
15.	A	39.	A	63.	A	87.	A
16.	A	40.	D	64.	A	88.	D
17.	A	41.	D	65.	D	89.	A
18.	A	42.	A	66.	D	90.	A
19.	D	43.	A	67.	A	91.	A
20.	D	44.	D	68.	A	92.	A
21.	D	45.	A	69.	D	93.	D
22.	A	46.	A	70.	A	94.	D
23.	D	47.	A	71.	D	95.	A
24.	D	48.	D	72.	D		

PART B—MEMORY FOR ADDRESSES

List 1

1.	E	17.	D	33.	A	49.	C
2.	D	18.	C	34.	C	50.	E
3.	E	19.	D	35.	A	51.	B
4.	D	20.	A	36.	A	52.	D
5.	A	21.	C	37.	B	53.	A
6.	B	22.	D	38.	B	54.	A
7.	E	23.	C	39.	B	55.	A
8.	C	24.	B	40.	E	56.	B
9.	C	25.	D	41.	D	57.	E
10.	D	26.	B	42.	D	58.	C
11.	B	27.	B	43.	C	59.	A
12.	A	28.	E	44.	C	60.	E
13.	A	29.	E	45.	A	61.	C
14.	B	30.	A	46.	B	62.	C
15.	E	31.	D	47.	C	63.	D
16.	E	32.	D	48.	A	64.	C

65.	A	71.	C	77.	D	83.	E
66.	D	72.	A	78.	D	84.	A
67.	C	73.	C	79.	B	85.	E
68.	B	74.	A	80.	E	86.	E
69.	C	75.	A	81.	B	87.	D
70.	D	76.	C	82.	E	88.	B

List 2

1.	D	23.	B	45.	B	67.	A
2.	A	24.	B	46.	B	68.	B
3.	D	25.	E	47.	E	69.	B
4.	A	26.	E	48.	B	70.	E
5.	A	27.	B	49.	A	71.	D
6.	C	28.	B	50.	A	72.	C
7.	C	29.	C	51.	C	73.	A
8.	C	30.	A	52.	E	74.	A
9.	C	31.	C	53.	E	75.	A
10.	A	32.	D	54.	D	76.	C
11.	E	33.	D	55.	A	77.	A
12.	D	34.	B	56.	B	78.	D
13.	E	35.	C	57.	C	79.	B
14.	E	36.	D	58.	D	80.	D
15.	A	37.	E	59.	B	81.	E
16.	B	38.	C	60.	E	82.	B
17.	C	39.	A	61.	C	83.	C
18.	C	40.	A	62.	D	84.	D
19.	E	41.	B	63.	C	85.	A
20.	D	42.	E	64.	C	86.	D
21.	D	43.	E	65.	C	87.	A
22.	B	44.	D	66.	E	88.	D

EVALUATING YOUR PROGRESS

PART A

Computing Your Score

Check your answers against the Answer Key. Score yourself by using this formula:

Number right
− Number wrong
YOUR SCORE

For example, if you completed 52 questions and got 8 wrong,

Number right 44
− Number wrong ..... − 8
YOUR SCORE = 36

Notice that you do *not* figure in the questions you did not answer.

Guidelines

How good is the score you just made?

52 or higher..............Good
Between 32 and 52 ......Fair
Below 32 ....You need to improve

These are commonly accepted figures. We believe, however, that you should not be satisfied with anything *less* than 52. Our experience in training many people to prepare for this test shows that most serious test candidates who use the preparation program described in this book will be able to raise their score to the upper sixties and seventies.

Personal Progress Record

As was mentioned before, one of the most satisfying things that can happen while you are working toward a goal is to see signs of progress. By this time, you should have seen improvement on Address Checking by examining the scores you made on the practice tests and exercises in this book. If you have not yet reached a score of 52 on the practice tests, or would still like to improve your score, you may wish to repeat some of the practice tests and exercises. Additional answer sheets may be found on pages 243 through 278. In any case, refer to the Personal Progress Record on page 231 to record your scores.

A sample of this Personal Progress Record may be found on the next page in order to familiarize you with it. The entries on this sample are based on the example above.

Personal Progress Record—Sample

	ADDRESS CHECKING									
	Initial Tests						Repeated Tests			
Date	Test	Number Completed	Number Correct	− Number Wrong	= Score		Date	Score	Date	Score
5/15	Diagnostic Practice Test	52	44	− 8	= 36					
5/16	Practice Test 1	64	54	− 10	= 44					
5/18	Practice Test 2	66	57	− 9	= 48					
5/20	Practice Test 3	70	60	− 10	= 50					
	Practice Test 4			−	=					
	Practice Test 5			−	=					

Now turn to page 231. Look at the table entitled "Personal Progress Record—Address Checking." Make the proper entries on the line for Practice Test 5 which you just took. Note that there is also space on the right-hand side to keep a record of your scores if you decide to take the practice tests more than once.

PART B

Computing Your Score

Check the answers on your answer sheet against the Answer Key. Calculate your score by using these four steps:

1. Enter the number of answers you got right ...._____
2. Enter the number of answers you got wrong ...._____
3. Divide the number wrong by 4 (or multiply by ¼) .... −_____
4. Subtract Line 3 from Line 1....................YOUR SCORE = _____

Follow this example to make sure that you have figured your score correctly. We will assume that you completed 32 questions, of which you got 24 right and 8 wrong.

> Line 1.......Number right................... 24
> Line 2.......Number wrong............... 8
> Line 3.......¼ of line 2 = ¼ × 8... −2
> Line 4.......24 − 2 ...YOUR SCORE = 22

Notice that just as for Address Checking, questions that are not answered are *not* taken into account.

Guidelines

How good is the score you just made?

> 44 or more ....Good
> 26 to 43 ....Fair
> 25 or less ....You need to improve

By this time, you should have seen improvement on Memory for Addresses by examining the scores you made on the practice tests and exercises in this book. If you have not yet reached a score of 44 on the practice tests, or would still like to improve your score, you may wish to repeat some of the practice tests and exercises. Additional answer sheets may be found on pages 243 through 278. In any case, refer to the Personal Progress Record on page 231 to record your scores.

Personal Progress Record

Turn to page 231. Look at the table entitled "Personal Progress Card— Memory for Addresses." A sample is printed below to familiarize you with it. The entries are based on the preceding example.

Personal Progress Record—Sample

		MEMORY FOR ADDRESSES									
		Initial Tests							Repeated Tests		
Date	Test	Number Completed	Number Correct **A**	Number Wrong	$\times$ ¼ $=$	Points off **B**	Score **(A − B)**	Date	Score	Date	Score
5/15	Diagnostic Practice Test	32	24	8	$\times$ ¼ $=$	2	22				
5/16	Practice Test 1	46	38	8	$\times$ ¼ $=$	2	36				
5/18	Practice Test 2	58	52	6	$\times$ ¼ $=$	1½	50½				
5/20	Practice Test 3	64	60	4	$\times$ ¼ $=$	1	59				
	Practice Test 4				$\times$ ¼ $=$						
	Practice Test 5				$\times$ ¼ $=$						

Make the proper entries on the record for Practice Test 5 that you just took. Note that there is also space on the right-hand side to keep a record of your scores if you decide to take the practice tests more than once.

DIAGNOSTIC CHART

PART A—ADDRESS CHECKING

Type of Difference	"D" Questions	"D" Questions Wrong		
		TRIAL 1	TRIAL 2	TRIAL 3
Numbers: transposed	8, 21, 33, 71, 78			
changed	1, 35, 40, 54, 61, 76, 81			
omitted	65			
Directions	29, 79, 84			
Abbreviations: streets, roads, avenues, etc.	20, 38, 48, 75, 80, 94			
states	44, 56, 58			
Spelling: single letters	2, 11, 14, 24, 25, 32, 41, 60, 62, 69, 77, 85, 93			
groups of letters	3, 19, 23, 30, 36, 49, 51, 57, 66, 72			
Total Number of Each Type	48			
	Use the columns on the right to enter the question numbers of those "A" you marked "D"			

This chart will help you to pinpoint the kinds of errors you have made on this Practice Test. Use it as directed below after you have taken and marked the test.

The first column on the left, "Type of Difference," contains the same categories whereby addresses may differ shown on page 30 in Chapter 2. On the same line across, the second column gives the number of the questions that fall within each category. In the third column, you are to enter the number of the questions you had wrong. Do not include those you did not do. Use the space indicated in this column to list the number of any "A" questions you answered as "D." Checking these addresses may reveal a problem on which you will want to work.

After you've made all the entries, you will be able to see the areas in which you need to improve. Then turn to the appropriate part of Chapter 3,

Address Checking: How to Improve Your Score, and re-read it. Then repeat those drills that can help. For example, if you find you have been making too many errors picking out number differences, read pages 38 to 40 and do Drills 18 through 21. If you have a problem with single letters because of reversals like *b* and *d*, or if you have been overlooking the difference between *a, e,* and *o*, read pages 38 to 40. Examine the table on page 49 and work on Drills 10 and 11 if the problem persists.

Remember that this chart is designed for diagnostic purposes and guidance on further practice. It has been drawn so that you can enter the results each time you retake a Practice Test. In this way you will be able to see how you are progressing. It is not necessary to try to score it. That is best done by using the Personal Progress Record Card.

PART B—MEMORY FOR ADDRESSES

Kind of Address		Number of Questions	Number Wrong		
			TRIAL 1	TRIAL 2	TRIAL 3
Direct:					
	list 1	43			
	list 2	45			
Numbered:					
	list 1	43			
	list 2	45			

The purpose of this chart is to help you evaluate your performance on the two kinds of memory questions that appear in the Practice Test—the questions on the direct (name) addresses and the questions on the numbered addresses. Use it as directed below after you have taken and marked the entire test.

The first column on the left, "Kind of Address," is divided by category into "Direct Address" versus "Numbered Address." The second column gives the number of questions in each category. Use the third column to enter the total number of questions in each category that you answered incorrectly. There is room for you to make additional entries if you take the Practice Test more than once.

At a glance, you will be able to see which area you need to concentrate on and how well you are progressing as you take repeat trials. Use Chapter 4 and the drills in it to improve your memory for the direct addresses. Use Chapter 5 for the numbered addresses.

Remember to use the Personal Progress Record Card (Memory for Addresses) to keep track of your actual scores as you keep studying and practicing.

Appendix

STATE AND TERRITORY
ABBREVIATIONS

Look over the table. It is not necessary to memorize it. Rather, practice your speed and accuracy of perception by looking at two or more adjoining abbreviations at a glance. Then, look away and jot down what you saw. Because many of these begin with the same letter, you will be getting good practice in avoiding confusion should they appear on the test.

State	Abbreviation	State	Abbreviation
Alabama	AL	Nebraska	NE
Alaska	AK	Nevada	NV
Arizona	AZ	New Hampshire	NH
Arkansas	AR	New Jersey	NJ
American Samoa	AS	New Mexico	NM
California	CA	New York	NY
Colorado	CO	North Carolina	NC
Connecticut	CT	North Dakota	ND
Delaware	DE	Northern Mariana Islands	CM
District of Columbia	DC	Ohio	OH
Florida	FL	Oklahoma	OK
Georgia	GA	Oregon	OR
Guam	GU	Pennsylvania	PA
Hawaii	HI	Puerto Rico	PR
Idaho	ID	Rhode Island	RI
Illinois	IL	South Carolina	SC
Indiana	IN	South Dakota	SD
Iowa	IA	Tennessee	TN
Kansas	KS	Trust Territory	TT
Kentucky	KY	Texas	TX
Louisiana	LA	Utah	UT
Maine	ME	Vermont	VT
Maryland	MD	Virginia	VA
Massachusetts	MA	Virgin Islands	VI
Michigan	MI	Washington	WA
Minnesota	MN	West Virginia	WV
Mississippi	MS	Wisconsin	WI
Missouri	MO	Wyoming	WY
Montana	MT		

EYE SPAN SELECTORS

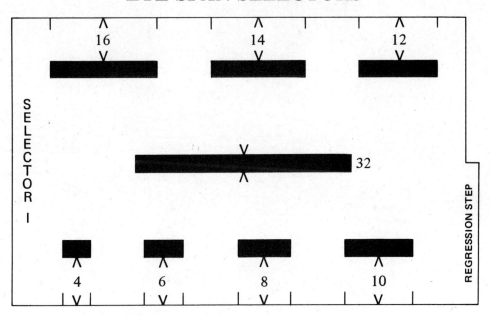

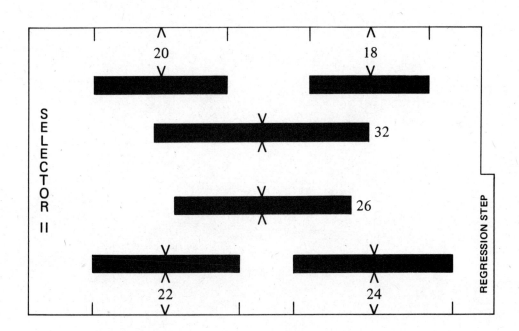

HOW TO USE THIS SELECTOR IN THE DRILLS ON PAGES 59 THROUGH 64

1. Cut out both selectors on page 227. Trace the outline of each selector onto cardboard, and then cut the cardboard to the same size. Tape each selector to a separate piece of cardboard. This will provide each selector with a firm backing. Now cut out each slot window.
2. Select one of the twelve slot windows with a width that just about matches your present eye span, or is even a trifle wider.
3. Place the window over the first address line so that the beginning of the address and the left edge of the slot line up.
4. You should now see part of the address framed in the slot. Notice that there is a small arrow that indicates the middle of the slot.
5. Quickly scan the part of the address you see. Use your peripheral vision to see the beginning and end letters or numbers. Remember, your task is to compare whatever you see with the line below.
6. Make the comparison of the address either by (a) moving the Selector back and forth from the top line to the one below until you've scanned the entire address, or (b) moving the Selector horizontally along each part of the entire address and *then* checking what you saw against each part of the line below.
7. In either case, indicate your answer choice, Ⓐ alike, or Ⓓ different, in the spaces available. (Cover the line of answers you have already completed so that they do not influence you on your second and third trials.)
8. If you wish, you may use the "guidelines" scribed along the edge of the Selectors. The space between each pair of lines exactly corresponds in width to the slot adjoining it. The center of each width is indicated by an arrow. The "guidelines" may be used for exactly the same purpose as the window slots. It is strictly a matter of preference in deciding which method to use. Incidentally, the Selectors may be used for practice when you are reading *any* printed matter—your favorite newspaper, magazine or book.
9. The important thing is to keep drilling until you've mastered a certain width. Then move on to the next larger size. Keep increasing the size of the slots until you reach one that brings you consistently good results. You will, therefore, progress from Selector I to Selector II.
10. Do away with the Selector as soon as you can. It is only a tool designed to help develop new habits. At every opportunity drill for awhile *without* it. Soon, you will find your new skills are a really natural part of the way you read.

HOW TO USE THE SELECTOR TO PREVENT REGRESSION IN THE DRILLS ON PAGES 67 THROUGH 69

Assuming that you will be checking each address using two fixations, use the following procedure.

1. Hold the Selector *above the first line of address* on the page. Line up the edge of the little "step" with the dotted guide line (see Position 1). Scan the left half of the address in Column 1. Compare it to the left half of the address in Column 2 while moving the Selector down one line to Position 2.
2. Scan the *remaining portion of the address*, and compare it to Column 2. Now mark your answer as to whether the items are Ⓐ alike, or Ⓓ different.
3. The Selector is now in the correct position for you to begin checking the *next line*. Now repeat steps 1 and 2 above.

PERSONAL PROGRESS RECORD

TESTS

ADDRESS CHECKING

		Initial Tests				Repeated Tests			
Date	Test	Number Completed	Number Correct −	Number Wrong	= Score	Date	Score	Date	Score
	Diagnostic Practice Test		−		=				
	Practice Test 1		−		=				
	Practice Test 2		−		=				
	Practice Test 3		−		=				
	Practice Test 4		−		=				
	Practice Test 5		−		=				

MEMORY FOR ADDRESSES

		Initial Tests					Repeated Tests			
Date	Test	Number Completed	Number Correct **A**	Number Wrong $\times$ $\frac{1}{4}$ =	Points off **B**	Score **(A − B)**	Date	Score	Date	Score
	Diagnostic Practice Test			$\times$ $\frac{1}{4}$ =						
	Practice Test 1			$\times$ $\frac{1}{4}$ =						
	Practice Test 2			$\times$ $\frac{1}{4}$ =						
	Practice Test 3			$\times$ $\frac{1}{4}$ =						
	Practice Test 4			$\times$ $\frac{1}{4}$ =						
	Practice Test 5			$\times$ $\frac{1}{4}$ =						

Address Checking

Computing Your Score

Check your answers against the Answer Key. Score yourself by using this formula:

$$\begin{array}{r} \text{Number right} \\ -\text{Number wrong} \\ \hline \text{YOUR SCORE} \end{array}$$

For example, if you completed 52 questions and got 8 wrong,

$$\begin{array}{r} \text{Number right} \ldots\ldots \quad 44 \\ -\text{Number wrong} \ldots\ldots - \quad 8 \\ \hline \text{YOUR SCORE} = \quad 36 \end{array}$$

Notice that you do *not* figure in the questions you did not answer.

Guidelines

How good is the score you just made?

> 52 or higher...............Good
> Between 32 and 52 ......Fair
> Below 32 ....You need to improve

These are commonly accepted figures. We believe, however, that you should not be satisfied with anything *less* than 52. Our experience in training many people to prepare for this test shows that most serious test candidates who use the preparation program described in this book will be able to raise their score to the upper sixties and seventies.

Memory for Addresses

Computing Your Score

Check the answers on your answer sheet against the Answer Key. Calculate your score by using these four steps:

1. Enter the number of answers you got right ...._____
2. Enter the number of answers you got wrong ...._____
3. Divide the number wrong by 4 (or multiply by ¼) .... −_____
4. Subtract Line 3 from Line 1.....................YOUR SCORE =_____

Follow this example to make sure that you have figured your score correctly. We will assume that you completed 32 questions, of which you got 24 right and 8 wrong.

> Line 1.......Number right................... 24
> Line 2.......Number wrong.............. 8
> Line 3.......¼ of line 2 = ¼ × 8... −2
> Line 4.......24 − 2....YOUR SCORE = 22

Notice that just as for Address Checking, questions that are not answered are *not* taken into account.

Guidelines

How good is the score you just made?

> 44 or more ....Good
> 26 to 43..............Fair
> 25 or less............You need to improve

These are commonly accepted figures. We believe, however, that you should not be satisfied with anything *less* than 44.

DRILLS

ADDRESS CHECKING

Date	Drill Number	Number Done	Number Correct	Number Incorrect	Raw Score	Time Taken	Calcu-lation	Final Score	Date	Score	Date	Score
		Initial Drills							*Repeated Drills*			
	SAMPLE	—	80	—	—	—	—	80				
	Drill 1											
	Drill 2											
	Drill 3											
	Drill 4											
	Drill 5											
	Drill 6											
	Drill 7											
	Drill 8											
	Drill 9											
	SAMPLE	No entries needed										
	Drill 10											
	Drill 11											
	Drill 12											
	SAMPLE	10	8	—	—	30 sec.	$8 \times \dfrac{60}{30} = 16$					
	Drill 13											
	Drill 14											
	Drill 15											
	Drill 16											
	Drill 17											
	Drill 18											
	Drill 19											
	Drill 20											
	Drill 21											
	SAMPLE	No entries needed										
	Drill 22											
	Drill 23											

ADDRESS CHECKING

Date	Drill Number	Number Done	Number Correct	Number Incorrect	Raw Score	Time Taken	Calculation	Final Score	Date	Score	Date	Score
					Initial Drills					*Repeated Drills*		
SAMPLE		20	18	2	16	80 sec.	$16 \times \frac{60}{80} = 12$					
	Drill 24											
	Drill 25											
	Drill 26											
	Drill 27											
	Drill 28											
	Drill 29											
	Drill 30											
	Drill 31											
SAMPLE		No entries needed										
	Drill 32											

MEMORY FOR *DIRECT* ADDRESSES

Date	Drill Number	Number Done	Number Correct	Number Incorrect	Raw Score	Time Taken	Calculation	Final Score	Date	Score	Date	Score
					Initial Drills					*Repeated Drills*		
SAMPLE		No entries needed										
	Drill 1											
	Drill 2											
	Drill 3											
	Drill 4											
	Drill 5											
	Drill 6											
SAMPLE		40	28	12			$28 - \frac{1}{4}(12) = 25$					
	Drill 7											
	Drill 8											
	Drill 9											
	Drill 10											
	Drill 11											

MEMORY FOR *DIRECT* ADDRESSES

		Initial Drills							Repeated Drills			
Date	Drill Number	Number Done	Number Correct	Number Incorrect	Raw Score	Time Taken	Calcu-lation	Final Score	Date	Score	Date	Score
	Drill 12											
	Drill 13											
	Drill 14											
	Drill 15											
	Drill 16											
	Drill 17											
	Drill 18											
	Drill 19											
	Drill 20											
	Drill 21											
	Drill 22											

MEMORY FOR *NUMBERED* ADDRESSES

		Initial Drills							Repeated Drills			
Date	Drill Number	Number Done	Number Correct	Number Incorrect	Raw Score	Time Taken	Calcu-lation	Final Score	Date	Score	Date	Score
SAMPLE	No entries needed											
	Drill 1											
	Drill 2											
SAMPLE		44	35	9	—	—	$35 - \frac{1}{3} \times 9 = 32$					
	Drill 3											
	Drill 4											
	Drill 5											
	Drill 6											
	Drill 7											
	Drill 8											
	Drill 9											
	Drill 10											
	Drill 11											
	Drill 12											

MEMORY FOR *NUMBERED* ADDRESSES

| Date | Drill Number | Initial Drills | | | | | | | Repeated Drills | | | |
		Number Done	Number Correct	Number Incorrect	Raw Score	Time Taken	Calcu-lation	Final Score	Date	Score	Date	Score
	Drill 13											
	Drill 14											
	Drill 15											
	Drill 16											
	Drill 17											
SAMPLE		No entries needed										
	Drill 18											
SAMPLE		12	10	—	—	—	—	10				
	Drill 19											
	Drill 20											
	Drill 21											
	Drill 22											
	Drill 23											
	Drill 24											
	Drill 25											
	Drill 26											
	Drill 27											
	Drill 28											
	Drill 29											
	Drill 30											
	Drill 31											
	Drill 32											
	Drill 33											

Keeping a record of your drill scores is important. Below are guidelines, with examples, to help you enter and interpret your drill scores. Each example is also shown on the actual progress chart for drills.

Address Checking

These drills are designed to help you develop skills in *different* categories. Although all of them contribute, and are connected to how well you do on address checking, do *not* try to compare the results of one drill to another. That would be like judging a ball player's batting average by examining his fielding average. Both skills are important to his overall ability as a ball player, but they are, of course, entirely different. Rather, compare your results from one trial of a drill to another trial of it.

Drills 1—9: pencil markings. Enter the number of satisfactory marks you make during one minute, in the column marked "Number Correct." Because the timing is constant (one minute), your "Final Score" will be the same.

> *Sample:* Assume that you made 80 satisfactory marks in 1 minute on Drill 1. Your score would be 80.

Drills 10—12: No entries are needed.

Drills 13—17: word differentiation. In these drills, the time you need to complete each drill will keep decreasing as you build speed. Use the formula below to adjust your score so that it comes out in terms of correct answers per minute. In this way, the scores you make on Drills 13 to 17 can be compared with each other more accurately.

> *Formula: Your Final Score* = Number of Correct Answers $\times \dfrac{60 \text{ (seconds)}}{\text{time taken (seconds)}}$

> *Sample:*   On Drill 13, assume you had 8 correct answers in a 30-second trial test.
>
> *Your Final Score* $= 8 \times \dfrac{60}{30} = 16$.

Drills 18—21: number differentiation. Use the same instructions as for Drills 13 to 17 above.

Drills 22 and 23. No entries are needed.

Drills 24—29: eye span. On these drills, you are checking complete addresses, the same as you do on the practice tests. They are rated like Drills 13 to 17 and Drills 18 to 21, but with one additional step:

> Step 1: Number Right − Number Wrong = Raw Score
>
> Step 2: Raw Score $\times \dfrac{60 \text{ (seconds)}}{\text{time taken (seconds)}}$ = Final Score

> *Sample:* Assume you had 18 correct answers and 2 wrong ones when you did Drill 24, and that it took you 80 seconds to do it.
>
> Step 1: 18 − 2 = 16 (Raw Score)
>
> Step 2: $16 \times \dfrac{60}{80} = 12$ (Final Score)

Drills 30 and 31: regression. Use the same instructions as for Drills 24 to 29 above.

Drill 32: miscellaneous. No entries are needed.

Memory for Addresses

Although these drills (like the address-checking drills), are arranged by category, the results on most of them can be compared to each other.

Direct Name Addresses

Drills 1—6: drills for association. No entries are needed.

Drills 7—12: drills using association and imagery, loci, reduction coding.

> *Formula:* *Your Final Score* = Number Correct − ¼ of the Number Wrong
>
> *Sample:* Assume you got 28 questions correct and 12 incorrect. Take ¼ of the number incorrect, ¼(12) = 3, and subtract this from the number correct, 28. The answer is 25.

Drills 13—22: drills for making up stories and slogans. Use the same scoring method as for Drills 7 through 12, but make sure that only the letters that are placed in the *original* position shown in the question, are counted as correct.

Numbered Addresses

Drills 1 and 2. No entries are needed.

Drills 3—17: using 4-digit chunks. The ability to remember 4-digit chunks is common to all categories of these drills. However, because the number of chunks and other conditions vary, compare your scores only within the *same* category, i.e., Drills 3 to 5; Drills 6 to 8, etc.

   The scoring formula is the same for all Drills 3 to 17. It reflects the fact that you have four choices instead of five. The formula to use is:

> *Formula:* *Your Final Score* = Number Right − ⅓ of the Number Wrong.
>
> *Sample:* Assume that you answered 35 of the 44 questions in Drill 3 correctly.
> Your Score = 35 − ⅓ × 9 = 32

Drill 18. No entries are needed.

Drills 19—33: using 6-digit chunks. The ability to remember 6-digit chunks is common to all categories of these drills. Do not, however, compare the results between categories (19 to 21, 22 to 24, etc.) for the same reasons given above.

Use a simplified scoring formula which is the same for Drills 19—33. Allow 1 point for each letter entry you make that is in the original position shown in the box for the question. Then, your final score is simply equal to the total number of letters you placed in the correct position.

Sample: Assume you had correctly entered ten of the original 12 letters in Drill 28: Your Score = 10.

NOTE: Some of the instructions above require a little arithmetic. If you do not wish to go through the arithmetic, you can get an approximate, but useful, idea of your progress as follows: Merely check the Drill Record Charts to see how many you finally get correct (Raw Score) against the "Time Taken." If the number of correct answers increases (or even if it stays the same) while the time taken decreases, you know that you are making progress.

TIMING METHODS FOR PRACTICE TESTS AND DRILLS

The best method for timing your practice tests and drills is to have someone else do it for you. In that way, you will be free from the distraction and loss of time involved in looking at a timepiece. It will help prevent you from losing your rhythm or your place on the question and answer sheets. (On the actual test, one of the monitors directs all the timing.)

If you cannot get someone to time you, you can minimize the disadvantages of working alone by following some of these suggestions:

1. Use a timer that can be pre-set so that when the time is up for a particular study or practice period, an alarm sounds or flashes to alert you;
2. Use an ordinary wall clock, with a face large enough for you to see the numerals clearly from your seat. Mount it at eye-level, in a position where you can see it without moving your head or searching for it. It must have a sweep second-hand or a continuous digital readout in seconds. Clocks without this feature allow too much margin for error.
3. Use a wristwatch, taking it off your wrist and setting it in front of you before you begin work. It, too, must show the passage of seconds as well as minutes, and have a clear, easy-to-read display.
4. Use a stopwatch or chronometer that can be pre-set for an exact time period. It insures extreme accuracy.
5. Use a metronome for the drills and practice tests on address checking. You can develop a rhythm for working that will help you move along at a consistent pace. (See pages 43 to 44.)
6. Do *not* use egg timers or spring wound kitchen timers. They do not keep time accurately and consistently. Being even a few seconds off can make an appreciable difference in your final score.

ADDITIONAL ANSWER SHEETS FOR
PRACTICE TESTS
(TRIALS 2 AND 3)

ANSWER SHEET—DIAGNOSTIC
PRACTICE TEST
TRIAL 2

PART A—ADDRESS CHECKING   DATE _____

1 Ⓐ Ⓓ	25 Ⓐ Ⓓ	49 Ⓐ Ⓓ	73 Ⓐ Ⓓ
2 Ⓐ Ⓓ	26 Ⓐ Ⓓ	50 Ⓐ Ⓓ	74 Ⓐ Ⓓ
3 Ⓐ Ⓓ	27 Ⓐ Ⓓ	51 Ⓐ Ⓓ	75 Ⓐ Ⓓ
4 Ⓐ Ⓓ	28 Ⓐ Ⓓ	52 Ⓐ Ⓓ	76 Ⓐ Ⓓ
5 Ⓐ Ⓓ	29 Ⓐ Ⓓ	53 Ⓐ Ⓓ	77 Ⓐ Ⓓ
6 Ⓐ Ⓓ	30 Ⓐ Ⓓ	54 Ⓐ Ⓓ	78 Ⓐ Ⓓ
7 Ⓐ Ⓓ	31 Ⓐ Ⓓ	55 Ⓐ Ⓓ	79 Ⓐ Ⓓ
8 Ⓐ Ⓓ	32 Ⓐ Ⓓ	56 Ⓐ Ⓓ	80 Ⓐ Ⓓ
9 Ⓐ Ⓓ	33 Ⓐ Ⓓ	57 Ⓐ Ⓓ	81 Ⓐ Ⓓ
10 Ⓐ Ⓓ	34 Ⓐ Ⓓ	58 Ⓐ Ⓓ	82 Ⓐ Ⓓ
11 Ⓐ Ⓓ	35 Ⓐ Ⓓ	59 Ⓐ Ⓓ	83 Ⓐ Ⓓ
12 Ⓐ Ⓓ	36 Ⓐ Ⓓ	60 Ⓐ Ⓓ	84 Ⓐ Ⓓ
13 Ⓐ Ⓓ	37 Ⓐ Ⓓ	61 Ⓐ Ⓓ	85 Ⓐ Ⓓ
14 Ⓐ Ⓓ	38 Ⓐ Ⓓ	62 Ⓐ Ⓓ	86 Ⓐ Ⓓ
15 Ⓐ Ⓓ	39 Ⓐ Ⓓ	63 Ⓐ Ⓓ	87 Ⓐ Ⓓ
16 Ⓐ Ⓓ	40 Ⓐ Ⓓ	64 Ⓐ Ⓓ	88 Ⓐ Ⓓ
17 Ⓐ Ⓓ	41 Ⓐ Ⓓ	65 Ⓐ Ⓓ	89 Ⓐ Ⓓ
18 Ⓐ Ⓓ	42 Ⓐ Ⓓ	66 Ⓐ Ⓓ	90 Ⓐ Ⓓ
19 Ⓐ Ⓓ	43 Ⓐ Ⓓ	67 Ⓐ Ⓓ	91 Ⓐ Ⓓ
20 Ⓐ Ⓓ	44 Ⓐ Ⓓ	68 Ⓐ Ⓓ	92 Ⓐ Ⓓ
21 Ⓐ Ⓓ	45 Ⓐ Ⓓ	69 Ⓐ Ⓓ	93 Ⓐ Ⓓ
22 Ⓐ Ⓓ	46 Ⓐ Ⓓ	70 Ⓐ Ⓓ	94 Ⓐ Ⓓ
23 Ⓐ Ⓓ	47 Ⓐ Ⓓ	71 Ⓐ Ⓓ	95 Ⓐ Ⓓ
24 Ⓐ Ⓓ	48 Ⓐ Ⓓ	72 Ⓐ Ⓓ	

ANSWER SHEET—DIAGNOSTIC
PRACTICE TEST
TRIAL 3

PART A—ADDRESS CHECKING   DATE _____

1 Ⓐ Ⓓ	25 Ⓐ Ⓓ	49 Ⓐ Ⓓ	73 Ⓐ Ⓓ
2 Ⓐ Ⓓ	26 Ⓐ Ⓓ	50 Ⓐ Ⓓ	74 Ⓐ Ⓓ
3 Ⓐ Ⓓ	27 Ⓐ Ⓓ	51 Ⓐ Ⓓ	75 Ⓐ Ⓓ
4 Ⓐ Ⓓ	28 Ⓐ Ⓓ	52 Ⓐ Ⓓ	76 Ⓐ Ⓓ
5 Ⓐ Ⓓ	29 Ⓐ Ⓓ	53 Ⓐ Ⓓ	77 Ⓐ Ⓓ
6 Ⓐ Ⓓ	30 Ⓐ Ⓓ	54 Ⓐ Ⓓ	78 Ⓐ Ⓓ
7 Ⓐ Ⓓ	31 Ⓐ Ⓓ	55 Ⓐ Ⓓ	79 Ⓐ Ⓓ
8 Ⓐ Ⓓ	32 Ⓐ Ⓓ	56 Ⓐ Ⓓ	80 Ⓐ Ⓓ
9 Ⓐ Ⓓ	33 Ⓐ Ⓓ	57 Ⓐ Ⓓ	81 Ⓐ Ⓓ
10 Ⓐ Ⓓ	34 Ⓐ Ⓓ	58 Ⓐ Ⓓ	82 Ⓐ Ⓓ
11 Ⓐ Ⓓ	35 Ⓐ Ⓓ	59 Ⓐ Ⓓ	83 Ⓐ Ⓓ
12 Ⓐ Ⓓ	36 Ⓐ Ⓓ	60 Ⓐ Ⓓ	84 Ⓐ Ⓓ
13 Ⓐ Ⓓ	37 Ⓐ Ⓓ	61 Ⓐ Ⓓ	85 Ⓐ Ⓓ
14 Ⓐ Ⓓ	38 Ⓐ Ⓓ	62 Ⓐ Ⓓ	86 Ⓐ Ⓓ
15 Ⓐ Ⓓ	39 Ⓐ Ⓓ	63 Ⓐ Ⓓ	87 Ⓐ Ⓓ
16 Ⓐ Ⓓ	40 Ⓐ Ⓓ	64 Ⓐ Ⓓ	88 Ⓐ Ⓓ
17 Ⓐ Ⓓ	41 Ⓐ Ⓓ	65 Ⓐ Ⓓ	89 Ⓐ Ⓓ
18 Ⓐ Ⓓ	42 Ⓐ Ⓓ	66 Ⓐ Ⓓ	90 Ⓐ Ⓓ
19 Ⓐ Ⓓ	43 Ⓐ Ⓓ	67 Ⓐ Ⓓ	91 Ⓐ Ⓓ
20 Ⓐ Ⓓ	44 Ⓐ Ⓓ	68 Ⓐ Ⓓ	92 Ⓐ Ⓓ
21 Ⓐ Ⓓ	45 Ⓐ Ⓓ	69 Ⓐ Ⓓ	93 Ⓐ Ⓓ
22 Ⓐ Ⓓ	46 Ⓐ Ⓓ	70 Ⓐ Ⓓ	94 Ⓐ Ⓓ
23 Ⓐ Ⓓ	47 Ⓐ Ⓓ	71 Ⓐ Ⓓ	95 Ⓐ Ⓓ
24 Ⓐ Ⓓ	48 Ⓐ Ⓓ	72 Ⓐ Ⓓ	

ANSWER SHEET—PRACTICE TEST 1
TRIAL 2

PART A—ADDRESS CHECKING   DATE _____

1 Ⓐ Ⓓ	25 Ⓐ Ⓓ	49 Ⓐ Ⓓ	73 Ⓐ Ⓓ
2 Ⓐ Ⓓ	26 Ⓐ Ⓓ	50 Ⓐ Ⓓ	74 Ⓐ Ⓓ
3 Ⓐ Ⓓ	27 Ⓐ Ⓓ	51 Ⓐ Ⓓ	75 Ⓐ Ⓓ
4 Ⓐ Ⓓ	28 Ⓐ Ⓓ	52 Ⓐ Ⓓ	76 Ⓐ Ⓓ
5 Ⓐ Ⓓ	29 Ⓐ Ⓓ	53 Ⓐ Ⓓ	77 Ⓐ Ⓓ
6 Ⓐ Ⓓ	30 Ⓐ Ⓓ	54 Ⓐ Ⓓ	78 Ⓐ Ⓓ
7 Ⓐ Ⓓ	31 Ⓐ Ⓓ	55 Ⓐ Ⓓ	79 Ⓐ Ⓓ
8 Ⓐ Ⓓ	32 Ⓐ Ⓓ	56 Ⓐ Ⓓ	80 Ⓐ Ⓓ
9 Ⓐ Ⓓ	33 Ⓐ Ⓓ	57 Ⓐ Ⓓ	81 Ⓐ Ⓓ
10 Ⓐ Ⓓ	34 Ⓐ Ⓓ	58 Ⓐ Ⓓ	82 Ⓐ Ⓓ
11 Ⓐ Ⓓ	35 Ⓐ Ⓓ	59 Ⓐ Ⓓ	83 Ⓐ Ⓓ
12 Ⓐ Ⓓ	36 Ⓐ Ⓓ	60 Ⓐ Ⓓ	84 Ⓐ Ⓓ
13 Ⓐ Ⓓ	37 Ⓐ Ⓓ	61 Ⓐ Ⓓ	85 Ⓐ Ⓓ
14 Ⓐ Ⓓ	38 Ⓐ Ⓓ	62 Ⓐ Ⓓ	86 Ⓐ Ⓓ
15 Ⓐ Ⓓ	39 Ⓐ Ⓓ	63 Ⓐ Ⓓ	87 Ⓐ Ⓓ
16 Ⓐ Ⓓ	40 Ⓐ Ⓓ	64 Ⓐ Ⓓ	88 Ⓐ Ⓓ
17 Ⓐ Ⓓ	41 Ⓐ Ⓓ	65 Ⓐ Ⓓ	89 Ⓐ Ⓓ
18 Ⓐ Ⓓ	42 Ⓐ Ⓓ	66 Ⓐ Ⓓ	90 Ⓐ Ⓓ
19 Ⓐ Ⓓ	43 Ⓐ Ⓓ	67 Ⓐ Ⓓ	91 Ⓐ Ⓓ
20 Ⓐ Ⓓ	44 Ⓐ Ⓓ	68 Ⓐ Ⓓ	92 Ⓐ Ⓓ
21 Ⓐ Ⓓ	45 Ⓐ Ⓓ	69 Ⓐ Ⓓ	93 Ⓐ Ⓓ
22 Ⓐ Ⓓ	46 Ⓐ Ⓓ	70 Ⓐ Ⓓ	94 Ⓐ Ⓓ
23 Ⓐ Ⓓ	47 Ⓐ Ⓓ	71 Ⓐ Ⓓ	95 Ⓐ Ⓓ
24 Ⓐ Ⓓ	48 Ⓐ Ⓓ	72 Ⓐ Ⓓ	

ANSWER SHEET—PRACTICE TEST 1
TRIAL 3

PART A—ADDRESS CHECKING   DATE _____

1 Ⓐ Ⓓ	25 Ⓐ Ⓓ	49 Ⓐ Ⓓ	73 Ⓐ Ⓓ
2 Ⓐ Ⓓ	26 Ⓐ Ⓓ	50 Ⓐ Ⓓ	74 Ⓐ Ⓓ
3 Ⓐ Ⓓ	27 Ⓐ Ⓓ	51 Ⓐ Ⓓ	75 Ⓐ Ⓓ
4 Ⓐ Ⓓ	28 Ⓐ Ⓓ	52 Ⓐ Ⓓ	76 Ⓐ Ⓓ
5 Ⓐ Ⓓ	29 Ⓐ Ⓓ	53 Ⓐ Ⓓ	77 Ⓐ Ⓓ
6 Ⓐ Ⓓ	30 Ⓐ Ⓓ	54 Ⓐ Ⓓ	78 Ⓐ Ⓓ
7 Ⓐ Ⓓ	31 Ⓐ Ⓓ	55 Ⓐ Ⓓ	79 Ⓐ Ⓓ
8 Ⓐ Ⓓ	32 Ⓐ Ⓓ	56 Ⓐ Ⓓ	80 Ⓐ Ⓓ
9 Ⓐ Ⓓ	33 Ⓐ Ⓓ	57 Ⓐ Ⓓ	81 Ⓐ Ⓓ
10 Ⓐ Ⓓ	34 Ⓐ Ⓓ	58 Ⓐ Ⓓ	82 Ⓐ Ⓓ
11 Ⓐ Ⓓ	35 Ⓐ Ⓓ	59 Ⓐ Ⓓ	83 Ⓐ Ⓓ
12 Ⓐ Ⓓ	36 Ⓐ Ⓓ	60 Ⓐ Ⓓ	84 Ⓐ Ⓓ
13 Ⓐ Ⓓ	37 Ⓐ Ⓓ	61 Ⓐ Ⓓ	85 Ⓐ Ⓓ
14 Ⓐ Ⓓ	38 Ⓐ Ⓓ	62 Ⓐ Ⓓ	86 Ⓐ Ⓓ
15 Ⓐ Ⓓ	39 Ⓐ Ⓓ	63 Ⓐ Ⓓ	87 Ⓐ Ⓓ
16 Ⓐ Ⓓ	40 Ⓐ Ⓓ	64 Ⓐ Ⓓ	88 Ⓐ Ⓓ
17 Ⓐ Ⓓ	41 Ⓐ Ⓓ	65 Ⓐ Ⓓ	89 Ⓐ Ⓓ
18 Ⓐ Ⓓ	42 Ⓐ Ⓓ	66 Ⓐ Ⓓ	90 Ⓐ Ⓓ
19 Ⓐ Ⓓ	43 Ⓐ Ⓓ	67 Ⓐ Ⓓ	91 Ⓐ Ⓓ
20 Ⓐ Ⓓ	44 Ⓐ Ⓓ	68 Ⓐ Ⓓ	92 Ⓐ Ⓓ
21 Ⓐ Ⓓ	45 Ⓐ Ⓓ	69 Ⓐ Ⓓ	93 Ⓐ Ⓓ
22 Ⓐ Ⓓ	46 Ⓐ Ⓓ	70 Ⓐ Ⓓ	94 Ⓐ Ⓓ
23 Ⓐ Ⓓ	47 Ⓐ Ⓓ	71 Ⓐ Ⓓ	95 Ⓐ Ⓓ
24 Ⓐ Ⓓ	48 Ⓐ Ⓓ	72 Ⓐ Ⓓ	

ANSWER SHEET—PRACTICE TEST 2
TRIAL 2

PART A—ADDRESS CHECKING   DATE _____

1 Ⓐ Ⓓ	25 Ⓐ Ⓓ	49 Ⓐ Ⓓ	73 Ⓐ Ⓓ
2 Ⓐ Ⓓ	26 Ⓐ Ⓓ	50 Ⓐ Ⓓ	74 Ⓐ Ⓓ
3 Ⓐ Ⓓ	27 Ⓐ Ⓓ	51 Ⓐ Ⓓ	75 Ⓐ Ⓓ
4 Ⓐ Ⓓ	28 Ⓐ Ⓓ	52 Ⓐ Ⓓ	76 Ⓐ Ⓓ
5 Ⓐ Ⓓ	29 Ⓐ Ⓓ	53 Ⓐ Ⓓ	77 Ⓐ Ⓓ
6 Ⓐ Ⓓ	30 Ⓐ Ⓓ	54 Ⓐ Ⓓ	78 Ⓐ Ⓓ
7 Ⓐ Ⓓ	31 Ⓐ Ⓓ	55 Ⓐ Ⓓ	79 Ⓐ Ⓓ
8 Ⓐ Ⓓ	32 Ⓐ Ⓓ	56 Ⓐ Ⓓ	80 Ⓐ Ⓓ
9 Ⓐ Ⓓ	33 Ⓐ Ⓓ	57 Ⓐ Ⓓ	81 Ⓐ Ⓓ
10 Ⓐ Ⓓ	34 Ⓐ Ⓓ	58 Ⓐ Ⓓ	82 Ⓐ Ⓓ
11 Ⓐ Ⓓ	35 Ⓐ Ⓓ	59 Ⓐ Ⓓ	83 Ⓐ Ⓓ
12 Ⓐ Ⓓ	36 Ⓐ Ⓓ	60 Ⓐ Ⓓ	84 Ⓐ Ⓓ
13 Ⓐ Ⓓ	37 Ⓐ Ⓓ	61 Ⓐ Ⓓ	85 Ⓐ Ⓓ
14 Ⓐ Ⓓ	38 Ⓐ Ⓓ	62 Ⓐ Ⓓ	86 Ⓐ Ⓓ
15 Ⓐ Ⓓ	39 Ⓐ Ⓓ	63 Ⓐ Ⓓ	87 Ⓐ Ⓓ
16 Ⓐ Ⓓ	40 Ⓐ Ⓓ	64 Ⓐ Ⓓ	88 Ⓐ Ⓓ
17 Ⓐ Ⓓ	41 Ⓐ Ⓓ	65 Ⓐ Ⓓ	89 Ⓐ Ⓓ
18 Ⓐ Ⓓ	42 Ⓐ Ⓓ	66 Ⓐ Ⓓ	90 Ⓐ Ⓓ
19 Ⓐ Ⓓ	43 Ⓐ Ⓓ	67 Ⓐ Ⓓ	91 Ⓐ Ⓓ
20 Ⓐ Ⓓ	44 Ⓐ Ⓓ	68 Ⓐ Ⓓ	92 Ⓐ Ⓓ
21 Ⓐ Ⓓ	45 Ⓐ Ⓓ	69 Ⓐ Ⓓ	93 Ⓐ Ⓓ
22 Ⓐ Ⓓ	46 Ⓐ Ⓓ	70 Ⓐ Ⓓ	94 Ⓐ Ⓓ
23 Ⓐ Ⓓ	47 Ⓐ Ⓓ	71 Ⓐ Ⓓ	95 Ⓐ Ⓓ
24 Ⓐ Ⓓ	48 Ⓐ Ⓓ	72 Ⓐ Ⓓ	

ANSWER SHEET—PRACTICE TEST 2
TRIAL 3

PART A—ADDRESS CHECKING   DATE _____

1 Ⓐ Ⓓ	25 Ⓐ Ⓓ	49 Ⓐ Ⓓ	73 Ⓐ Ⓓ
2 Ⓐ Ⓓ	26 Ⓐ Ⓓ	50 Ⓐ Ⓓ	74 Ⓐ Ⓓ
3 Ⓐ Ⓓ	27 Ⓐ Ⓓ	51 Ⓐ Ⓓ	75 Ⓐ Ⓓ
4 Ⓐ Ⓓ	28 Ⓐ Ⓓ	52 Ⓐ Ⓓ	76 Ⓐ Ⓓ
5 Ⓐ Ⓓ	29 Ⓐ Ⓓ	53 Ⓐ Ⓓ	77 Ⓐ Ⓓ
6 Ⓐ Ⓓ	30 Ⓐ Ⓓ	54 Ⓐ Ⓓ	78 Ⓐ Ⓓ
7 Ⓐ Ⓓ	31 Ⓐ Ⓓ	55 Ⓐ Ⓓ	79 Ⓐ Ⓓ
8 Ⓐ Ⓓ	32 Ⓐ Ⓓ	56 Ⓐ Ⓓ	80 Ⓐ Ⓓ
9 Ⓐ Ⓓ	33 Ⓐ Ⓓ	57 Ⓐ Ⓓ	81 Ⓐ Ⓓ
10 Ⓐ Ⓓ	34 Ⓐ Ⓓ	58 Ⓐ Ⓓ	82 Ⓐ Ⓓ
11 Ⓐ Ⓓ	35 Ⓐ Ⓓ	59 Ⓐ Ⓓ	83 Ⓐ Ⓓ
12 Ⓐ Ⓓ	36 Ⓐ Ⓓ	60 Ⓐ Ⓓ	84 Ⓐ Ⓓ
13 Ⓐ Ⓓ	37 Ⓐ Ⓓ	61 Ⓐ Ⓓ	85 Ⓐ Ⓓ
14 Ⓐ Ⓓ	38 Ⓐ Ⓓ	62 Ⓐ Ⓓ	86 Ⓐ Ⓓ
15 Ⓐ Ⓓ	39 Ⓐ Ⓓ	63 Ⓐ Ⓓ	87 Ⓐ Ⓓ
16 Ⓐ Ⓓ	40 Ⓐ Ⓓ	64 Ⓐ Ⓓ	88 Ⓐ Ⓓ
17 Ⓐ Ⓓ	41 Ⓐ Ⓓ	65 Ⓐ Ⓓ	89 Ⓐ Ⓓ
18 Ⓐ Ⓓ	42 Ⓐ Ⓓ	66 Ⓐ Ⓓ	90 Ⓐ Ⓓ
19 Ⓐ Ⓓ	43 Ⓐ Ⓓ	67 Ⓐ Ⓓ	91 Ⓐ Ⓓ
20 Ⓐ Ⓓ	44 Ⓐ Ⓓ	68 Ⓐ Ⓓ	92 Ⓐ Ⓓ
21 Ⓐ Ⓓ	45 Ⓐ Ⓓ	69 Ⓐ Ⓓ	93 Ⓐ Ⓓ
22 Ⓐ Ⓓ	46 Ⓐ Ⓓ	70 Ⓐ Ⓓ	94 Ⓐ Ⓓ
23 Ⓐ Ⓓ	47 Ⓐ Ⓓ	71 Ⓐ Ⓓ	95 Ⓐ Ⓓ
24 Ⓐ Ⓓ	48 Ⓐ Ⓓ	72 Ⓐ Ⓓ	

ANSWER SHEET—PRACTICE TEST 3
TRIAL 2

PART A—ADDRESS CHECKING   DATE _____

1 Ⓐ Ⓓ	25 Ⓐ Ⓓ	49 Ⓐ Ⓓ	73 Ⓐ Ⓓ
2 Ⓐ Ⓓ	26 Ⓐ Ⓓ	50 Ⓐ Ⓓ	74 Ⓐ Ⓓ
3 Ⓐ Ⓓ	27 Ⓐ Ⓓ	51 Ⓐ Ⓓ	75 Ⓐ Ⓓ
4 Ⓐ Ⓓ	28 Ⓐ Ⓓ	52 Ⓐ Ⓓ	76 Ⓐ Ⓓ
5 Ⓐ Ⓓ	29 Ⓐ Ⓓ	53 Ⓐ Ⓓ	77 Ⓐ Ⓓ
6 Ⓐ Ⓓ	30 Ⓐ Ⓓ	54 Ⓐ Ⓓ	78 Ⓐ Ⓓ
7 Ⓐ Ⓓ	31 Ⓐ Ⓓ	55 Ⓐ Ⓓ	79 Ⓐ Ⓓ
8 Ⓐ Ⓓ	32 Ⓐ Ⓓ	56 Ⓐ Ⓓ	80 Ⓐ Ⓓ
9 Ⓐ Ⓓ	33 Ⓐ Ⓓ	57 Ⓐ Ⓓ	81 Ⓐ Ⓓ
10 Ⓐ Ⓓ	34 Ⓐ Ⓓ	58 Ⓐ Ⓓ	82 Ⓐ Ⓓ
11 Ⓐ Ⓓ	35 Ⓐ Ⓓ	59 Ⓐ Ⓓ	83 Ⓐ Ⓓ
12 Ⓐ Ⓓ	36 Ⓐ Ⓓ	60 Ⓐ Ⓓ	84 Ⓐ Ⓓ
13 Ⓐ Ⓓ	37 Ⓐ Ⓓ	61 Ⓐ Ⓓ	85 Ⓐ Ⓓ
14 Ⓐ Ⓓ	38 Ⓐ Ⓓ	62 Ⓐ Ⓓ	86 Ⓐ Ⓓ
15 Ⓐ Ⓓ	39 Ⓐ Ⓓ	63 Ⓐ Ⓓ	87 Ⓐ Ⓓ
16 Ⓐ Ⓓ	40 Ⓐ Ⓓ	64 Ⓐ Ⓓ	88 Ⓐ Ⓓ
17 Ⓐ Ⓓ	41 Ⓐ Ⓓ	65 Ⓐ Ⓓ	89 Ⓐ Ⓓ
18 Ⓐ Ⓓ	42 Ⓐ Ⓓ	66 Ⓐ Ⓓ	90 Ⓐ Ⓓ
19 Ⓐ Ⓓ	43 Ⓐ Ⓓ	67 Ⓐ Ⓓ	91 Ⓐ Ⓓ
20 Ⓐ Ⓓ	44 Ⓐ Ⓓ	68 Ⓐ Ⓓ	92 Ⓐ Ⓓ
21 Ⓐ Ⓓ	45 Ⓐ Ⓓ	69 Ⓐ Ⓓ	93 Ⓐ Ⓓ
22 Ⓐ Ⓓ	46 Ⓐ Ⓓ	70 Ⓐ Ⓓ	94 Ⓐ Ⓓ
23 Ⓐ Ⓓ	47 Ⓐ Ⓓ	71 Ⓐ Ⓓ	95 Ⓐ Ⓓ
24 Ⓐ Ⓓ	48 Ⓐ Ⓓ	72 Ⓐ Ⓓ	

ANSWER SHEET—PRACTICE TEST 3
TRIAL 3

PART A—ADDRESS CHECKING   DATE _____

1 ⒶⒹ	25 ⒶⒹ	49 ⒶⒹ	73 ⒶⒹ
2 ⒶⒹ	26 ⒶⒹ	50 ⒶⒹ	74 ⒶⒹ
3 ⒶⒹ	27 ⒶⒹ	51 ⒶⒹ	75 ⒶⒹ
4 ⒶⒹ	28 ⒶⒹ	52 ⒶⒹ	76 ⒶⒹ
5 ⒶⒹ	29 ⒶⒹ	53 ⒶⒹ	77 ⒶⒹ
6 ⒶⒹ	30 ⒶⒹ	54 ⒶⒹ	78 ⒶⒹ
7 ⒶⒹ	31 ⒶⒹ	55 ⒶⒹ	79 ⒶⒹ
8 ⒶⒹ	32 ⒶⒹ	56 ⒶⒹ	80 ⒶⒹ
9 ⒶⒹ	33 ⒶⒹ	57 ⒶⒹ	81 ⒶⒹ
10 ⒶⒹ	34 ⒶⒹ	58 ⒶⒹ	82 ⒶⒹ
11 ⒶⒹ	35 ⒶⒹ	59 ⒶⒹ	83 ⒶⒹ
12 ⒶⒹ	36 ⒶⒹ	60 ⒶⒹ	84 ⒶⒹ
13 ⒶⒹ	37 ⒶⒹ	61 ⒶⒹ	85 ⒶⒹ
14 ⒶⒹ	38 ⒶⒹ	62 ⒶⒹ	86 ⒶⒹ
15 ⒶⒹ	39 ⒶⒹ	63 ⒶⒹ	87 ⒶⒹ
16 ⒶⒹ	40 ⒶⒹ	64 ⒶⒹ	88 ⒶⒹ
17 ⒶⒹ	41 ⒶⒹ	65 ⒶⒹ	89 ⒶⒹ
18 ⒶⒹ	42 ⒶⒹ	66 ⒶⒹ	90 ⒶⒹ
19 ⒶⒹ	43 ⒶⒹ	67 ⒶⒹ	91 ⒶⒹ
20 ⒶⒹ	44 ⒶⒹ	68 ⒶⒹ	92 ⒶⒹ
21 ⒶⒹ	45 ⒶⒹ	69 ⒶⒹ	93 ⒶⒹ
22 ⒶⒹ	46 ⒶⒹ	70 ⒶⒹ	94 ⒶⒹ
23 ⒶⒹ	47 ⒶⒹ	71 ⒶⒹ	95 ⒶⒹ
24 ⒶⒹ	48 ⒶⒹ	72 ⒶⒹ	

ANSWER SHEET—PRACTICE TEST 4
TRIAL 2

PART A—ADDRESS CHECKING   DATE _____

1 Ⓐ Ⓓ	25 Ⓐ Ⓓ	49 Ⓐ Ⓓ	73 Ⓐ Ⓓ
2 Ⓐ Ⓓ	26 Ⓐ Ⓓ	50 Ⓐ Ⓓ	74 Ⓐ Ⓓ
3 Ⓐ Ⓓ	27 Ⓐ Ⓓ	51 Ⓐ Ⓓ	75 Ⓐ Ⓓ
4 Ⓐ Ⓓ	28 Ⓐ Ⓓ	52 Ⓐ Ⓓ	76 Ⓐ Ⓓ
5 Ⓐ Ⓓ	29 Ⓐ Ⓓ	53 Ⓐ Ⓓ	77 Ⓐ Ⓓ
6 Ⓐ Ⓓ	30 Ⓐ Ⓓ	54 Ⓐ Ⓓ	78 Ⓐ Ⓓ
7 Ⓐ Ⓓ	31 Ⓐ Ⓓ	55 Ⓐ Ⓓ	79 Ⓐ Ⓓ
8 Ⓐ Ⓓ	32 Ⓐ Ⓓ	56 Ⓐ Ⓓ	80 Ⓐ Ⓓ
9 Ⓐ Ⓓ	33 Ⓐ Ⓓ	57 Ⓐ Ⓓ	81 Ⓐ Ⓓ
10 Ⓐ Ⓓ	34 Ⓐ Ⓓ	58 Ⓐ Ⓓ	82 Ⓐ Ⓓ
11 Ⓐ Ⓓ	35 Ⓐ Ⓓ	59 Ⓐ Ⓓ	83 Ⓐ Ⓓ
12 Ⓐ Ⓓ	36 Ⓐ Ⓓ	60 Ⓐ Ⓓ	84 Ⓐ Ⓓ
13 Ⓐ Ⓓ	37 Ⓐ Ⓓ	61 Ⓐ Ⓓ	85 Ⓐ Ⓓ
14 Ⓐ Ⓓ	38 Ⓐ Ⓓ	62 Ⓐ Ⓓ	86 Ⓐ Ⓓ
15 Ⓐ Ⓓ	39 Ⓐ Ⓓ	63 Ⓐ Ⓓ	87 Ⓐ Ⓓ
16 Ⓐ Ⓓ	40 Ⓐ Ⓓ	64 Ⓐ Ⓓ	88 Ⓐ Ⓓ
17 Ⓐ Ⓓ	41 Ⓐ Ⓓ	65 Ⓐ Ⓓ	89 Ⓐ Ⓓ
18 Ⓐ Ⓓ	42 Ⓐ Ⓓ	66 Ⓐ Ⓓ	90 Ⓐ Ⓓ
19 Ⓐ Ⓓ	43 Ⓐ Ⓓ	67 Ⓐ Ⓓ	91 Ⓐ Ⓓ
20 Ⓐ Ⓓ	44 Ⓐ Ⓓ	68 Ⓐ Ⓓ	92 Ⓐ Ⓓ
21 Ⓐ Ⓓ	45 Ⓐ Ⓓ	69 Ⓐ Ⓓ	93 Ⓐ Ⓓ
22 Ⓐ Ⓓ	46 Ⓐ Ⓓ	70 Ⓐ Ⓓ	94 Ⓐ Ⓓ
23 Ⓐ Ⓓ	47 Ⓐ Ⓓ	71 Ⓐ Ⓓ	95 Ⓐ Ⓓ
24 Ⓐ Ⓓ	48 Ⓐ Ⓓ	72 Ⓐ Ⓓ	

ANSWER SHEET—PRACTICE TEST 4
TRIAL 3

PART A—ADDRESS CHECKING   DATE _____

1 Ⓐ Ⓓ	25 Ⓐ Ⓓ	49 Ⓐ Ⓓ	73 Ⓐ Ⓓ
2 Ⓐ Ⓓ	26 Ⓐ Ⓓ	50 Ⓐ Ⓓ	74 Ⓐ Ⓓ
3 Ⓐ Ⓓ	27 Ⓐ Ⓓ	51 Ⓐ Ⓓ	75 Ⓐ Ⓓ
4 Ⓐ Ⓓ	28 Ⓐ Ⓓ	52 Ⓐ Ⓓ	76 Ⓐ Ⓓ
5 Ⓐ Ⓓ	29 Ⓐ Ⓓ	53 Ⓐ Ⓓ	77 Ⓐ Ⓓ
6 Ⓐ Ⓓ	30 Ⓐ Ⓓ	54 Ⓐ Ⓓ	78 Ⓐ Ⓓ
7 Ⓐ Ⓓ	31 Ⓐ Ⓓ	55 Ⓐ Ⓓ	79 Ⓐ Ⓓ
8 Ⓐ Ⓓ	32 Ⓐ Ⓓ	56 Ⓐ Ⓓ	80 Ⓐ Ⓓ
9 Ⓐ Ⓓ	33 Ⓐ Ⓓ	57 Ⓐ Ⓓ	81 Ⓐ Ⓓ
10 Ⓐ Ⓓ	34 Ⓐ Ⓓ	58 Ⓐ Ⓓ	82 Ⓐ Ⓓ
11 Ⓐ Ⓓ	35 Ⓐ Ⓓ	59 Ⓐ Ⓓ	83 Ⓐ Ⓓ
12 Ⓐ Ⓓ	36 Ⓐ Ⓓ	60 Ⓐ Ⓓ	84 Ⓐ Ⓓ
13 Ⓐ Ⓓ	37 Ⓐ Ⓓ	61 Ⓐ Ⓓ	85 Ⓐ Ⓓ
14 Ⓐ Ⓓ	38 Ⓐ Ⓓ	62 Ⓐ Ⓓ	86 Ⓐ Ⓓ
15 Ⓐ Ⓓ	39 Ⓐ Ⓓ	63 Ⓐ Ⓓ	87 Ⓐ Ⓓ
16 Ⓐ Ⓓ	40 Ⓐ Ⓓ	64 Ⓐ Ⓓ	88 Ⓐ Ⓓ
17 Ⓐ Ⓓ	41 Ⓐ Ⓓ	65 Ⓐ Ⓓ	89 Ⓐ Ⓓ
18 Ⓐ Ⓓ	42 Ⓐ Ⓓ	66 Ⓐ Ⓓ	90 Ⓐ Ⓓ
19 Ⓐ Ⓓ	43 Ⓐ Ⓓ	67 Ⓐ Ⓓ	91 Ⓐ Ⓓ
20 Ⓐ Ⓓ	44 Ⓐ Ⓓ	68 Ⓐ Ⓓ	92 Ⓐ Ⓓ
21 Ⓐ Ⓓ	45 Ⓐ Ⓓ	69 Ⓐ Ⓓ	93 Ⓐ Ⓓ
22 Ⓐ Ⓓ	46 Ⓐ Ⓓ	70 Ⓐ Ⓓ	94 Ⓐ Ⓓ
23 Ⓐ Ⓓ	47 Ⓐ Ⓓ	71 Ⓐ Ⓓ	95 Ⓐ Ⓓ
24 Ⓐ Ⓓ	48 Ⓐ Ⓓ	72 Ⓐ Ⓓ	

ANSWER SHEET—PRACTICE TEST 5
TRIAL 2

PART A—ADDRESS CHECKING   DATE _____

1 Ⓐ Ⓓ	25 Ⓐ Ⓓ	49 Ⓐ Ⓓ	73 Ⓐ Ⓓ
2 Ⓐ Ⓓ	26 Ⓐ Ⓓ	50 Ⓐ Ⓓ	74 Ⓐ Ⓓ
3 Ⓐ Ⓓ	27 Ⓐ Ⓓ	51 Ⓐ Ⓓ	75 Ⓐ Ⓓ
4 Ⓐ Ⓓ	28 Ⓐ Ⓓ	52 Ⓐ Ⓓ	76 Ⓐ Ⓓ
5 Ⓐ Ⓓ	29 Ⓐ Ⓓ	53 Ⓐ Ⓓ	77 Ⓐ Ⓓ
6 Ⓐ Ⓓ	30 Ⓐ Ⓓ	54 Ⓐ Ⓓ	78 Ⓐ Ⓓ
7 Ⓐ Ⓓ	31 Ⓐ Ⓓ	55 Ⓐ Ⓓ	79 Ⓐ Ⓓ
8 Ⓐ Ⓓ	32 Ⓐ Ⓓ	56 Ⓐ Ⓓ	80 Ⓐ Ⓓ
9 Ⓐ Ⓓ	33 Ⓐ Ⓓ	57 Ⓐ Ⓓ	81 Ⓐ Ⓓ
10 Ⓐ Ⓓ	34 Ⓐ Ⓓ	58 Ⓐ Ⓓ	82 Ⓐ Ⓓ
11 Ⓐ Ⓓ	35 Ⓐ Ⓓ	59 Ⓐ Ⓓ	83 Ⓐ Ⓓ
12 Ⓐ Ⓓ	36 Ⓐ Ⓓ	60 Ⓐ Ⓓ	84 Ⓐ Ⓓ
13 Ⓐ Ⓓ	37 Ⓐ Ⓓ	61 Ⓐ Ⓓ	85 Ⓐ Ⓓ
14 Ⓐ Ⓓ	38 Ⓐ Ⓓ	62 Ⓐ Ⓓ	86 Ⓐ Ⓓ
15 Ⓐ Ⓓ	39 Ⓐ Ⓓ	63 Ⓐ Ⓓ	87 Ⓐ Ⓓ
16 Ⓐ Ⓓ	40 Ⓐ Ⓓ	64 Ⓐ Ⓓ	88 Ⓐ Ⓓ
17 Ⓐ Ⓓ	41 Ⓐ Ⓓ	65 Ⓐ Ⓓ	89 Ⓐ Ⓓ
18 Ⓐ Ⓓ	42 Ⓐ Ⓓ	66 Ⓐ Ⓓ	90 Ⓐ Ⓓ
19 Ⓐ Ⓓ	43 Ⓐ Ⓓ	67 Ⓐ Ⓓ	91 Ⓐ Ⓓ
20 Ⓐ Ⓓ	44 Ⓐ Ⓓ	68 Ⓐ Ⓓ	92 Ⓐ Ⓓ
21 Ⓐ Ⓓ	45 Ⓐ Ⓓ	69 Ⓐ Ⓓ	93 Ⓐ Ⓓ
22 Ⓐ Ⓓ	46 Ⓐ Ⓓ	70 Ⓐ Ⓓ	94 Ⓐ Ⓓ
23 Ⓐ Ⓓ	47 Ⓐ Ⓓ	71 Ⓐ Ⓓ	95 Ⓐ Ⓓ
24 Ⓐ Ⓓ	48 Ⓐ Ⓓ	72 Ⓐ Ⓓ	

ANSWER SHEET—PRACTICE TEST 5
TRIAL 3

PART A—ADDRESS CHECKING   DATE _____

1 Ⓐ Ⓓ	25 Ⓐ Ⓓ	49 Ⓐ Ⓓ	73 Ⓐ Ⓓ
2 Ⓐ Ⓓ	26 Ⓐ Ⓓ	50 Ⓐ Ⓓ	74 Ⓐ Ⓓ
3 Ⓐ Ⓓ	27 Ⓐ Ⓓ	51 Ⓐ Ⓓ	75 Ⓐ Ⓓ
4 Ⓐ Ⓓ	28 Ⓐ Ⓓ	52 Ⓐ Ⓓ	76 Ⓐ Ⓓ
5 Ⓐ Ⓓ	29 Ⓐ Ⓓ	53 Ⓐ Ⓓ	77 Ⓐ Ⓓ
6 Ⓐ Ⓓ	30 Ⓐ Ⓓ	54 Ⓐ Ⓓ	78 Ⓐ Ⓓ
7 Ⓐ Ⓓ	31 Ⓐ Ⓓ	55 Ⓐ Ⓓ	79 Ⓐ Ⓓ
8 Ⓐ Ⓓ	32 Ⓐ Ⓓ	56 Ⓐ Ⓓ	80 Ⓐ Ⓓ
9 Ⓐ Ⓓ	33 Ⓐ Ⓓ	57 Ⓐ Ⓓ	81 Ⓐ Ⓓ
10 Ⓐ Ⓓ	34 Ⓐ Ⓓ	58 Ⓐ Ⓓ	82 Ⓐ Ⓓ
11 Ⓐ Ⓓ	35 Ⓐ Ⓓ	59 Ⓐ Ⓓ	83 Ⓐ Ⓓ
12 Ⓐ Ⓓ	36 Ⓐ Ⓓ	60 Ⓐ Ⓓ	84 Ⓐ Ⓓ
13 Ⓐ Ⓓ	37 Ⓐ Ⓓ	61 Ⓐ Ⓓ	85 Ⓐ Ⓓ
14 Ⓐ Ⓓ	38 Ⓐ Ⓓ	62 Ⓐ Ⓓ	86 Ⓐ Ⓓ
15 Ⓐ Ⓓ	39 Ⓐ Ⓓ	63 Ⓐ Ⓓ	87 Ⓐ Ⓓ
16 Ⓐ Ⓓ	40 Ⓐ Ⓓ	64 Ⓐ Ⓓ	88 Ⓐ Ⓓ
17 Ⓐ Ⓓ	41 Ⓐ Ⓓ	65 Ⓐ Ⓓ	89 Ⓐ Ⓓ
18 Ⓐ Ⓓ	42 Ⓐ Ⓓ	66 Ⓐ Ⓓ	90 Ⓐ Ⓓ
19 Ⓐ Ⓓ	43 Ⓐ Ⓓ	67 Ⓐ Ⓓ	91 Ⓐ Ⓓ
20 Ⓐ Ⓓ	44 Ⓐ Ⓓ	68 Ⓐ Ⓓ	92 Ⓐ Ⓓ
21 Ⓐ Ⓓ	45 Ⓐ Ⓓ	69 Ⓐ Ⓓ	93 Ⓐ Ⓓ
22 Ⓐ Ⓓ	46 Ⓐ Ⓓ	70 Ⓐ Ⓓ	94 Ⓐ Ⓓ
23 Ⓐ Ⓓ	47 Ⓐ Ⓓ	71 Ⓐ Ⓓ	95 Ⓐ Ⓓ
24 Ⓐ Ⓓ	48 Ⓐ Ⓓ	72 Ⓐ Ⓓ	

ANSWER SHEET—DIAGNOSTIC
PRACTICE TEST
TRIAL 2

PART B—MEMORY FOR ADDRESSES
LIST 1   DATE _____

1 Ⓐ Ⓑ Ⓒ Ⓓ Ⓔ	31 Ⓐ Ⓑ Ⓒ Ⓓ Ⓔ	61 Ⓐ Ⓑ Ⓒ Ⓓ Ⓔ
2 Ⓐ Ⓑ Ⓒ Ⓓ Ⓔ	32 Ⓐ Ⓑ Ⓒ Ⓓ Ⓔ	62 Ⓐ Ⓑ Ⓒ Ⓓ Ⓔ
3 Ⓐ Ⓑ Ⓒ Ⓓ Ⓔ	33 Ⓐ Ⓑ Ⓒ Ⓓ Ⓔ	63 Ⓐ Ⓑ Ⓒ Ⓓ Ⓔ
4 Ⓐ Ⓑ Ⓒ Ⓓ Ⓔ	34 Ⓐ Ⓑ Ⓒ Ⓓ Ⓔ	64 Ⓐ Ⓑ Ⓒ Ⓓ Ⓔ
5 Ⓐ Ⓑ Ⓒ Ⓓ Ⓔ	35 Ⓐ Ⓑ Ⓒ Ⓓ Ⓔ	65 Ⓐ Ⓑ Ⓒ Ⓓ Ⓔ
6 Ⓐ Ⓑ Ⓒ Ⓓ Ⓔ	36 Ⓐ Ⓑ Ⓒ Ⓓ Ⓔ	66 Ⓐ Ⓑ Ⓒ Ⓓ Ⓔ
7 Ⓐ Ⓑ Ⓒ Ⓓ Ⓔ	37 Ⓐ Ⓑ Ⓒ Ⓓ Ⓔ	67 Ⓐ Ⓑ Ⓒ Ⓓ Ⓔ
8 Ⓐ Ⓑ Ⓒ Ⓓ Ⓔ	38 Ⓐ Ⓑ Ⓒ Ⓓ Ⓔ	68 Ⓐ Ⓑ Ⓒ Ⓓ Ⓔ
9 Ⓐ Ⓑ Ⓒ Ⓓ Ⓔ	39 Ⓐ Ⓑ Ⓒ Ⓓ Ⓔ	69 Ⓐ Ⓑ Ⓒ Ⓓ Ⓔ
10 Ⓐ Ⓑ Ⓒ Ⓓ Ⓔ	40 Ⓐ Ⓑ Ⓒ Ⓓ Ⓔ	70 Ⓐ Ⓑ Ⓒ Ⓓ Ⓔ
11 Ⓐ Ⓑ Ⓒ Ⓓ Ⓔ	41 Ⓐ Ⓑ Ⓒ Ⓓ Ⓔ	71 Ⓐ Ⓑ Ⓒ Ⓓ Ⓔ
12 Ⓐ Ⓑ Ⓒ Ⓓ Ⓔ	42 Ⓐ Ⓑ Ⓒ Ⓓ Ⓔ	72 Ⓐ Ⓑ Ⓒ Ⓓ Ⓔ
13 Ⓐ Ⓑ Ⓒ Ⓓ Ⓔ	43 Ⓐ Ⓑ Ⓒ Ⓓ Ⓔ	73 Ⓐ Ⓑ Ⓒ Ⓓ Ⓔ
14 Ⓐ Ⓑ Ⓒ Ⓓ Ⓔ	44 Ⓐ Ⓑ Ⓒ Ⓓ Ⓔ	74 Ⓐ Ⓑ Ⓒ Ⓓ Ⓔ
15 Ⓐ Ⓑ Ⓒ Ⓓ Ⓔ	45 Ⓐ Ⓑ Ⓒ Ⓓ Ⓔ	75 Ⓐ Ⓑ Ⓒ Ⓓ Ⓔ
16 Ⓐ Ⓑ Ⓒ Ⓓ Ⓔ	46 Ⓐ Ⓑ Ⓒ Ⓓ Ⓔ	76 Ⓐ Ⓑ Ⓒ Ⓓ Ⓔ
17 Ⓐ Ⓑ Ⓒ Ⓓ Ⓔ	47 Ⓐ Ⓑ Ⓒ Ⓓ Ⓔ	77 Ⓐ Ⓑ Ⓒ Ⓓ Ⓔ
18 Ⓐ Ⓑ Ⓒ Ⓓ Ⓔ	48 Ⓐ Ⓑ Ⓒ Ⓓ Ⓔ	78 Ⓐ Ⓑ Ⓒ Ⓓ Ⓔ
19 Ⓐ Ⓑ Ⓒ Ⓓ Ⓔ	49 Ⓐ Ⓑ Ⓒ Ⓓ Ⓔ	79 Ⓐ Ⓑ Ⓒ Ⓓ Ⓔ
20 Ⓐ Ⓑ Ⓒ Ⓓ Ⓔ	50 Ⓐ Ⓑ Ⓒ Ⓓ Ⓔ	80 Ⓐ Ⓑ Ⓒ Ⓓ Ⓔ
21 Ⓐ Ⓑ Ⓒ Ⓓ Ⓔ	51 Ⓐ Ⓑ Ⓒ Ⓓ Ⓔ	81 Ⓐ Ⓑ Ⓒ Ⓓ Ⓔ
22 Ⓐ Ⓑ Ⓒ Ⓓ Ⓔ	52 Ⓐ Ⓑ Ⓒ Ⓓ Ⓔ	82 Ⓐ Ⓑ Ⓒ Ⓓ Ⓔ
23 Ⓐ Ⓑ Ⓒ Ⓓ Ⓔ	53 Ⓐ Ⓑ Ⓒ Ⓓ Ⓔ	83 Ⓐ Ⓑ Ⓒ Ⓓ Ⓔ
24 Ⓐ Ⓑ Ⓒ Ⓓ Ⓔ	54 Ⓐ Ⓑ Ⓒ Ⓓ Ⓔ	84 Ⓐ Ⓑ Ⓒ Ⓓ Ⓔ
25 Ⓐ Ⓑ Ⓒ Ⓓ Ⓔ	55 Ⓐ Ⓑ Ⓒ Ⓓ Ⓔ	85 Ⓐ Ⓑ Ⓒ Ⓓ Ⓔ
26 Ⓐ Ⓑ Ⓒ Ⓓ Ⓔ	56 Ⓐ Ⓑ Ⓒ Ⓓ Ⓔ	86 Ⓐ Ⓑ Ⓒ Ⓓ Ⓔ
27 Ⓐ Ⓑ Ⓒ Ⓓ Ⓔ	57 Ⓐ Ⓑ Ⓒ Ⓓ Ⓔ	87 Ⓐ Ⓑ Ⓒ Ⓓ Ⓔ
28 Ⓐ Ⓑ Ⓒ Ⓓ Ⓔ	58 Ⓐ Ⓑ Ⓒ Ⓓ Ⓔ	88 Ⓐ Ⓑ Ⓒ Ⓓ Ⓔ
29 Ⓐ Ⓑ Ⓒ Ⓓ Ⓔ	59 Ⓐ Ⓑ Ⓒ Ⓓ Ⓔ	
30 Ⓐ Ⓑ Ⓒ Ⓓ Ⓔ	60 Ⓐ Ⓑ Ⓒ Ⓓ Ⓔ	

ANSWER SHEET—DIAGNOSTIC
PRACTICE TEST
TRIAL 3

PART B—MEMORY FOR ADDRESSES
LIST 1　　　　　　　　　　DATE _____

1 Ⓐ Ⓑ Ⓒ Ⓓ Ⓔ	31 Ⓐ Ⓑ Ⓒ Ⓓ Ⓔ	61 Ⓐ Ⓑ Ⓒ Ⓓ Ⓔ
2 Ⓐ Ⓑ Ⓒ Ⓓ Ⓔ	32 Ⓐ Ⓑ Ⓒ Ⓓ Ⓔ	62 Ⓐ Ⓑ Ⓒ Ⓓ Ⓔ
3 Ⓐ Ⓑ Ⓒ Ⓓ Ⓔ	33 Ⓐ Ⓑ Ⓒ Ⓓ Ⓔ	63 Ⓐ Ⓑ Ⓒ Ⓓ Ⓔ
4 Ⓐ Ⓑ Ⓒ Ⓓ Ⓔ	34 Ⓐ Ⓑ Ⓒ Ⓓ Ⓔ	64 Ⓐ Ⓑ Ⓒ Ⓓ Ⓔ
5 Ⓐ Ⓑ Ⓒ Ⓓ Ⓔ	35 Ⓐ Ⓑ Ⓒ Ⓓ Ⓔ	65 Ⓐ Ⓑ Ⓒ Ⓓ Ⓔ
6 Ⓐ Ⓑ Ⓒ Ⓓ Ⓔ	36 Ⓐ Ⓑ Ⓒ Ⓓ Ⓔ	66 Ⓐ Ⓑ Ⓒ Ⓓ Ⓔ
7 Ⓐ Ⓑ Ⓒ Ⓓ Ⓔ	37 Ⓐ Ⓑ Ⓒ Ⓓ Ⓔ	67 Ⓐ Ⓑ Ⓒ Ⓓ Ⓔ
8 Ⓐ Ⓑ Ⓒ Ⓓ Ⓔ	38 Ⓐ Ⓑ Ⓒ Ⓓ Ⓔ	68 Ⓐ Ⓑ Ⓒ Ⓓ Ⓔ
9 Ⓐ Ⓑ Ⓒ Ⓓ Ⓔ	39 Ⓐ Ⓑ Ⓒ Ⓓ Ⓔ	69 Ⓐ Ⓑ Ⓒ Ⓓ Ⓔ
10 Ⓐ Ⓑ Ⓒ Ⓓ Ⓔ	40 Ⓐ Ⓑ Ⓒ Ⓓ Ⓔ	70 Ⓐ Ⓑ Ⓒ Ⓓ Ⓔ
11 Ⓐ Ⓑ Ⓒ Ⓓ Ⓔ	41 Ⓐ Ⓑ Ⓒ Ⓓ Ⓔ	71 Ⓐ Ⓑ Ⓒ Ⓓ Ⓔ
12 Ⓐ Ⓑ Ⓒ Ⓓ Ⓔ	42 Ⓐ Ⓑ Ⓒ Ⓓ Ⓔ	72 Ⓐ Ⓑ Ⓒ Ⓓ Ⓔ
13 Ⓐ Ⓑ Ⓒ Ⓓ Ⓔ	43 Ⓐ Ⓑ Ⓒ Ⓓ Ⓔ	73 Ⓐ Ⓑ Ⓒ Ⓓ Ⓔ
14 Ⓐ Ⓑ Ⓒ Ⓓ Ⓔ	44 Ⓐ Ⓑ Ⓒ Ⓓ Ⓔ	74 Ⓐ Ⓑ Ⓒ Ⓓ Ⓔ
15 Ⓐ Ⓑ Ⓒ Ⓓ Ⓔ	45 Ⓐ Ⓑ Ⓒ Ⓓ Ⓔ	75 Ⓐ Ⓑ Ⓒ Ⓓ Ⓔ
16 Ⓐ Ⓑ Ⓒ Ⓓ Ⓔ	46 Ⓐ Ⓑ Ⓒ Ⓓ Ⓔ	76 Ⓐ Ⓑ Ⓒ Ⓓ Ⓔ
17 Ⓐ Ⓑ Ⓒ Ⓓ Ⓔ	47 Ⓐ Ⓑ Ⓒ Ⓓ Ⓔ	77 Ⓐ Ⓑ Ⓒ Ⓓ Ⓔ
18 Ⓐ Ⓑ Ⓒ Ⓓ Ⓔ	48 Ⓐ Ⓑ Ⓒ Ⓓ Ⓔ	78 Ⓐ Ⓑ Ⓒ Ⓓ Ⓔ
19 Ⓐ Ⓑ Ⓒ Ⓓ Ⓔ	49 Ⓐ Ⓑ Ⓒ Ⓓ Ⓔ	79 Ⓐ Ⓑ Ⓒ Ⓓ Ⓔ
20 Ⓐ Ⓑ Ⓒ Ⓓ Ⓔ	50 Ⓐ Ⓑ Ⓒ Ⓓ Ⓔ	80 Ⓐ Ⓑ Ⓒ Ⓓ Ⓔ
21 Ⓐ Ⓑ Ⓒ Ⓓ Ⓔ	51 Ⓐ Ⓑ Ⓒ Ⓓ Ⓔ	81 Ⓐ Ⓑ Ⓒ Ⓓ Ⓔ
22 Ⓐ Ⓑ Ⓒ Ⓓ Ⓔ	52 Ⓐ Ⓑ Ⓒ Ⓓ Ⓔ	82 Ⓐ Ⓑ Ⓒ Ⓓ Ⓔ
23 Ⓐ Ⓑ Ⓒ Ⓓ Ⓔ	53 Ⓐ Ⓑ Ⓒ Ⓓ Ⓔ	83 Ⓐ Ⓑ Ⓒ Ⓓ Ⓔ
24 Ⓐ Ⓑ Ⓒ Ⓓ Ⓔ	54 Ⓐ Ⓑ Ⓒ Ⓓ Ⓔ	84 Ⓐ Ⓑ Ⓒ Ⓓ Ⓔ
25 Ⓐ Ⓑ Ⓒ Ⓓ Ⓔ	55 Ⓐ Ⓑ Ⓒ Ⓓ Ⓔ	85 Ⓐ Ⓑ Ⓒ Ⓓ Ⓔ
26 Ⓐ Ⓑ Ⓒ Ⓓ Ⓔ	56 Ⓐ Ⓑ Ⓒ Ⓓ Ⓔ	86 Ⓐ Ⓑ Ⓒ Ⓓ Ⓔ
27 Ⓐ Ⓑ Ⓒ Ⓓ Ⓔ	57 Ⓐ Ⓑ Ⓒ Ⓓ Ⓔ	87 Ⓐ Ⓑ Ⓒ Ⓓ Ⓔ
28 Ⓐ Ⓑ Ⓒ Ⓓ Ⓔ	58 Ⓐ Ⓑ Ⓒ Ⓓ Ⓔ	88 Ⓐ Ⓑ Ⓒ Ⓓ Ⓔ
29 Ⓐ Ⓑ Ⓒ Ⓓ Ⓔ	59 Ⓐ Ⓑ Ⓒ Ⓓ Ⓔ	
30 Ⓐ Ⓑ Ⓒ Ⓓ Ⓔ	60 Ⓐ Ⓑ Ⓒ Ⓓ Ⓔ	

ANSWER SHEET—PRACTICE TEST 1
TRIAL 2

PART B—MEMORY FOR ADDRESSES
LIST 1   DATE _____

1 Ⓐ Ⓑ Ⓒ Ⓓ Ⓔ	31 Ⓐ Ⓑ Ⓒ Ⓓ Ⓔ	61 Ⓐ Ⓑ Ⓒ Ⓓ Ⓔ
2 Ⓐ Ⓑ Ⓒ Ⓓ Ⓔ	32 Ⓐ Ⓑ Ⓒ Ⓓ Ⓔ	62 Ⓐ Ⓑ Ⓒ Ⓓ Ⓔ
3 Ⓐ Ⓑ Ⓒ Ⓓ Ⓔ	33 Ⓐ Ⓑ Ⓒ Ⓓ Ⓔ	63 Ⓐ Ⓑ Ⓒ Ⓓ Ⓔ
4 Ⓐ Ⓑ Ⓒ Ⓓ Ⓔ	34 Ⓐ Ⓑ Ⓒ Ⓓ Ⓔ	64 Ⓐ Ⓑ Ⓒ Ⓓ Ⓔ
5 Ⓐ Ⓑ Ⓒ Ⓓ Ⓔ	35 Ⓐ Ⓑ Ⓒ Ⓓ Ⓔ	65 Ⓐ Ⓑ Ⓒ Ⓓ Ⓔ
6 Ⓐ Ⓑ Ⓒ Ⓓ Ⓔ	36 Ⓐ Ⓑ Ⓒ Ⓓ Ⓔ	66 Ⓐ Ⓑ Ⓒ Ⓓ Ⓔ
7 Ⓐ Ⓑ Ⓒ Ⓓ Ⓔ	37 Ⓐ Ⓑ Ⓒ Ⓓ Ⓔ	67 Ⓐ Ⓑ Ⓒ Ⓓ Ⓔ
8 Ⓐ Ⓑ Ⓒ Ⓓ Ⓔ	38 Ⓐ Ⓑ Ⓒ Ⓓ Ⓔ	68 Ⓐ Ⓑ Ⓒ Ⓓ Ⓔ
9 Ⓐ Ⓑ Ⓒ Ⓓ Ⓔ	39 Ⓐ Ⓑ Ⓒ Ⓓ Ⓔ	69 Ⓐ Ⓑ Ⓒ Ⓓ Ⓔ
10 Ⓐ Ⓑ Ⓒ Ⓓ Ⓔ	40 Ⓐ Ⓑ Ⓒ Ⓓ Ⓔ	70 Ⓐ Ⓑ Ⓒ Ⓓ Ⓔ
11 Ⓐ Ⓑ Ⓒ Ⓓ Ⓔ	41 Ⓐ Ⓑ Ⓒ Ⓓ Ⓔ	71 Ⓐ Ⓑ Ⓒ Ⓓ Ⓔ
12 Ⓐ Ⓑ Ⓒ Ⓓ Ⓔ	42 Ⓐ Ⓑ Ⓒ Ⓓ Ⓔ	72 Ⓐ Ⓑ Ⓒ Ⓓ Ⓔ
13 Ⓐ Ⓑ Ⓒ Ⓓ Ⓔ	43 Ⓐ Ⓑ Ⓒ Ⓓ Ⓔ	73 Ⓐ Ⓑ Ⓒ Ⓓ Ⓔ
14 Ⓐ Ⓑ Ⓒ Ⓓ Ⓔ	44 Ⓐ Ⓑ Ⓒ Ⓓ Ⓔ	74 Ⓐ Ⓑ Ⓒ Ⓓ Ⓔ
15 Ⓐ Ⓑ Ⓒ Ⓓ Ⓔ	45 Ⓐ Ⓑ Ⓒ Ⓓ Ⓔ	75 Ⓐ Ⓑ Ⓒ Ⓓ Ⓔ
16 Ⓐ Ⓑ Ⓒ Ⓓ Ⓔ	46 Ⓐ Ⓑ Ⓒ Ⓓ Ⓔ	76 Ⓐ Ⓑ Ⓒ Ⓓ Ⓔ
17 Ⓐ Ⓑ Ⓒ Ⓓ Ⓔ	47 Ⓐ Ⓑ Ⓒ Ⓓ Ⓔ	77 Ⓐ Ⓑ Ⓒ Ⓓ Ⓔ
18 Ⓐ Ⓑ Ⓒ Ⓓ Ⓔ	48 Ⓐ Ⓑ Ⓒ Ⓓ Ⓔ	78 Ⓐ Ⓑ Ⓒ Ⓓ Ⓔ
19 Ⓐ Ⓑ Ⓒ Ⓓ Ⓔ	49 Ⓐ Ⓑ Ⓒ Ⓓ Ⓔ	79 Ⓐ Ⓑ Ⓒ Ⓓ Ⓔ
20 Ⓐ Ⓑ Ⓒ Ⓓ Ⓔ	50 Ⓐ Ⓑ Ⓒ Ⓓ Ⓔ	80 Ⓐ Ⓑ Ⓒ Ⓓ Ⓔ
21 Ⓐ Ⓑ Ⓒ Ⓓ Ⓔ	51 Ⓐ Ⓑ Ⓒ Ⓓ Ⓔ	81 Ⓐ Ⓑ Ⓒ Ⓓ Ⓔ
22 Ⓐ Ⓑ Ⓒ Ⓓ Ⓔ	52 Ⓐ Ⓑ Ⓒ Ⓓ Ⓔ	82 Ⓐ Ⓑ Ⓒ Ⓓ Ⓔ
23 Ⓐ Ⓑ Ⓒ Ⓓ Ⓔ	53 Ⓐ Ⓑ Ⓒ Ⓓ Ⓔ	83 Ⓐ Ⓑ Ⓒ Ⓓ Ⓔ
24 Ⓐ Ⓑ Ⓒ Ⓓ Ⓔ	54 Ⓐ Ⓑ Ⓒ Ⓓ Ⓔ	84 Ⓐ Ⓑ Ⓒ Ⓓ Ⓔ
25 Ⓐ Ⓑ Ⓒ Ⓓ Ⓔ	55 Ⓐ Ⓑ Ⓒ Ⓓ Ⓔ	85 Ⓐ Ⓑ Ⓒ Ⓓ Ⓔ
26 Ⓐ Ⓑ Ⓒ Ⓓ Ⓔ	56 Ⓐ Ⓑ Ⓒ Ⓓ Ⓔ	86 Ⓐ Ⓑ Ⓒ Ⓓ Ⓔ
27 Ⓐ Ⓑ Ⓒ Ⓓ Ⓔ	57 Ⓐ Ⓑ Ⓒ Ⓓ Ⓔ	87 Ⓐ Ⓑ Ⓒ Ⓓ Ⓔ
28 Ⓐ Ⓑ Ⓒ Ⓓ Ⓔ	58 Ⓐ Ⓑ Ⓒ Ⓓ Ⓔ	88 Ⓐ Ⓑ Ⓒ Ⓓ Ⓔ
29 Ⓐ Ⓑ Ⓒ Ⓓ Ⓔ	59 Ⓐ Ⓑ Ⓒ Ⓓ Ⓔ	
30 Ⓐ Ⓑ Ⓒ Ⓓ Ⓔ	60 Ⓐ Ⓑ Ⓒ Ⓓ Ⓔ	

ANSWER SHEET—PRACTICE TEST 1
TRIAL 3

PART B—MEMORY FOR ADDRESSES
LIST 1   DATE _____

1 Ⓐ Ⓑ Ⓒ Ⓓ Ⓔ	31 Ⓐ Ⓑ Ⓒ Ⓓ Ⓔ	61 Ⓐ Ⓑ Ⓒ Ⓓ Ⓔ
2 Ⓐ Ⓑ Ⓒ Ⓓ Ⓔ	32 Ⓐ Ⓑ Ⓒ Ⓓ Ⓔ	62 Ⓐ Ⓑ Ⓒ Ⓓ Ⓔ
3 Ⓐ Ⓑ Ⓒ Ⓓ Ⓔ	33 Ⓐ Ⓑ Ⓒ Ⓓ Ⓔ	63 Ⓐ Ⓑ Ⓒ Ⓓ Ⓔ
4 Ⓐ Ⓑ Ⓒ Ⓓ Ⓔ	34 Ⓐ Ⓑ Ⓒ Ⓓ Ⓔ	64 Ⓐ Ⓑ Ⓒ Ⓓ Ⓔ
5 Ⓐ Ⓑ Ⓒ Ⓓ Ⓔ	35 Ⓐ Ⓑ Ⓒ Ⓓ Ⓔ	65 Ⓐ Ⓑ Ⓒ Ⓓ Ⓔ
6 Ⓐ Ⓑ Ⓒ Ⓓ Ⓔ	36 Ⓐ Ⓑ Ⓒ Ⓓ Ⓔ	66 Ⓐ Ⓑ Ⓒ Ⓓ Ⓔ
7 Ⓐ Ⓑ Ⓒ Ⓓ Ⓔ	37 Ⓐ Ⓑ Ⓒ Ⓓ Ⓔ	67 Ⓐ Ⓑ Ⓒ Ⓓ Ⓔ
8 Ⓐ Ⓑ Ⓒ Ⓓ Ⓔ	38 Ⓐ Ⓑ Ⓒ Ⓓ Ⓔ	68 Ⓐ Ⓑ Ⓒ Ⓓ Ⓔ
9 Ⓐ Ⓑ Ⓒ Ⓓ Ⓔ	39 Ⓐ Ⓑ Ⓒ Ⓓ Ⓔ	69 Ⓐ Ⓑ Ⓒ Ⓓ Ⓔ
10 Ⓐ Ⓑ Ⓒ Ⓓ Ⓔ	40 Ⓐ Ⓑ Ⓒ Ⓓ Ⓔ	70 Ⓐ Ⓑ Ⓒ Ⓓ Ⓔ
11 Ⓐ Ⓑ Ⓒ Ⓓ Ⓔ	41 Ⓐ Ⓑ Ⓒ Ⓓ Ⓔ	71 Ⓐ Ⓑ Ⓒ Ⓓ Ⓔ
12 Ⓐ Ⓑ Ⓒ Ⓓ Ⓔ	42 Ⓐ Ⓑ Ⓒ Ⓓ Ⓔ	72 Ⓐ Ⓑ Ⓒ Ⓓ Ⓔ
13 Ⓐ Ⓑ Ⓒ Ⓓ Ⓔ	43 Ⓐ Ⓑ Ⓒ Ⓓ Ⓔ	73 Ⓐ Ⓑ Ⓒ Ⓓ Ⓔ
14 Ⓐ Ⓑ Ⓒ Ⓓ Ⓔ	44 Ⓐ Ⓑ Ⓒ Ⓓ Ⓔ	74 Ⓐ Ⓑ Ⓒ Ⓓ Ⓔ
15 Ⓐ Ⓑ Ⓒ Ⓓ Ⓔ	45 Ⓐ Ⓑ Ⓒ Ⓓ Ⓔ	75 Ⓐ Ⓑ Ⓒ Ⓓ Ⓔ
16 Ⓐ Ⓑ Ⓒ Ⓓ Ⓔ	46 Ⓐ Ⓑ Ⓒ Ⓓ Ⓔ	76 Ⓐ Ⓑ Ⓒ Ⓓ Ⓔ
17 Ⓐ Ⓑ Ⓒ Ⓓ Ⓔ	47 Ⓐ Ⓑ Ⓒ Ⓓ Ⓔ	77 Ⓐ Ⓑ Ⓒ Ⓓ Ⓔ
18 Ⓐ Ⓑ Ⓒ Ⓓ Ⓔ	48 Ⓐ Ⓑ Ⓒ Ⓓ Ⓔ	78 Ⓐ Ⓑ Ⓒ Ⓓ Ⓔ
19 Ⓐ Ⓑ Ⓒ Ⓓ Ⓔ	49 Ⓐ Ⓑ Ⓒ Ⓓ Ⓔ	79 Ⓐ Ⓑ Ⓒ Ⓓ Ⓔ
20 Ⓐ Ⓑ Ⓒ Ⓓ Ⓔ	50 Ⓐ Ⓑ Ⓒ Ⓓ Ⓔ	80 Ⓐ Ⓑ Ⓒ Ⓓ Ⓔ
21 Ⓐ Ⓑ Ⓒ Ⓓ Ⓔ	51 Ⓐ Ⓑ Ⓒ Ⓓ Ⓔ	81 Ⓐ Ⓑ Ⓒ Ⓓ Ⓔ
22 Ⓐ Ⓑ Ⓒ Ⓓ Ⓔ	52 Ⓐ Ⓑ Ⓒ Ⓓ Ⓔ	82 Ⓐ Ⓑ Ⓒ Ⓓ Ⓔ
23 Ⓐ Ⓑ Ⓒ Ⓓ Ⓔ	53 Ⓐ Ⓑ Ⓒ Ⓓ Ⓔ	83 Ⓐ Ⓑ Ⓒ Ⓓ Ⓔ
24 Ⓐ Ⓑ Ⓒ Ⓓ Ⓔ	54 Ⓐ Ⓑ Ⓒ Ⓓ Ⓔ	84 Ⓐ Ⓑ Ⓒ Ⓓ Ⓔ
25 Ⓐ Ⓑ Ⓒ Ⓓ Ⓔ	55 Ⓐ Ⓑ Ⓒ Ⓓ Ⓔ	85 Ⓐ Ⓑ Ⓒ Ⓓ Ⓔ
26 Ⓐ Ⓑ Ⓒ Ⓓ Ⓔ	56 Ⓐ Ⓑ Ⓒ Ⓓ Ⓔ	86 Ⓐ Ⓑ Ⓒ Ⓓ Ⓔ
27 Ⓐ Ⓑ Ⓒ Ⓓ Ⓔ	57 Ⓐ Ⓑ Ⓒ Ⓓ Ⓔ	87 Ⓐ Ⓑ Ⓒ Ⓓ Ⓔ
28 Ⓐ Ⓑ Ⓒ Ⓓ Ⓔ	58 Ⓐ Ⓑ Ⓒ Ⓓ Ⓔ	88 Ⓐ Ⓑ Ⓒ Ⓓ Ⓔ
29 Ⓐ Ⓑ Ⓒ Ⓓ Ⓔ	59 Ⓐ Ⓑ Ⓒ Ⓓ Ⓔ	
30 Ⓐ Ⓑ Ⓒ Ⓓ Ⓔ	60 Ⓐ Ⓑ Ⓒ Ⓓ Ⓔ	

ANSWER SHEET—PRACTICE TEST 2
TRIAL 2

PART B—MEMORY FOR ADDRESSES
LIST 1   DATE _____

1 Ⓐ Ⓑ Ⓒ Ⓓ Ⓔ	31 Ⓐ Ⓑ Ⓒ Ⓓ Ⓔ	61 Ⓐ Ⓑ Ⓒ Ⓓ Ⓔ
2 Ⓐ Ⓑ Ⓒ Ⓓ Ⓔ	32 Ⓐ Ⓑ Ⓒ Ⓓ Ⓔ	62 Ⓐ Ⓑ Ⓒ Ⓓ Ⓔ
3 Ⓐ Ⓑ Ⓒ Ⓓ Ⓔ	33 Ⓐ Ⓑ Ⓒ Ⓓ Ⓔ	63 Ⓐ Ⓑ Ⓒ Ⓓ Ⓔ
4 Ⓐ Ⓑ Ⓒ Ⓓ Ⓔ	34 Ⓐ Ⓑ Ⓒ Ⓓ Ⓔ	64 Ⓐ Ⓑ Ⓒ Ⓓ Ⓔ
5 Ⓐ Ⓑ Ⓒ Ⓓ Ⓔ	35 Ⓐ Ⓑ Ⓒ Ⓓ Ⓔ	65 Ⓐ Ⓑ Ⓒ Ⓓ Ⓔ
6 Ⓐ Ⓑ Ⓒ Ⓓ Ⓔ	36 Ⓐ Ⓑ Ⓒ Ⓓ Ⓔ	66 Ⓐ Ⓑ Ⓒ Ⓓ Ⓔ
7 Ⓐ Ⓑ Ⓒ Ⓓ Ⓔ	37 Ⓐ Ⓑ Ⓒ Ⓓ Ⓔ	67 Ⓐ Ⓑ Ⓒ Ⓓ Ⓔ
8 Ⓐ Ⓑ Ⓒ Ⓓ Ⓔ	38 Ⓐ Ⓑ Ⓒ Ⓓ Ⓔ	68 Ⓐ Ⓑ Ⓒ Ⓓ Ⓔ
9 Ⓐ Ⓑ Ⓒ Ⓓ Ⓔ	39 Ⓐ Ⓑ Ⓒ Ⓓ Ⓔ	69 Ⓐ Ⓑ Ⓒ Ⓓ Ⓔ
10 Ⓐ Ⓑ Ⓒ Ⓓ Ⓔ	40 Ⓐ Ⓑ Ⓒ Ⓓ Ⓔ	70 Ⓐ Ⓑ Ⓒ Ⓓ Ⓔ
11 Ⓐ Ⓑ Ⓒ Ⓓ Ⓔ	41 Ⓐ Ⓑ Ⓒ Ⓓ Ⓔ	71 Ⓐ Ⓑ Ⓒ Ⓓ Ⓔ
12 Ⓐ Ⓑ Ⓒ Ⓓ Ⓔ	42 Ⓐ Ⓑ Ⓒ Ⓓ Ⓔ	72 Ⓐ Ⓑ Ⓒ Ⓓ Ⓔ
13 Ⓐ Ⓑ Ⓒ Ⓓ Ⓔ	43 Ⓐ Ⓑ Ⓒ Ⓓ Ⓔ	73 Ⓐ Ⓑ Ⓒ Ⓓ Ⓔ
14 Ⓐ Ⓑ Ⓒ Ⓓ Ⓔ	44 Ⓐ Ⓑ Ⓒ Ⓓ Ⓔ	74 Ⓐ Ⓑ Ⓒ Ⓓ Ⓔ
15 Ⓐ Ⓑ Ⓒ Ⓓ Ⓔ	45 Ⓐ Ⓑ Ⓒ Ⓓ Ⓔ	75 Ⓐ Ⓑ Ⓒ Ⓓ Ⓔ
16 Ⓐ Ⓑ Ⓒ Ⓓ Ⓔ	46 Ⓐ Ⓑ Ⓒ Ⓓ Ⓔ	76 Ⓐ Ⓑ Ⓒ Ⓓ Ⓔ
17 Ⓐ Ⓑ Ⓒ Ⓓ Ⓔ	47 Ⓐ Ⓑ Ⓒ Ⓓ Ⓔ	77 Ⓐ Ⓑ Ⓒ Ⓓ Ⓔ
18 Ⓐ Ⓑ Ⓒ Ⓓ Ⓔ	48 Ⓐ Ⓑ Ⓒ Ⓓ Ⓔ	78 Ⓐ Ⓑ Ⓒ Ⓓ Ⓔ
19 Ⓐ Ⓑ Ⓒ Ⓓ Ⓔ	49 Ⓐ Ⓑ Ⓒ Ⓓ Ⓔ	79 Ⓐ Ⓑ Ⓒ Ⓓ Ⓔ
20 Ⓐ Ⓑ Ⓒ Ⓓ Ⓔ	50 Ⓐ Ⓑ Ⓒ Ⓓ Ⓔ	80 Ⓐ Ⓑ Ⓒ Ⓓ Ⓔ
21 Ⓐ Ⓑ Ⓒ Ⓓ Ⓔ	51 Ⓐ Ⓑ Ⓒ Ⓓ Ⓔ	81 Ⓐ Ⓑ Ⓒ Ⓓ Ⓔ
22 Ⓐ Ⓑ Ⓒ Ⓓ Ⓔ	52 Ⓐ Ⓑ Ⓒ Ⓓ Ⓔ	82 Ⓐ Ⓑ Ⓒ Ⓓ Ⓔ
23 Ⓐ Ⓑ Ⓒ Ⓓ Ⓔ	53 Ⓐ Ⓑ Ⓒ Ⓓ Ⓔ	83 Ⓐ Ⓑ Ⓒ Ⓓ Ⓔ
24 Ⓐ Ⓑ Ⓒ Ⓓ Ⓔ	54 Ⓐ Ⓑ Ⓒ Ⓓ Ⓔ	84 Ⓐ Ⓑ Ⓒ Ⓓ Ⓔ
25 Ⓐ Ⓑ Ⓒ Ⓓ Ⓔ	55 Ⓐ Ⓑ Ⓒ Ⓓ Ⓔ	85 Ⓐ Ⓑ Ⓒ Ⓓ Ⓔ
26 Ⓐ Ⓑ Ⓒ Ⓓ Ⓔ	56 Ⓐ Ⓑ Ⓒ Ⓓ Ⓔ	86 Ⓐ Ⓑ Ⓒ Ⓓ Ⓔ
27 Ⓐ Ⓑ Ⓒ Ⓓ Ⓔ	57 Ⓐ Ⓑ Ⓒ Ⓓ Ⓔ	87 Ⓐ Ⓑ Ⓒ Ⓓ Ⓔ
28 Ⓐ Ⓑ Ⓒ Ⓓ Ⓔ	58 Ⓐ Ⓑ Ⓒ Ⓓ Ⓔ	88 Ⓐ Ⓑ Ⓒ Ⓓ Ⓔ
29 Ⓐ Ⓑ Ⓒ Ⓓ Ⓔ	59 Ⓐ Ⓑ Ⓒ Ⓓ Ⓔ	
30 Ⓐ Ⓑ Ⓒ Ⓓ Ⓔ	60 Ⓐ Ⓑ Ⓒ Ⓓ Ⓔ	

ANSWER SHEET—PRACTICE TEST 2
TRIAL 3

PART B—MEMORY FOR ADDRESSES
LIST 1   DATE _____

1 Ⓐ Ⓑ Ⓒ Ⓓ Ⓔ	31 Ⓐ Ⓑ Ⓒ Ⓓ Ⓔ	61 Ⓐ Ⓑ Ⓒ Ⓓ Ⓔ
2 Ⓐ Ⓑ Ⓒ Ⓓ Ⓔ	32 Ⓐ Ⓑ Ⓒ Ⓓ Ⓔ	62 Ⓐ Ⓑ Ⓒ Ⓓ Ⓔ
3 Ⓐ Ⓑ Ⓒ Ⓓ Ⓔ	33 Ⓐ Ⓑ Ⓒ Ⓓ Ⓔ	63 Ⓐ Ⓑ Ⓒ Ⓓ Ⓔ
4 Ⓐ Ⓑ Ⓒ Ⓓ Ⓔ	34 Ⓐ Ⓑ Ⓒ Ⓓ Ⓔ	64 Ⓐ Ⓑ Ⓒ Ⓓ Ⓔ
5 Ⓐ Ⓑ Ⓒ Ⓓ Ⓔ	35 Ⓐ Ⓑ Ⓒ Ⓓ Ⓔ	65 Ⓐ Ⓑ Ⓒ Ⓓ Ⓔ
6 Ⓐ Ⓑ Ⓒ Ⓓ Ⓔ	36 Ⓐ Ⓑ Ⓒ Ⓓ Ⓔ	66 Ⓐ Ⓑ Ⓒ Ⓓ Ⓔ
7 Ⓐ Ⓑ Ⓒ Ⓓ Ⓔ	37 Ⓐ Ⓑ Ⓒ Ⓓ Ⓔ	67 Ⓐ Ⓑ Ⓒ Ⓓ Ⓔ
8 Ⓐ Ⓑ Ⓒ Ⓓ Ⓔ	38 Ⓐ Ⓑ Ⓒ Ⓓ Ⓔ	68 Ⓐ Ⓑ Ⓒ Ⓓ Ⓔ
9 Ⓐ Ⓑ Ⓒ Ⓓ Ⓔ	39 Ⓐ Ⓑ Ⓒ Ⓓ Ⓔ	69 Ⓐ Ⓑ Ⓒ Ⓓ Ⓔ
10 Ⓐ Ⓑ Ⓒ Ⓓ Ⓔ	40 Ⓐ Ⓑ Ⓒ Ⓓ Ⓔ	70 Ⓐ Ⓑ Ⓒ Ⓓ Ⓔ
11 Ⓐ Ⓑ Ⓒ Ⓓ Ⓔ	41 Ⓐ Ⓑ Ⓒ Ⓓ Ⓔ	71 Ⓐ Ⓑ Ⓒ Ⓓ Ⓔ
12 Ⓐ Ⓑ Ⓒ Ⓓ Ⓔ	42 Ⓐ Ⓑ Ⓒ Ⓓ Ⓔ	72 Ⓐ Ⓑ Ⓒ Ⓓ Ⓔ
13 Ⓐ Ⓑ Ⓒ Ⓓ Ⓔ	43 Ⓐ Ⓑ Ⓒ Ⓓ Ⓔ	73 Ⓐ Ⓑ Ⓒ Ⓓ Ⓔ
14 Ⓐ Ⓑ Ⓒ Ⓓ Ⓔ	44 Ⓐ Ⓑ Ⓒ Ⓓ Ⓔ	74 Ⓐ Ⓑ Ⓒ Ⓓ Ⓔ
15 Ⓐ Ⓑ Ⓒ Ⓓ Ⓔ	45 Ⓐ Ⓑ Ⓒ Ⓓ Ⓔ	75 Ⓐ Ⓑ Ⓒ Ⓓ Ⓔ
16 Ⓐ Ⓑ Ⓒ Ⓓ Ⓔ	46 Ⓐ Ⓑ Ⓒ Ⓓ Ⓔ	76 Ⓐ Ⓑ Ⓒ Ⓓ Ⓔ
17 Ⓐ Ⓑ Ⓒ Ⓓ Ⓔ	47 Ⓐ Ⓑ Ⓒ Ⓓ Ⓔ	77 Ⓐ Ⓑ Ⓒ Ⓓ Ⓔ
18 Ⓐ Ⓑ Ⓒ Ⓓ Ⓔ	48 Ⓐ Ⓑ Ⓒ Ⓓ Ⓔ	78 Ⓐ Ⓑ Ⓒ Ⓓ Ⓔ
19 Ⓐ Ⓑ Ⓒ Ⓓ Ⓔ	49 Ⓐ Ⓑ Ⓒ Ⓓ Ⓔ	79 Ⓐ Ⓑ Ⓒ Ⓓ Ⓔ
20 Ⓐ Ⓑ Ⓒ Ⓓ Ⓔ	50 Ⓐ Ⓑ Ⓒ Ⓓ Ⓔ	80 Ⓐ Ⓑ Ⓒ Ⓓ Ⓔ
21 Ⓐ Ⓑ Ⓒ Ⓓ Ⓔ	51 Ⓐ Ⓑ Ⓒ Ⓓ Ⓔ	81 Ⓐ Ⓑ Ⓒ Ⓓ Ⓔ
22 Ⓐ Ⓑ Ⓒ Ⓓ Ⓔ	52 Ⓐ Ⓑ Ⓒ Ⓓ Ⓔ	82 Ⓐ Ⓑ Ⓒ Ⓓ Ⓔ
23 Ⓐ Ⓑ Ⓒ Ⓓ Ⓔ	53 Ⓐ Ⓑ Ⓒ Ⓓ Ⓔ	83 Ⓐ Ⓑ Ⓒ Ⓓ Ⓔ
24 Ⓐ Ⓑ Ⓒ Ⓓ Ⓔ	54 Ⓐ Ⓑ Ⓒ Ⓓ Ⓔ	84 Ⓐ Ⓑ Ⓒ Ⓓ Ⓔ
25 Ⓐ Ⓑ Ⓒ Ⓓ Ⓔ	55 Ⓐ Ⓑ Ⓒ Ⓓ Ⓔ	85 Ⓐ Ⓑ Ⓒ Ⓓ Ⓔ
26 Ⓐ Ⓑ Ⓒ Ⓓ Ⓔ	56 Ⓐ Ⓑ Ⓒ Ⓓ Ⓔ	86 Ⓐ Ⓑ Ⓒ Ⓓ Ⓔ
27 Ⓐ Ⓑ Ⓒ Ⓓ Ⓔ	57 Ⓐ Ⓑ Ⓒ Ⓓ Ⓔ	87 Ⓐ Ⓑ Ⓒ Ⓓ Ⓔ
28 Ⓐ Ⓑ Ⓒ Ⓓ Ⓔ	58 Ⓐ Ⓑ Ⓒ Ⓓ Ⓔ	88 Ⓐ Ⓑ Ⓒ Ⓓ Ⓔ
29 Ⓐ Ⓑ Ⓒ Ⓓ Ⓔ	59 Ⓐ Ⓑ Ⓒ Ⓓ Ⓔ	
30 Ⓐ Ⓑ Ⓒ Ⓓ Ⓔ	60 Ⓐ Ⓑ Ⓒ Ⓓ Ⓔ	

ANSWER SHEET—PRACTICE TEST 3
TRIAL 2

PART B—MEMORY FOR ADDRESSES
LIST 1   DATE _____

1 Ⓐ Ⓑ Ⓒ Ⓓ Ⓔ
2 Ⓐ Ⓑ Ⓒ Ⓓ Ⓔ
3 Ⓐ Ⓑ Ⓒ Ⓓ Ⓔ
4 Ⓐ Ⓑ Ⓒ Ⓓ Ⓔ
5 Ⓐ Ⓑ Ⓒ Ⓓ Ⓔ
6 Ⓐ Ⓑ Ⓒ Ⓓ Ⓔ
7 Ⓐ Ⓑ Ⓒ Ⓓ Ⓔ
8 Ⓐ Ⓑ Ⓒ Ⓓ Ⓔ
9 Ⓐ Ⓑ Ⓒ Ⓓ Ⓔ
10 Ⓐ Ⓑ Ⓒ Ⓓ Ⓔ
11 Ⓐ Ⓑ Ⓒ Ⓓ Ⓔ
12 Ⓐ Ⓑ Ⓒ Ⓓ Ⓔ
13 Ⓐ Ⓑ Ⓒ Ⓓ Ⓔ
14 Ⓐ Ⓑ Ⓒ Ⓓ Ⓔ
15 Ⓐ Ⓑ Ⓒ Ⓓ Ⓔ
16 Ⓐ Ⓑ Ⓒ Ⓓ Ⓔ
17 Ⓐ Ⓑ Ⓒ Ⓓ Ⓔ
18 Ⓐ Ⓑ Ⓒ Ⓓ Ⓔ
19 Ⓐ Ⓑ Ⓒ Ⓓ Ⓔ
20 Ⓐ Ⓑ Ⓒ Ⓓ Ⓔ
21 Ⓐ Ⓑ Ⓒ Ⓓ Ⓔ
22 Ⓐ Ⓑ Ⓒ Ⓓ Ⓔ
23 Ⓐ Ⓑ Ⓒ Ⓓ Ⓔ
24 Ⓐ Ⓑ Ⓒ Ⓓ Ⓔ
25 Ⓐ Ⓑ Ⓒ Ⓓ Ⓔ
26 Ⓐ Ⓑ Ⓒ Ⓓ Ⓔ
27 Ⓐ Ⓑ Ⓒ Ⓓ Ⓔ
28 Ⓐ Ⓑ Ⓒ Ⓓ Ⓔ
29 Ⓐ Ⓑ Ⓒ Ⓓ Ⓔ
30 Ⓐ Ⓑ Ⓒ Ⓓ Ⓔ

31 Ⓐ Ⓑ Ⓒ Ⓓ Ⓔ
32 Ⓐ Ⓑ Ⓒ Ⓓ Ⓔ
33 Ⓐ Ⓑ Ⓒ Ⓓ Ⓔ
34 Ⓐ Ⓑ Ⓒ Ⓓ Ⓔ
35 Ⓐ Ⓑ Ⓒ Ⓓ Ⓔ
36 Ⓐ Ⓑ Ⓒ Ⓓ Ⓔ
37 Ⓐ Ⓑ Ⓒ Ⓓ Ⓔ
38 Ⓐ Ⓑ Ⓒ Ⓓ Ⓔ
39 Ⓐ Ⓑ Ⓒ Ⓓ Ⓔ
40 Ⓐ Ⓑ Ⓒ Ⓓ Ⓔ
41 Ⓐ Ⓑ Ⓒ Ⓓ Ⓔ
42 Ⓐ Ⓑ Ⓒ Ⓓ Ⓔ
43 Ⓐ Ⓑ Ⓒ Ⓓ Ⓔ
44 Ⓐ Ⓑ Ⓒ Ⓓ Ⓔ
45 Ⓐ Ⓑ Ⓒ Ⓓ Ⓔ
46 Ⓐ Ⓑ Ⓒ Ⓓ Ⓔ
47 Ⓐ Ⓑ Ⓒ Ⓓ Ⓔ
48 Ⓐ Ⓑ Ⓒ Ⓓ Ⓔ
49 Ⓐ Ⓑ Ⓒ Ⓓ Ⓔ
50 Ⓐ Ⓑ Ⓒ Ⓓ Ⓔ
51 Ⓐ Ⓑ Ⓒ Ⓓ Ⓔ
52 Ⓐ Ⓑ Ⓒ Ⓓ Ⓔ
53 Ⓐ Ⓑ Ⓒ Ⓓ Ⓔ
54 Ⓐ Ⓑ Ⓒ Ⓓ Ⓔ
55 Ⓐ Ⓑ Ⓒ Ⓓ Ⓔ
56 Ⓐ Ⓑ Ⓒ Ⓓ Ⓔ
57 Ⓐ Ⓑ Ⓒ Ⓓ Ⓔ
58 Ⓐ Ⓑ Ⓒ Ⓓ Ⓔ
59 Ⓐ Ⓑ Ⓒ Ⓓ Ⓔ
60 Ⓐ Ⓑ Ⓒ Ⓓ Ⓔ

61 Ⓐ Ⓑ Ⓒ Ⓓ Ⓔ
62 Ⓐ Ⓑ Ⓒ Ⓓ Ⓔ
63 Ⓐ Ⓑ Ⓒ Ⓓ Ⓔ
64 Ⓐ Ⓑ Ⓒ Ⓓ Ⓔ
65 Ⓐ Ⓑ Ⓒ Ⓓ Ⓔ
66 Ⓐ Ⓑ Ⓒ Ⓓ Ⓔ
67 Ⓐ Ⓑ Ⓒ Ⓓ Ⓔ
68 Ⓐ Ⓑ Ⓒ Ⓓ Ⓔ
69 Ⓐ Ⓑ Ⓒ Ⓓ Ⓔ
70 Ⓐ Ⓑ Ⓒ Ⓓ Ⓔ
71 Ⓐ Ⓑ Ⓒ Ⓓ Ⓔ
72 Ⓐ Ⓑ Ⓒ Ⓓ Ⓔ
73 Ⓐ Ⓑ Ⓒ Ⓓ Ⓔ
74 Ⓐ Ⓑ Ⓒ Ⓓ Ⓔ
75 Ⓐ Ⓑ Ⓒ Ⓓ Ⓔ
76 Ⓐ Ⓑ Ⓒ Ⓓ Ⓔ
77 Ⓐ Ⓑ Ⓒ Ⓓ Ⓔ
78 Ⓐ Ⓑ Ⓒ Ⓓ Ⓔ
79 Ⓐ Ⓑ Ⓒ Ⓓ Ⓔ
80 Ⓐ Ⓑ Ⓒ Ⓓ Ⓔ
81 Ⓐ Ⓑ Ⓒ Ⓓ Ⓔ
82 Ⓐ Ⓑ Ⓒ Ⓓ Ⓔ
83 Ⓐ Ⓑ Ⓒ Ⓓ Ⓔ
84 Ⓐ Ⓑ Ⓒ Ⓓ Ⓔ
85 Ⓐ Ⓑ Ⓒ Ⓓ Ⓔ
86 Ⓐ Ⓑ Ⓒ Ⓓ Ⓔ
87 Ⓐ Ⓑ Ⓒ Ⓓ Ⓔ
88 Ⓐ Ⓑ Ⓒ Ⓓ Ⓔ

ANSWER SHEET—PRACTICE TEST 3
TRIAL 3

PART B—MEMORY FOR ADDRESSES
LIST 1   DATE _____

1 Ⓐ Ⓑ Ⓒ Ⓓ Ⓔ	31 Ⓐ Ⓑ Ⓒ Ⓓ Ⓔ	61 Ⓐ Ⓑ Ⓒ Ⓓ Ⓔ
2 Ⓐ Ⓑ Ⓒ Ⓓ Ⓔ	32 Ⓐ Ⓑ Ⓒ Ⓓ Ⓔ	62 Ⓐ Ⓑ Ⓒ Ⓓ Ⓔ
3 Ⓐ Ⓑ Ⓒ Ⓓ Ⓔ	33 Ⓐ Ⓑ Ⓒ Ⓓ Ⓔ	63 Ⓐ Ⓑ Ⓒ Ⓓ Ⓔ
4 Ⓐ Ⓑ Ⓒ Ⓓ Ⓔ	34 Ⓐ Ⓑ Ⓒ Ⓓ Ⓔ	64 Ⓐ Ⓑ Ⓒ Ⓓ Ⓔ
5 Ⓐ Ⓑ Ⓒ Ⓓ Ⓔ	35 Ⓐ Ⓑ Ⓒ Ⓓ Ⓔ	65 Ⓐ Ⓑ Ⓒ Ⓓ Ⓔ
6 Ⓐ Ⓑ Ⓒ Ⓓ Ⓔ	36 Ⓐ Ⓑ Ⓒ Ⓓ Ⓔ	66 Ⓐ Ⓑ Ⓒ Ⓓ Ⓔ
7 Ⓐ Ⓑ Ⓒ Ⓓ Ⓔ	37 Ⓐ Ⓑ Ⓒ Ⓓ Ⓔ	67 Ⓐ Ⓑ Ⓒ Ⓓ Ⓔ
8 Ⓐ Ⓑ Ⓒ Ⓓ Ⓔ	38 Ⓐ Ⓑ Ⓒ Ⓓ Ⓔ	68 Ⓐ Ⓑ Ⓒ Ⓓ Ⓔ
9 Ⓐ Ⓑ Ⓒ Ⓓ Ⓔ	39 Ⓐ Ⓑ Ⓒ Ⓓ Ⓔ	69 Ⓐ Ⓑ Ⓒ Ⓓ Ⓔ
10 Ⓐ Ⓑ Ⓒ Ⓓ Ⓔ	40 Ⓐ Ⓑ Ⓒ Ⓓ Ⓔ	70 Ⓐ Ⓑ Ⓒ Ⓓ Ⓔ
11 Ⓐ Ⓑ Ⓒ Ⓓ Ⓔ	41 Ⓐ Ⓑ Ⓒ Ⓓ Ⓔ	71 Ⓐ Ⓑ Ⓒ Ⓓ Ⓔ
12 Ⓐ Ⓑ Ⓒ Ⓓ Ⓔ	42 Ⓐ Ⓑ Ⓒ Ⓓ Ⓔ	72 Ⓐ Ⓑ Ⓒ Ⓓ Ⓔ
13 Ⓐ Ⓑ Ⓒ Ⓓ Ⓔ	43 Ⓐ Ⓑ Ⓒ Ⓓ Ⓔ	73 Ⓐ Ⓑ Ⓒ Ⓓ Ⓔ
14 Ⓐ Ⓑ Ⓒ Ⓓ Ⓔ	44 Ⓐ Ⓑ Ⓒ Ⓓ Ⓔ	74 Ⓐ Ⓑ Ⓒ Ⓓ Ⓔ
15 Ⓐ Ⓑ Ⓒ Ⓓ Ⓔ	45 Ⓐ Ⓑ Ⓒ Ⓓ Ⓔ	75 Ⓐ Ⓑ Ⓒ Ⓓ Ⓔ
16 Ⓐ Ⓑ Ⓒ Ⓓ Ⓔ	46 Ⓐ Ⓑ Ⓒ Ⓓ Ⓔ	76 Ⓐ Ⓑ Ⓒ Ⓓ Ⓔ
17 Ⓐ Ⓑ Ⓒ Ⓓ Ⓔ	47 Ⓐ Ⓑ Ⓒ Ⓓ Ⓔ	77 Ⓐ Ⓑ Ⓒ Ⓓ Ⓔ
18 Ⓐ Ⓑ Ⓒ Ⓓ Ⓔ	48 Ⓐ Ⓑ Ⓒ Ⓓ Ⓔ	78 Ⓐ Ⓑ Ⓒ Ⓓ Ⓔ
19 Ⓐ Ⓑ Ⓒ Ⓓ Ⓔ	49 Ⓐ Ⓑ Ⓒ Ⓓ Ⓔ	79 Ⓐ Ⓑ Ⓒ Ⓓ Ⓔ
20 Ⓐ Ⓑ Ⓒ Ⓓ Ⓔ	50 Ⓐ Ⓑ Ⓒ Ⓓ Ⓔ	80 Ⓐ Ⓑ Ⓒ Ⓓ Ⓔ
21 Ⓐ Ⓑ Ⓒ Ⓓ Ⓔ	51 Ⓐ Ⓑ Ⓒ Ⓓ Ⓔ	81 Ⓐ Ⓑ Ⓒ Ⓓ Ⓔ
22 Ⓐ Ⓑ Ⓒ Ⓓ Ⓔ	52 Ⓐ Ⓑ Ⓒ Ⓓ Ⓔ	82 Ⓐ Ⓑ Ⓒ Ⓓ Ⓔ
23 Ⓐ Ⓑ Ⓒ Ⓓ Ⓔ	53 Ⓐ Ⓑ Ⓒ Ⓓ Ⓔ	83 Ⓐ Ⓑ Ⓒ Ⓓ Ⓔ
24 Ⓐ Ⓑ Ⓒ Ⓓ Ⓔ	54 Ⓐ Ⓑ Ⓒ Ⓓ Ⓔ	84 Ⓐ Ⓑ Ⓒ Ⓓ Ⓔ
25 Ⓐ Ⓑ Ⓒ Ⓓ Ⓔ	55 Ⓐ Ⓑ Ⓒ Ⓓ Ⓔ	85 Ⓐ Ⓑ Ⓒ Ⓓ Ⓔ
26 Ⓐ Ⓑ Ⓒ Ⓓ Ⓔ	56 Ⓐ Ⓑ Ⓒ Ⓓ Ⓔ	86 Ⓐ Ⓑ Ⓒ Ⓓ Ⓔ
27 Ⓐ Ⓑ Ⓒ Ⓓ Ⓔ	57 Ⓐ Ⓑ Ⓒ Ⓓ Ⓔ	87 Ⓐ Ⓑ Ⓒ Ⓓ Ⓔ
28 Ⓐ Ⓑ Ⓒ Ⓓ Ⓔ	58 Ⓐ Ⓑ Ⓒ Ⓓ Ⓔ	88 Ⓐ Ⓑ Ⓒ Ⓓ Ⓔ
29 Ⓐ Ⓑ Ⓒ Ⓓ Ⓔ	59 Ⓐ Ⓑ Ⓒ Ⓓ Ⓔ	
30 Ⓐ Ⓑ Ⓒ Ⓓ Ⓔ	60 Ⓐ Ⓑ Ⓒ Ⓓ Ⓔ	

ANSWER SHEET—PRACTICE TEST 4
TRIAL 2

PART B—MEMORY FOR ADDRESSES
LIST 1   DATE _____

1 Ⓐ Ⓑ Ⓒ Ⓓ Ⓔ	31 Ⓐ Ⓑ Ⓒ Ⓓ Ⓔ	61 Ⓐ Ⓑ Ⓒ Ⓓ Ⓔ
2 Ⓐ Ⓑ Ⓒ Ⓓ Ⓔ	32 Ⓐ Ⓑ Ⓒ Ⓓ Ⓔ	62 Ⓐ Ⓑ Ⓒ Ⓓ Ⓔ
3 Ⓐ Ⓑ Ⓒ Ⓓ Ⓔ	33 Ⓐ Ⓑ Ⓒ Ⓓ Ⓔ	63 Ⓐ Ⓑ Ⓒ Ⓓ Ⓔ
4 Ⓐ Ⓑ Ⓒ Ⓓ Ⓔ	34 Ⓐ Ⓑ Ⓒ Ⓓ Ⓔ	64 Ⓐ Ⓑ Ⓒ Ⓓ Ⓔ
5 Ⓐ Ⓑ Ⓒ Ⓓ Ⓔ	35 Ⓐ Ⓑ Ⓒ Ⓓ Ⓔ	65 Ⓐ Ⓑ Ⓒ Ⓓ Ⓔ
6 Ⓐ Ⓑ Ⓒ Ⓓ Ⓔ	36 Ⓐ Ⓑ Ⓒ Ⓓ Ⓔ	66 Ⓐ Ⓑ Ⓒ Ⓓ Ⓔ
7 Ⓐ Ⓑ Ⓒ Ⓓ Ⓔ	37 Ⓐ Ⓑ Ⓒ Ⓓ Ⓔ	67 Ⓐ Ⓑ Ⓒ Ⓓ Ⓔ
8 Ⓐ Ⓑ Ⓒ Ⓓ Ⓔ	38 Ⓐ Ⓑ Ⓒ Ⓓ Ⓔ	68 Ⓐ Ⓑ Ⓒ Ⓓ Ⓔ
9 Ⓐ Ⓑ Ⓒ Ⓓ Ⓔ	39 Ⓐ Ⓑ Ⓒ Ⓓ Ⓔ	69 Ⓐ Ⓑ Ⓒ Ⓓ Ⓔ
10 Ⓐ Ⓑ Ⓒ Ⓓ Ⓔ	40 Ⓐ Ⓑ Ⓒ Ⓓ Ⓔ	70 Ⓐ Ⓑ Ⓒ Ⓓ Ⓔ
11 Ⓐ Ⓑ Ⓒ Ⓓ Ⓔ	41 Ⓐ Ⓑ Ⓒ Ⓓ Ⓔ	71 Ⓐ Ⓑ Ⓒ Ⓓ Ⓔ
12 Ⓐ Ⓑ Ⓒ Ⓓ Ⓔ	42 Ⓐ Ⓑ Ⓒ Ⓓ Ⓔ	72 Ⓐ Ⓑ Ⓒ Ⓓ Ⓔ
13 Ⓐ Ⓑ Ⓒ Ⓓ Ⓔ	43 Ⓐ Ⓑ Ⓒ Ⓓ Ⓔ	73 Ⓐ Ⓑ Ⓒ Ⓓ Ⓔ
14 Ⓐ Ⓑ Ⓒ Ⓓ Ⓔ	44 Ⓐ Ⓑ Ⓒ Ⓓ Ⓔ	74 Ⓐ Ⓑ Ⓒ Ⓓ Ⓔ
15 Ⓐ Ⓑ Ⓒ Ⓓ Ⓔ	45 Ⓐ Ⓑ Ⓒ Ⓓ Ⓔ	75 Ⓐ Ⓑ Ⓒ Ⓓ Ⓔ
16 Ⓐ Ⓑ Ⓒ Ⓓ Ⓔ	46 Ⓐ Ⓑ Ⓒ Ⓓ Ⓔ	76 Ⓐ Ⓑ Ⓒ Ⓓ Ⓔ
17 Ⓐ Ⓑ Ⓒ Ⓓ Ⓔ	47 Ⓐ Ⓑ Ⓒ Ⓓ Ⓔ	77 Ⓐ Ⓑ Ⓒ Ⓓ Ⓔ
18 Ⓐ Ⓑ Ⓒ Ⓓ Ⓔ	48 Ⓐ Ⓑ Ⓒ Ⓓ Ⓔ	78 Ⓐ Ⓑ Ⓒ Ⓓ Ⓔ
19 Ⓐ Ⓑ Ⓒ Ⓓ Ⓔ	49 Ⓐ Ⓑ Ⓒ Ⓓ Ⓔ	79 Ⓐ Ⓑ Ⓒ Ⓓ Ⓔ
20 Ⓐ Ⓑ Ⓒ Ⓓ Ⓔ	50 Ⓐ Ⓑ Ⓒ Ⓓ Ⓔ	80 Ⓐ Ⓑ Ⓒ Ⓓ Ⓔ
21 Ⓐ Ⓑ Ⓒ Ⓓ Ⓔ	51 Ⓐ Ⓑ Ⓒ Ⓓ Ⓔ	81 Ⓐ Ⓑ Ⓒ Ⓓ Ⓔ
22 Ⓐ Ⓑ Ⓒ Ⓓ Ⓔ	52 Ⓐ Ⓑ Ⓒ Ⓓ Ⓔ	82 Ⓐ Ⓑ Ⓒ Ⓓ Ⓔ
23 Ⓐ Ⓑ Ⓒ Ⓓ Ⓔ	53 Ⓐ Ⓑ Ⓒ Ⓓ Ⓔ	83 Ⓐ Ⓑ Ⓒ Ⓓ Ⓔ
24 Ⓐ Ⓑ Ⓒ Ⓓ Ⓔ	54 Ⓐ Ⓑ Ⓒ Ⓓ Ⓔ	84 Ⓐ Ⓑ Ⓒ Ⓓ Ⓔ
25 Ⓐ Ⓑ Ⓒ Ⓓ Ⓔ	55 Ⓐ Ⓑ Ⓒ Ⓓ Ⓔ	85 Ⓐ Ⓑ Ⓒ Ⓓ Ⓔ
26 Ⓐ Ⓑ Ⓒ Ⓓ Ⓔ	56 Ⓐ Ⓑ Ⓒ Ⓓ Ⓔ	86 Ⓐ Ⓑ Ⓒ Ⓓ Ⓔ
27 Ⓐ Ⓑ Ⓒ Ⓓ Ⓔ	57 Ⓐ Ⓑ Ⓒ Ⓓ Ⓔ	87 Ⓐ Ⓑ Ⓒ Ⓓ Ⓔ
28 Ⓐ Ⓑ Ⓒ Ⓓ Ⓔ	58 Ⓐ Ⓑ Ⓒ Ⓓ Ⓔ	88 Ⓐ Ⓑ Ⓒ Ⓓ Ⓔ
29 Ⓐ Ⓑ Ⓒ Ⓓ Ⓔ	59 Ⓐ Ⓑ Ⓒ Ⓓ Ⓔ	
30 Ⓐ Ⓑ Ⓒ Ⓓ Ⓔ	60 Ⓐ Ⓑ Ⓒ Ⓓ Ⓔ	

ANSWER SHEET—PRACTICE TEST 4
TRIAL 3

PART B—MEMORY FOR ADDRESSES
LIST 1   DATE _____

1 Ⓐ Ⓑ Ⓒ Ⓓ Ⓔ	31 Ⓐ Ⓑ Ⓒ Ⓓ Ⓔ	61 Ⓐ Ⓑ Ⓒ Ⓓ Ⓔ
2 Ⓐ Ⓑ Ⓒ Ⓓ Ⓔ	32 Ⓐ Ⓑ Ⓒ Ⓓ Ⓔ	62 Ⓐ Ⓑ Ⓒ Ⓓ Ⓔ
3 Ⓐ Ⓑ Ⓒ Ⓓ Ⓔ	33 Ⓐ Ⓑ Ⓒ Ⓓ Ⓔ	63 Ⓐ Ⓑ Ⓒ Ⓓ Ⓔ
4 Ⓐ Ⓑ Ⓒ Ⓓ Ⓔ	34 Ⓐ Ⓑ Ⓒ Ⓓ Ⓔ	64 Ⓐ Ⓑ Ⓒ Ⓓ Ⓔ
5 Ⓐ Ⓑ Ⓒ Ⓓ Ⓔ	35 Ⓐ Ⓑ Ⓒ Ⓓ Ⓔ	65 Ⓐ Ⓑ Ⓒ Ⓓ Ⓔ
6 Ⓐ Ⓑ Ⓒ Ⓓ Ⓔ	36 Ⓐ Ⓑ Ⓒ Ⓓ Ⓔ	66 Ⓐ Ⓑ Ⓒ Ⓓ Ⓔ
7 Ⓐ Ⓑ Ⓒ Ⓓ Ⓔ	37 Ⓐ Ⓑ Ⓒ Ⓓ Ⓔ	67 Ⓐ Ⓑ Ⓒ Ⓓ Ⓔ
8 Ⓐ Ⓑ Ⓒ Ⓓ Ⓔ	38 Ⓐ Ⓑ Ⓒ Ⓓ Ⓔ	68 Ⓐ Ⓑ Ⓒ Ⓓ Ⓔ
9 Ⓐ Ⓑ Ⓒ Ⓓ Ⓔ	39 Ⓐ Ⓑ Ⓒ Ⓓ Ⓔ	69 Ⓐ Ⓑ Ⓒ Ⓓ Ⓔ
10 Ⓐ Ⓑ Ⓒ Ⓓ Ⓔ	40 Ⓐ Ⓑ Ⓒ Ⓓ Ⓔ	70 Ⓐ Ⓑ Ⓒ Ⓓ Ⓔ
11 Ⓐ Ⓑ Ⓒ Ⓓ Ⓔ	41 Ⓐ Ⓑ Ⓒ Ⓓ Ⓔ	71 Ⓐ Ⓑ Ⓒ Ⓓ Ⓔ
12 Ⓐ Ⓑ Ⓒ Ⓓ Ⓔ	42 Ⓐ Ⓑ Ⓒ Ⓓ Ⓔ	72 Ⓐ Ⓑ Ⓒ Ⓓ Ⓔ
13 Ⓐ Ⓑ Ⓒ Ⓓ Ⓔ	43 Ⓐ Ⓑ Ⓒ Ⓓ Ⓔ	73 Ⓐ Ⓑ Ⓒ Ⓓ Ⓔ
14 Ⓐ Ⓑ Ⓒ Ⓓ Ⓔ	44 Ⓐ Ⓑ Ⓒ Ⓓ Ⓔ	74 Ⓐ Ⓑ Ⓒ Ⓓ Ⓔ
15 Ⓐ Ⓑ Ⓒ Ⓓ Ⓔ	45 Ⓐ Ⓑ Ⓒ Ⓓ Ⓔ	75 Ⓐ Ⓑ Ⓒ Ⓓ Ⓔ
16 Ⓐ Ⓑ Ⓒ Ⓓ Ⓔ	46 Ⓐ Ⓑ Ⓒ Ⓓ Ⓔ	76 Ⓐ Ⓑ Ⓒ Ⓓ Ⓔ
17 Ⓐ Ⓑ Ⓒ Ⓓ Ⓔ	47 Ⓐ Ⓑ Ⓒ Ⓓ Ⓔ	77 Ⓐ Ⓑ Ⓒ Ⓓ Ⓔ
18 Ⓐ Ⓑ Ⓒ Ⓓ Ⓔ	48 Ⓐ Ⓑ Ⓒ Ⓓ Ⓔ	78 Ⓐ Ⓑ Ⓒ Ⓓ Ⓔ
19 Ⓐ Ⓑ Ⓒ Ⓓ Ⓔ	49 Ⓐ Ⓑ Ⓒ Ⓓ Ⓔ	79 Ⓐ Ⓑ Ⓒ Ⓓ Ⓔ
20 Ⓐ Ⓑ Ⓒ Ⓓ Ⓔ	50 Ⓐ Ⓑ Ⓒ Ⓓ Ⓔ	80 Ⓐ Ⓑ Ⓒ Ⓓ Ⓔ
21 Ⓐ Ⓑ Ⓒ Ⓓ Ⓔ	51 Ⓐ Ⓑ Ⓒ Ⓓ Ⓔ	81 Ⓐ Ⓑ Ⓒ Ⓓ Ⓔ
22 Ⓐ Ⓑ Ⓒ Ⓓ Ⓔ	52 Ⓐ Ⓑ Ⓒ Ⓓ Ⓔ	82 Ⓐ Ⓑ Ⓒ Ⓓ Ⓔ
23 Ⓐ Ⓑ Ⓒ Ⓓ Ⓔ	53 Ⓐ Ⓑ Ⓒ Ⓓ Ⓔ	83 Ⓐ Ⓑ Ⓒ Ⓓ Ⓔ
24 Ⓐ Ⓑ Ⓒ Ⓓ Ⓔ	54 Ⓐ Ⓑ Ⓒ Ⓓ Ⓔ	84 Ⓐ Ⓑ Ⓒ Ⓓ Ⓔ
25 Ⓐ Ⓑ Ⓒ Ⓓ Ⓔ	55 Ⓐ Ⓑ Ⓒ Ⓓ Ⓔ	85 Ⓐ Ⓑ Ⓒ Ⓓ Ⓔ
26 Ⓐ Ⓑ Ⓒ Ⓓ Ⓔ	56 Ⓐ Ⓑ Ⓒ Ⓓ Ⓔ	86 Ⓐ Ⓑ Ⓒ Ⓓ Ⓔ
27 Ⓐ Ⓑ Ⓒ Ⓓ Ⓔ	57 Ⓐ Ⓑ Ⓒ Ⓓ Ⓔ	87 Ⓐ Ⓑ Ⓒ Ⓓ Ⓔ
28 Ⓐ Ⓑ Ⓒ Ⓓ Ⓔ	58 Ⓐ Ⓑ Ⓒ Ⓓ Ⓔ	88 Ⓐ Ⓑ Ⓒ Ⓓ Ⓔ
29 Ⓐ Ⓑ Ⓒ Ⓓ Ⓔ	59 Ⓐ Ⓑ Ⓒ Ⓓ Ⓔ	
30 Ⓐ Ⓑ Ⓒ Ⓓ Ⓔ	60 Ⓐ Ⓑ Ⓒ Ⓓ Ⓔ	

ANSWER SHEET—PRACTICE TEST 5
TRIAL 2

PART B—MEMORY FOR ADDRESSES
LIST 1   DATE _____

1 Ⓐ Ⓑ Ⓒ Ⓓ Ⓔ	31 Ⓐ Ⓑ Ⓒ Ⓓ Ⓔ	61 Ⓐ Ⓑ Ⓒ Ⓓ Ⓔ
2 Ⓐ Ⓑ Ⓒ Ⓓ Ⓔ	32 Ⓐ Ⓑ Ⓒ Ⓓ Ⓔ	62 Ⓐ Ⓑ Ⓒ Ⓓ Ⓔ
3 Ⓐ Ⓑ Ⓒ Ⓓ Ⓔ	33 Ⓐ Ⓑ Ⓒ Ⓓ Ⓔ	63 Ⓐ Ⓑ Ⓒ Ⓓ Ⓔ
4 Ⓐ Ⓑ Ⓒ Ⓓ Ⓔ	34 Ⓐ Ⓑ Ⓒ Ⓓ Ⓔ	64 Ⓐ Ⓑ Ⓒ Ⓓ Ⓔ
5 Ⓐ Ⓑ Ⓒ Ⓓ Ⓔ	35 Ⓐ Ⓑ Ⓒ Ⓓ Ⓔ	65 Ⓐ Ⓑ Ⓒ Ⓓ Ⓔ
6 Ⓐ Ⓑ Ⓒ Ⓓ Ⓔ	36 Ⓐ Ⓑ Ⓒ Ⓓ Ⓔ	66 Ⓐ Ⓑ Ⓒ Ⓓ Ⓔ
7 Ⓐ Ⓑ Ⓒ Ⓓ Ⓔ	37 Ⓐ Ⓑ Ⓒ Ⓓ Ⓔ	67 Ⓐ Ⓑ Ⓒ Ⓓ Ⓔ
8 Ⓐ Ⓑ Ⓒ Ⓓ Ⓔ	38 Ⓐ Ⓑ Ⓒ Ⓓ Ⓔ	68 Ⓐ Ⓑ Ⓒ Ⓓ Ⓔ
9 Ⓐ Ⓑ Ⓒ Ⓓ Ⓔ	39 Ⓐ Ⓑ Ⓒ Ⓓ Ⓔ	69 Ⓐ Ⓑ Ⓒ Ⓓ Ⓔ
10 Ⓐ Ⓑ Ⓒ Ⓓ Ⓔ	40 Ⓐ Ⓑ Ⓒ Ⓓ Ⓔ	70 Ⓐ Ⓑ Ⓒ Ⓓ Ⓔ
11 Ⓐ Ⓑ Ⓒ Ⓓ Ⓔ	41 Ⓐ Ⓑ Ⓒ Ⓓ Ⓔ	71 Ⓐ Ⓑ Ⓒ Ⓓ Ⓔ
12 Ⓐ Ⓑ Ⓒ Ⓓ Ⓔ	42 Ⓐ Ⓑ Ⓒ Ⓓ Ⓔ	72 Ⓐ Ⓑ Ⓒ Ⓓ Ⓔ
13 Ⓐ Ⓑ Ⓒ Ⓓ Ⓔ	43 Ⓐ Ⓑ Ⓒ Ⓓ Ⓔ	73 Ⓐ Ⓑ Ⓒ Ⓓ Ⓔ
14 Ⓐ Ⓑ Ⓒ Ⓓ Ⓔ	44 Ⓐ Ⓑ Ⓒ Ⓓ Ⓔ	74 Ⓐ Ⓑ Ⓒ Ⓓ Ⓔ
15 Ⓐ Ⓑ Ⓒ Ⓓ Ⓔ	45 Ⓐ Ⓑ Ⓒ Ⓓ Ⓔ	75 Ⓐ Ⓑ Ⓒ Ⓓ Ⓔ
16 Ⓐ Ⓑ Ⓒ Ⓓ Ⓔ	46 Ⓐ Ⓑ Ⓒ Ⓓ Ⓔ	76 Ⓐ Ⓑ Ⓒ Ⓓ Ⓔ
17 Ⓐ Ⓑ Ⓒ Ⓓ Ⓔ	47 Ⓐ Ⓑ Ⓒ Ⓓ Ⓔ	77 Ⓐ Ⓑ Ⓒ Ⓓ Ⓔ
18 Ⓐ Ⓑ Ⓒ Ⓓ Ⓔ	48 Ⓐ Ⓑ Ⓒ Ⓓ Ⓔ	78 Ⓐ Ⓑ Ⓒ Ⓓ Ⓔ
19 Ⓐ Ⓑ Ⓒ Ⓓ Ⓔ	49 Ⓐ Ⓑ Ⓒ Ⓓ Ⓔ	79 Ⓐ Ⓑ Ⓒ Ⓓ Ⓔ
20 Ⓐ Ⓑ Ⓒ Ⓓ Ⓔ	50 Ⓐ Ⓑ Ⓒ Ⓓ Ⓔ	80 Ⓐ Ⓑ Ⓒ Ⓓ Ⓔ
21 Ⓐ Ⓑ Ⓒ Ⓓ Ⓔ	51 Ⓐ Ⓑ Ⓒ Ⓓ Ⓔ	81 Ⓐ Ⓑ Ⓒ Ⓓ Ⓔ
22 Ⓐ Ⓑ Ⓒ Ⓓ Ⓔ	52 Ⓐ Ⓑ Ⓒ Ⓓ Ⓔ	82 Ⓐ Ⓑ Ⓒ Ⓓ Ⓔ
23 Ⓐ Ⓑ Ⓒ Ⓓ Ⓔ	53 Ⓐ Ⓑ Ⓒ Ⓓ Ⓔ	83 Ⓐ Ⓑ Ⓒ Ⓓ Ⓔ
24 Ⓐ Ⓑ Ⓒ Ⓓ Ⓔ	54 Ⓐ Ⓑ Ⓒ Ⓓ Ⓔ	84 Ⓐ Ⓑ Ⓒ Ⓓ Ⓔ
25 Ⓐ Ⓑ Ⓒ Ⓓ Ⓔ	55 Ⓐ Ⓑ Ⓒ Ⓓ Ⓔ	85 Ⓐ Ⓑ Ⓒ Ⓓ Ⓔ
26 Ⓐ Ⓑ Ⓒ Ⓓ Ⓔ	56 Ⓐ Ⓑ Ⓒ Ⓓ Ⓔ	86 Ⓐ Ⓑ Ⓒ Ⓓ Ⓔ
27 Ⓐ Ⓑ Ⓒ Ⓓ Ⓔ	57 Ⓐ Ⓑ Ⓒ Ⓓ Ⓔ	87 Ⓐ Ⓑ Ⓒ Ⓓ Ⓔ
28 Ⓐ Ⓑ Ⓒ Ⓓ Ⓔ	58 Ⓐ Ⓑ Ⓒ Ⓓ Ⓔ	88 Ⓐ Ⓑ Ⓒ Ⓓ Ⓔ
29 Ⓐ Ⓑ Ⓒ Ⓓ Ⓔ	59 Ⓐ Ⓑ Ⓒ Ⓓ Ⓔ	
30 Ⓐ Ⓑ Ⓒ Ⓓ Ⓔ	60 Ⓐ Ⓑ Ⓒ Ⓓ Ⓔ	

ANSWER SHEET—PRACTICE TEST 5
TRIAL 3

PART B—MEMORY FOR ADDRESSES
LIST 1   DATE _____

1 Ⓐ Ⓑ Ⓒ Ⓓ Ⓔ	31 Ⓐ Ⓑ Ⓒ Ⓓ Ⓔ	61 Ⓐ Ⓑ Ⓒ Ⓓ Ⓔ
2 Ⓐ Ⓑ Ⓒ Ⓓ Ⓔ	32 Ⓐ Ⓑ Ⓒ Ⓓ Ⓔ	62 Ⓐ Ⓑ Ⓒ Ⓓ Ⓔ
3 Ⓐ Ⓑ Ⓒ Ⓓ Ⓔ	33 Ⓐ Ⓑ Ⓒ Ⓓ Ⓔ	63 Ⓐ Ⓑ Ⓒ Ⓓ Ⓔ
4 Ⓐ Ⓑ Ⓒ Ⓓ Ⓔ	34 Ⓐ Ⓑ Ⓒ Ⓓ Ⓔ	64 Ⓐ Ⓑ Ⓒ Ⓓ Ⓔ
5 Ⓐ Ⓑ Ⓒ Ⓓ Ⓔ	35 Ⓐ Ⓑ Ⓒ Ⓓ Ⓔ	65 Ⓐ Ⓑ Ⓒ Ⓓ Ⓔ
6 Ⓐ Ⓑ Ⓒ Ⓓ Ⓔ	36 Ⓐ Ⓑ Ⓒ Ⓓ Ⓔ	66 Ⓐ Ⓑ Ⓒ Ⓓ Ⓔ
7 Ⓐ Ⓑ Ⓒ Ⓓ Ⓔ	37 Ⓐ Ⓑ Ⓒ Ⓓ Ⓔ	67 Ⓐ Ⓑ Ⓒ Ⓓ Ⓔ
8 Ⓐ Ⓑ Ⓒ Ⓓ Ⓔ	38 Ⓐ Ⓑ Ⓒ Ⓓ Ⓔ	68 Ⓐ Ⓑ Ⓒ Ⓓ Ⓔ
9 Ⓐ Ⓑ Ⓒ Ⓓ Ⓔ	39 Ⓐ Ⓑ Ⓒ Ⓓ Ⓔ	69 Ⓐ Ⓑ Ⓒ Ⓓ Ⓔ
10 Ⓐ Ⓑ Ⓒ Ⓓ Ⓔ	40 Ⓐ Ⓑ Ⓒ Ⓓ Ⓔ	70 Ⓐ Ⓑ Ⓒ Ⓓ Ⓔ
11 Ⓐ Ⓑ Ⓒ Ⓓ Ⓔ	41 Ⓐ Ⓑ Ⓒ Ⓓ Ⓔ	71 Ⓐ Ⓑ Ⓒ Ⓓ Ⓔ
12 Ⓐ Ⓑ Ⓒ Ⓓ Ⓔ	42 Ⓐ Ⓑ Ⓒ Ⓓ Ⓔ	72 Ⓐ Ⓑ Ⓒ Ⓓ Ⓔ
13 Ⓐ Ⓑ Ⓒ Ⓓ Ⓔ	43 Ⓐ Ⓑ Ⓒ Ⓓ Ⓔ	73 Ⓐ Ⓑ Ⓒ Ⓓ Ⓔ
14 Ⓐ Ⓑ Ⓒ Ⓓ Ⓔ	44 Ⓐ Ⓑ Ⓒ Ⓓ Ⓔ	74 Ⓐ Ⓑ Ⓒ Ⓓ Ⓔ
15 Ⓐ Ⓑ Ⓒ Ⓓ Ⓔ	45 Ⓐ Ⓑ Ⓒ Ⓓ Ⓔ	75 Ⓐ Ⓑ Ⓒ Ⓓ Ⓔ
16 Ⓐ Ⓑ Ⓒ Ⓓ Ⓔ	46 Ⓐ Ⓑ Ⓒ Ⓓ Ⓔ	76 Ⓐ Ⓑ Ⓒ Ⓓ Ⓔ
17 Ⓐ Ⓑ Ⓒ Ⓓ Ⓔ	47 Ⓐ Ⓑ Ⓒ Ⓓ Ⓔ	77 Ⓐ Ⓑ Ⓒ Ⓓ Ⓔ
18 Ⓐ Ⓑ Ⓒ Ⓓ Ⓔ	48 Ⓐ Ⓑ Ⓒ Ⓓ Ⓔ	78 Ⓐ Ⓑ Ⓒ Ⓓ Ⓔ
19 Ⓐ Ⓑ Ⓒ Ⓓ Ⓔ	49 Ⓐ Ⓑ Ⓒ Ⓓ Ⓔ	79 Ⓐ Ⓑ Ⓒ Ⓓ Ⓔ
20 Ⓐ Ⓑ Ⓒ Ⓓ Ⓔ	50 Ⓐ Ⓑ Ⓒ Ⓓ Ⓔ	80 Ⓐ Ⓑ Ⓒ Ⓓ Ⓔ
21 Ⓐ Ⓑ Ⓒ Ⓓ Ⓔ	51 Ⓐ Ⓑ Ⓒ Ⓓ Ⓔ	81 Ⓐ Ⓑ Ⓒ Ⓓ Ⓔ
22 Ⓐ Ⓑ Ⓒ Ⓓ Ⓔ	52 Ⓐ Ⓑ Ⓒ Ⓓ Ⓔ	82 Ⓐ Ⓑ Ⓒ Ⓓ Ⓔ
23 Ⓐ Ⓑ Ⓒ Ⓓ Ⓔ	53 Ⓐ Ⓑ Ⓒ Ⓓ Ⓔ	83 Ⓐ Ⓑ Ⓒ Ⓓ Ⓔ
24 Ⓐ Ⓑ Ⓒ Ⓓ Ⓔ	54 Ⓐ Ⓑ Ⓒ Ⓓ Ⓔ	84 Ⓐ Ⓑ Ⓒ Ⓓ Ⓔ
25 Ⓐ Ⓑ Ⓒ Ⓓ Ⓔ	55 Ⓐ Ⓑ Ⓒ Ⓓ Ⓔ	85 Ⓐ Ⓑ Ⓒ Ⓓ Ⓔ
26 Ⓐ Ⓑ Ⓒ Ⓓ Ⓔ	56 Ⓐ Ⓑ Ⓒ Ⓓ Ⓔ	86 Ⓐ Ⓑ Ⓒ Ⓓ Ⓔ
27 Ⓐ Ⓑ Ⓒ Ⓓ Ⓔ	57 Ⓐ Ⓑ Ⓒ Ⓓ Ⓔ	87 Ⓐ Ⓑ Ⓒ Ⓓ Ⓔ
28 Ⓐ Ⓑ Ⓒ Ⓓ Ⓔ	58 Ⓐ Ⓑ Ⓒ Ⓓ Ⓔ	88 Ⓐ Ⓑ Ⓒ Ⓓ Ⓔ
29 Ⓐ Ⓑ Ⓒ Ⓓ Ⓔ	59 Ⓐ Ⓑ Ⓒ Ⓓ Ⓔ	
30 Ⓐ Ⓑ Ⓒ Ⓓ Ⓔ	60 Ⓐ Ⓑ Ⓒ Ⓓ Ⓔ	

ANSWER SHEET—DIAGNOSTIC
PRACTICE TEST
TRIAL 2

PART B—MEMORY FOR ADDRESSES
LIST 2   DATE _____

1 Ⓐ Ⓑ Ⓒ Ⓓ Ⓔ	31 Ⓐ Ⓑ Ⓒ Ⓓ Ⓔ	61 Ⓐ Ⓑ Ⓒ Ⓓ Ⓔ
2 Ⓐ Ⓑ Ⓒ Ⓓ Ⓔ	32 Ⓐ Ⓑ Ⓒ Ⓓ Ⓔ	62 Ⓐ Ⓑ Ⓒ Ⓓ Ⓔ
3 Ⓐ Ⓑ Ⓒ Ⓓ Ⓔ	33 Ⓐ Ⓑ Ⓒ Ⓓ Ⓔ	63 Ⓐ Ⓑ Ⓒ Ⓓ Ⓔ
4 Ⓐ Ⓑ Ⓒ Ⓓ Ⓔ	34 Ⓐ Ⓑ Ⓒ Ⓓ Ⓔ	64 Ⓐ Ⓑ Ⓒ Ⓓ Ⓔ
5 Ⓐ Ⓑ Ⓒ Ⓓ Ⓔ	35 Ⓐ Ⓑ Ⓒ Ⓓ Ⓔ	65 Ⓐ Ⓑ Ⓒ Ⓓ Ⓔ
6 Ⓐ Ⓑ Ⓒ Ⓓ Ⓔ	36 Ⓐ Ⓑ Ⓒ Ⓓ Ⓔ	66 Ⓐ Ⓑ Ⓒ Ⓓ Ⓔ
7 Ⓐ Ⓑ Ⓒ Ⓓ Ⓔ	37 Ⓐ Ⓑ Ⓒ Ⓓ Ⓔ	67 Ⓐ Ⓑ Ⓒ Ⓓ Ⓔ
8 Ⓐ Ⓑ Ⓒ Ⓓ Ⓔ	38 Ⓐ Ⓑ Ⓒ Ⓓ Ⓔ	68 Ⓐ Ⓑ Ⓒ Ⓓ Ⓔ
9 Ⓐ Ⓑ Ⓒ Ⓓ Ⓔ	39 Ⓐ Ⓑ Ⓒ Ⓓ Ⓔ	69 Ⓐ Ⓑ Ⓒ Ⓓ Ⓔ
10 Ⓐ Ⓑ Ⓒ Ⓓ Ⓔ	40 Ⓐ Ⓑ Ⓒ Ⓓ Ⓔ	70 Ⓐ Ⓑ Ⓒ Ⓓ Ⓔ
11 Ⓐ Ⓑ Ⓒ Ⓓ Ⓔ	41 Ⓐ Ⓑ Ⓒ Ⓓ Ⓔ	71 Ⓐ Ⓑ Ⓒ Ⓓ Ⓔ
12 Ⓐ Ⓑ Ⓒ Ⓓ Ⓔ	42 Ⓐ Ⓑ Ⓒ Ⓓ Ⓔ	72 Ⓐ Ⓑ Ⓒ Ⓓ Ⓔ
13 Ⓐ Ⓑ Ⓒ Ⓓ Ⓔ	43 Ⓐ Ⓑ Ⓒ Ⓓ Ⓔ	73 Ⓐ Ⓑ Ⓒ Ⓓ Ⓔ
14 Ⓐ Ⓑ Ⓒ Ⓓ Ⓔ	44 Ⓐ Ⓑ Ⓒ Ⓓ Ⓔ	74 Ⓐ Ⓑ Ⓒ Ⓓ Ⓔ
15 Ⓐ Ⓑ Ⓒ Ⓓ Ⓔ	45 Ⓐ Ⓑ Ⓒ Ⓓ Ⓔ	75 Ⓐ Ⓑ Ⓒ Ⓓ Ⓔ
16 Ⓐ Ⓑ Ⓒ Ⓓ Ⓔ	46 Ⓐ Ⓑ Ⓒ Ⓓ Ⓔ	76 Ⓐ Ⓑ Ⓒ Ⓓ Ⓔ
17 Ⓐ Ⓑ Ⓒ Ⓓ Ⓔ	47 Ⓐ Ⓑ Ⓒ Ⓓ Ⓔ	77 Ⓐ Ⓑ Ⓒ Ⓓ Ⓔ
18 Ⓐ Ⓑ Ⓒ Ⓓ Ⓔ	48 Ⓐ Ⓑ Ⓒ Ⓓ Ⓔ	78 Ⓐ Ⓑ Ⓒ Ⓓ Ⓔ
19 Ⓐ Ⓑ Ⓒ Ⓓ Ⓔ	49 Ⓐ Ⓑ Ⓒ Ⓓ Ⓔ	79 Ⓐ Ⓑ Ⓒ Ⓓ Ⓔ
20 Ⓐ Ⓑ Ⓒ Ⓓ Ⓔ	50 Ⓐ Ⓑ Ⓒ Ⓓ Ⓔ	80 Ⓐ Ⓑ Ⓒ Ⓓ Ⓔ
21 Ⓐ Ⓑ Ⓒ Ⓓ Ⓔ	51 Ⓐ Ⓑ Ⓒ Ⓓ Ⓔ	81 Ⓐ Ⓑ Ⓒ Ⓓ Ⓔ
22 Ⓐ Ⓑ Ⓒ Ⓓ Ⓔ	52 Ⓐ Ⓑ Ⓒ Ⓓ Ⓔ	82 Ⓐ Ⓑ Ⓒ Ⓓ Ⓔ
23 Ⓐ Ⓑ Ⓒ Ⓓ Ⓔ	53 Ⓐ Ⓑ Ⓒ Ⓓ Ⓔ	83 Ⓐ Ⓑ Ⓒ Ⓓ Ⓔ
24 Ⓐ Ⓑ Ⓒ Ⓓ Ⓔ	54 Ⓐ Ⓑ Ⓒ Ⓓ Ⓔ	84 Ⓐ Ⓑ Ⓒ Ⓓ Ⓔ
25 Ⓐ Ⓑ Ⓒ Ⓓ Ⓔ	55 Ⓐ Ⓑ Ⓒ Ⓓ Ⓔ	85 Ⓐ Ⓑ Ⓒ Ⓓ Ⓔ
26 Ⓐ Ⓑ Ⓒ Ⓓ Ⓔ	56 Ⓐ Ⓑ Ⓒ Ⓓ Ⓔ	86 Ⓐ Ⓑ Ⓒ Ⓓ Ⓔ
27 Ⓐ Ⓑ Ⓒ Ⓓ Ⓔ	57 Ⓐ Ⓑ Ⓒ Ⓓ Ⓔ	87 Ⓐ Ⓑ Ⓒ Ⓓ Ⓔ
28 Ⓐ Ⓑ Ⓒ Ⓓ Ⓔ	58 Ⓐ Ⓑ Ⓒ Ⓓ Ⓔ	88 Ⓐ Ⓑ Ⓒ Ⓓ Ⓔ
29 Ⓐ Ⓑ Ⓒ Ⓓ Ⓔ	59 Ⓐ Ⓑ Ⓒ Ⓓ Ⓔ	
30 Ⓐ Ⓑ Ⓒ Ⓓ Ⓔ	60 Ⓐ Ⓑ Ⓒ Ⓓ Ⓔ	

ANSWER SHEET—DIAGNOSTIC
PRACTICE TEST
TRIAL 3

PART B—MEMORY FOR ADDRESSES
LIST 2   DATE _____

1 Ⓐ Ⓑ Ⓒ Ⓓ Ⓔ	31 Ⓐ Ⓑ Ⓒ Ⓓ Ⓔ	61 Ⓐ Ⓑ Ⓒ Ⓓ Ⓔ
2 Ⓐ Ⓑ Ⓒ Ⓓ Ⓔ	32 Ⓐ Ⓑ Ⓒ Ⓓ Ⓔ	62 Ⓐ Ⓑ Ⓒ Ⓓ Ⓔ
3 Ⓐ Ⓑ Ⓒ Ⓓ Ⓔ	33 Ⓐ Ⓑ Ⓒ Ⓓ Ⓔ	63 Ⓐ Ⓑ Ⓒ Ⓓ Ⓔ
4 Ⓐ Ⓑ Ⓒ Ⓓ Ⓔ	34 Ⓐ Ⓑ Ⓒ Ⓓ Ⓔ	64 Ⓐ Ⓑ Ⓒ Ⓓ Ⓔ
5 Ⓐ Ⓑ Ⓒ Ⓓ Ⓔ	35 Ⓐ Ⓑ Ⓒ Ⓓ Ⓔ	65 Ⓐ Ⓑ Ⓒ Ⓓ Ⓔ
6 Ⓐ Ⓑ Ⓒ Ⓓ Ⓔ	36 Ⓐ Ⓑ Ⓒ Ⓓ Ⓔ	66 Ⓐ Ⓑ Ⓒ Ⓓ Ⓔ
7 Ⓐ Ⓑ Ⓒ Ⓓ Ⓔ	37 Ⓐ Ⓑ Ⓒ Ⓓ Ⓔ	67 Ⓐ Ⓑ Ⓒ Ⓓ Ⓔ
8 Ⓐ Ⓑ Ⓒ Ⓓ Ⓔ	38 Ⓐ Ⓑ Ⓒ Ⓓ Ⓔ	68 Ⓐ Ⓑ Ⓒ Ⓓ Ⓔ
9 Ⓐ Ⓑ Ⓒ Ⓓ Ⓔ	39 Ⓐ Ⓑ Ⓒ Ⓓ Ⓔ	69 Ⓐ Ⓑ Ⓒ Ⓓ Ⓔ
10 Ⓐ Ⓑ Ⓒ Ⓓ Ⓔ	40 Ⓐ Ⓑ Ⓒ Ⓓ Ⓔ	70 Ⓐ Ⓑ Ⓒ Ⓓ Ⓔ
11 Ⓐ Ⓑ Ⓒ Ⓓ Ⓔ	41 Ⓐ Ⓑ Ⓒ Ⓓ Ⓔ	71 Ⓐ Ⓑ Ⓒ Ⓓ Ⓔ
12 Ⓐ Ⓑ Ⓒ Ⓓ Ⓔ	42 Ⓐ Ⓑ Ⓒ Ⓓ Ⓔ	72 Ⓐ Ⓑ Ⓒ Ⓓ Ⓔ
13 Ⓐ Ⓑ Ⓒ Ⓓ Ⓔ	43 Ⓐ Ⓑ Ⓒ Ⓓ Ⓔ	73 Ⓐ Ⓑ Ⓒ Ⓓ Ⓔ
14 Ⓐ Ⓑ Ⓒ Ⓓ Ⓔ	44 Ⓐ Ⓑ Ⓒ Ⓓ Ⓔ	74 Ⓐ Ⓑ Ⓒ Ⓓ Ⓔ
15 Ⓐ Ⓑ Ⓒ Ⓓ Ⓔ	45 Ⓐ Ⓑ Ⓒ Ⓓ Ⓔ	75 Ⓐ Ⓑ Ⓒ Ⓓ Ⓔ
16 Ⓐ Ⓑ Ⓒ Ⓓ Ⓔ	46 Ⓐ Ⓑ Ⓒ Ⓓ Ⓔ	76 Ⓐ Ⓑ Ⓒ Ⓓ Ⓔ
17 Ⓐ Ⓑ Ⓒ Ⓓ Ⓔ	47 Ⓐ Ⓑ Ⓒ Ⓓ Ⓔ	77 Ⓐ Ⓑ Ⓒ Ⓓ Ⓔ
18 Ⓐ Ⓑ Ⓒ Ⓓ Ⓔ	48 Ⓐ Ⓑ Ⓒ Ⓓ Ⓔ	78 Ⓐ Ⓑ Ⓒ Ⓓ Ⓔ
19 Ⓐ Ⓑ Ⓒ Ⓓ Ⓔ	49 Ⓐ Ⓑ Ⓒ Ⓓ Ⓔ	79 Ⓐ Ⓑ Ⓒ Ⓓ Ⓔ
20 Ⓐ Ⓑ Ⓒ Ⓓ Ⓔ	50 Ⓐ Ⓑ Ⓒ Ⓓ Ⓔ	80 Ⓐ Ⓑ Ⓒ Ⓓ Ⓔ
21 Ⓐ Ⓑ Ⓒ Ⓓ Ⓔ	51 Ⓐ Ⓑ Ⓒ Ⓓ Ⓔ	81 Ⓐ Ⓑ Ⓒ Ⓓ Ⓔ
22 Ⓐ Ⓑ Ⓒ Ⓓ Ⓔ	52 Ⓐ Ⓑ Ⓒ Ⓓ Ⓔ	82 Ⓐ Ⓑ Ⓒ Ⓓ Ⓔ
23 Ⓐ Ⓑ Ⓒ Ⓓ Ⓔ	53 Ⓐ Ⓑ Ⓒ Ⓓ Ⓔ	83 Ⓐ Ⓑ Ⓒ Ⓓ Ⓔ
24 Ⓐ Ⓑ Ⓒ Ⓓ Ⓔ	54 Ⓐ Ⓑ Ⓒ Ⓓ Ⓔ	84 Ⓐ Ⓑ Ⓒ Ⓓ Ⓔ
25 Ⓐ Ⓑ Ⓒ Ⓓ Ⓔ	55 Ⓐ Ⓑ Ⓒ Ⓓ Ⓔ	85 Ⓐ Ⓑ Ⓒ Ⓓ Ⓔ
26 Ⓐ Ⓑ Ⓒ Ⓓ Ⓔ	56 Ⓐ Ⓑ Ⓒ Ⓓ Ⓔ	86 Ⓐ Ⓑ Ⓒ Ⓓ Ⓔ
27 Ⓐ Ⓑ Ⓒ Ⓓ Ⓔ	57 Ⓐ Ⓑ Ⓒ Ⓓ Ⓔ	87 Ⓐ Ⓑ Ⓒ Ⓓ Ⓔ
28 Ⓐ Ⓑ Ⓒ Ⓓ Ⓔ	58 Ⓐ Ⓑ Ⓒ Ⓓ Ⓔ	88 Ⓐ Ⓑ Ⓒ Ⓓ Ⓔ
29 Ⓐ Ⓑ Ⓒ Ⓓ Ⓔ	59 Ⓐ Ⓑ Ⓒ Ⓓ Ⓔ	
30 Ⓐ Ⓑ Ⓒ Ⓓ Ⓔ	60 Ⓐ Ⓑ Ⓒ Ⓓ Ⓔ	

ANSWER SHEET—PRACTICE TEST 1
TRIAL 2

PART B—MEMORY FOR ADDRESSES
LIST 2   DATE _____

1 Ⓐ Ⓑ Ⓒ Ⓓ Ⓔ	31 Ⓐ Ⓑ Ⓒ Ⓓ Ⓔ	61 Ⓐ Ⓑ Ⓒ Ⓓ Ⓔ
2 Ⓐ Ⓑ Ⓒ Ⓓ Ⓔ	32 Ⓐ Ⓑ Ⓒ Ⓓ Ⓔ	62 Ⓐ Ⓑ Ⓒ Ⓓ Ⓔ
3 Ⓐ Ⓑ Ⓒ Ⓓ Ⓔ	33 Ⓐ Ⓑ Ⓒ Ⓓ Ⓔ	63 Ⓐ Ⓑ Ⓒ Ⓓ Ⓔ
4 Ⓐ Ⓑ Ⓒ Ⓓ Ⓔ	34 Ⓐ Ⓑ Ⓒ Ⓓ Ⓔ	64 Ⓐ Ⓑ Ⓒ Ⓓ Ⓔ
5 Ⓐ Ⓑ Ⓒ Ⓓ Ⓔ	35 Ⓐ Ⓑ Ⓒ Ⓓ Ⓔ	65 Ⓐ Ⓑ Ⓒ Ⓓ Ⓔ
6 Ⓐ Ⓑ Ⓒ Ⓓ Ⓔ	36 Ⓐ Ⓑ Ⓒ Ⓓ Ⓔ	66 Ⓐ Ⓑ Ⓒ Ⓓ Ⓔ
7 Ⓐ Ⓑ Ⓒ Ⓓ Ⓔ	37 Ⓐ Ⓑ Ⓒ Ⓓ Ⓔ	67 Ⓐ Ⓑ Ⓒ Ⓓ Ⓔ
8 Ⓐ Ⓑ Ⓒ Ⓓ Ⓔ	38 Ⓐ Ⓑ Ⓒ Ⓓ Ⓔ	68 Ⓐ Ⓑ Ⓒ Ⓓ Ⓔ
9 Ⓐ Ⓑ Ⓒ Ⓓ Ⓔ	39 Ⓐ Ⓑ Ⓒ Ⓓ Ⓔ	69 Ⓐ Ⓑ Ⓒ Ⓓ Ⓔ
10 Ⓐ Ⓑ Ⓒ Ⓓ Ⓔ	40 Ⓐ Ⓑ Ⓒ Ⓓ Ⓔ	70 Ⓐ Ⓑ Ⓒ Ⓓ Ⓔ
11 Ⓐ Ⓑ Ⓒ Ⓓ Ⓔ	41 Ⓐ Ⓑ Ⓒ Ⓓ Ⓔ	71 Ⓐ Ⓑ Ⓒ Ⓓ Ⓔ
12 Ⓐ Ⓑ Ⓒ Ⓓ Ⓔ	42 Ⓐ Ⓑ Ⓒ Ⓓ Ⓔ	72 Ⓐ Ⓑ Ⓒ Ⓓ Ⓔ
13 Ⓐ Ⓑ Ⓒ Ⓓ Ⓔ	43 Ⓐ Ⓑ Ⓒ Ⓓ Ⓔ	73 Ⓐ Ⓑ Ⓒ Ⓓ Ⓔ
14 Ⓐ Ⓑ Ⓒ Ⓓ Ⓔ	44 Ⓐ Ⓑ Ⓒ Ⓓ Ⓔ	74 Ⓐ Ⓑ Ⓒ Ⓓ Ⓔ
15 Ⓐ Ⓑ Ⓒ Ⓓ Ⓔ	45 Ⓐ Ⓑ Ⓒ Ⓓ Ⓔ	75 Ⓐ Ⓑ Ⓒ Ⓓ Ⓔ
16 Ⓐ Ⓑ Ⓒ Ⓓ Ⓔ	46 Ⓐ Ⓑ Ⓒ Ⓓ Ⓔ	76 Ⓐ Ⓑ Ⓒ Ⓓ Ⓔ
17 Ⓐ Ⓑ Ⓒ Ⓓ Ⓔ	47 Ⓐ Ⓑ Ⓒ Ⓓ Ⓔ	77 Ⓐ Ⓑ Ⓒ Ⓓ Ⓔ
18 Ⓐ Ⓑ Ⓒ Ⓓ Ⓔ	48 Ⓐ Ⓑ Ⓒ Ⓓ Ⓔ	78 Ⓐ Ⓑ Ⓒ Ⓓ Ⓔ
19 Ⓐ Ⓑ Ⓒ Ⓓ Ⓔ	49 Ⓐ Ⓑ Ⓒ Ⓓ Ⓔ	79 Ⓐ Ⓑ Ⓒ Ⓓ Ⓔ
20 Ⓐ Ⓑ Ⓒ Ⓓ Ⓔ	50 Ⓐ Ⓑ Ⓒ Ⓓ Ⓔ	80 Ⓐ Ⓑ Ⓒ Ⓓ Ⓔ
21 Ⓐ Ⓑ Ⓒ Ⓓ Ⓔ	51 Ⓐ Ⓑ Ⓒ Ⓓ Ⓔ	81 Ⓐ Ⓑ Ⓒ Ⓓ Ⓔ
22 Ⓐ Ⓑ Ⓒ Ⓓ Ⓔ	52 Ⓐ Ⓑ Ⓒ Ⓓ Ⓔ	82 Ⓐ Ⓑ Ⓒ Ⓓ Ⓔ
23 Ⓐ Ⓑ Ⓒ Ⓓ Ⓔ	53 Ⓐ Ⓑ Ⓒ Ⓓ Ⓔ	83 Ⓐ Ⓑ Ⓒ Ⓓ Ⓔ
24 Ⓐ Ⓑ Ⓒ Ⓓ Ⓔ	54 Ⓐ Ⓑ Ⓒ Ⓓ Ⓔ	84 Ⓐ Ⓑ Ⓒ Ⓓ Ⓔ
25 Ⓐ Ⓑ Ⓒ Ⓓ Ⓔ	55 Ⓐ Ⓑ Ⓒ Ⓓ Ⓔ	85 Ⓐ Ⓑ Ⓒ Ⓓ Ⓔ
26 Ⓐ Ⓑ Ⓒ Ⓓ Ⓔ	56 Ⓐ Ⓑ Ⓒ Ⓓ Ⓔ	86 Ⓐ Ⓑ Ⓒ Ⓓ Ⓔ
27 Ⓐ Ⓑ Ⓒ Ⓓ Ⓔ	57 Ⓐ Ⓑ Ⓒ Ⓓ Ⓔ	87 Ⓐ Ⓑ Ⓒ Ⓓ Ⓔ
28 Ⓐ Ⓑ Ⓒ Ⓓ Ⓔ	58 Ⓐ Ⓑ Ⓒ Ⓓ Ⓔ	88 Ⓐ Ⓑ Ⓒ Ⓓ Ⓔ
29 Ⓐ Ⓑ Ⓒ Ⓓ Ⓔ	59 Ⓐ Ⓑ Ⓒ Ⓓ Ⓔ	
30 Ⓐ Ⓑ Ⓒ Ⓓ Ⓔ	60 Ⓐ Ⓑ Ⓒ Ⓓ Ⓔ	

ANSWER SHEET—PRACTICE TEST 1
TRIAL 3

PART B—MEMORY FOR ADDRESSES
LIST 2   DATE _____

1 Ⓐ Ⓑ Ⓒ Ⓓ Ⓔ	31 Ⓐ Ⓑ Ⓒ Ⓓ Ⓔ	61 Ⓐ Ⓑ Ⓒ Ⓓ Ⓔ
2 Ⓐ Ⓑ Ⓒ Ⓓ Ⓔ	32 Ⓐ Ⓑ Ⓒ Ⓓ Ⓔ	62 Ⓐ Ⓑ Ⓒ Ⓓ Ⓔ
3 Ⓐ Ⓑ Ⓒ Ⓓ Ⓔ	33 Ⓐ Ⓑ Ⓒ Ⓓ Ⓔ	63 Ⓐ Ⓑ Ⓒ Ⓓ Ⓔ
4 Ⓐ Ⓑ Ⓒ Ⓓ Ⓔ	34 Ⓐ Ⓑ Ⓒ Ⓓ Ⓔ	64 Ⓐ Ⓑ Ⓒ Ⓓ Ⓔ
5 Ⓐ Ⓑ Ⓒ Ⓓ Ⓔ	35 Ⓐ Ⓑ Ⓒ Ⓓ Ⓔ	65 Ⓐ Ⓑ Ⓒ Ⓓ Ⓔ
6 Ⓐ Ⓑ Ⓒ Ⓓ Ⓔ	36 Ⓐ Ⓑ Ⓒ Ⓓ Ⓔ	66 Ⓐ Ⓑ Ⓒ Ⓓ Ⓔ
7 Ⓐ Ⓑ Ⓒ Ⓓ Ⓔ	37 Ⓐ Ⓑ Ⓒ Ⓓ Ⓔ	67 Ⓐ Ⓑ Ⓒ Ⓓ Ⓔ
8 Ⓐ Ⓑ Ⓒ Ⓓ Ⓔ	38 Ⓐ Ⓑ Ⓒ Ⓓ Ⓔ	68 Ⓐ Ⓑ Ⓒ Ⓓ Ⓔ
9 Ⓐ Ⓑ Ⓒ Ⓓ Ⓔ	39 Ⓐ Ⓑ Ⓒ Ⓓ Ⓔ	69 Ⓐ Ⓑ Ⓒ Ⓓ Ⓔ
10 Ⓐ Ⓑ Ⓒ Ⓓ Ⓔ	40 Ⓐ Ⓑ Ⓒ Ⓓ Ⓔ	70 Ⓐ Ⓑ Ⓒ Ⓓ Ⓔ
11 Ⓐ Ⓑ Ⓒ Ⓓ Ⓔ	41 Ⓐ Ⓑ Ⓒ Ⓓ Ⓔ	71 Ⓐ Ⓑ Ⓒ Ⓓ Ⓔ
12 Ⓐ Ⓑ Ⓒ Ⓓ Ⓔ	42 Ⓐ Ⓑ Ⓒ Ⓓ Ⓔ	72 Ⓐ Ⓑ Ⓒ Ⓓ Ⓔ
13 Ⓐ Ⓑ Ⓒ Ⓓ Ⓔ	43 Ⓐ Ⓑ Ⓒ Ⓓ Ⓔ	73 Ⓐ Ⓑ Ⓒ Ⓓ Ⓔ
14 Ⓐ Ⓑ Ⓒ Ⓓ Ⓔ	44 Ⓐ Ⓑ Ⓒ Ⓓ Ⓔ	74 Ⓐ Ⓑ Ⓒ Ⓓ Ⓔ
15 Ⓐ Ⓑ Ⓒ Ⓓ Ⓔ	45 Ⓐ Ⓑ Ⓒ Ⓓ Ⓔ	75 Ⓐ Ⓑ Ⓒ Ⓓ Ⓔ
16 Ⓐ Ⓑ Ⓒ Ⓓ Ⓔ	46 Ⓐ Ⓑ Ⓒ Ⓓ Ⓔ	76 Ⓐ Ⓑ Ⓒ Ⓓ Ⓔ
17 Ⓐ Ⓑ Ⓒ Ⓓ Ⓔ	47 Ⓐ Ⓑ Ⓒ Ⓓ Ⓔ	77 Ⓐ Ⓑ Ⓒ Ⓓ Ⓔ
18 Ⓐ Ⓑ Ⓒ Ⓓ Ⓔ	48 Ⓐ Ⓑ Ⓒ Ⓓ Ⓔ	78 Ⓐ Ⓑ Ⓒ Ⓓ Ⓔ
19 Ⓐ Ⓑ Ⓒ Ⓓ Ⓔ	49 Ⓐ Ⓑ Ⓒ Ⓓ Ⓔ	79 Ⓐ Ⓑ Ⓒ Ⓓ Ⓔ
20 Ⓐ Ⓑ Ⓒ Ⓓ Ⓔ	50 Ⓐ Ⓑ Ⓒ Ⓓ Ⓔ	80 Ⓐ Ⓑ Ⓒ Ⓓ Ⓔ
21 Ⓐ Ⓑ Ⓒ Ⓓ Ⓔ	51 Ⓐ Ⓑ Ⓒ Ⓓ Ⓔ	81 Ⓐ Ⓑ Ⓒ Ⓓ Ⓔ
22 Ⓐ Ⓑ Ⓒ Ⓓ Ⓔ	52 Ⓐ Ⓑ Ⓒ Ⓓ Ⓔ	82 Ⓐ Ⓑ Ⓒ Ⓓ Ⓔ
23 Ⓐ Ⓑ Ⓒ Ⓓ Ⓔ	53 Ⓐ Ⓑ Ⓒ Ⓓ Ⓔ	83 Ⓐ Ⓑ Ⓒ Ⓓ Ⓔ
24 Ⓐ Ⓑ Ⓒ Ⓓ Ⓔ	54 Ⓐ Ⓑ Ⓒ Ⓓ Ⓔ	84 Ⓐ Ⓑ Ⓒ Ⓓ Ⓔ
25 Ⓐ Ⓑ Ⓒ Ⓓ Ⓔ	55 Ⓐ Ⓑ Ⓒ Ⓓ Ⓔ	85 Ⓐ Ⓑ Ⓒ Ⓓ Ⓔ
26 Ⓐ Ⓑ Ⓒ Ⓓ Ⓔ	56 Ⓐ Ⓑ Ⓒ Ⓓ Ⓔ	86 Ⓐ Ⓑ Ⓒ Ⓓ Ⓔ
27 Ⓐ Ⓑ Ⓒ Ⓓ Ⓔ	57 Ⓐ Ⓑ Ⓒ Ⓓ Ⓔ	87 Ⓐ Ⓑ Ⓒ Ⓓ Ⓔ
28 Ⓐ Ⓑ Ⓒ Ⓓ Ⓔ	58 Ⓐ Ⓑ Ⓒ Ⓓ Ⓔ	88 Ⓐ Ⓑ Ⓒ Ⓓ Ⓔ
29 Ⓐ Ⓑ Ⓒ Ⓓ Ⓔ	59 Ⓐ Ⓑ Ⓒ Ⓓ Ⓔ	
30 Ⓐ Ⓑ Ⓒ Ⓓ Ⓔ	60 Ⓐ Ⓑ Ⓒ Ⓓ Ⓔ	

ANSWER SHEET—PRACTICE TEST 2
TRIAL 2

PART B—MEMORY FOR ADDRESSES
LIST 2   DATE _____

1 Ⓐ Ⓑ Ⓒ Ⓓ Ⓔ	31 Ⓐ Ⓑ Ⓒ Ⓓ Ⓔ	61 Ⓐ Ⓑ Ⓒ Ⓓ Ⓔ
2 Ⓐ Ⓑ Ⓒ Ⓓ Ⓔ	32 Ⓐ Ⓑ Ⓒ Ⓓ Ⓔ	62 Ⓐ Ⓑ Ⓒ Ⓓ Ⓔ
3 Ⓐ Ⓑ Ⓒ Ⓓ Ⓔ	33 Ⓐ Ⓑ Ⓒ Ⓓ Ⓔ	63 Ⓐ Ⓑ Ⓒ Ⓓ Ⓔ
4 Ⓐ Ⓑ Ⓒ Ⓓ Ⓔ	34 Ⓐ Ⓑ Ⓒ Ⓓ Ⓔ	64 Ⓐ Ⓑ Ⓒ Ⓓ Ⓔ
5 Ⓐ Ⓑ Ⓒ Ⓓ Ⓔ	35 Ⓐ Ⓑ Ⓒ Ⓓ Ⓔ	65 Ⓐ Ⓑ Ⓒ Ⓓ Ⓔ
6 Ⓐ Ⓑ Ⓒ Ⓓ Ⓔ	36 Ⓐ Ⓑ Ⓒ Ⓓ Ⓔ	66 Ⓐ Ⓑ Ⓒ Ⓓ Ⓔ
7 Ⓐ Ⓑ Ⓒ Ⓓ Ⓔ	37 Ⓐ Ⓑ Ⓒ Ⓓ Ⓔ	67 Ⓐ Ⓑ Ⓒ Ⓓ Ⓔ
8 Ⓐ Ⓑ Ⓒ Ⓓ Ⓔ	38 Ⓐ Ⓑ Ⓒ Ⓓ Ⓔ	68 Ⓐ Ⓑ Ⓒ Ⓓ Ⓔ
9 Ⓐ Ⓑ Ⓒ Ⓓ Ⓔ	39 Ⓐ Ⓑ Ⓒ Ⓓ Ⓔ	69 Ⓐ Ⓑ Ⓒ Ⓓ Ⓔ
10 Ⓐ Ⓑ Ⓒ Ⓓ Ⓔ	40 Ⓐ Ⓑ Ⓒ Ⓓ Ⓔ	70 Ⓐ Ⓑ Ⓒ Ⓓ Ⓔ
11 Ⓐ Ⓑ Ⓒ Ⓓ Ⓔ	41 Ⓐ Ⓑ Ⓒ Ⓓ Ⓔ	71 Ⓐ Ⓑ Ⓒ Ⓓ Ⓔ
12 Ⓐ Ⓑ Ⓒ Ⓓ Ⓔ	42 Ⓐ Ⓑ Ⓒ Ⓓ Ⓔ	72 Ⓐ Ⓑ Ⓒ Ⓓ Ⓔ
13 Ⓐ Ⓑ Ⓒ Ⓓ Ⓔ	43 Ⓐ Ⓑ Ⓒ Ⓓ Ⓔ	73 Ⓐ Ⓑ Ⓒ Ⓓ Ⓔ
14 Ⓐ Ⓑ Ⓒ Ⓓ Ⓔ	44 Ⓐ Ⓑ Ⓒ Ⓓ Ⓔ	74 Ⓐ Ⓑ Ⓒ Ⓓ Ⓔ
15 Ⓐ Ⓑ Ⓒ Ⓓ Ⓔ	45 Ⓐ Ⓑ Ⓒ Ⓓ Ⓔ	75 Ⓐ Ⓑ Ⓒ Ⓓ Ⓔ
16 Ⓐ Ⓑ Ⓒ Ⓓ Ⓔ	46 Ⓐ Ⓑ Ⓒ Ⓓ Ⓔ	76 Ⓐ Ⓑ Ⓒ Ⓓ Ⓔ
17 Ⓐ Ⓑ Ⓒ Ⓓ Ⓔ	47 Ⓐ Ⓑ Ⓒ Ⓓ Ⓔ	77 Ⓐ Ⓑ Ⓒ Ⓓ Ⓔ
18 Ⓐ Ⓑ Ⓒ Ⓓ Ⓔ	48 Ⓐ Ⓑ Ⓒ Ⓓ Ⓔ	78 Ⓐ Ⓑ Ⓒ Ⓓ Ⓔ
19 Ⓐ Ⓑ Ⓒ Ⓓ Ⓔ	49 Ⓐ Ⓑ Ⓒ Ⓓ Ⓔ	79 Ⓐ Ⓑ Ⓒ Ⓓ Ⓔ
20 Ⓐ Ⓑ Ⓒ Ⓓ Ⓔ	50 Ⓐ Ⓑ Ⓒ Ⓓ Ⓔ	80 Ⓐ Ⓑ Ⓒ Ⓓ Ⓔ
21 Ⓐ Ⓑ Ⓒ Ⓓ Ⓔ	51 Ⓐ Ⓑ Ⓒ Ⓓ Ⓔ	81 Ⓐ Ⓑ Ⓒ Ⓓ Ⓔ
22 Ⓐ Ⓑ Ⓒ Ⓓ Ⓔ	52 Ⓐ Ⓑ Ⓒ Ⓓ Ⓔ	82 Ⓐ Ⓑ Ⓒ Ⓓ Ⓔ
23 Ⓐ Ⓑ Ⓒ Ⓓ Ⓔ	53 Ⓐ Ⓑ Ⓒ Ⓓ Ⓔ	83 Ⓐ Ⓑ Ⓒ Ⓓ Ⓔ
24 Ⓐ Ⓑ Ⓒ Ⓓ Ⓔ	54 Ⓐ Ⓑ Ⓒ Ⓓ Ⓔ	84 Ⓐ Ⓑ Ⓒ Ⓓ Ⓔ
25 Ⓐ Ⓑ Ⓒ Ⓓ Ⓔ	55 Ⓐ Ⓑ Ⓒ Ⓓ Ⓔ	85 Ⓐ Ⓑ Ⓒ Ⓓ Ⓔ
26 Ⓐ Ⓑ Ⓒ Ⓓ Ⓔ	56 Ⓐ Ⓑ Ⓒ Ⓓ Ⓔ	86 Ⓐ Ⓑ Ⓒ Ⓓ Ⓔ
27 Ⓐ Ⓑ Ⓒ Ⓓ Ⓔ	57 Ⓐ Ⓑ Ⓒ Ⓓ Ⓔ	87 Ⓐ Ⓑ Ⓒ Ⓓ Ⓔ
28 Ⓐ Ⓑ Ⓒ Ⓓ Ⓔ	58 Ⓐ Ⓑ Ⓒ Ⓓ Ⓔ	88 Ⓐ Ⓑ Ⓒ Ⓓ Ⓔ
29 Ⓐ Ⓑ Ⓒ Ⓓ Ⓔ	59 Ⓐ Ⓑ Ⓒ Ⓓ Ⓔ	
30 Ⓐ Ⓑ Ⓒ Ⓓ Ⓔ	60 Ⓐ Ⓑ Ⓒ Ⓓ Ⓔ	

ANSWER SHEET—PRACTICE TEST 2
TRIAL 3

PART B—MEMORY FOR ADDRESSES
LIST 2   DATE _____

1 Ⓐ Ⓑ Ⓒ Ⓓ Ⓔ	31 Ⓐ Ⓑ Ⓒ Ⓓ Ⓔ	61 Ⓐ Ⓑ Ⓒ Ⓓ Ⓔ
2 Ⓐ Ⓑ Ⓒ Ⓓ Ⓔ	32 Ⓐ Ⓑ Ⓒ Ⓓ Ⓔ	62 Ⓐ Ⓑ Ⓒ Ⓓ Ⓔ
3 Ⓐ Ⓑ Ⓒ Ⓓ Ⓔ	33 Ⓐ Ⓑ Ⓒ Ⓓ Ⓔ	63 Ⓐ Ⓑ Ⓒ Ⓓ Ⓔ
4 Ⓐ Ⓑ Ⓒ Ⓓ Ⓔ	34 Ⓐ Ⓑ Ⓒ Ⓓ Ⓔ	64 Ⓐ Ⓑ Ⓒ Ⓓ Ⓔ
5 Ⓐ Ⓑ Ⓒ Ⓓ Ⓔ	35 Ⓐ Ⓑ Ⓒ Ⓓ Ⓔ	65 Ⓐ Ⓑ Ⓒ Ⓓ Ⓔ
6 Ⓐ Ⓑ Ⓒ Ⓓ Ⓔ	36 Ⓐ Ⓑ Ⓒ Ⓓ Ⓔ	66 Ⓐ Ⓑ Ⓒ Ⓓ Ⓔ
7 Ⓐ Ⓑ Ⓒ Ⓓ Ⓔ	37 Ⓐ Ⓑ Ⓒ Ⓓ Ⓔ	67 Ⓐ Ⓑ Ⓒ Ⓓ Ⓔ
8 Ⓐ Ⓑ Ⓒ Ⓓ Ⓔ	38 Ⓐ Ⓑ Ⓒ Ⓓ Ⓔ	68 Ⓐ Ⓑ Ⓒ Ⓓ Ⓔ
9 Ⓐ Ⓑ Ⓒ Ⓓ Ⓔ	39 Ⓐ Ⓑ Ⓒ Ⓓ Ⓔ	69 Ⓐ Ⓑ Ⓒ Ⓓ Ⓔ
10 Ⓐ Ⓑ Ⓒ Ⓓ Ⓔ	40 Ⓐ Ⓑ Ⓒ Ⓓ Ⓔ	70 Ⓐ Ⓑ Ⓒ Ⓓ Ⓔ
11 Ⓐ Ⓑ Ⓒ Ⓓ Ⓔ	41 Ⓐ Ⓑ Ⓒ Ⓓ Ⓔ	71 Ⓐ Ⓑ Ⓒ Ⓓ Ⓔ
12 Ⓐ Ⓑ Ⓒ Ⓓ Ⓔ	42 Ⓐ Ⓑ Ⓒ Ⓓ Ⓔ	72 Ⓐ Ⓑ Ⓒ Ⓓ Ⓔ
13 Ⓐ Ⓑ Ⓒ Ⓓ Ⓔ	43 Ⓐ Ⓑ Ⓒ Ⓓ Ⓔ	73 Ⓐ Ⓑ Ⓒ Ⓓ Ⓔ
14 Ⓐ Ⓑ Ⓒ Ⓓ Ⓔ	44 Ⓐ Ⓑ Ⓒ Ⓓ Ⓔ	74 Ⓐ Ⓑ Ⓒ Ⓓ Ⓔ
15 Ⓐ Ⓑ Ⓒ Ⓓ Ⓔ	45 Ⓐ Ⓑ Ⓒ Ⓓ Ⓔ	75 Ⓐ Ⓑ Ⓒ Ⓓ Ⓔ
16 Ⓐ Ⓑ Ⓒ Ⓓ Ⓔ	46 Ⓐ Ⓑ Ⓒ Ⓓ Ⓔ	76 Ⓐ Ⓑ Ⓒ Ⓓ Ⓔ
17 Ⓐ Ⓑ Ⓒ Ⓓ Ⓔ	47 Ⓐ Ⓑ Ⓒ Ⓓ Ⓔ	77 Ⓐ Ⓑ Ⓒ Ⓓ Ⓔ
18 Ⓐ Ⓑ Ⓒ Ⓓ Ⓔ	48 Ⓐ Ⓑ Ⓒ Ⓓ Ⓔ	78 Ⓐ Ⓑ Ⓒ Ⓓ Ⓔ
19 Ⓐ Ⓑ Ⓒ Ⓓ Ⓔ	49 Ⓐ Ⓑ Ⓒ Ⓓ Ⓔ	79 Ⓐ Ⓑ Ⓒ Ⓓ Ⓔ
20 Ⓐ Ⓑ Ⓒ Ⓓ Ⓔ	50 Ⓐ Ⓑ Ⓒ Ⓓ Ⓔ	80 Ⓐ Ⓑ Ⓒ Ⓓ Ⓔ
21 Ⓐ Ⓑ Ⓒ Ⓓ Ⓔ	51 Ⓐ Ⓑ Ⓒ Ⓓ Ⓔ	81 Ⓐ Ⓑ Ⓒ Ⓓ Ⓔ
22 Ⓐ Ⓑ Ⓒ Ⓓ Ⓔ	52 Ⓐ Ⓑ Ⓒ Ⓓ Ⓔ	82 Ⓐ Ⓑ Ⓒ Ⓓ Ⓔ
23 Ⓐ Ⓑ Ⓒ Ⓓ Ⓔ	53 Ⓐ Ⓑ Ⓒ Ⓓ Ⓔ	83 Ⓐ Ⓑ Ⓒ Ⓓ Ⓔ
24 Ⓐ Ⓑ Ⓒ Ⓓ Ⓔ	54 Ⓐ Ⓑ Ⓒ Ⓓ Ⓔ	84 Ⓐ Ⓑ Ⓒ Ⓓ Ⓔ
25 Ⓐ Ⓑ Ⓒ Ⓓ Ⓔ	55 Ⓐ Ⓑ Ⓒ Ⓓ Ⓔ	85 Ⓐ Ⓑ Ⓒ Ⓓ Ⓔ
26 Ⓐ Ⓑ Ⓒ Ⓓ Ⓔ	56 Ⓐ Ⓑ Ⓒ Ⓓ Ⓔ	86 Ⓐ Ⓑ Ⓒ Ⓓ Ⓔ
27 Ⓐ Ⓑ Ⓒ Ⓓ Ⓔ	57 Ⓐ Ⓑ Ⓒ Ⓓ Ⓔ	87 Ⓐ Ⓑ Ⓒ Ⓓ Ⓔ
28 Ⓐ Ⓑ Ⓒ Ⓓ Ⓔ	58 Ⓐ Ⓑ Ⓒ Ⓓ Ⓔ	88 Ⓐ Ⓑ Ⓒ Ⓓ Ⓔ
29 Ⓐ Ⓑ Ⓒ Ⓓ Ⓔ	59 Ⓐ Ⓑ Ⓒ Ⓓ Ⓔ	
30 Ⓐ Ⓑ Ⓒ Ⓓ Ⓔ	60 Ⓐ Ⓑ Ⓒ Ⓓ Ⓔ	

ANSWER SHEET—PRACTICE TEST 3
TRIAL 2

PART B—MEMORY FOR ADDRESSES
LIST 2   DATE _____

1 Ⓐ Ⓑ Ⓒ Ⓓ Ⓔ	31 Ⓐ Ⓑ Ⓒ Ⓓ Ⓔ	61 Ⓐ Ⓑ Ⓒ Ⓓ Ⓔ
2 Ⓐ Ⓑ Ⓒ Ⓓ Ⓔ	32 Ⓐ Ⓑ Ⓒ Ⓓ Ⓔ	62 Ⓐ Ⓑ Ⓒ Ⓓ Ⓔ
3 Ⓐ Ⓑ Ⓒ Ⓓ Ⓔ	33 Ⓐ Ⓑ Ⓒ Ⓓ Ⓔ	63 Ⓐ Ⓑ Ⓒ Ⓓ Ⓔ
4 Ⓐ Ⓑ Ⓒ Ⓓ Ⓔ	34 Ⓐ Ⓑ Ⓒ Ⓓ Ⓔ	64 Ⓐ Ⓑ Ⓒ Ⓓ Ⓔ
5 Ⓐ Ⓑ Ⓒ Ⓓ Ⓔ	35 Ⓐ Ⓑ Ⓒ Ⓓ Ⓔ	65 Ⓐ Ⓑ Ⓒ Ⓓ Ⓔ
6 Ⓐ Ⓑ Ⓒ Ⓓ Ⓔ	36 Ⓐ Ⓑ Ⓒ Ⓓ Ⓔ	66 Ⓐ Ⓑ Ⓒ Ⓓ Ⓔ
7 Ⓐ Ⓑ Ⓒ Ⓓ Ⓔ	37 Ⓐ Ⓑ Ⓒ Ⓓ Ⓔ	67 Ⓐ Ⓑ Ⓒ Ⓓ Ⓔ
8 Ⓐ Ⓑ Ⓒ Ⓓ Ⓔ	38 Ⓐ Ⓑ Ⓒ Ⓓ Ⓔ	68 Ⓐ Ⓑ Ⓒ Ⓓ Ⓔ
9 Ⓐ Ⓑ Ⓒ Ⓓ Ⓔ	39 Ⓐ Ⓑ Ⓒ Ⓓ Ⓔ	69 Ⓐ Ⓑ Ⓒ Ⓓ Ⓔ
10 Ⓐ Ⓑ Ⓒ Ⓓ Ⓔ	40 Ⓐ Ⓑ Ⓒ Ⓓ Ⓔ	70 Ⓐ Ⓑ Ⓒ Ⓓ Ⓔ
11 Ⓐ Ⓑ Ⓒ Ⓓ Ⓔ	41 Ⓐ Ⓑ Ⓒ Ⓓ Ⓔ	71 Ⓐ Ⓑ Ⓒ Ⓓ Ⓔ
12 Ⓐ Ⓑ Ⓒ Ⓓ Ⓔ	42 Ⓐ Ⓑ Ⓒ Ⓓ Ⓔ	72 Ⓐ Ⓑ Ⓒ Ⓓ Ⓔ
13 Ⓐ Ⓑ Ⓒ Ⓓ Ⓔ	43 Ⓐ Ⓑ Ⓒ Ⓓ Ⓔ	73 Ⓐ Ⓑ Ⓒ Ⓓ Ⓔ
14 Ⓐ Ⓑ Ⓒ Ⓓ Ⓔ	44 Ⓐ Ⓑ Ⓒ Ⓓ Ⓔ	74 Ⓐ Ⓑ Ⓒ Ⓓ Ⓔ
15 Ⓐ Ⓑ Ⓒ Ⓓ Ⓔ	45 Ⓐ Ⓑ Ⓒ Ⓓ Ⓔ	75 Ⓐ Ⓑ Ⓒ Ⓓ Ⓔ
16 Ⓐ Ⓑ Ⓒ Ⓓ Ⓔ	46 Ⓐ Ⓑ Ⓒ Ⓓ Ⓔ	76 Ⓐ Ⓑ Ⓒ Ⓓ Ⓔ
17 Ⓐ Ⓑ Ⓒ Ⓓ Ⓔ	47 Ⓐ Ⓑ Ⓒ Ⓓ Ⓔ	77 Ⓐ Ⓑ Ⓒ Ⓓ Ⓔ
18 Ⓐ Ⓑ Ⓒ Ⓓ Ⓔ	48 Ⓐ Ⓑ Ⓒ Ⓓ Ⓔ	78 Ⓐ Ⓑ Ⓒ Ⓓ Ⓔ
19 Ⓐ Ⓑ Ⓒ Ⓓ Ⓔ	49 Ⓐ Ⓑ Ⓒ Ⓓ Ⓔ	79 Ⓐ Ⓑ Ⓒ Ⓓ Ⓔ
20 Ⓐ Ⓑ Ⓒ Ⓓ Ⓔ	50 Ⓐ Ⓑ Ⓒ Ⓓ Ⓔ	80 Ⓐ Ⓑ Ⓒ Ⓓ Ⓔ
21 Ⓐ Ⓑ Ⓒ Ⓓ Ⓔ	51 Ⓐ Ⓑ Ⓒ Ⓓ Ⓔ	81 Ⓐ Ⓑ Ⓒ Ⓓ Ⓔ
22 Ⓐ Ⓑ Ⓒ Ⓓ Ⓔ	52 Ⓐ Ⓑ Ⓒ Ⓓ Ⓔ	82 Ⓐ Ⓑ Ⓒ Ⓓ Ⓔ
23 Ⓐ Ⓑ Ⓒ Ⓓ Ⓔ	53 Ⓐ Ⓑ Ⓒ Ⓓ Ⓔ	83 Ⓐ Ⓑ Ⓒ Ⓓ Ⓔ
24 Ⓐ Ⓑ Ⓒ Ⓓ Ⓔ	54 Ⓐ Ⓑ Ⓒ Ⓓ Ⓔ	84 Ⓐ Ⓑ Ⓒ Ⓓ Ⓔ
25 Ⓐ Ⓑ Ⓒ Ⓓ Ⓔ	55 Ⓐ Ⓑ Ⓒ Ⓓ Ⓔ	85 Ⓐ Ⓑ Ⓒ Ⓓ Ⓔ
26 Ⓐ Ⓑ Ⓒ Ⓓ Ⓔ	56 Ⓐ Ⓑ Ⓒ Ⓓ Ⓔ	86 Ⓐ Ⓑ Ⓒ Ⓓ Ⓔ
27 Ⓐ Ⓑ Ⓒ Ⓓ Ⓔ	57 Ⓐ Ⓑ Ⓒ Ⓓ Ⓔ	87 Ⓐ Ⓑ Ⓒ Ⓓ Ⓔ
28 Ⓐ Ⓑ Ⓒ Ⓓ Ⓔ	58 Ⓐ Ⓑ Ⓒ Ⓓ Ⓔ	88 Ⓐ Ⓑ Ⓒ Ⓓ Ⓔ
29 Ⓐ Ⓑ Ⓒ Ⓓ Ⓔ	59 Ⓐ Ⓑ Ⓒ Ⓓ Ⓔ	
30 Ⓐ Ⓑ Ⓒ Ⓓ Ⓔ	60 Ⓐ Ⓑ Ⓒ Ⓓ Ⓔ	

ANSWER SHEET—PRACTICE TEST 3
TRIAL 3

PART B—MEMORY FOR ADDRESSES
LIST 2   DATE _____

1 Ⓐ Ⓑ Ⓒ Ⓓ Ⓔ	31 Ⓐ Ⓑ Ⓒ Ⓓ Ⓔ	61 Ⓐ Ⓑ Ⓒ Ⓓ Ⓔ
2 Ⓐ Ⓑ Ⓒ Ⓓ Ⓔ	32 Ⓐ Ⓑ Ⓒ Ⓓ Ⓔ	62 Ⓐ Ⓑ Ⓒ Ⓓ Ⓔ
3 Ⓐ Ⓑ Ⓒ Ⓓ Ⓔ	33 Ⓐ Ⓑ Ⓒ Ⓓ Ⓔ	63 Ⓐ Ⓑ Ⓒ Ⓓ Ⓔ
4 Ⓐ Ⓑ Ⓒ Ⓓ Ⓔ	34 Ⓐ Ⓑ Ⓒ Ⓓ Ⓔ	64 Ⓐ Ⓑ Ⓒ Ⓓ Ⓔ
5 Ⓐ Ⓑ Ⓒ Ⓓ Ⓔ	35 Ⓐ Ⓑ Ⓒ Ⓓ Ⓔ	65 Ⓐ Ⓑ Ⓒ Ⓓ Ⓔ
6 Ⓐ Ⓑ Ⓒ Ⓓ Ⓔ	36 Ⓐ Ⓑ Ⓒ Ⓓ Ⓔ	66 Ⓐ Ⓑ Ⓒ Ⓓ Ⓔ
7 Ⓐ Ⓑ Ⓒ Ⓓ Ⓔ	37 Ⓐ Ⓑ Ⓒ Ⓓ Ⓔ	67 Ⓐ Ⓑ Ⓒ Ⓓ Ⓔ
8 Ⓐ Ⓑ Ⓒ Ⓓ Ⓔ	38 Ⓐ Ⓑ Ⓒ Ⓓ Ⓔ	68 Ⓐ Ⓑ Ⓒ Ⓓ Ⓔ
9 Ⓐ Ⓑ Ⓒ Ⓓ Ⓔ	39 Ⓐ Ⓑ Ⓒ Ⓓ Ⓔ	69 Ⓐ Ⓑ Ⓒ Ⓓ Ⓔ
10 Ⓐ Ⓑ Ⓒ Ⓓ Ⓔ	40 Ⓐ Ⓑ Ⓒ Ⓓ Ⓔ	70 Ⓐ Ⓑ Ⓒ Ⓓ Ⓔ
11 Ⓐ Ⓑ Ⓒ Ⓓ Ⓔ	41 Ⓐ Ⓑ Ⓒ Ⓓ Ⓔ	71 Ⓐ Ⓑ Ⓒ Ⓓ Ⓔ
12 Ⓐ Ⓑ Ⓒ Ⓓ Ⓔ	42 Ⓐ Ⓑ Ⓒ Ⓓ Ⓔ	72 Ⓐ Ⓑ Ⓒ Ⓓ Ⓔ
13 Ⓐ Ⓑ Ⓒ Ⓓ Ⓔ	43 Ⓐ Ⓑ Ⓒ Ⓓ Ⓔ	73 Ⓐ Ⓑ Ⓒ Ⓓ Ⓔ
14 Ⓐ Ⓑ Ⓒ Ⓓ Ⓔ	44 Ⓐ Ⓑ Ⓒ Ⓓ Ⓔ	74 Ⓐ Ⓑ Ⓒ Ⓓ Ⓔ
15 Ⓐ Ⓑ Ⓒ Ⓓ Ⓔ	45 Ⓐ Ⓑ Ⓒ Ⓓ Ⓔ	75 Ⓐ Ⓑ Ⓒ Ⓓ Ⓔ
16 Ⓐ Ⓑ Ⓒ Ⓓ Ⓔ	46 Ⓐ Ⓑ Ⓒ Ⓓ Ⓔ	76 Ⓐ Ⓑ Ⓒ Ⓓ Ⓔ
17 Ⓐ Ⓑ Ⓒ Ⓓ Ⓔ	47 Ⓐ Ⓑ Ⓒ Ⓓ Ⓔ	77 Ⓐ Ⓑ Ⓒ Ⓓ Ⓔ
18 Ⓐ Ⓑ Ⓒ Ⓓ Ⓔ	48 Ⓐ Ⓑ Ⓒ Ⓓ Ⓔ	78 Ⓐ Ⓑ Ⓒ Ⓓ Ⓔ
19 Ⓐ Ⓑ Ⓒ Ⓓ Ⓔ	49 Ⓐ Ⓑ Ⓒ Ⓓ Ⓔ	79 Ⓐ Ⓑ Ⓒ Ⓓ Ⓔ
20 Ⓐ Ⓑ Ⓒ Ⓓ Ⓔ	50 Ⓐ Ⓑ Ⓒ Ⓓ Ⓔ	80 Ⓐ Ⓑ Ⓒ Ⓓ Ⓔ
21 Ⓐ Ⓑ Ⓒ Ⓓ Ⓔ	51 Ⓐ Ⓑ Ⓒ Ⓓ Ⓔ	81 Ⓐ Ⓑ Ⓒ Ⓓ Ⓔ
22 Ⓐ Ⓑ Ⓒ Ⓓ Ⓔ	52 Ⓐ Ⓑ Ⓒ Ⓓ Ⓔ	82 Ⓐ Ⓑ Ⓒ Ⓓ Ⓔ
23 Ⓐ Ⓑ Ⓒ Ⓓ Ⓔ	53 Ⓐ Ⓑ Ⓒ Ⓓ Ⓔ	83 Ⓐ Ⓑ Ⓒ Ⓓ Ⓔ
24 Ⓐ Ⓑ Ⓒ Ⓓ Ⓔ	54 Ⓐ Ⓑ Ⓒ Ⓓ Ⓔ	84 Ⓐ Ⓑ Ⓒ Ⓓ Ⓔ
25 Ⓐ Ⓑ Ⓒ Ⓓ Ⓔ	55 Ⓐ Ⓑ Ⓒ Ⓓ Ⓔ	85 Ⓐ Ⓑ Ⓒ Ⓓ Ⓔ
26 Ⓐ Ⓑ Ⓒ Ⓓ Ⓔ	56 Ⓐ Ⓑ Ⓒ Ⓓ Ⓔ	86 Ⓐ Ⓑ Ⓒ Ⓓ Ⓔ
27 Ⓐ Ⓑ Ⓒ Ⓓ Ⓔ	57 Ⓐ Ⓑ Ⓒ Ⓓ Ⓔ	87 Ⓐ Ⓑ Ⓒ Ⓓ Ⓔ
28 Ⓐ Ⓑ Ⓒ Ⓓ Ⓔ	58 Ⓐ Ⓑ Ⓒ Ⓓ Ⓔ	88 Ⓐ Ⓑ Ⓒ Ⓓ Ⓔ
29 Ⓐ Ⓑ Ⓒ Ⓓ Ⓔ	59 Ⓐ Ⓑ Ⓒ Ⓓ Ⓔ	
30 Ⓐ Ⓑ Ⓒ Ⓓ Ⓔ	60 Ⓐ Ⓑ Ⓒ Ⓓ Ⓔ	

ANSWER SHEET—PRACTICE TEST 4
TRIAL 2

PART B—MEMORY FOR ADDRESSES
LIST 2   DATE _____

1 Ⓐ Ⓑ Ⓒ Ⓓ Ⓔ	31 Ⓐ Ⓑ Ⓒ Ⓓ Ⓔ	61 Ⓐ Ⓑ Ⓒ Ⓓ Ⓔ
2 Ⓐ Ⓑ Ⓒ Ⓓ Ⓔ	32 Ⓐ Ⓑ Ⓒ Ⓓ Ⓔ	62 Ⓐ Ⓑ Ⓒ Ⓓ Ⓔ
3 Ⓐ Ⓑ Ⓒ Ⓓ Ⓔ	33 Ⓐ Ⓑ Ⓒ Ⓓ Ⓔ	63 Ⓐ Ⓑ Ⓒ Ⓓ Ⓔ
4 Ⓐ Ⓑ Ⓒ Ⓓ Ⓔ	34 Ⓐ Ⓑ Ⓒ Ⓓ Ⓔ	64 Ⓐ Ⓑ Ⓒ Ⓓ Ⓔ
5 Ⓐ Ⓑ Ⓒ Ⓓ Ⓔ	35 Ⓐ Ⓑ Ⓒ Ⓓ Ⓔ	65 Ⓐ Ⓑ Ⓒ Ⓓ Ⓔ
6 Ⓐ Ⓑ Ⓒ Ⓓ Ⓔ	36 Ⓐ Ⓑ Ⓒ Ⓓ Ⓔ	66 Ⓐ Ⓑ Ⓒ Ⓓ Ⓔ
7 Ⓐ Ⓑ Ⓒ Ⓓ Ⓔ	37 Ⓐ Ⓑ Ⓒ Ⓓ Ⓔ	67 Ⓐ Ⓑ Ⓒ Ⓓ Ⓔ
8 Ⓐ Ⓑ Ⓒ Ⓓ Ⓔ	38 Ⓐ Ⓑ Ⓒ Ⓓ Ⓔ	68 Ⓐ Ⓑ Ⓒ Ⓓ Ⓔ
9 Ⓐ Ⓑ Ⓒ Ⓓ Ⓔ	39 Ⓐ Ⓑ Ⓒ Ⓓ Ⓔ	69 Ⓐ Ⓑ Ⓒ Ⓓ Ⓔ
10 Ⓐ Ⓑ Ⓒ Ⓓ Ⓔ	40 Ⓐ Ⓑ Ⓒ Ⓓ Ⓔ	70 Ⓐ Ⓑ Ⓒ Ⓓ Ⓔ
11 Ⓐ Ⓑ Ⓒ Ⓓ Ⓔ	41 Ⓐ Ⓑ Ⓒ Ⓓ Ⓔ	71 Ⓐ Ⓑ Ⓒ Ⓓ Ⓔ
12 Ⓐ Ⓑ Ⓒ Ⓓ Ⓔ	42 Ⓐ Ⓑ Ⓒ Ⓓ Ⓔ	72 Ⓐ Ⓑ Ⓒ Ⓓ Ⓔ
13 Ⓐ Ⓑ Ⓒ Ⓓ Ⓔ	43 Ⓐ Ⓑ Ⓒ Ⓓ Ⓔ	73 Ⓐ Ⓑ Ⓒ Ⓓ Ⓔ
14 Ⓐ Ⓑ Ⓒ Ⓓ Ⓔ	44 Ⓐ Ⓑ Ⓒ Ⓓ Ⓔ	74 Ⓐ Ⓑ Ⓒ Ⓓ Ⓔ
15 Ⓐ Ⓑ Ⓒ Ⓓ Ⓔ	45 Ⓐ Ⓑ Ⓒ Ⓓ Ⓔ	75 Ⓐ Ⓑ Ⓒ Ⓓ Ⓔ
16 Ⓐ Ⓑ Ⓒ Ⓓ Ⓔ	46 Ⓐ Ⓑ Ⓒ Ⓓ Ⓔ	76 Ⓐ Ⓑ Ⓒ Ⓓ Ⓔ
17 Ⓐ Ⓑ Ⓒ Ⓓ Ⓔ	47 Ⓐ Ⓑ Ⓒ Ⓓ Ⓔ	77 Ⓐ Ⓑ Ⓒ Ⓓ Ⓔ
18 Ⓐ Ⓑ Ⓒ Ⓓ Ⓔ	48 Ⓐ Ⓑ Ⓒ Ⓓ Ⓔ	78 Ⓐ Ⓑ Ⓒ Ⓓ Ⓔ
19 Ⓐ Ⓑ Ⓒ Ⓓ Ⓔ	49 Ⓐ Ⓑ Ⓒ Ⓓ Ⓔ	79 Ⓐ Ⓑ Ⓒ Ⓓ Ⓔ
20 Ⓐ Ⓑ Ⓒ Ⓓ Ⓔ	50 Ⓐ Ⓑ Ⓒ Ⓓ Ⓔ	80 Ⓐ Ⓑ Ⓒ Ⓓ Ⓔ
21 Ⓐ Ⓑ Ⓒ Ⓓ Ⓔ	51 Ⓐ Ⓑ Ⓒ Ⓓ Ⓔ	81 Ⓐ Ⓑ Ⓒ Ⓓ Ⓔ
22 Ⓐ Ⓑ Ⓒ Ⓓ Ⓔ	52 Ⓐ Ⓑ Ⓒ Ⓓ Ⓔ	82 Ⓐ Ⓑ Ⓒ Ⓓ Ⓔ
23 Ⓐ Ⓑ Ⓒ Ⓓ Ⓔ	53 Ⓐ Ⓑ Ⓒ Ⓓ Ⓔ	83 Ⓐ Ⓑ Ⓒ Ⓓ Ⓔ
24 Ⓐ Ⓑ Ⓒ Ⓓ Ⓔ	54 Ⓐ Ⓑ Ⓒ Ⓓ Ⓔ	84 Ⓐ Ⓑ Ⓒ Ⓓ Ⓔ
25 Ⓐ Ⓑ Ⓒ Ⓓ Ⓔ	55 Ⓐ Ⓑ Ⓒ Ⓓ Ⓔ	85 Ⓐ Ⓑ Ⓒ Ⓓ Ⓔ
26 Ⓐ Ⓑ Ⓒ Ⓓ Ⓔ	56 Ⓐ Ⓑ Ⓒ Ⓓ Ⓔ	86 Ⓐ Ⓑ Ⓒ Ⓓ Ⓔ
27 Ⓐ Ⓑ Ⓒ Ⓓ Ⓔ	57 Ⓐ Ⓑ Ⓒ Ⓓ Ⓔ	87 Ⓐ Ⓑ Ⓒ Ⓓ Ⓔ
28 Ⓐ Ⓑ Ⓒ Ⓓ Ⓔ	58 Ⓐ Ⓑ Ⓒ Ⓓ Ⓔ	88 Ⓐ Ⓑ Ⓒ Ⓓ Ⓔ
29 Ⓐ Ⓑ Ⓒ Ⓓ Ⓔ	59 Ⓐ Ⓑ Ⓒ Ⓓ Ⓔ	
30 Ⓐ Ⓑ Ⓒ Ⓓ Ⓔ	60 Ⓐ Ⓑ Ⓒ Ⓓ Ⓔ	

ANSWER SHEET—PRACTICE TEST 4
TRIAL 3

PART B—MEMORY FOR ADDRESSES
LIST 2   DATE _____

1 Ⓐ Ⓑ Ⓒ Ⓓ Ⓔ	31 Ⓐ Ⓑ Ⓒ Ⓓ Ⓔ	61 Ⓐ Ⓑ Ⓒ Ⓓ Ⓔ
2 Ⓐ Ⓑ Ⓒ Ⓓ Ⓔ	32 Ⓐ Ⓑ Ⓒ Ⓓ Ⓔ	62 Ⓐ Ⓑ Ⓒ Ⓓ Ⓔ
3 Ⓐ Ⓑ Ⓒ Ⓓ Ⓔ	33 Ⓐ Ⓑ Ⓒ Ⓓ Ⓔ	63 Ⓐ Ⓑ Ⓒ Ⓓ Ⓔ
4 Ⓐ Ⓑ Ⓒ Ⓓ Ⓔ	34 Ⓐ Ⓑ Ⓒ Ⓓ Ⓔ	64 Ⓐ Ⓑ Ⓒ Ⓓ Ⓔ
5 Ⓐ Ⓑ Ⓒ Ⓓ Ⓔ	35 Ⓐ Ⓑ Ⓒ Ⓓ Ⓔ	65 Ⓐ Ⓑ Ⓒ Ⓓ Ⓔ
6 Ⓐ Ⓑ Ⓒ Ⓓ Ⓔ	36 Ⓐ Ⓑ Ⓒ Ⓓ Ⓔ	66 Ⓐ Ⓑ Ⓒ Ⓓ Ⓔ
7 Ⓐ Ⓑ Ⓒ Ⓓ Ⓔ	37 Ⓐ Ⓑ Ⓒ Ⓓ Ⓔ	67 Ⓐ Ⓑ Ⓒ Ⓓ Ⓔ
8 Ⓐ Ⓑ Ⓒ Ⓓ Ⓔ	38 Ⓐ Ⓑ Ⓒ Ⓓ Ⓔ	68 Ⓐ Ⓑ Ⓒ Ⓓ Ⓔ
9 Ⓐ Ⓑ Ⓒ Ⓓ Ⓔ	39 Ⓐ Ⓑ Ⓒ Ⓓ Ⓔ	69 Ⓐ Ⓑ Ⓒ Ⓓ Ⓔ
10 Ⓐ Ⓑ Ⓒ Ⓓ Ⓔ	40 Ⓐ Ⓑ Ⓒ Ⓓ Ⓔ	70 Ⓐ Ⓑ Ⓒ Ⓓ Ⓔ
11 Ⓐ Ⓑ Ⓒ Ⓓ Ⓔ	41 Ⓐ Ⓑ Ⓒ Ⓓ Ⓔ	71 Ⓐ Ⓑ Ⓒ Ⓓ Ⓔ
12 Ⓐ Ⓑ Ⓒ Ⓓ Ⓔ	42 Ⓐ Ⓑ Ⓒ Ⓓ Ⓔ	72 Ⓐ Ⓑ Ⓒ Ⓓ Ⓔ
13 Ⓐ Ⓑ Ⓒ Ⓓ Ⓔ	43 Ⓐ Ⓑ Ⓒ Ⓓ Ⓔ	73 Ⓐ Ⓑ Ⓒ Ⓓ Ⓔ
14 Ⓐ Ⓑ Ⓒ Ⓓ Ⓔ	44 Ⓐ Ⓑ Ⓒ Ⓓ Ⓔ	74 Ⓐ Ⓑ Ⓒ Ⓓ Ⓔ
15 Ⓐ Ⓑ Ⓒ Ⓓ Ⓔ	45 Ⓐ Ⓑ Ⓒ Ⓓ Ⓔ	75 Ⓐ Ⓑ Ⓒ Ⓓ Ⓔ
16 Ⓐ Ⓑ Ⓒ Ⓓ Ⓔ	46 Ⓐ Ⓑ Ⓒ Ⓓ Ⓔ	76 Ⓐ Ⓑ Ⓒ Ⓓ Ⓔ
17 Ⓐ Ⓑ Ⓒ Ⓓ Ⓔ	47 Ⓐ Ⓑ Ⓒ Ⓓ Ⓔ	77 Ⓐ Ⓑ Ⓒ Ⓓ Ⓔ
18 Ⓐ Ⓑ Ⓒ Ⓓ Ⓔ	48 Ⓐ Ⓑ Ⓒ Ⓓ Ⓔ	78 Ⓐ Ⓑ Ⓒ Ⓓ Ⓔ
19 Ⓐ Ⓑ Ⓒ Ⓓ Ⓔ	49 Ⓐ Ⓑ Ⓒ Ⓓ Ⓔ	79 Ⓐ Ⓑ Ⓒ Ⓓ Ⓔ
20 Ⓐ Ⓑ Ⓒ Ⓓ Ⓔ	50 Ⓐ Ⓑ Ⓒ Ⓓ Ⓔ	80 Ⓐ Ⓑ Ⓒ Ⓓ Ⓔ
21 Ⓐ Ⓑ Ⓒ Ⓓ Ⓔ	51 Ⓐ Ⓑ Ⓒ Ⓓ Ⓔ	81 Ⓐ Ⓑ Ⓒ Ⓓ Ⓔ
22 Ⓐ Ⓑ Ⓒ Ⓓ Ⓔ	52 Ⓐ Ⓑ Ⓒ Ⓓ Ⓔ	82 Ⓐ Ⓑ Ⓒ Ⓓ Ⓔ
23 Ⓐ Ⓑ Ⓒ Ⓓ Ⓔ	53 Ⓐ Ⓑ Ⓒ Ⓓ Ⓔ	83 Ⓐ Ⓑ Ⓒ Ⓓ Ⓔ
24 Ⓐ Ⓑ Ⓒ Ⓓ Ⓔ	54 Ⓐ Ⓑ Ⓒ Ⓓ Ⓔ	84 Ⓐ Ⓑ Ⓒ Ⓓ Ⓔ
25 Ⓐ Ⓑ Ⓒ Ⓓ Ⓔ	55 Ⓐ Ⓑ Ⓒ Ⓓ Ⓔ	85 Ⓐ Ⓑ Ⓒ Ⓓ Ⓔ
26 Ⓐ Ⓑ Ⓒ Ⓓ Ⓔ	56 Ⓐ Ⓑ Ⓒ Ⓓ Ⓔ	86 Ⓐ Ⓑ Ⓒ Ⓓ Ⓔ
27 Ⓐ Ⓑ Ⓒ Ⓓ Ⓔ	57 Ⓐ Ⓑ Ⓒ Ⓓ Ⓔ	87 Ⓐ Ⓑ Ⓒ Ⓓ Ⓔ
28 Ⓐ Ⓑ Ⓒ Ⓓ Ⓔ	58 Ⓐ Ⓑ Ⓒ Ⓓ Ⓔ	88 Ⓐ Ⓑ Ⓒ Ⓓ Ⓔ
29 Ⓐ Ⓑ Ⓒ Ⓓ Ⓔ	59 Ⓐ Ⓑ Ⓒ Ⓓ Ⓔ	
30 Ⓐ Ⓑ Ⓒ Ⓓ Ⓔ	60 Ⓐ Ⓑ Ⓒ Ⓓ Ⓔ	

ANSWER SHEET—PRACTICE TEST 5
TRIAL 2

PART B—MEMORY FOR ADDRESSES
LIST 2   DATE _____

1 Ⓐ Ⓑ Ⓒ Ⓓ Ⓔ	31 Ⓐ Ⓑ Ⓒ Ⓓ Ⓔ	61 Ⓐ Ⓑ Ⓒ Ⓓ Ⓔ
2 Ⓐ Ⓑ Ⓒ Ⓓ Ⓔ	32 Ⓐ Ⓑ Ⓒ Ⓓ Ⓔ	62 Ⓐ Ⓑ Ⓒ Ⓓ Ⓔ
3 Ⓐ Ⓑ Ⓒ Ⓓ Ⓔ	33 Ⓐ Ⓑ Ⓒ Ⓓ Ⓔ	63 Ⓐ Ⓑ Ⓒ Ⓓ Ⓔ
4 Ⓐ Ⓑ Ⓒ Ⓓ Ⓔ	34 Ⓐ Ⓑ Ⓒ Ⓓ Ⓔ	64 Ⓐ Ⓑ Ⓒ Ⓓ Ⓔ
5 Ⓐ Ⓑ Ⓒ Ⓓ Ⓔ	35 Ⓐ Ⓑ Ⓒ Ⓓ Ⓔ	65 Ⓐ Ⓑ Ⓒ Ⓓ Ⓔ
6 Ⓐ Ⓑ Ⓒ Ⓓ Ⓔ	36 Ⓐ Ⓑ Ⓒ Ⓓ Ⓔ	66 Ⓐ Ⓑ Ⓒ Ⓓ Ⓔ
7 Ⓐ Ⓑ Ⓒ Ⓓ Ⓔ	37 Ⓐ Ⓑ Ⓒ Ⓓ Ⓔ	67 Ⓐ Ⓑ Ⓒ Ⓓ Ⓔ
8 Ⓐ Ⓑ Ⓒ Ⓓ Ⓔ	38 Ⓐ Ⓑ Ⓒ Ⓓ Ⓔ	68 Ⓐ Ⓑ Ⓒ Ⓓ Ⓔ
9 Ⓐ Ⓑ Ⓒ Ⓓ Ⓔ	39 Ⓐ Ⓑ Ⓒ Ⓓ Ⓔ	69 Ⓐ Ⓑ Ⓒ Ⓓ Ⓔ
10 Ⓐ Ⓑ Ⓒ Ⓓ Ⓔ	40 Ⓐ Ⓑ Ⓒ Ⓓ Ⓔ	70 Ⓐ Ⓑ Ⓒ Ⓓ Ⓔ
11 Ⓐ Ⓑ Ⓒ Ⓓ Ⓔ	41 Ⓐ Ⓑ Ⓒ Ⓓ Ⓔ	71 Ⓐ Ⓑ Ⓒ Ⓓ Ⓔ
12 Ⓐ Ⓑ Ⓒ Ⓓ Ⓔ	42 Ⓐ Ⓑ Ⓒ Ⓓ Ⓔ	72 Ⓐ Ⓑ Ⓒ Ⓓ Ⓔ
13 Ⓐ Ⓑ Ⓒ Ⓓ Ⓔ	43 Ⓐ Ⓑ Ⓒ Ⓓ Ⓔ	73 Ⓐ Ⓑ Ⓒ Ⓓ Ⓔ
14 Ⓐ Ⓑ Ⓒ Ⓓ Ⓔ	44 Ⓐ Ⓑ Ⓒ Ⓓ Ⓔ	74 Ⓐ Ⓑ Ⓒ Ⓓ Ⓔ
15 Ⓐ Ⓑ Ⓒ Ⓓ Ⓔ	45 Ⓐ Ⓑ Ⓒ Ⓓ Ⓔ	75 Ⓐ Ⓑ Ⓒ Ⓓ Ⓔ
16 Ⓐ Ⓑ Ⓒ Ⓓ Ⓔ	46 Ⓐ Ⓑ Ⓒ Ⓓ Ⓔ	76 Ⓐ Ⓑ Ⓒ Ⓓ Ⓔ
17 Ⓐ Ⓑ Ⓒ Ⓓ Ⓔ	47 Ⓐ Ⓑ Ⓒ Ⓓ Ⓔ	77 Ⓐ Ⓑ Ⓒ Ⓓ Ⓔ
18 Ⓐ Ⓑ Ⓒ Ⓓ Ⓔ	48 Ⓐ Ⓑ Ⓒ Ⓓ Ⓔ	78 Ⓐ Ⓑ Ⓒ Ⓓ Ⓔ
19 Ⓐ Ⓑ Ⓒ Ⓓ Ⓔ	49 Ⓐ Ⓑ Ⓒ Ⓓ Ⓔ	79 Ⓐ Ⓑ Ⓒ Ⓓ Ⓔ
20 Ⓐ Ⓑ Ⓒ Ⓓ Ⓔ	50 Ⓐ Ⓑ Ⓒ Ⓓ Ⓔ	80 Ⓐ Ⓑ Ⓒ Ⓓ Ⓔ
21 Ⓐ Ⓑ Ⓒ Ⓓ Ⓔ	51 Ⓐ Ⓑ Ⓒ Ⓓ Ⓔ	81 Ⓐ Ⓑ Ⓒ Ⓓ Ⓔ
22 Ⓐ Ⓑ Ⓒ Ⓓ Ⓔ	52 Ⓐ Ⓑ Ⓒ Ⓓ Ⓔ	82 Ⓐ Ⓑ Ⓒ Ⓓ Ⓔ
23 Ⓐ Ⓑ Ⓒ Ⓓ Ⓔ	53 Ⓐ Ⓑ Ⓒ Ⓓ Ⓔ	83 Ⓐ Ⓑ Ⓒ Ⓓ Ⓔ
24 Ⓐ Ⓑ Ⓒ Ⓓ Ⓔ	54 Ⓐ Ⓑ Ⓒ Ⓓ Ⓔ	84 Ⓐ Ⓑ Ⓒ Ⓓ Ⓔ
25 Ⓐ Ⓑ Ⓒ Ⓓ Ⓔ	55 Ⓐ Ⓑ Ⓒ Ⓓ Ⓔ	85 Ⓐ Ⓑ Ⓒ Ⓓ Ⓔ
26 Ⓐ Ⓑ Ⓒ Ⓓ Ⓔ	56 Ⓐ Ⓑ Ⓒ Ⓓ Ⓔ	86 Ⓐ Ⓑ Ⓒ Ⓓ Ⓔ
27 Ⓐ Ⓑ Ⓒ Ⓓ Ⓔ	57 Ⓐ Ⓑ Ⓒ Ⓓ Ⓔ	87 Ⓐ Ⓑ Ⓒ Ⓓ Ⓔ
28 Ⓐ Ⓑ Ⓒ Ⓓ Ⓔ	58 Ⓐ Ⓑ Ⓒ Ⓓ Ⓔ	88 Ⓐ Ⓑ Ⓒ Ⓓ Ⓔ
29 Ⓐ Ⓑ Ⓒ Ⓓ Ⓔ	59 Ⓐ Ⓑ Ⓒ Ⓓ Ⓔ	
30 Ⓐ Ⓑ Ⓒ Ⓓ Ⓔ	60 Ⓐ Ⓑ Ⓒ Ⓓ Ⓔ	

ANSWER SHEET—PRACTICE TEST 5
TRIAL 3

PART B—MEMORY FOR ADDRESSES
LIST 2   DATE _____

1 Ⓐ Ⓑ Ⓒ Ⓓ Ⓔ	31 Ⓐ Ⓑ Ⓒ Ⓓ Ⓔ	61 Ⓐ Ⓑ Ⓒ Ⓓ Ⓔ
2 Ⓐ Ⓑ Ⓒ Ⓓ Ⓔ	32 Ⓐ Ⓑ Ⓒ Ⓓ Ⓔ	62 Ⓐ Ⓑ Ⓒ Ⓓ Ⓔ
3 Ⓐ Ⓑ Ⓒ Ⓓ Ⓔ	33 Ⓐ Ⓑ Ⓒ Ⓓ Ⓔ	63 Ⓐ Ⓑ Ⓒ Ⓓ Ⓔ
4 Ⓐ Ⓑ Ⓒ Ⓓ Ⓔ	34 Ⓐ Ⓑ Ⓒ Ⓓ Ⓔ	64 Ⓐ Ⓑ Ⓒ Ⓓ Ⓔ
5 Ⓐ Ⓑ Ⓒ Ⓓ Ⓔ	35 Ⓐ Ⓑ Ⓒ Ⓓ Ⓔ	65 Ⓐ Ⓑ Ⓒ Ⓓ Ⓔ
6 Ⓐ Ⓑ Ⓒ Ⓓ Ⓔ	36 Ⓐ Ⓑ Ⓒ Ⓓ Ⓔ	66 Ⓐ Ⓑ Ⓒ Ⓓ Ⓔ
7 Ⓐ Ⓑ Ⓒ Ⓓ Ⓔ	37 Ⓐ Ⓑ Ⓒ Ⓓ Ⓔ	67 Ⓐ Ⓑ Ⓒ Ⓓ Ⓔ
8 Ⓐ Ⓑ Ⓒ Ⓓ Ⓔ	38 Ⓐ Ⓑ Ⓒ Ⓓ Ⓔ	68 Ⓐ Ⓑ Ⓒ Ⓓ Ⓔ
9 Ⓐ Ⓑ Ⓒ Ⓓ Ⓔ	39 Ⓐ Ⓑ Ⓒ Ⓓ Ⓔ	69 Ⓐ Ⓑ Ⓒ Ⓓ Ⓔ
10 Ⓐ Ⓑ Ⓒ Ⓓ Ⓔ	40 Ⓐ Ⓑ Ⓒ Ⓓ Ⓔ	70 Ⓐ Ⓑ Ⓒ Ⓓ Ⓔ
11 Ⓐ Ⓑ Ⓒ Ⓓ Ⓔ	41 Ⓐ Ⓑ Ⓒ Ⓓ Ⓔ	71 Ⓐ Ⓑ Ⓒ Ⓓ Ⓔ
12 Ⓐ Ⓑ Ⓒ Ⓓ Ⓔ	42 Ⓐ Ⓑ Ⓒ Ⓓ Ⓔ	72 Ⓐ Ⓑ Ⓒ Ⓓ Ⓔ
13 Ⓐ Ⓑ Ⓒ Ⓓ Ⓔ	43 Ⓐ Ⓑ Ⓒ Ⓓ Ⓔ	73 Ⓐ Ⓑ Ⓒ Ⓓ Ⓔ
14 Ⓐ Ⓑ Ⓒ Ⓓ Ⓔ	44 Ⓐ Ⓑ Ⓒ Ⓓ Ⓔ	74 Ⓐ Ⓑ Ⓒ Ⓓ Ⓔ
15 Ⓐ Ⓑ Ⓒ Ⓓ Ⓔ	45 Ⓐ Ⓑ Ⓒ Ⓓ Ⓔ	75 Ⓐ Ⓑ Ⓒ Ⓓ Ⓔ
16 Ⓐ Ⓑ Ⓒ Ⓓ Ⓔ	46 Ⓐ Ⓑ Ⓒ Ⓓ Ⓔ	76 Ⓐ Ⓑ Ⓒ Ⓓ Ⓔ
17 Ⓐ Ⓑ Ⓒ Ⓓ Ⓔ	47 Ⓐ Ⓑ Ⓒ Ⓓ Ⓔ	77 Ⓐ Ⓑ Ⓒ Ⓓ Ⓔ
18 Ⓐ Ⓑ Ⓒ Ⓓ Ⓔ	48 Ⓐ Ⓑ Ⓒ Ⓓ Ⓔ	78 Ⓐ Ⓑ Ⓒ Ⓓ Ⓔ
19 Ⓐ Ⓑ Ⓒ Ⓓ Ⓔ	49 Ⓐ Ⓑ Ⓒ Ⓓ Ⓔ	79 Ⓐ Ⓑ Ⓒ Ⓓ Ⓔ
20 Ⓐ Ⓑ Ⓒ Ⓓ Ⓔ	50 Ⓐ Ⓑ Ⓒ Ⓓ Ⓔ	80 Ⓐ Ⓑ Ⓒ Ⓓ Ⓔ
21 Ⓐ Ⓑ Ⓒ Ⓓ Ⓔ	51 Ⓐ Ⓑ Ⓒ Ⓓ Ⓔ	81 Ⓐ Ⓑ Ⓒ Ⓓ Ⓔ
22 Ⓐ Ⓑ Ⓒ Ⓓ Ⓔ	52 Ⓐ Ⓑ Ⓒ Ⓓ Ⓔ	82 Ⓐ Ⓑ Ⓒ Ⓓ Ⓔ
23 Ⓐ Ⓑ Ⓒ Ⓓ Ⓔ	53 Ⓐ Ⓑ Ⓒ Ⓓ Ⓔ	83 Ⓐ Ⓑ Ⓒ Ⓓ Ⓔ
24 Ⓐ Ⓑ Ⓒ Ⓓ Ⓔ	54 Ⓐ Ⓑ Ⓒ Ⓓ Ⓔ	84 Ⓐ Ⓑ Ⓒ Ⓓ Ⓔ
25 Ⓐ Ⓑ Ⓒ Ⓓ Ⓔ	55 Ⓐ Ⓑ Ⓒ Ⓓ Ⓔ	85 Ⓐ Ⓑ Ⓒ Ⓓ Ⓔ
26 Ⓐ Ⓑ Ⓒ Ⓓ Ⓔ	56 Ⓐ Ⓑ Ⓒ Ⓓ Ⓔ	86 Ⓐ Ⓑ Ⓒ Ⓓ Ⓔ
27 Ⓐ Ⓑ Ⓒ Ⓓ Ⓔ	57 Ⓐ Ⓑ Ⓒ Ⓓ Ⓔ	87 Ⓐ Ⓑ Ⓒ Ⓓ Ⓔ
28 Ⓐ Ⓑ Ⓒ Ⓓ Ⓔ	58 Ⓐ Ⓑ Ⓒ Ⓓ Ⓔ	88 Ⓐ Ⓑ Ⓒ Ⓓ Ⓔ
29 Ⓐ Ⓑ Ⓒ Ⓓ Ⓔ	59 Ⓐ Ⓑ Ⓒ Ⓓ Ⓔ	
30 Ⓐ Ⓑ Ⓒ Ⓓ Ⓔ	60 Ⓐ Ⓑ Ⓒ Ⓓ Ⓔ	